Respectable Professionals

Hispanic Studies: Culture and Ideas

Volume **59**

Edited by
Claudio Canaparo

PETER LANG
Oxford · Bern · Berlin · Bruxelles · New York · Wien

Raquel Sánchez and David Martínez-Vilches
(eds)

Respectable Professionals

The Origins of the Liberal Professions in Nineteenth-Century Spain

PETER LANG
Oxford · Bern · Berlin · Bruxelles · New York · Wien

Bibliographic information published by Die Deutsche Nationalbibliothek.
Die Deutsche Nationalbibliothek lists this publication in the Deutsche Nationalbibliografie; detailed bibliographic data is available on the Internet at http://dnb.d-nb.de.

A catalogue record for this book is available from the British Library.

Library of Congress Cataloging-in-Publication Data

Names: Sánchez, Raquel, 1968- editor. | Martínez-Vilches, David, 1994- editor.
Title: Respectable professionals : the origins of the liberal professions in nineteenth-century Spain / [edited by] Raquel Sánchez and David Martínez-Vilches.
Description: Oxford ; New York : Peter Lang, 2022. | Series: Hispanic studies: culture and ideas, 1661-4720 ; volume 59 | Includes bibliographical references and index.
Identifiers: LCCN 2021034091 (print) | LCCN 2021034092 (ebook) | ISBN 9781800794504 (paperback) | ISBN 9781800794511 (ebook) | ISBN 9781800794528 (epub)
Subjects: LCSH: Labor market--Spain--History--19th century. | Professional ethics--Spain--History--19th century. | Respect--History--19th century.
Classification: LCC HD5807 .R48 2022 (print) | LCC HD5807 (ebook) | DDC 331.12--dc23
LC record available at https://lccn.loc.gov/2021034091
LC ebook record available at https://lccn.loc.gov/2021034092

Cover image: 'El doctor Simarro ante el microscopio', by Joaquín Sorolla (1897). Patrimonio Histórico Universidad Complutense de Madrid.
Cover design by Peter Lang Ltd.

ISSN 1661-4720
ISBN 978-1-80079-450-4 (print)
ISBN 978-1-80079-451-1 (ePDF)
ISBN 978-1-80079-452-8 (ePub)

Published by Peter Lang Ltd, International Academic Publishers,
52 St Giles, Oxford, OX1 3LU, United Kingdom
oxford@peterlang.com, www.peterlang.com

This publication has been peer reviewed.

Contents

DAVID MARTÍNEZ-VILCHES AND RAQUEL SÁNCHEZ

History and Sociology of Professions

An Introductory Approach

There is no doubt that one of the events for which the twenty-first century will be remembered is the pandemic we are currently experiencing. It has led to very significant changes on the international scene, reduced mobility of individuals, curtailed citizens' rights, changed government priorities, etc. Among these changes are transformations in the world of work. The pandemic has accelerated a process towards teleworking that had already been underway for some years. Many workers had turned their homes into offices and their personal computers into work tools. Online meetings have become a common, almost daily occurrence. The mobile phone, already indispensable for almost everyone, has been transmuted into an organ of the human body, like an artificial extension of the hand. Microphones, cameras and headphones are part of the ancillary accessories of our daily existence. Simultaneously, some jobs have disappeared; others will soon. New occupations are already emerging and more will follow that we cannot yet imagine. In short, we are witnessing an accelerated major change in the world of work, a change that should make us reflect on its consequences and the social and mental transformations that it is generating. We will have to rethink everything from the educational system to the meaning of what we conventionally understand by 'work', including labour legislation, the regulation of working hours and productivity, to mention only the most obvious issues.

Rarely do major changes occur suddenly. We are now experiencing one of those rare occasions and we do not always understand the unstable reality we are witnessing. Looking back into the past can be very helpful to appreciate such phenomena and that is precisely the origin of this book: a reflection on how these processes of change in the labour area have occurred in other historical moments and how the mentality of an era was transformed through them. At this point, the question arises as to why focus on the nineteenth century? The nineteenth century saw the birth of the modern world through a profound transformation of the political and socio-economic reality. The liberalization of the regulations of the Old Regime, as well as the innovations resulting from industrialization, gave way to the creation of new jobs and the redefinition of existing ones, generated new spaces for economic activity, reformulated social relations under new criteria, gave rise to new needs to be covered by professions that had not yet been known and so on. In fact, as Harold Perkin explained in his classical study about the rise of the professional society in England, it was in nineteenth century when the 'professional ideal' was born, facing the outdated 'aristocratic ideal' and the new entrepreneurial and working-class ideals. The professional ideal is based 'on human capital rather than passive or active property, highly skilled and differentiated labour rather than simple labour theory of value, and selection by merit defined as trained and certified expertise'. These three ideals (entrepreneurial, working class and professional) competed in the social and economic markets for resources, power and status.[1] In a certain sense, professional practice and, therefore, professionalism itself became a structuring element of modern society.

The sociology of the professions has dealt extensively with these issues, with a special focus on changes in the world of work in the twentieth century, consolidating itself as a solid field of study that has developed a broad corpus in which various theories and schools of thought have coexisted and debated. Developed on the basis of case studies, these theories have displayed different realities on the economic sectors that have been the object of their interest.[2] One of the biases that most clearly marks

1 Harold Perkin, *The Rise of Professional Society. England since 1880* (London/New York: Routledge, 2002), 4.

2 See Michael Burrage and Rolf Torstendahl, eds, *Professions in Theory and History: Rethinking the Study of the Professions* (London: Sage Publications, 1990); Eliot Freidon, *Professionalism: The Third Logic. In the Practice of Knowledge* (Chicago: University of Chicago Press, 2001); Claude Dubar, Pierre Tripier and

the distinction between them is the framework of analysis: Continental European or Anglo-Saxon. To a large extent, the differences are mainly due to the role attributed to the State in shaping a particular professional field. In the study of the sociology of the professions, the State (as a public power) plays a very important role, since it is the source of the regulations governing the exercise of a profession and, in some cases, the control of training processes and ways of access to professional practice. The State also demands services for professionals and generates specialized jobs for its own internal needs, as the civil service shows. At the same time, the role of the State in the study of the different professional sectors refers to an analysis based on the nation-state, which does not invalidate the influences and transfer of practices, customs and regulations from one country to another.[3]

Historical analysis has fruitfully contributed to the sociology of the professions, sometimes from the perspective of their social history, sometimes from the analysis of the evolution of their regulatory frameworks.[4] In any case, the historical perspective reveals the fragility of the borders established by the great theoretical constructions and the importance of flexibility in the meaning of commonly accepted concepts among specialists, such as profession, professionalization and corporatism.[5] At the same time,

---

Valérie Boussard, *Sociologie des professions* (París: Armand Colin, 2015). A general analysis in Ricardo González Leandri, *Las profesiones: entre la vocación y el interés corporativo* (Madrid: Catriel, 1999); Florent Champy, *Nouvelle théorie sociologique des professions* (Paris: Presses Universitaires de France, 2011); Lucila Finkel, *La sociología de las profesiones: legados y perspectivas* (Madrid: UCM, 2015).

3 The State as a framework of analysis for the study of the professions has been discussed by Thomas Le Bianic in 'La division spatiale des professions: un point d'aveugle de l'analyse sociologique?' in Jean-Paul Barrière and Hervé Leuwer, eds, *La construction des professions juridiques et médicales: Europe occidentale XVIIIe-XXe siècle* (Villeneuve d'Ascq: Presses Universitaires du Septentrion, 2020), 33–56.

4 Some reflections in Hannes Siegrist, 'Professionalization as a Process: Patterns, Progressions and Discontinuity', in Burrage and Torstendahl, eds, *Professions in Theory and History*, 177–202; and 'Professionalization / Professions in History', *International Encyclopedia of the Social and Behavioral Sciences* (Amsterdam: Elsevier, 2002), 12154–60.

5 Even comparisons should be made with caution, as each profession has its own dynamics, as has already been studied by Andrew Abbott in *The System of Professions*.

it allows us to trace the genealogy of notions such as meritocracy and reflect on its historicity, to link the practice of certain professions and the condition of active citizenship, or to study the process of feminization of some professions, such as teaching and primary healthcare (especially nursing). As we said above, the nineteenth century is a privileged observatory for understanding these processes, which link the end of the Old Regime with a world, our world, also in the midst of a process of transformation. The nineteenth century witnessed the consolidation of the nation-state, the disappearance of guilds and, therefore, the liberalization of the labour market and the mechanization of production processes, which had so many consequences for the remodelling of the structure of the labour market, particularly in terms of unskilled jobs. On the other hand, the value of personal effort and work as vehicles for social advancement contributed to the old duality between manual and intellectual work acquiring new profiles, the latter being associated with high levels of educational training and, depending on the case, social prestige. This also leads us to consider the conceptual differences between work, profession and trade.

The development of this process follows a relatively similar line in the countries of the Western world, which includes Spain, the subject of this book. Spanish historiography has long been concerned with the social history of professions. It is not one of the most explored areas, but its study has never waned, as evidenced by the works published on the subject since the 1980s.[6] However, research in this field – and as far as the

---

An Essay on the Division of Expert Labor (Chicago: University of Chicago Press, 1988).

6 Among them, and for the nineteenth and twentieth century, the following should be mentioned: Francisco Villacorta Baños, *Profesionales y burócratas: estado y poder corporativo en la España del siglo XX, 1890–1923* (Madrid: Siglo Veintiuno de España, 1989); Mercedes Cabrera and Fernando del Rey, *El poder de los empresarios: política e intereses económicos en la España contemporánea, 1875–2000* (Madrid: Taurus, 2002); Raquel Sánchez, *El autor en España 1900–1936* (Madrid: Editorial Fundamentos, 2008); Stephen Jacobson, *Catalonia's Advocates: Lawyers, Society, and Politics in Barcelona, 1759–1900* (Chapel Hill: University of North Carolina Press, 2009); Jesús A. Martínez Martín, *Vivir de la pluma: la profesionalización del escritor, 1836–1936* (Madrid: Marcial Pons Historia, 2009); Darina Martykánová, *Los ingenieros en España y en el Imperio Otomano en el siglo XIX: Una historia*

nineteenth century is concerned – has two gaps that this book aims to fill. On the one hand, there is a lack of collective work that would allow us to compare the Spanish professional ecosystem with the situation in other European countries.[7] On the other hand, no attention has been paid to certain activities which, from a strict conception of what a 'profession' is, have not been considered as such. In some cases, because they are associated with activities outside the productive world (such as the priesthood), and in other cases, because they are difficult to define (such as professions linked to business and artistic creation).[8] *Respectable Professionals*, therefore, moves away from theoretical rigidities to show a global picture of the evolution of the activities that are known as 'liberal professions' in a

---

comparada (Madrid: UAM, 2010); Santiago Muñoz Machado, ed., *Historia de la abogacía española* (Cizur Menor: Aranzadi, 2015), vol. 2.

7 Examples of collective work on national contexts: Gerald L. Geison, ed., *Professions and the French State, 1700–1900* (Philadelphia: University of Pennsylvania Press, 1984); Harold James Perkin, *The Rise of Professional Society: England since 1880* (London: Routledge, 1989, 2002); Konrad H. Jarausch and Geoffrey Cocks, eds, *German Professions, 1800–1950* (Oxford: Oxford University Press, 1990); Charles E. McClelland, *The German Experience of Professionalization: Modern Learned Professions and Their Organizations from the Early Nineteenth Century to the Hitler Era* (Cambridge: Cambridge University Press, 1991); Maria M. Kovacs, *Liberal Professions and Illiberal Politics: Hungary from the Habsburgs to the Holocaust* (Oxford: Oxford University Press, 1994); Penelope J. Corfield, *Power and the Professions in Britain, 1700–1850* (London/New York: Routledge, 1995); Maria Malatesta dir., *Society and the Professions in Italy, 1860–1914* (Cambridge: Cambridge University Press, 1995); Harvey Balzer, ed., *Russia's Missing Middle Class: The Professions in Russian History* (New York/London: Armonk, 1996). The extensive bibliography by professional sectors is not mentioned in order to avoid overloading the text, but it is of great interest for comparative studies.

8 By a strict conception of what a profession is, we refer to the proposal that emerges from, among others, the work of Burrage, Torstendahl and Siegrist. A liberal professional must meet these requirements: be the holder of the academic qualifications that enable them to carry out this work, be dedicated to this activity on a full-time basis, have a monopoly in the exercise of this activity in the labour marked due to their expert knowledge, be autonomous with respect to external agents and obtain both material and symbolic rewards in a society that recognizes the value of this specialized knowledge. Many of the professions discussed in this book meet these criteria, although others do not meet all of them.

broad sense.[9] In this book, we will refer to professions that require prior training – to a greater or lesser extent – and that are carried out by their performers as independent professionals, public employees or employees of a company. In other words, jobs that are not essentially manual, which required a particular specialization in a particular area of economic activity and for which income was received in various forms (salaries, fees and other remuneration).

In addition to the sociological considerations that the authors of this book make according to the peculiarities of their field, it also includes cultural analyses that can help to better understand the place of these professionals in the society of their time. Methodologically speaking, the title itself indicates the path chosen. The concept of 'respectable professionals' articulates the study on the basis of 'respectability' as an objective pursued by the individuals who carried out these activities. As various authors have indicated, from the second half of the eighteenth century onwards, we can speak of the emergence of the 'modern regime of selfhood', which would imply a reformulation of the consciousness of the individual self and the concepts that had traditionally been associated with the relationship of the subject with the social whole. Among these concepts is 'honour', a criterion of distinction that in the Old Regime was linked to the status and family lineage to which one belonged and that, from the second half of the eighteenth century, began to be ascribed to the individual subject. The way in which the subject, deprived of the protection of his nobility title, had to show their value and social utility (another key concept of the eighteenth century) was through their own actions, as well as their capacity to create wealth and to contribute to the general welfare, in other words, the external manifestation of their activity. The complexity of this change and its consequences cannot be explained in a short paragraph, so we refer the interested reader to specialized literature.[10] In a simplified way, it could be

9 We could also call them 'intellectual professions', as does Maria Malatesta in *Professional Men, Professional Women. The European Professions from the 19th Century until Today* (Bologna: University of Bologna Press, 2011).

10 See Charles Taylor, *Sources of the Self: The Making of the Modern Identity* (Cambridge: Cambridge University Press, 1989); Anthony Giddens, *Modernity and Self-Identity: Self and Society in the Late Modern Age* (Stanford: Stanford University

said that this was projected onto a new model of civility that disciplined interpersonal relations on more horizontal criteria and on the consideration of work and its economic results as the regulatory mechanism of social progress, which found its legitimizing element in the discourse of meritocracy. It can even be said that it was the enlightened monarchy itself that promoted this change of values, not for the sake of social democratization, but the welfare and economic progress of the country. In Spain, the Royal Decree of 18 March 1783, which positively valued the exercise of certain manual professions and, therefore, work, can be considered a symbol of these new ideas.[11]

Therefore, the key is to be found in the redefinition of the concept of honour that, as early as the nineteenth century, manifested itself in the social status achieved by individual activities, the respect deserved from others and the need to maintain that public image, which came to be identified with the subject himself as their 'social self'. In other words, we are talking about a concept of honour identified with a person's public reputation, with the opinion they project outwards or generates in others. Reputation and honour would ultimately condition the inclusion of individuals in the elite, understood in a broad sense. Honour would come to surpass the principle of nobility as a criterion of social distinction, the

Press, 1991); Alexander Welsh, *What Is Honor? A Question of Moral Imperatives* (London/New Haven: Yale University Press, 2008); Robert L. Oprisko, *Honor: A Phenomenology* (Nueva York: Routledge, 2012); some studies based on British experience in John O. Lyons, *The Invention of the Self: The Hinge of Consciousness in the Eighteenth Century* (Carbondale: Southern Illinois University Press, 1978); and Dror Wahrman, *The Making of the Modern Self: Identity and Culture in Eighteenth-Century England* (New Haven/London: Yale University Press, 2006). Some reflections on the Spanish case: Carlos Maza Ozcoidi, 'La definición del concepto de honor: su entidad como objeto de investigación histórica', *Espacio, Tiempo y Forma. Serie IV, Historia moderna* 9 (1995), 191–210.

11 On these issues, see: Javier Guillamón Álvarez, *Honor y honra en la España del siglo XVIII* (Madrid: UCM, 1981); Fernando Ampudia de Haro, *Las bridas de la conducta: una aproximación al proceso civilizatorio español* (Madrid: Centro de Investigaciones Sociológicas, 2007); Mónica Bolufer Peruga, *Arte y artificio de la vida en común. Los modelos de comportamiento y sus tensiones en el Siglo de las Luces* (Madrid: Marcial Pons, 2019).

latter becoming a secondary element, more ornamental than truly operative.[12] Insofar as it constituted one of the most obvious public activities of the subject, the professional practice became one of the defining criteria of public reputation. The profession, the path through which it had been reached, the prestige that its practice had in society and the economic remuneration it could provide were the pillars on which public reputations were built in the nineteenth century.[13] It could be said that the more closed the access – with long training periods and complex qualifying tests or exams – the more prestige the profession attained. Usually, those who were already practising the activity regulated the access to it and were, therefore, the most interested in maintaining strict selection criteria to safeguard the exclusivity of this circle. In this way, intrusion was the object of the harshest attacks because, on the one hand, intruders acted outside the channels of legitimization established for the practice of the profession; on the other hand, the possible malpractice of these individuals could compromise the reputation of the entire professional collective. Professions that did not have restricted channels of access – the so-called 'open professions' – generally enjoyed less prestige, except in the case of those individuals who managed to achieve high salaries for their work.

This process was accompanied by a redefinition of the roles attributable to men and women in bourgeois society. Reputation acquired a different meaning depending on the social role of each sex, which is particularly evident in relation to the world of work. As is well known, professional practice was forbidden to women of the middle and upper classes. This does not mean that there were no women involved in certain labour activities, but it was not the rule. In the case of men, bourgeois masculinity, based on common characteristics, manifested itself in different ways in the world

12 See Pablo Ortega-del-Cerro, 'Del honor a la honradez: un recorrido por el cambio de valores sociales en la España de los siglos XVIII y XIX', *Cuadernos de Ilustración y Romanticismo* 24 (2018), 597–618.

13 Woodruff D. Smith, *Respectability as Moral Map and Public Discourse in the Nineteenth Century* (London: Routledge, 2017), 154. The concept of honour in the historical study of professions has been used – from a different approach – by Samuel Haber in his book *The Quest for Authority and Honor in the American Professions, 1750–1900* (Chicago: Chicago University Press, 1991).

of work, as will be seen throughout this book. Based on a shared corpus, the peculiarities of the different professions gave the individuals who exercised them specific masculine attributes that modelled a way of being in the public space and, specifically, in the workplace. The profiles were very diverse: from scientific intellectuality and rationality to physical courage and risk-taking, as well as an artistic sensibility duly channelled by academic institutions. In any case, the respectable bourgeois male responded to the canons of professionalism understood as a combination of broad competence in his field (demonstrated by his official qualifications), seriousness in the exercise of his profession (accredited by his clients and recognized by his peers) and a solid social position that guaranteed his economic independence. This was symbolically displayed through an adequate home and attire, a code of conduct and language appropriate to their status and membership of professional organizations for self-recognition as a group.[14] In the words of Bourdieu, these codes of conduct refer to the development of an 'habitus' linked not only to professional men but to each profession. Naturally, what is described here is the ideal standard, which did not always correspond to the more complex and nuanced reality.

The book *Respectable Professionals* tries to show all these facets through the study of various professional groups. On the one hand, it deals with the professions that best fit the stereotype described above: engineering and law. To facilitate the understanding of the study, we will group them under the label of 'liberal professions', even though they do not always conform to what we conventionally understand as such. As will be seen in the following pages, these professions exhibit a great diversity of situations that lead us to rethink the theoretical frameworks that sociology offers us to introduce other, more flexible dynamics that facilitate their analysis. In the case of Spain, as in other European countries (especially those in the south of the continent), the figure of the engineer was at the time the emblem of modernity because it united science with the physical transformation of space, with the ultimate aim of improving the living conditions of the population. Dr Martykánová and Dr Pan-Montojo explain how these men

14 For the British case see John Tosh, 'Masculinities in an Industrializing Society: Britain, 1800–1914', *Journal of British Studies* 44/2 (2005), 330–42.

of science became the hope for the physical and intellectual regeneration of the country at a time when its image as a nation was being redefined. Lawyers, for their part, are studied by Dr González Fuertes. They were the architects of the construction of the liberal state, the pillars of the new bourgeois society. In Spain, the legal profession became the breadbasket of civil servants and politicians, embodying the clearest example of bourgeois respectability.

A second group is comprised of the war-related professions and, in particular, the Naval Officer Corps and Military Corps, studied by Dr Ortega-del-Cerro, Tribaldos and Cameno. Among the Spanish military forces, the Naval Officer Corps always enjoyed the highest prestige. Filled with aristocrats in other centuries, in this chapter we will learn how it adapted from the end of the eighteenth century to the new realities of the enlightened monarchy, first, and the liberal state, later. Of particular importance, in this case, is the assumption of a concept of honour that had begun to evolve towards new significances. Meanwhile, the study of the Military Corps offers a very intriguing picture of the modernization process of the Spanish military forces. This allows us to analyse how the process of professionalization of the Army unfolded through the specialization of its elite corps. At the same time, we wanted to find out what image they projected in the society to gauge how they were perceived at a time when civilian and military power were closely intertwined in the management of political affairs.

The healthcare professions constitute the third group to be analysed and, specifically, doctors and women linked to the world of medicine. Throughout the nineteenth century, this sector underwent a profound process of change associated with advances in medical research and improvements in techniques for treating the sick. Sociologically, this was an area in which there was a progressive masculinization of activities previously carried out by women, such as childbirth care. At the same time, there was a growing presence of women in secondary tasks previously carried out by priests and nuns, tasks which thus underwent a process of specialization. Dr Núñez-García provides an insight into the plurality of situations related to the medical profession, paying special attention to the image of the doctor as a scientific hero, capable of improving the living conditions of the population. For their part, Dr Mirón and Dr González Canalejo offer us a panoramic view of what they call 'the healthcare middle class', in order to understand, from a gender perspective, the hidden realities of this group.

Professions related to creation constitute another section. Three categories have been selected: actors, painters and journalists. Throughout the nineteenth century, the cultural sector underwent extensive development between the protection of the State and the market projection. Culture was both a political instrument and a consumer good. Through the study of theatrical performance, and under the guidance of Dr Álvarez Barrientos, we will delve into the process by which an old profession with very little social prestige eventually became a respected profession, although it was still associated with old prejudices about the moral conduct of actors and actresses. Among other reasons, this was due to the interpreters' awareness of the value of their work and the need to assert it in a society of professionals. Next, Dr Gilarranz examines the painting world to explain how the modern professional painter was forged in a highly complex artistic environment in which ancient courtly and academic practices were combined with the modern idea of genius, the art market and the role of the State as a provider of commissions. Finally, Dr Raquel Sánchez studies journalism as one of the multiple facets of the work of intellectuals, together with critique, erudition and literary writing (novels, poetry and plays). Throughout the nineteenth century, the journalistic profession gradually developed its own profiles. Although it never ceased to be linked to literary activities, it gradually gained its own autonomy until it acquired a specific identity within the intellectual professions. Broadly speaking, the jobs related to creation present some very interesting peculiarities as they were open professions, based on problematic concepts (such as literary property) and with great instability due to their continuous dependence on institutions and agents that contributed to their legitimization (academies, patrons, public, readers, etc.).

The fifth professional group analysed is related to the teaching profession. Considerable rhetoric has been produced around this group in relation to the role of education as a social lift, but which concealed very difficult living and working conditions. Dr Eduardo Higueras deals with the teachers, their access to education and the efforts they made to give prestige to a profession that, socially speaking, was closely associated with economic precariousness. Especially from the 1860s onwards, this group showed a growing political commitment in which their professional demands converged with the importance they attached to education as a vehicle for improving the living conditions of the most deprived Spanish population. The situation of female teachers is studied by Dr Cristina del Prado. Her work shows that the difficulties in professional practice were even greater for female teachers. This explains the emergence of initiatives to promote female education, subject of important debates in the Spain of the second half of the nineteenth century. Projects such as the Asociación para la Enseñanza de la Mujer [Association for the Education of Women] were conceived as a mechanism to provide women with professional training that would enable them to have a respectable job in the event that, due to various circumstances, they were obliged to earn a living.

The book closes with a section that deals with two professions difficult to classify, but important for what their analysis reveals about the social reality of nineteenth-century Spain. Firstly, parish priests, studied by Dr David Martínez-Vilches. Secondly, businessmen, analysed by Dr David San Narciso. With regard to the former, and taking into account the important role played by the Catholic Church in nineteenth-century Spain, the parish clergy went from being the bottom rung of a privileged class to a kind of 'professional' for the spiritual well-being of citizens, 'doctors of the soul' whose religious vocation was of benefit to others. In this sense, while Church and State ensured the training of priests and the creation of a sustainable parish system, parish priests adapted their model of celibate masculinity to modern society and claimed a respectable public image. On the other hand, when approaching business people, as with other 'open' professions, we encounter a wide variety of activities carried out by a diverse group of individuals from different backgrounds and educational levels. It is indeed difficult to label them as a 'profession' in a narrow sense. However, it is a field in turmoil that shows better than any other the economic and cultural changes of the period, precisely because of the diversity of situations that can be encountered. In this chapter, the reader will learn about the scenario in which the economic elites moved, how they reinterpreted the codes of conduct of the old aristocratic elites and adapted them to their needs for legitimization as a group. They thus constructed a discourse in which the value of work, effort and reputation served as the basis for their real power and symbolic influence.

We finish these introductory lines outlining that this book aims to contribute to the knowledge of the Spanish professional world in the nineteenth century through the study of the most significant professions of the time. Both the selection of these professions and the theoretical approaches taken by both the editors and authors may be debatable. In any case, the purpose of the editors and authors is to provide ideas and arguments for debate and comparative study in a field of great interest to historians.

This book presents the results of the research project 'Culture of Honour, Politics and Public Sphere in Liberal Spain (1833–1890)', funded by the Ministry of Science, Innovation and Universities of Spain (PGC2018-093698-B-I00).

PART I

Renewed Professions

DARINA MARTYKÁNOVÁ AND JUAN PAN-MONTOJO

Between the State and the Market

Engineers in Nineteenth-Century Spain

ABSTRACT

The history of engineering as a profession in nineteenth-century Spain is a success story. While there were very few engineers except for the military and navy men in the beginning of the century, by the end of it, engineering was one of the most prestigious and desirable professions in Spain. Not only was it considered suitable for a son of a gentleman, it was also deemed useful and necessary for the country. Our chapter examines how the engineers negotiated their social standing in a society in which bourgeois masculinity and active citizenship were linked to ownership rather than to work. We argue that they succeeded due to a combination of factors, including the state's policies in public works, the power of the state corps and their schools and the link between the engineering and scientific education. From this solid basis they were able to establish themselves in both public and private sector as one of the few elite professions.

Introduction[1]

Engineering is a profession held in high esteem in Spain and engineering degrees are among the most prestigious ones in higher education. In fact, a diploma in engineering, particularly in the traditional branches such as industrial, mining or civil (in the sense of ponts-et-chaussées, *caminos*) engineering,[2] serve as credentials of capacity for persons, mostly men,

1 The chapter is product of research and discussions within TRANSCAP: The Transnational Construction of Capitalism during the Long 19th Century. An Approach from Two Peripheral Regions – The Iberian World and the Mediterranean [PGC2018-097023-B-100], a research project funded by the Ministry of Universities, Science and Innovation of Spain.

2 For the plurality of meanings of the term 'civil engineering', see Peter Lundgreen, 'Engineering Education in Europe and in the USA, 1750–1930: The Rise to

who often strive to become executive managers in the private sector, rather than build bridges or design machinery. The references to intelligence and hard work – qualities one cannot supposedly do without when trying to obtain an engineering diploma – as well as meritocratic selection throughout the education process, are used today to legitimize the access to posts that guarantee a high social standing. Frequently, these noble principles hide the workings of family and social class networks and affinities that play a key role in explaining why a specific person comes to hold a post in top management in the Spain of the twenty-first century.[3] Pointing to this mechanism of elite reproduction does not mean that the fact that a degree in engineering plays this legitimizing role is without significance. The path of a degree or a profession to such prestige and high social status has by no means been a straightforward one. There is nothing obvious about a degree specifically in engineering becoming a mechanism to legitimize the reproduction of social elites, presenting their high social status as well deserved within the framework of meritocratic discourse. Among us historians, the case of England where degrees in Classics and History from Oxford and Cambridge represent a privileged way of access to high-raking posts in the public administration, is well known. The notion of engineering as elite profession, well established in Spain, does not exist in Germany or the USA, but it is observable in France and Portugal, too.

To explain the prestige and elite status engineering profession has enjoyed in some countries including Spain, and the role it has played in legitimizing social elites, this chapter invites the readers to turn their glance to the nineteenth century. It was at that time when engineering became a profession in the modern sense.[4] It was a complex process that led to a

Dominance of Schools Culture and the Engineering Profession', *Annals of Science* 47 (1990), 33–75.

3 Pedro Pablo Ortúñez and Jorge Lafuente, 'Leopoldo Calvo-Sotelo: ingeniero, empresario y político frente a la integración europea', *Historia y Política* 43 (2020), 121–55. On how meritocratic selection processes hide often other social filters, see Pierre Bourdieu, *La noblesse d'état. Grandes écoles et esprit de corps* (Paris: Les éditions de Minuit, 1989).

4 André Grelon and Irina Gouzévitch, 'Reflexión sobre el ingeniero europeo en el siglo XIX: retos, problemáticas e historiografías', in Manuel Silva Suárez, ed.,

great variety of professional configurations all around the world, a variety that did not prevent mutual recognition and collaboration across national, ethnic and, in the twentieth century, also gender barriers.

Ingenious men: Engineers in the Early Modern Era

A profession is generally understood as a stable link between a paid occupation and a person who has achieved special skills in this occupation due to his/her training. Furthermore, in many cultural and historical contexts, a distinction is made between profession and a trade (*métier* in French and *oficio* in Spanish), in which profession is assigned higher social status, often due to being considered as requiring intellectual, rather than manual capacity. All these definitions are unstable and historically contingent. Therefore, history of professions needs to pay attention to issues such as class and gender when interpreting the shifting differences in social status and prestige of different occupations, and, specifically, between different liberal professions.[5]

When compared to lawyers or physicians, the consolidation of engineering as a profession took place rather late. We do find engineers in Ancient Rome, in Al-Andalus or in the Renaissance Italy, but it was one of those blurred occupational categories that aspired to pin down and classify the useful knowledge of a man.[6] The category of engineer only acquired certain stability via titles granted by the rulers to men charged with a series of tasks that required such 'ingeniousness', mostly in the art of war and in hydraulic

---

Técnica e ingeniería en España, 9 vols (Zaragoza: Real Academia de Ingeniería/ Institución 'Fernando el Católico'/Prensas Universitarias de Zaragoza, 2004–2019), vol. 4, 269–321.

5 A summary of some of the important debates in the history of professions in M. Burrage and R. Torstendhal, eds, *Professions in Theory and History. Rethinking the Study of the Professions* (London/New Delhi: Sage Publications, 1990).

6 For the Iberian lands, see the encyclopaedic work by Silva Suárez, ed., *Técnica e Ingeniería en España*.

works applied to irrigation, navigation and mining.[7] There was no clear link for the engineers between a more or less standardized education, on the one hand, and a professional category on the other. Such link existed in Western Christendom between medical and law professions and university education, though both in medicine and in law many people were recognized by the community, by the authorities and by their university-trained colleagues as legal or medical professionals without such education. Medical practitioners and surgeons acquired their knowledge and skills by training with senior professionals, assisting them in their everyday practice. They could also broaden their knowledge through reading and travels of learning. The engineers had to rely almost exclusively on this path of informal learning to build a reputation for themselves and be acknowledged as experts in their field. Engineering could not be studied at a university. There were many ways of becoming an engineer, and, at the same time, most of the engineers' work could also be done by people who did not even call themselves engineers.

Since the late seventeenth century, empires such as Russia, France, Spain, Portugal or the Ottoman Empire began to put in place stable structures that regulated the ways to become and to work as engineer for the sovereign. Official titles of engineer were granted to those appointed for expert posts, engineering corps and academies that trained the members of these corps in applied mathematics and in engineering theory and practice.[8] While the division between the civil and the military was still rather blurred, these institutions contributed to promote the link between engineering and the art of war. Moreover, engineering was thus institutionalized in many countries as a career at the service of the Crown, often a military one, rather than a liberal profession operating at the market. The image of engineer as an officer, supported by this tradition and institutional framework, was to

7 Hélène Verin, *La gloire des ingénieurs. L'intelligence technique du XVIe au XVIIIe siècle* (Paris: Albin Michel, 1993).

8 Irina Gouzévitch, Ana Cardoso de Matos and Darina Martykánová, 'La Russie, l'Espagne, le Portugal et l'Empire Ottoman: deux siècles de politiques technoscientifiques à l'épreuve des approches comparatistes', in Mina Kleiche-Dray, ed., *Les ancrages nationaux de la science mondiale, XVIIIe-XXIe siècles* (Paris/Marseille: EAC/IDR, 2017), 239–86.

play a key role in the consolidation during the nineteenth century of the civil corps of state engineers as the 'state nobility' (*noblesse d'État*), to use the words of Pierre Bourdieu for the new elites within the expanding administrative apparatus, in empires such as France, Spain or Russia.[9]

At the same time, the rulers continued to make use of men with proven knowledge of and skills in hydraulic works. Canals became, so to say, an extremely fashionable government initiative in the eighteenth century. Complex machinery, including steam engine, was applied to strategic sectors such as mining. The men who built and managed these works and supervised the operation of these machines were often called engineers, too. Their education tended to be eclectic and diverse, a combination of studying mathematics and physics and practical training and experimentation. Unlike lawyers and physicians, professions where there existed a clear – although not exclusive – path towards the title via university diploma, becoming an engineer was a process in which one studied, trained and worked to create an expert reputation for himself. The men who worked for the political powers in relatively prestigious posts were, in great part, self-taught gentlemen, who studied relevant disciplines working with acknowledged experts, reading, travelling and training by observation in locations where similar works and machines were in operation. For their activity as inventors, for their learned publications and for their style as refined men of the Enlightenment, these *savants* were able to get acknowledged as members of the Republic of Letters, a trans-imperial space of intellectual sociability that encompassed Europe, America and many foci

9 Antoine Picon, *L'invention de l'ingénieur moderne. L'École de Ponts et Chaussées 1747–1851* (Paris: Presses de l'Ecole Nationale des Ponts et Chaussées, 1992); Ken Alder, *Engineering the Revolution: Arms and Enlightenment in France, 1763–1815* (Pinceton: Princeton University Press, 1999); Irina Gouzévitch, 'L'institut des ingénieurs des Vois de communication de Saint-Petersburg: des modèles étrangers à l'école nationale (1809–1836)', in Irina Gouzévitch, André Grelon and Anousheh Karvar, eds, *La formation des ingénieurs en perspective. Modèles de référence et réseaux e médiation (XVIIIe-XXe siècles)* (Rennes: Presses Universitaires de Rennes, 2004), 127–39; Dmitri Gouzévitch and Irina Gouzévitch, 'Les corps d'ingénieurs comme forme d'organisation professionnelle en Russie: Genèse, évolution, spécificité: XVIIIe et XIXe siècles', *Cahiers du monde russe* 41/4 (2000), 569–614.

all over the world.[10] The self-fashioning of engineers as learned gentlemen (*savants*) who were capable of making their knowledge useful, for the Crown or for mankind, was to become another of the pillars that sustained the construction of engineering as an elite profession in some countries, including Spain.

In parallel, and in dialogue with both figures linked to the government, a professional profile generally known as civil engineer was emerging in the areas of industrial development in Europe, America, West Asia and North Africa. They were men who put their know-how into practice at the market, selling their inventions or providing expert services to entrepreneurs and companies engaged in activities that required a sophisticated technical management. Sugar plantations in the colonies and mines were among the first such spaces, before the expansion of privately operated transport infrastructures. In countries where the industrialization was very limited, the consolidation of this professional profile was not easy. Few industrialists or owners of plantations or estates were ready to hire an engineer and pay him according to his self-perception as gentleman of certain standing, as they did not perceive a clear need for his expert technical knowledge. England, with its *Society of Civil Engineers* created in 1771, was rather an exception, due to the early and particularly widespread impact of the first industrial revolution.[11]

10 Agustín de Betancourt is a striking example of a Spaniard who was particularly successful in gaining acknowledgement as member of the Republic of Letters and whose se career as engineer was truly trans-imperial. The best monograph on Betancourt still awaits translation to Spanish: Irina Gouzévitch, *Planète "Betancourt"* (Paris: Habilitation à diriger les recherches/ Université Paris Diderot, 2018). Peter Jones has explored the clash between the sociability and intellectual exchange among gentleman savants, with the new logic of patenting endorsed by men who strove to make a living from their inventions. Peter Jones, 'Commerce des Lumières': The International Trade in Technology, 1763–1815', *Quaderns d'Història de l'Enginyeria* 10 (2009), 67–82.

11 For an overview of the ways of being an engineer in the eighteenth century, see Irina Gouzévitch Irina and Hélène Verin, 'Sobre la institución y el desarrollo de la ingeniería: una perspectiva europea', in Silva Suárez, ed., *Técnica e ingeniería en España,* vol. 3, 115–63.

Becoming an engineer in nineteenth-century Spain

In nineteenth-century Spain, there were several ways of becoming an engineer. Engineers were the officers of the military corps of engineers (army engineers and naval engineers) who, in principle, had been trained in special academies and then received an empirical training in the regiments and arsenals. Not all the Spanish military engineers had gone through institutions of formal training: some of them had been promoted from lower ranks or had been directly accepted as officers in engineering units, especially during the war on both sides of the Atlantic and had acquired their expertise in the field.[12]

In contrast to the relative uniformity of military engineers, civilian engineers were a heterogeneous group. The term *ingenieros civiles* was used to distinguish them from military men, unlike in France where *ingénieur civil* referred to a man working in private sector, in contrast to the state engineers. First and foremost, among these civilian engineers there were practitioners, Spanish and foreign, who had trained as engineers working at engineering works in Spain and abroad, high-skilled mechanics, specialized workers and successful inventors. These men called themselves engineers and were able to get acknowledged as such by society and by the people who were ready to pay for their services, but, as we will outline below, in the nineteenth century their entitlement to call themselves engineers was to come under attack by their peers who had acquired higher technical education.

12 Horacio Capel, Luis García et al., *Los ingenieros militares en España. Siglo XVIII. Repertorio biográfico e inventario de su labor científica y espacial* (Barcelona: Publicacions i edicions de la Universität de Barcelona, 1983); Horacio Capel, Joan Eugeni Sánchez and Omar Moncada, *De Palas a Minerva. La formación científica y la estructura institucional de los ingenieros militares en el siglo XVIII* (Barcelona-Madrid: Ediciones del Serbal-CSIC, 1988); José Ignacio Muro Morales, 'Ingenieros militares: la formación y la práctica profesional de unos oficiales facultativos', in Silva Suárez, ed., *Técnica e ingeniería en España*, vol. 4, 589–643; Martine Galland-Seguela, *Les ingénieurs militaires espagnoles de1710 à 1803. Etude prosopographique et sociale d'un corps d'élite* (Madrid: Bibliothèque de la Casa de Velázquez, 2008).

The second group of the civilian engineers, probably the most exclusive one, were people – Spanish men, to be exact – who had graduated from the different Spanish schools of engineering, called special schools, which were created outside university. The first non-military school, aimed at training ponts-et-chaussées engineers (*ingenieros de caminos*), opened in Madrid for the first time in 1802 and, after different interruptions, was re-opened as Escuela de Ingenieros de Caminos in 1834. Mining engineers had various training centres from 1777 onwards, including a dynamic institution of higher learning in the city of Mexico, in the colonial New Spain, although in 1835, the only national school for mining engineers was established in Madrid. Following the models of the other two branches, in 1846 a school for forestry engineers was created in Villaviciosa de Odón, not far from Madrid. Between 1850 and 1867, the Real Instituto Industrial de Madrid, acted as the school for industrial engineers. This branch of engineering, which, as we will see, had many other peculiar traits (including the non-existence of a public corps until the twentieth century), was the only one that, after 1857, had other centres where the title could be obtained: Barcelona, Gijón, Seville, Valencia and Vergara. However, the School of Barcelona was the sole school that had continuity, because of the willingness of local authorities to contribute to its funding, and most of the nineteenth-century industrial engineers graduated from this school.[13] Only in 1899 started its classes a new school of Industrial Engineers in Bilbao and two years later a similar centre was created in Madrid. Finally, in 1855 a General School of Agriculture opened in Aranjuez (Madrid) to prepare engineers-agronomists or agricultural engineers. In 1869, it was transferred to Madrid, and called Escuela de Ingenieros Agrónomos.[14]

Finally, there were those engineers who had obtained their title in France, Belgium, Switzerland, the German states, Austria-Hungary, Great Britain and other countries. Many of them were foreign, but there were as

13 Guillermo Lusa Monforte, 'La difícil consolidación de las enseñanzas industriales (1855–1873)', *Documentos de la Escuela de Ingenieros Industriales de Barcelona* 7 (1997), 114–9.

14 Juan Pan-Montojo, *Apostolado, profesión y tecnología. Una historia de los ingenieros agrónomos en España* (Madrid: Asociación Nacional de Ingenieros Agrónomos, 2005).

well quite a few Spaniards, although we do not know the exact number.[15] In 1901, there were 206 foreign engineers working in Spain, according to an inquiry organized by the Ministry of Education, although the minister himself estimated that the real number was twice the one the inquiry determined.[16] In the same year, according to the same source, there were 1,386 foreign technicians; among them, many carried out what the Spanish legislation – or the consensus among Spanish engineers – considered as engineering tasks.

As for the Spaniards with a foreign title, besides those who had gone to foreign schools before schools catering for the private sector were founded in Spain,[17] many did so because their families, or themselves, preferred the education they could obtain abroad. Others were just the outcome of a system that, outside industrial engineering, linked expert education to state corps. Those who wished to avoid sitting the entrance exams in a tough competition for scarce places, or failed the exams, had no option left, but travelling abroad and getting a title that did not enable them to enter any administrative career, since the validation of titles was very difficult.

As the century advanced and the power of the state technical corps recruited through the special schools grew (ponts-et-chaussées and mining engineering since the mid-1830s, forestry engineering since the 1850s, engineers-agronomists since 1879), more and more legal barriers were imposed on the engineers with foreign diplomas while the acknowledgement as engineers was straightforwardly denied to men without a diploma, particularly if they were Spaniards. Spanish engineers from the special schools regarded this struggle as a part of their campaigns against *intrusismo* [intruder-ism]. This term, which has no exact equivalent in other languages, was and is used to define the exercise of a profession by

15 Aingeru Zabala Uriarte, 'Una inversión: estudiar en el extranjero: ingenieros españoles del siglo XIX', *Quaderns d'història de l'enginyeria* 13 (2012), 287–347.

16 Francisco Villacorta Baños, *Profesionales y burócratas. Estado y poder corporativo en la España del siglo XX, 1890–1923* (Madrid: Siglo XXI, 1989), 113.

17 Darina Martykánová, 'Global Engineers: Professional Trajectories of the Graduates of the École Centrale des Arts et Manufactures (1830s–1920s)', in David Pretel and Lino Camprubí, eds, *Technology and Globalisation. Networks of Experts in World History* (London: Palgrave Macmillan, 2018), 75–104.

people who, despite not having acquired the credentials fixed by the law, dare to use professional titles (physicians,[18] *ingenieros* …) or to undertake the projects and tasks defined as professional by those who have the competence to do so. By those recognized as 'genuine' professionals by the law or by the bodies entitled to dictate who is a professional. The fight against 'intruders' became a political issue from the 1890s onwards. The growth of the industrial sector, as well as a mining boom in the first years of the twentieth century, brought about tensions between military and civilian engineers and between Spanish engineers with Spanish titles and the rest of the engineers.[19] By 1900, according to the Census, there were 5,414 engineers and architects in the country (although this figure was a result of self-identification in the census questionnaires) and 784 active engineers in the state corps.[20] The latter number was a minimum and the Census figure was inflated, since it included architects, but still they give us a picture of a socio-professional group whose members had, in a proportion of 3–4 to one, not studied engineering in the Spanish schools.[21]

Engineering in nineteenth-century Spain: A profession?

Spanish engineering followed in the nineteenth century the trajectory of professionalization. The concept of profession, both in its nineteenth-century definition and in the sociology of professions, underlines a

18 See Víctor M. Núñez-García, 'A Physician and a Gentleman: Individual Dimension of the Collective Pursuit of Social Standing', in this volume.

19 Baños, *Profesionales y burócratas*, 113–25.

20 The Census data from Dirección general del Instituto Geográfico y Estadístico. Ministerio de Instrucción Pública y Bellas Artes, *Censo de la población de España en 1900 según el empadronamiento hecho el 31 de diciembre de 1900* (Madrid: Imprenta del Instituto Geográfico y Estadístico, 1907), vol. 4, 214, and the ones concerning the public corps in Villacorta Baños, *Profesionales y burócratas*, 113–25.

21 Those engineers who belonged to the corps but did not work in public positions allocated to the corps – for instance, those teaching in universities, or doing official tasks in the colonies – were not included.

connection between an occupation for which one receives either fees (honorariums) for their services or a salary and a specific training acknowledged by peers. *Capitalistas* [capitalists], *fabricantes* [industrialists], *comerciantes* [traders] or *empresarios* [impresarios or public concession holders] were not professionals: these figures, with their different nuances, were linked to ownership rather than to knowledge, as was the *terrateniente* [landowner] or the *rentista* [somebody living off rents, normally land, buildings or public debt].[22] In fact, they were grouped under the term *propietario* [proprietor] if they could live off their property. Professionals defined themselves in contrast to these specific figures (not to the one of proprietor, although they would not present themselves as such, unless they wanted to underline that they were not exercising their profession), emphasizing their expert knowledge, which they brought to the market and for which they demanded a remuneration corresponding to a gentleman. In the electoral systems based on the taxes payed (*census suffrage*), they also demanded and achieved an exception based on their knowledge and its usefulness for the country, under the name in Spain of *capacidades* [capacities].

A profession was not a public office, either. Nonetheless, in nineteenth-century Spain, the so-called expert corps (*cuerpos facultativos*) contributed decisively to the consolidation of engineering as a liberal profession when engineers had hard times living off their work in the private sector, in the market. Those corps existed for the mining engineers (1833), the ponts-et-chaussées engineers (1799/1836), the forestry engineers (1853), the engineers-agronomists or agricultural engineers (1879) and the industrial engineers (1911), although these last ones did not have direct access to the civil service and needed an *oposición* or selection procedure. Until the mid-nineteenth century, only few men were able to earn a good living as engineers in the private sector, precisely because they claimed a payment corresponding to a gentleman. Most of these engineers who worked outside

22 On these terms and their use in the nineteenth century, see Carmen García García, 'El lenguaje económico: empresarios, fabricantes, capitalistas, propietarios y comerciantes en el siglo XIX español', in Manuel Pérez Ledesma, ed., *Lenguajes de la modernidad en la Península Ibérica* (Madrid: Ediciones Universidad Autónoma de Madrid, 2012), 431–57.

the public institutions were either self-employed, in their own firm or estate, or foreign. Spanish men who came from well-off families that had been able to fund their higher education in engineering, such as the members of wealthy Andalusian industrial families Larios and Heredia who had studied at the *École centrale des arts et manufactures* in Paris, did not work as liberal professionals once their finished their studies, mostly in prestigious schools abroad. Instead, they ran their family businesses and expanded and modernized them, paying other people to implement technological innovation.[23] In some cases, particularly in Catalonia, sons of industrial entrepreneurs worked as engineers in the family company. Those who had no such family connections and did achieve to make a good living as engineers operating in the incipient techno-scientific labour market in Spain were foreigners, with or without an engineering diploma. They mobilized the prestige of the countries where they came from or where they studied, as industrial hotbeds, to achieve local business partners and invest in enterprises related to their expertise or to get a well-paid job in mostly foreign mining and infrastructure companies. Thus, for instance, Bartolomé, Paradas and Mirás-Araujo have shown the importance of foreign engineers in the first stages of introduction of gas in the cities of Spain.[24] Pretel and Fernández de Pinedo have explored how the prosperous and expanding sugar industry in the colonial Cuba turned the island into a land of opportunities for the engineers from many European countries.[25] The situation began to change in the second half of the nineteenth century, particularly in its last third, when the demand for engineers and the willingness to pay good fees and salaries for their services grew rapidly.[26]

23 Martykánová, 'Global Engineers', 75–104.

24 Bartolomé Rodríguez, Isabel, Mercedes Fernández Paradas and Jesús Mirás-Araujo, eds, *Globalización, nacionalización y liberación de la industria del gas en la Europa latina (siglos XIX–XXI)* (Madrid: Marcial Pons, 2017).

25 Pretel David and Nadia Fernández de Pinedo, 'Technology Transfer and Expert Migration in Nineteenth-Century Cuba', *EUI Working Papers, MWP* 34 (2013).

26 Garrabou, Ramón, *Enginyers industrials, modernització econòmica i burgesia a Catalunya (1850 – inicis del segle XX)* (Barcelona: L'Avenç/Collegi d'Enginyers Industrials, 1982).

Another important group of men who succeeded in creating a space for themselves on the limited and competitive engineering labour market were the state engineers. They either engaged in private business while working for the state, or, after having worked as expert public employees decided to switch to the private sector, a decision that could be reverted if there were vacant posts.

Table 1 contains information on the different branches of engineering in the 1880s and their situation, from the point of view of work. In the case of civil, mining and forestry engineers, it shows the official data on

Table 1. Graduates from the Spanish special schools of engineering in the public and private sector in Spain and the overseas Spanish possessions

	Civil (1880)	Agricultural (1892)	Industrial (1885)	Mining (1880)	Forestry (1883)
Active in the state corps (a) or in the public administration (b)	247 (a)	243 (b)	120 (b)	153 (a)	151 (a)
Supernumerary	97			24	27
Private companies		1	196		
Their own firms/estates		6	60		
Unknown			92		
Total	344	250	468	177	178

Sources: Manuel Silva Suárez and Guillermo Lusa Monforte, 'Cuerpos facultativos del Estado *versus* profesión liberal: la singularidad de la ingeniería industrial', in Silva Suárez, ed., *Técnica e ingeniería en España*, vol. 4, 372; Eduardo de la Sotilla and Gabriel del Valle, *Guía del Servicio Agronómico* (Madrid: Imprenta de la Viuda de Minuesa de los Ríos, 1892), 222–37; *Cuadro del Servicio Facultativo del Ramo de Minas en Febrero de 1880* (Madrid: Revista Minera, 1880); *Escalafón del Cuerpo de Ingenieros de Montes* (Madrid: Imprenta del Colegio Nacional de Sordo-mudos y de Ciegos, 1883); 'Escalafón del cuerpo de ingenieros de caminos', *Gaceta de Madrid* 3 (3 January 1881), 25–6.

members of the state corps, and therefore it only conveys the distinction between those engineers who were active in positions officially allocated to the corps and those who either worked in the private sector or held a political office or worked for the State in posts that did not belong to their corps (universities, high schools, colonial service ...): the so-called supernumerary engineers. In the case of industrial and agricultural engineers, we have data from the Association of Industrial Engineers and from a book written by an agricultural engineer, and hence the distinction between those who worked for the Public Administration in corps positions and those who did too, but were in other posts, is not made. Despite these differences, Table 1 clearly shows three types of relations between engineers with a Spanish title and the public/private sectors. Industrial engineers were basically private sector professionals, although around a 25 per cent worked for the State. Ponts-et-chaussées engineers worked for the State, but a maximum of a third (most probably around a 20 per cent), in 1880, were liberal professionals or employed professionals. The other types of engineers (mining, forestry and agronomists) had fewer chances of earning an 'adequate' living outside the public administration, and only about a 10 per cent (even less when we talk about agronomists-engineers) were employed elsewhere, or self-employed.

The state-corps engineers who worked outside the State founded their own companies, joined forces with private investors or accepted well-paid management jobs. In this process, which the French sociologists call *pantouflage*, they left the state service taking with them a well-established social standing and expert reputation that the state engineers enjoyed as a group, but also useful contacts and networks created during their public service, ready to be exploited for private gain. In fact, the full-blown *pantouflage* was a late nineteenth-century phenomenon and, as we have explained, with wide differences among specialities. In the previous decades, the engineers preferred to keep their comfortable public salary while, at the same time, engaging in all sort of businesses, from running private academies that prepared wealthy young candidates for entry exams to engineering schools, to providing consult services to companies or commercializing their inventions. The repeated efforts to legislate on this matter are a sign of the growing perception of such practice as problematic, but also of the uselessness of the efforts to limit it or put an end to it.[27]

The sociology of professions has traditionally identified several features of the process of professionalization: (1) the effort to clearly define a field of expertise and practice; (2) the link between a remunerated occupation and specific training; (3) public acknowledgement and legal sanction of a limited and regulated access to professional practice; (4) professional self-regulation (professional chambers and associations); (5) professional discourse and its platforms (professional press). Taken these into consideration, was engineering a profession in nineteenth-century Spain? The link between training and professional practice was not enforced in the private sector, despite the effort of the engineers who had been trained in an institution of higher education to make a diploma from an engineering school a mandatory requirement. After the period when the demand for engineers in the private sector was very low, the growing willingness since the 1860s to pay for an engineer's services started to create opportunities for foreign and local men of very diverse training. Working as an engineer was in practice available to self-trained people, to those who had trained in a workshop or working with an expert engineer and, of course, to those who held a diploma from an institution of higher learning in Spain or abroad. Nonetheless, unlike their colleagues in many other countries, Spanish engineers – like their French counterparts – were able to establish a monopoly on the access to expert posts in the public sector. From this privileged position, they were able not only to achieve useful contacts of high value if they switched to the private sector, but also to promote the

27 The 1863 Regulation of the corps of the ponts-et-chaussées engineers (*caminos*) addressed the issue of a conflict of interest, establishing that while an engineer remained public employee, he could not apply for public works nor participate in the execution of public contracts, at the state, provincial or municipal levels. The 1863 Regulation, title 2, chapter 5, article 61. 'Reglamento orgánico del Cuerpo de Ingenieros de Caminos, canales y puertos', *Revista de Obras Públicas* 22 (1863), 257–71. State engineers could, however, apply for an authorization to complement their salary working in private sector and many of them did so. The 22 June 1877 made public service compatible with free professional practice. Overall, the incompatibility legislation often changed and was interpreted with great flexibility throughout the nineteenth century.

notion of engineering as an elite profession that should only be accessed via higher education and to restrict competition through the enforcement of regulation to fight *intrusismo*.

Training, collective action, useful science and identity: The plural world of engineers aiming at becoming a social elite

The emphasis on a specialized higher education had to do with two intertwined, albeit apparently contradictory concerns. The first concern was to safeguard the professions' elite social status, so that it was an occupation suitable for a gentleman. University education had been traditionally established as a signifier of a certain social status. The newly founded special schools and academies strove to equal and surpass the prestige – and political rights – university education granted to men. It was an important socio-economic filter in a society where only the privileged few could afford to get through the different levels of education and reach the highest level, and even fewer were able to fund several years of engineering studies often far from their hometown. The second concern was to make the elite status which they claimed for the whole profession, appear as based on individual merit. Higher education was to provide legitimizing mechanisms for the engineers' aspirations to social status, power and expert authority, by granting standard expert knowledge certified by a diploma and including meritocratic procedures such as exam-based selection throughout the learning process.

The discourse of nineteenth-century Spanish engineers was full of references to how demanding their training had been and how much it had shaped their character, making them resistant to sloth and corruption.[28] They used the 'long years at school' as an argument against the liberalization of the access to expert public posts and in their struggle with *intrusismo*.

28 Darina Martykánová, 'Shaping a New Man: The Schools for the State Engineers in Nineteenth-Century Spain (1830s–1900)', *Engineering Studies* 7 (2014), 87–107.

This strategy, that must be interpreted taking to consideration that in the private sector, engineering was not a regulated profession and any man, local and foreign, who was able to convince an entrepreneur to hire him or pay for his services as engineer, could do so. Only when it came to making a contract with the State or producing an expert report before a court or certifying technical aspects of an activity or an establishment, the signature of somebody with a title of engineer might become necessary.

The epic of becoming an engineer was reinforced by two factors: the entrance exams and the fact that future engineers were taught almost exclusively by engineers. In all the engineering branches which had a public corps connected to the schools (that is to say, where those who graduated became automatically applicants to the corps, ordered by their ranking within each year group [*promoción*], and had to be admitted as soon as there was any vacancy), the number of admittances were severely curtailed. There had to be a certain relationship between graduates and short-term vacancies. Hence, even counting with failures and abandonments, very few places were on offer each year. Therefore, there were many more applicants than places and an entrance exam was created to filter them. For this reason, young people started to prepare the entrance exam when still receiving secondary education and often had to continue their preparation for one or more years, whilst the members of their generations were already at university or enjoying their youth in social meetings, accumulating conquests or searching for adequate fiancées. Quite a few engineers worked as instructors for the applicants, earning extra money and strengthening their authority over people who might eventually become their younger colleagues. Moreover, once the exam was passed and the young students entered the school, their teachers in almost every course were engineers, and their study and exercises were directed by the older students. Obviously, in the first years of every school it was necessary to hire professors coming from the university faculties or other pre-existing institutions. Gradually, all schools managed to have a staff made up by engineers, who not only had the right qualifications (how else, coming from such a selective world, they would argue), but also the right values and outlook. Among the forestry engineers, it was well known that the initial staff –who included amateur botanists, gardeners … – received a symbolic admittance as forestry engineers, known as the 'consecration of bishops', since it was understood that otherwise they were not able to award the title to the students.[29]

Furthermore, the meritocratic ritual of exams did not cease once a candidate was admitted to the school. The students were frequently examined and ordered according to their performance, which strengthened the *esprit de corps* based on a hierarchy combining seniority (an impersonal criterion) with meritocratic elements. The joint suffering did so, too. True, the engineers' memoirs emphasize the iron discipline in the engineering schools in comparison with the chaos and idleness reigning at the university and gloss over the confirmed cases of protests and systematic misbehaviour among engineering students.[30] However, the mandatory attendance, frequent examinations and, in case of the forestry engineers, the isolation in a boarding school far from the lights of the city, did limit the students' social lives in comparison to their university counterparts.[31] Unsurprisingly, they used these peculiarities of their school years when presenting their position within the state apparatus and their social standing as a well-deserved right, rather than a privilege.[32]

In these circumstances and given the benefits of getting the title of engineer, the reader might be surprised by the engineers' lack of effort to establish a professional association, let alone a self-regulating professional body (a chamber – *colegio*). It was not until the early twentieth century that an engineering association eventually saw the light of the day. The Instituto de Ingenieros Civiles de España was created in 1905 by the associations of the

29 There is a picture at the Escuela Superior Técnica de Ingenieros de Montes, in Madrid, that represents the scene of the 'consecration of the bishops', painted by Miguel Sanguino. It is reproduced in Silva Suárez, ed., *Técnica e ingeniería en España*, vol. 5, 410.

30 Martykánová, 'Shaping a New Man', 87–107.

31 Amador Montenegro López, ed., *Memorias de un ingeniero del siglo XIX: Eduardo Cabello Ebrentz* (Madrid: Colegio de Ingenieros de Caminos, Canales y Puertos, 1991).

32 Among many self-flattering defences, see, for instance, the article in which a ponts-et-chaussées engineer defends the three civil cops (mines, ponts-et-chaussées and forestry) from an accusation in a newspaper of being privileged and rather useless 'friars of our time': O.N., 'Los ingenieros civiles (1)', *Revista de obras públicas* 17 (1872), 198–9.

different specialities, although two of them (the Asociación de Ingenieros de Caminos and the Asociación de Ingenieros de Minas) were set up for this purpose, to put on an equal footing their branches with the oldest association: those of the industrial engineers (established in 1861), the agricultural engineers (1872) and the forestry engineers (1889). It seems that the creation of the Instituto de Ingenieros Civiles was a result of the long debate with military engineers, who from the 1893 were officially authorized to work as civil engineers in the different fields.[33]

As Manuel Silva has convincingly argued, the long-lasting lack of a joint association of engineers, and the fact that once it appeared it was built as a federation of the different branches, was due to the great power held by the state engineers. State engineers, organized in civil and military engineering corps, monopolized public employment and did not wish to open it up to the engineers from the schools (firstly the *escuelas de ingenieros industriales* and then the *escuela de ingenieros agrónomos*) that were supposed to supply the private sector. Therefore, the different groups of engineers did not have a strong common interest. Moreover, each of the state corps had a strong *esprit de corps* forged in the respective special school and the engineers identified themselves mostly with these specific engineering 'careers' (the corps of army and naval engineers; the corps of ponts-et-chaussées, mines and forestry engineers, and, much later, in 1879, engineers-agronomists) and organized themselves along these lines, rather than acting in common.

This division based on engineering branches shaped the professional discourses and their platforms, too. Professional journals tended to be private initiatives but were often fast endorsed by the engineers who came out of the same state school, both if they continued in active public service or worked in the private sector (*Revista de obras públicas*, *Revista Minera*). Only the industrial engineers, whose school was not linked to a state corps and was supposed to supply the private sector to begin with, created several journals that were at the same time a platform of professional debate and learning and a vehicle of techno-scientific dissemination (*Gaceta industrial*). While more open to general public, they tended to have a more

33 See Muro Morales, 'Ingenieros militares', 589–643.

specific ideological profile and were often short-lived precisely because they lacked the backing of a strong, coherent engineering corps.

One way or another, this plural scene, on which the state corps, particularly the civilian ones, wielded great power and set the tone, was a space of professionalization of engineering in Spain. By the end of the nineteenth century, the engineer was a clearly recognizable figure in the Spanish social imaginary and one of an elite status, too. While the industrial engineers complained bitterly about the state engineers monopolizing expert posts in the public sector, they, at the same time, benefited greatly from the elite profile the state engineers had first been able to achieve and embody. The latter mobilized the traditional prestige the service to the sovereign entailed and combined it with patriotic discourse that presented them as 'disinterested' civil servants defending common good. They fashioned themselves as an aristocracy of the new era that, thanks to their expert knowledge, pushed Spain forwards on the path of the progress of civilization.[34]

In Spain, as well as in Portugal, Russia and several other countries, engineering thus emerged from the nineteenth century as an elite profession, besides law and medicine that had held the status of a gentlemanly occupation for centuries. We have not only the engineers' own statements to attest for this; contemporary novels are full of examples of the sons from well-off families being sent to study medicine, law or engineering to the big cities. While engineering was a newcomer to this privileged group of gentlemanly professions, the novelty had its comparative advantages. While lawyers were often perceived as vacuous and parasitical, fanning conflict and disorder for their material gain, engineers' work was perceived as tangible and useful. The long-standing tradition of medicine and law as a suitable occupation for sons of the well-off families led to the existence of a great number of professionals on a highly competitive market, and to the co-existence of rich and poor professionals. This inequality was a major challenge for the self-image of both professions (the relative poverty of rural physicians was of great concern to physicians as a professional

34 Darina Martykánová and Víctor M. Núñez-García, 'Ciencia, patria y honor: los médicos e ingenieros y la masculinidad romántica en España (1820–1860)', *Studia Historica. Historia contemporánea* 38 (2020), 45–75.

group, as it could endanger the gentlemanly profile of medical profession).[35] Comparatively, as there were few engineering schools in Spain and the access was strictly limited – something the engineers generally supported as it helped them keep the hard-won elite profile – the engineers were much less in number than the physicians or the lawyers. Furthermore, an important part of them held a well-paid public post. Nonetheless, as soon as the number of private-sector engineers increased, the notion emerged of Spain as a country where an engineer could not easily commercialize his ingeniousness, due to both lack of opportunities and the lack of honesty of local entrepreneurs.[36] This narrative co-existed in parallel with the real-life success stories of Spanish engineers taking over the technical management of some of the industries first launched mostly by foreigners, such as gas or urban infrastructures.[37] Another success story, and an example of *pantouflage*, is that of former state engineers getting rich by creating prosperous private companies that dealt in innovative technology (hydroelectricity, sugar factories, industrial sawmills …).

The real consolidation of engineering as a profession took place at the very end of the nineteenth century, and at the beginning of the twentieth, when innovative technology expanded due to institutional changes. Between 1898 and 1903, thanks to the inflow of capital from the lost colonies of Cuba, Puerto Rico, and the Philippines and to the end of the conflict with the USA, there was a peak in investment in Spain. It served to accelerate the construction of modern industrial companies, which so far had only existed in the railways and the mining sector.[38] 'Modern companies' are, according to Chandler, those with two features: the existence of different operative units within the company and the direction of those units by a hierarchy of executives hired for a wage.[39] Many of those

35 Núñez-García, 'A Physician and a Gentleman', this volume.

36 Pío Baroja, *El árbol de la ciencia* (Madrid: Rafael Caro Raggio, 1911).

37 Bartolomé Rodríguez, Fernández Paradas and Mirás-Araujo, *Globalización, nacionalización*.

38 Albert Carreras and Xavier Tafunell, *Historia económica de la España contemporánea (1789–2009)* (Barcelona: Crítica, 2010), 199.

39 Alfred D. Chandler, *The Visible Hand. The Managerial Revolution in American Business* (Cambridge: Belknapp, 1977).

companies expanded in the sector attached to the second industrial revolution, in which techno-science played a key role, since production was very complex and implied a deep understanding of chemical and physical processes. Graduates from the university faculties of sciences provided in some countries the necessary technical staff, whereas in Spain engineers managed to monopolize the leading positions and the best wages (those a gentleman could expect). After all, they had convinced society that they were an elite constructed around the 'useful science', that is, the applied sciences and technology, what was needed to import and adapt solutions for the new companies. Moreover, when the State created a special programme to send young students to foreign universities and research centres, in response to the demand of its involvement in the field of techno-scientific production to overcome what many public voices after the crisis provoked by the loss of the empire, had called 'the backwardness of the country', a special programme was created for engineers.[40]

The public image of engineers bore its fruits for all its branches, although not to the same extent. Industrial engineers were the most demanded ones, but the other engineering branches found also many new outlets in the private sector. The prominent position in the state administration, enabled them as a group (as the creation of the Instituto de Ingenieros Civiles conveyed) to enter the expanding world of industrial and public services companies in a hegemonic position that was to consolidate a path-dependency, a self-reproducing tendency, for the twentieth and even for the twenty-first centuries in Spain.

Being an engineer in Spain: A discrete professional style?

The nineteenth century is, in a way, a period of transition in professional regulation. In principle, the guild control was abolished, and professions and 'arts' were liberalized during the age of revolutions. Even if many of

40 Francisco Villacorta Baños, *La regeneración técnica: la Junta de pensiones de ingenieros y obreros en el extranjero (1910–1936)* (Madrid: CSIC, 2012).

them were fervent partisans of liberal regimes, elite professionals were not willing to accept free access to professional practice of law and medicine. They argued that their long and costly education guaranteed the correct professional practice and had to be established as a mandatory requirement for professional practice. Therefore, rather than a liberalization, established elite professional underwent the redefinition of existing professional regulation according to the new logic of equality before the Law, in which the exclusivity of access could only be based on nationality, sex, good health and acceptable physical appearance, and a clearly defined merit. Examination in front of self-regulating professional bodies was often to be replaced or accompanied with the requirement of a diploma from an institution of specialized higher education, either a university or a special school. The growing emphasis on formal, standardized training certified by a diploma is known as credentialism.

Engineering, as we have discussed above, was not a guild-regulated 'art'. Neither was it an established elite profession with long-standing links to university education like law and medicine, even if these two professions could and were still practiced without a university degree in nineteenth-century Europe and its colonial domains. Informal factors played an extremely important role in getting acknowledgement – as they still do, for instance, in history: a historian is not a necessarily a person with degree in history but needs to establish herself or himself as such by engaging in a series of practices. In the nineteenth century, very few elite professions had a clear ritual of becoming, as described by Pierre Bourdieu: you sit the final exam and then either you pass and become an engineer/physician/lawyer or you fail and are denied the honour.[41] In the case of engineering, the state corps came to operate this way, but they by no means monopolized the profession of engineer in Spain. As we have already stressed, in that period an engineer was a man able to get paid for working as engineer. Even the field of expertise and practice was blurred and shifting. There was no clear notion of engineering as a field, however vast and plural, like the art of healing. What was considered engineering was negotiated on transnational and national levels, often influenced by the creation of state

41 Bourdieu, *La noblesse*, 140.

schools and corps. Thus, for example, in some countries agronomy and forestry developed as engineering branches, and in others they did not; the same is true for chemistry and chemical engineering. The hierarchy of prestige of different engineering branches also varied in different cultural contexts, often shaped by the state's policies and/or by the impact of the attitudes of foreign economic agents.

The country of origin of the credentials and of the person was a key factor of importance in one's acknowledgement as engineer, too. As Martykánová has studied at both global and national/imperial levels, one's nationality could seriously shape his options to be acknowledged as engineer in a specific context.[42] For instance, in the Spain of the 1840s, an Englishman without formal credentials (engineering diploma) had it much easier to get hired as engineer in the private sector than a Spaniard in the same situation, due to the reputation of Great Britain as an industrial powerhouse and/or to the contacts with British investors and companies. The diploma from a French engineering school, in turn, made it possible for a Russian or Ottoman Jew to get a well-paid job as engineer in Spain, just like a Spaniard who had studied in France could do in Russia or in France itself. As the century progressed, credentialism was on the rise, helping overcome national, ethnoreligious and racial barriers – while reaffirming class and –albeit temporarily – gender ones. Nonetheless, there was still a plenty of space for alternative ways of acknowledgement and hierarchies of prestige.

Therefore, the engineers' style was an important part of getting acknowledgement and asserting professional authority. The knowledge and know-how themselves did not automatically grant an 'engineer' treatment. To begin with, one had to be a man. Particularly in the USA some of the daughters and wives of workshop-trained engineers also acquired such training in the family workshop and, de facto, worked as engineers in the family business.[43] But to get hired or paid as an individual for one's

42 Martykánová, 'Global Engineers', 75–104; Darina Martykánová and Meltem Kocaman, 'A Land of Opportunities: Foreign Engineers in the Ottoman Empire', in Concha Roldán, Daniel Brauer and Johannes Rohbeck, eds, *Philosophy of Globalization* (Paris: De Gruyter, 2018), 237–51.

43 Annie Canel, Ruth Oldenziel and Karin Zachmann, eds, *Crossing Boundaries, Building Bridges: Comparing the History of Women Engineers, (1870s–1920s)*

professional services in the market was quite a different issue. Things did not begin to change before the first decades of the twentieth century when women obtained engineering diplomas in Russia and France,[44] and much later in Spain, a country in which the access of women to engineering schools took place in the 1930s (to be reversed in practice by the Francoist dictatorship until the 1950s). Gender was not the only limiting factor. A man could have the knowledge and, particularly, know-how needed to perform a specific task, and yet be treated and paid as a foreman or mechanic, rather than as an engineer, were he identifiable as working class by his dress, speech and manners.

After the engineering schools were established and fully consolidated in the central decades of the nineteenth century, the insistence on official higher education was the safest way to establish and reproduce the elite status of engineering as a profession. Nonetheless, with titled engineers being in short supply, men trained through practice could get acknowledgement from their peers educated engineering schools in Spain and abroad. For that purpose, they needed to dress and talk the part, rather than simply show prowess in engineering. Their task was easier if they were, at the same time, nationals of a country admired for its industrial development or worked as engineers for a company from such a country.

The 'gentlemanly' dress, speech and manners were not the only ways to establish and assert authority. Years after their foundation, state engineering corps introduced a uniform to enhance the civilian engineers' authority vis à vis the workers and the other elite groups. The figure of an officer was held in great esteem in the first decades of the liberal regime. The reason was twofold. First, the officers inherited high status from the Ancien Regime when only noblemen could access such ranks. Moreover, military men were able to reconstruct and reaffirm this prestige and legitimacy in the context of the new constitutional regime, as they played an

(London/New York: Routledge, 2003). Specifically on the USA: Ruth Oldenziel, 'Multiple-Entry Visas: Gender and Engineering in the U.S. 1870–1945', in Canel, Oldenziel and Zachmann, eds, *Crossing Boundaries*, 11–49.

44 Dmitri Gouzévitch and Irina Gouzévitch, 'A Women's Challenge: The St. Petersburg Women's Polytechnic Institute, 1905–1918', in Canel, Oldenziel and Zachmann, eds, *Crossing Boundaries*, 103–26.

important and widely acknowledged role in the War of Independence, in the constitutional revolutionary movement and in the Carlist War.[45] The military features adopted and endorsed by the state engineers included not only the uniform, but also strict discipline in their schools, which they liked to contrast with the chaotic and boisterous lives of the university students, as well as hierarchy of ranks (*escalafón*) and detailed regulations of state service (*reglamento*). Moreover, they systematically emphasized their fitness, often in military terms. Thus, for example, the ponts-et-chaussées engineers fashioned themselves as indefatigable riders while forestry engineers' education included 'long marches' in the nature.[46] Private sector engineers had no such tools and in their professional practice they had to embody a more civilian bourgeois profile. It is remarkable, though, that what was for decades the only engineering school aimed at supplying the private sector, the *Escuela de Ingenieros Industriales* in Barcelona, funded by public authorities, also insisted on implementing a strict discipline among the students, well beyond the common practice at the university.

The manners were important, too. The engineer had to adopt the right kind of behaviour when interacting with other people professionally. He had to be assertive with business-owners and managers to gain their respect and authoritative with manual workers to mark the difference. As for the former, the engineers acquired a certain reputation for their arrogance in nineteenth-century Spain.[47] As their elite standing was fragile, they insisted on being an exceptional and underappreciated group among the contemporary Spanish elites. They argued that they were men

45 Similar trend can be observed in France during the same period. See Ainhoa Gilarranz, 'El buen doctor: cultura visual y defensa de la profesión médica en la Francia del siglo XIX', *Dynamis* 2 (2021), in press.

46 'Testamento forestal de Bernardo de la Torre Rojas, fundador y primer director de la Escuela de ingenieros de montes (1866)', reproduced in Erich Bauer Manderscheid, *Los montes de España en la Historia* (Madrid: Servicio de publicaciones agrarias/ Fundación Conde del Valle de Salazar, 1991), 519–28.

47 Javier Fornieles Alcáraz, *Trayectoria de un intelectual de la Restauración: José Echegaray* (Almería: Publicaciones de Cajalmería, 1989). Darina Martykánová, 'El amor condenado, el amor triunfante. El género en el discurso sobre la ciencia, la religión y la nación en tres obras de Benito Pérez Galdós', *Espacio, Tiempo y Forma* 29 (2017), 149–79.

of science in a country when the elites did not see the importance of sciences for the development of the country and presented themselves as the avant-garde of a modern Spain able to compete with the great powers of the time.[48] This self-fashioning, that proved quite successful as we may appreciate from it being reproduced and multiplied in contemporary novels and plays, was directed mostly towards the established elites, were they property-owners, high-ranking officials and officers or other liberal professionals such as lawyers.

Besides these intra-elite acknowledgement strategies, the engineers had to assert their authority among and over the workers. Some went about it in a soft way. Industrial engineers linked to the school in Barcelona established courses for foremen and workers that provided education in sciences as well as technical training. This way, the engineers helped the workers upgrade and certify their qualifications. At the same time, they showcased in front of these workers a vision of their work that included sciences as a useful element in the industrial production and thus reaffirmed the need for and the authority of an engineer, something that was, we should keep in mind, far from obvious for many workers and business-owners.

This was the sophisticated way of going about it, not surprisingly found in an urban environment where workers had access to revolutionary discourses and could organize an active resistance. In rural Spain – as well as in rural France, Portugal and the colonial domains – the engineers often wielded an almost feudal power over the workers. They liked to immortalize their position of authority as well as their contribution to progress by having their pictures taken, next to their works. In their everyday practice, they dressed as gentlemen, often with accessories such as a walking stick and a hat, making it clear that they did not need to bend and get dirty; they could just point the stick for the worker to fix whatever needed to be

48 Darina Martykánová, 'Remover los obstáculos. Los ingenieros de caminos españoles y sus visiones del Estado durante la segunda mitad del siglo XIX', *Historia y Política* 36 (2016), 49–73; Martykánová and Núñez-García, 'Ciencia, patria y honor', 45–75.

fixed. Sometimes they were assisted by the gendarmerie, particularly when they managed prisoners condemned to forced labour.[49]

Mining engineers were in a privileged position to engage in paternalist practices and, at the same time, they tended to be among the victims of the workers' resistance when the situation became unsustainable. Due to the isolation of many mining localities, small mining communities came to existence dominated by the engineer who managed the mine. Sometimes he did not restrict himself to ensure the smooth operation of the mine, but imposed moral rules like a self-styled patriarch, making use of the great power he had over the different aspects of the lives of the workers. Such interventionist engineers aspired to organize not only the work of the miners, but also their free time. As one of them stated: 'Here we do not want debauched workers, but workers devoted only and exclusively to the fulfilment of their duty and to caring for their families.' When the *Comisión de Reformas Sociales* [Social Reform Commission] asked the mining engineer Mariano Zuaznávar, expert-manager of the Orbó mining area, owned by the Esperanza de Reinosa Society, for data in order to improve the workers situation, the engineer adopted a hostile attitude towards what he considered as an intromission into his territory. He refused emphatically to ask the workers to provide information and to make them fill in and sign the questionnaires provided by the Commission. He argued that he was 'the only authority, an undisputable one, delegated by the Society's General Management'.[50] In his own report he proudly declared that while the workers were provided certain services to protect their health and their jobs were safe, 'the sale of drinks is not allowed on holidays and gambling and dance are not tolerated, unless stipulated conditions are fulfilled and under the always-paternal surveillance of the engineer and his employees'. Instead of dancing inappropriately, the miners, reduced to a child-like status, were forced to listen to engineer Zuaznávar playing the

49 Miguel Ángel González Gallego, *El Presidio del Canal de Isabel II en el contexto jurídico y penitenciario de la España isabelina (1851–1867)* (PhD. Thesis: Universidad Complutense de Madrid, 2021).

50 Mariano Zuaznávar, 'Informe del Ingeniero Jefe de las minas de Orbó', in *Reformas sociales. Información oral y escrita. 1889–1893*, vol. 5 (Madrid: Ministerio de Trabajo y Seguridad Social, 1985), 533–8.

organ on solemn occasions. Apparently, these music sessions did not have the desired cultivating effect. The workers, our engineer complained, were 'totally recalcitrant: none of them has a talent for music and the rhythm of their tunes is monotone and absurd. Their [musical] keys are savage.' Among the other proofs of the workers irredeemable inferiority was their lack of interest in public affairs and their inclination towards excessive wine consumption. These were issues that the engineer never linked publicly to the twelve-hour working day inside of the mine or from sunrise to sunset if they did tasks in the open air, or to the fact that the workload was incompatible with the older children's attendance to school. Not even the holidays were necessarily free: the engineer's fervent Catholicism did not prevent him from making people work on 'at least half' of the Sundays of the year. The engineer was more than satisfied with his small community ruled by the principles of order, work and piety, in which there was no 'separation or adultery and the marriage is the natural and perfect state without any scandals happening in the couples'. The tranquillity of the life in the mining area was only disturbed by discordant elements coming from outside, be them workers coming from the city, who soon realized they were 'outside of their environment' or by whichever useless commission insisting on breaking this natural balance with their impertinent questions and inquiries. The honourable engineer considered as

> a serious disturbance of the regime and discipline of the establishment that a so-called Commission would come to create it by listening to the workers. While in the industrial centres there exists a painful need to improve the condition of the working class, here everybody lives satisfied and happily, working in good health, educating one's children and saving small sums for the old age.[51]

Does the reader find it surprising that – amid such harmony and happiness – many mining companies employed private security or even funded a gendarmerie station in the mining areas to suffocate protests and labour movements in their origins?

Keeping an elite profile was an arduous but highly profitable task that, together with the decisive influence of the state engineering corps, allowed

51 Zuaznávar, 'Informe', 533–8.

the Spanish engineering transition from a being a military career of a few hundred to become one of the most prestigious and best-paid professions in the country.

Conclusion

The history of engineering as a profession in nineteenth-century Spain is a success story. While there were very few engineers except for the military and navy men in the beginning of the century, by the end of it, engineering was one of the most prestigious and desirable professions in Spain, not only considered suitable for a son of a gentleman, but also deemed useful and necessary for the country. This was due to a combination of factors. The role of the State in the institutionalization of engineering was indeed a relevant factor, but so was the skilful use by the engineers of the discourse that linked progress with public works, particularly infrastructures, as well as the meritocratic discourse and practices. They were combined with the implicit and explicit mobilization of class signifiers that identified engineers as respectable men of honour in the eyes of contemporary Spanish society.

The construction of engineering by the State, in order to supply the public administration with technicians, had other consequences. It restricted the capacity of the special schools of engineers to supply experts for the industrial firms and for companies in other economic sectors. Even industrial engineering, which was a branch not directly connected with any state corps, was influenced by this trend: it imported the model of a highly selective and demanding formation, limiting hence the number of graduates. The relatively scarce number of men who held the title of Spanish engineer was compensated by the entrance of foreign engineers, both with a formal education in engineering and without, and by the Spaniards who obtained credentials in foreign institutions or learned the profession through their working experience. Most of the engineers with the official Spanish title worked for the State, but they could also become professionals, either by taking a temporary or permanent leave or by combining their posts in the civil service with private projects and jobs.

The discourse of *intrusismo* shows that the professionalization of engineering in the nineteenth century took place at a market where opportunities were rather limited and, at the same time, shaped by two major features: the massive presence of foreign investors and companies in Spain and the Spanish titled engineers' aspirations to an elite status as individuals and as a professional group. The State was systematically called upon to regulate access to the professional practice, particularly to the most profitable jobs and commissions. The titled engineers strove to deny the working-class practitioners the category of engineer, but also intended to control and put strict limits on professional practice of foreigners and Spaniards who got their credentials abroad. While they could not impose their agenda, by the end of the nineteenth century they did prove successful in establishing engineering as an elite profession in Spain. They enacted this elite social standing in their everyday practice, dressing and acting according to what was expected from a gentleman, even if this could make actual engineering practice more complicated or fuel conflicts with the workers.

During the twentieth century, engineering as profession underwent major changes in Spain. The state corps became comparatively less powerful, the private sector employment expanded, including technical and managerial posts, and engineering education was integrated within the university system, which allowed for engineering to become a profession in the strictest sense. Women engineers appeared, although their numbers rose far more slowly than, for instance, the number of female lawyers. While twentieth-century Spain was never a professional society as described by Harold Perkin,[52] engineers played in designing some of the emblematic policies of the Francoist regime.[53] The trend observed by Bourdieu, Grelon

52 Harold Perkin, *The Rise of Professional Society, England since 1880* (London: Routledge, 1990).

53 Benjamin Brendel, 'Conexiones energéticas. Los ingenieros constructores de los pantanos de Franco como actores políticos y agentes del Estado en el contexto internacional', *Historia y Política* 43 (2020), 87–199. Lino Campubrí, *Los ingenieros de Franco: Ciencia, catolicismo y Guerra Fría en el Estado franquista* (Madrid: Crítica, 2017). Ortúñez and Lafuente, 'Leopoldo Calvo-Sotelo', 121–55.

and other French sociologists, of social prestige shifting from engineering as a profession exercised to engineering as an education granting meritocratic credentials to managers, is also clearly visible in Spain during the last decades.[54]

54 Darina Martykánová, 'Los ingenieros y el poder en la España contemporánea (presentación)', *Historia y Política* 43 (2020), 17–26. Ortúñez and Lafuente, 'Leopoldo Calvo-Sotelo', 121–55. Antoine Derouet Antoine et al., eds, *Les Ingénieurs: unité, expansion, fragmentation (XIXe-XXe siècles). Vol. I, La production d'un groupe social* (Paris: Garnier, 2018).

MANUEL AMADOR GONZÁLEZ FUERTES

The Century of Lawyers
The Making of Social Standing of Legal Professions in Spain (1789–1868)

ABSTRACT
This chapter approaches the process of professionalization of the legal profession in the nineteenth century from its roots in the legal practice of the Old Regime to its definitive consolidation during the liberal era. Our analysis focuses on three complementary dimensions in this field of work. Firstly, it examines the changes in lawyers' habits and attire that differentiated them from other forensic professionals and court staff. Secondly, it analyses the regulation of the bars, which were key institutions in controlling the practice of the profession and which, simultaneously, were subject to control by the administration of the liberal state. Finally, it studies the proliferation of publications on forensic oratory, a genre that reflected the internal hierarchy of this professional body, while providing valuable training for political and parliamentary activity.

Introduction[1]

It seems logical to think that legal knowledge would play an important role in the consolidation of the Spanish liberal regime, given the sublimation of the concept of law by its most influential thinkers as the basis of social organization, in contrast to the evident absence of regulation during the Old Regime. Whether or not such an objective character of legislation could exist in general terms or did exist virtually during the liberal period, such an exaltation would be a constitutive element of liberal ideology and a *desideratum* of its main ideologists.

1 I would like to thank Esther de Carlos Varona for her comments and the information provided.

However, it may be more complex to determine, as the title of this text states, that the legal profession was, within the legal field, the great beneficiary of this exaltation of the norm. A relatively simple explanation for this phenomenon would underline the novelty of a social group, lawyers, who were not organically linked to the established power and who, with their new 'bourgeois' social attitudes, represented an example of the new bourgeois – without the quotation marks – man – always male. The free exercise of the profession in a world marked by economic success and professional merit and linked to the incipient development of a 'civil society' would allow them to present themselves as a paradigm of this new liberal society that would struggle to escape from the corporative social orders of the still very enlightened and absolutist previous century.

But this interpretation, which would accentuate what we could call the modernizing aspect, even if it strips it of its finalist or contemporary vision, can be contrasted with another possible explanation that highlights the historical antecedents, looks into the corporate elements of the group, analyses the sources from the starting point rather than the arrival point and does not trace as inevitable the path towards future events whose protagonists could only imagine, in the best of cases. It is only a problem of the point of view from which it is observed, and perhaps it might be interesting to apply to what, as is acknowledged in the very title of this contribution, turned out to be one of the groups that benefited most from the implementation of the new liberal regime.

From this perspective, the analysis of the process of professionalization of the law throughout the nineteenth century – presented both from within the group, in terms of defining the tasks of the profession and delimiting it with from others, and from the outside, seeking social recognition of its specificity and positive value – can help us to understand the importance of inherited factors, the necessary adaptation to the changes of the new times and the inexcusable contextualization of the moment in which it developed. Therefore, it is as important to observe the steps taken by the lawyers to organize and present themselves in society as it is to observe their position among other professional groups that share the space of legal knowledge and the development of their relations over a broad period.

The starting point at the end of the Old Regime

In 1683, at the beginning of the Third Discourse, the last of his works, Melchor Cabrera Núñez de Guzmán, in his book on the 'perfect lawyer', presents a division of what he calls the 'profession of Jurisprudence', which can serve as a starting point for these lines:

> The profession of jurisprudence has various occupations, to which the inclination or convenience of those who study it leads. Some are judges, other professors, other *relatores* and other lawyers. And the purpose of all of them is to accumulate merits for the promotions destined for the legal experts; and since the judges and professors deal with a single ministry, the latter with the chair and the former with the court, all of them are found in the lawyers.[2]

The proposed division is significant, as it splits into four employment opportunities for law graduates in the world of civil jurisprudence. First, the performance of acts of justice through different tribunals, the framework of action of judges and magistrates. Second, the transmission of legal knowledge, which corresponds to university teaching. Third, the essential and scarcely studied work of procedural processing, carried out by the *relatores*, the only members of the justice administration who obtained their position through an objective test in which they demonstrated their knowledge. Finally, the performance of law defending the interests of others: the practice of law.

By the end of the seventeenth century, these four areas of law interacted with each other, orbiting one above the others according to the preeminence each had in social consideration, but the hierarchy was clear. At the top were the judges and, above all, the magistrates who, in the territorial

2 Melchor de Cabrera Núñez de Guzmán, *Idea de vn abogado perfecto, redvcida a practica, dedvcida de reglas, y disposiciones del Derecho, comprada con la autoridad de sus Interpretes. Ilvstrada Con letras Divinas, Santos, y Doctores, y Padres de la Iglesia. Esmaltada Con varias flores de todas letras. Y conforme A la Vida de San Ivon, Patron, y Patriarca de los Abogados* (Madrid: Oficina de Evgenio Rodriguez, 1683), 326. There is a facsimile edition published in Madrid by the Bar Association of Madrid in 1996 with an introduction by Luis Martí Mingarro.

courts or the councils, performed both judicial and governmental tasks and, in the most important cases, were part of the political apparatus of the Monarchy. The consideration of the small number of *relatores* was exclusively internal since in practice they were only recognized by the members of the administration of justice, as can be seen by the fact that they were included as a distinct group by Cabrera. As for the professors, beyond their teaching specialization, they acted in most cases as a breeding ground for future magistrates, especially if they belonged to the bar. Finally, lawyers were at the lowest rung of the pyramid, still trying to defend their nature against the, for them, intrusive work of proctors.

However, the second half of the eighteenth century saw significant changes that linked the evolution of the legal profession with the transformation of the judiciary planned by the enlightened rulers. Although the corporate representation of the Court' lawyers, its Colegio de Abogados [Bar Association], was given a new ordinance in 1732,[3] it was not until the designation of the Count of Aranda as president of the Council of Castile, after the 'Esquilache Riots' of 1766, that the situation of advocates began to change within the legal apparatus of the Monarchy. Firstly, even without new ordinances, a restructuring of the Bar's secretariat was approved, which accelerated the processing of its business.[4] These, meanwhile, increased as the Consejo de Castilla [Council of Castile] delegated significant tasks to it, such as the censorship of legal books and,[5] what is of most interest here, the exams for the incorporation of law school graduates into the profession.

The legislation issued by the Catholic Monarchs required three legal skills from the corps of lawyers: to study for a certain time some legal

3 Reproduced in *Estatutos, y acuerdos de el Ilustre Colegio de Abogados de la corte, y de los que se hallan incorporados con él por filiacion, en virtud de Reales Cédulas, en las Chancillerias de Valladolid, y Granada, Audiencias Reales de Sevilla, Aragon, Valencia, y Galicia. Aprobados por los señores del Real, y Supremo Consejo de Castilla* (Madrid: Imprenta de Antonio de Sancha, 1772), 3–20.

4 These instructions appear in manuscript in a copy preserved in the Archive of the Madrid Bar Association of the aforementioned edition of Sancha's *Statutes* of 1772. Archivo del Colegio de Abogados de Madrid (hereafter: AHICAM) Sig. 18-00781.

5 Javier Alvarado Planas, 'El Colegio de Abogados de Madrid y la censura de obras jurídicas a finales del Antiguo Régimen' in Santiago Muñoz Machado, ed., *Historia de la abogacía española* (Cizur: Aranzadi, 2015), II, 1089–130.

knowledge at university, to complete an internship with a lawyer and, finally, to pass an exam conducted by the Council of Castile at the Court and the territorial audiences and chanceries outside the Court. This provided the training that would later enable them to join the Colegio de Abogados de la Corte [Bar Association of the Court] or the territorial tribunals, which would ultimately allow them to practise law. The fact that legislation on these three points was extensive throughout the Early Modern Age and that it varied regarding the minimum time criteria and the contents of university training – hence our indeterminacy in setting them out above – only indicates the reality of their non-compliance in practice.[6]

Protective of their powers, which they had no reason to delegate, the Consejo de Castilla and the courts were in charge of conducting the exam thus ultimately controlling the number of lawyers and being able to set the criteria for admission. However, after having established that a certain Antonio Romero had cheated on his admission as a lawyer, the Bar Association of the Court received an order from the Consejo de Castilla stating

> That in order to avoid such factions and prejudices in the future, nine individuals of the highest satisfaction and credit will be appointed annually by the Colegio de Abogados of this Court [Madrid], who shall meet alternately each week until a minimum number of three is reached, to whom the candidates shall be referred for examination, after presenting to the Consejo the necessary documents and certification of four years of practice, as has been done heretofore, so that they may examine them especially in said practice on actions, suits and appeals, the method and way of libelling and introduction them, answering, deducting exceptions, directing and substantiating all kinds of trials, making accusations in criminal cases and everything else conducive to being able to form an opinion as to whether they are instructed in the practice, so that they may perform the duties of the job. In view of such report, which must be sent closed to the Chamber Clerk's Office, whoever proves to be competent is ordered to appear before the Council for regular examination to qualify the same concept.[7]

6 For the study of the legal profession in the Old Regime: María Paz Alonzo Romero and Carlos Garriga Acosta, *El régimen jurídico de la abogacía en Castilla (siglos XIII-XVIII)* (Madrid: Dykinson, 2013).

7 Reproduced in the handwritten part of *Estatutos, y acuerdos de el Ilustre Colegio de Abogados de la corte*, 6–7 (pencil pagination). AHICAM, Sig. 18-00781.

Although the competence of the Consejo de Castilla persisted, as the examination would continue to be held there, the introduction of a test with similar, if not identical, characteristics in the Colegio de Abogados of Madrid would lead to the latter controlling de facto the incorporation of new professionals, which at most could be limited by the Consejo de Castilla. Thus, in practice, the Colegio de Abogados was endowed with a basic prerogative: to control access to the profession, which would allow it to regulate itself. And all of this despite the possibility of obtaining the mercy of exemption from the examination – a route always present in the society of the Old Regime – appealing to criteria of professional qualification and legal knowledge.

The measure of 1770 must be seen in relation to a more profound change in the social role of lawyers that was taking place at that time, linked to the enlightened attempts to modify the apparatus of the administration of justice, and that, in the same process, was to provide them with new professional alternatives. As doctor Coronas points out,[8] 1770 was a key year in the implementation of the new 'judicial reform of Aranda' for the higher courts, which needed new personnel after the anti-bar policy headed by Pérez Bayer and supported by the monarch. In addition, since the 'Esquilache Riots', the number of legist *corregimientos* was increasing to the detriment of the political and military governments led by the so-called non-legist *corregidores* of *capa y espada*.

This need for new personnel with legal training was manifested, especially in the higher courts, through the less studied phenomenon of the gradual appointment by the Crown of 'simple' lawyers to judicial posts.[9] Within the general atmosphere of limiting the privileges of the *colegiales*

8 Santos Manuel Coronas González, 'La reforma judicial de Aranda (1766–1771)', *Anuario de Historia del Derecho Español* 68 (1998), 45–82.

9 Fundamental are the ideas put forward by Jean-Pierre Dedieu, 'La muerte del letrado', in Francisco José Aranda Pérez, ed., *Letrados, juristas y burócratas en la España moderna* (Cuenca: Servicio de Publicaciones de la Universidad de Castilla-La Mancha, 2005), 479–512, heavily criticized by Ana María Carabias Torres, '¿La muerte del letrado? Consideración sobre la tipología del oficial español en el siglo XVIII', in Salustiano de Dios and Eugenia Torijano, eds, *Cultura, política y práctica del derecho. Juristas de Salamanca, siglos XV-XX* (Salamanca: Ediciones de la Universidad de Salamanca, 2012), 143–238. A small contribution to this phenomenon, from a different perspective, in: Manuel Amador González Fuertes, '¿El

mayores and supported by their professional work in defence of the interests of prominent nobles or religious orders, the Secretaría del despacho de Gracia y Justicia [Secretariat of the Office of Grace and Justice], which was gradually replacing the Cámara de Castilla [Chamber of Castile] in the appointment of judicial posts, began to appoint these advocates to more important positions within the judicial career. Thus, from the first appointments to *alcaldía mayor* and *corregimientos*, the most fortunate lawyers moved on the corridors of audiences and chanceries and the most privileged even made it to the floors of the Court councils. Therefore, before the definitive crisis of the Old Regime and the difficult establishment of the liberal regime in Spain, the starting point of our protagonists could be described as hopeful, to say the least. This opened the door for the transition from the legal profession to the judiciary, which would be used by some to gain access to the highest positions in the administration and the more executive sphere of the courts' secretariats, a prelude to future ministries. But this would only be the first period of a development that would conclude with the establishment of the liberal regime in Spain in the nineteenth century, after the convulsive and zigzagging period of the Peninsular War and the reign of Fernando VII.[10]

---

hábito hace al monje? Institucionalización de la carrera judicial en España a finales del Antiguo Régimen', *Studia histórica. Historia moderna* 39/1 (2017), 229–62.

10 We exclude from the analysis the convulsive period between 1808 and 1833, which has its own characteristics marked precisely by the impossibility of generalization. The appearance of new men on the side of Fernando VII when the French invasion caused the majority of the judiciary to swear allegiance to José I favoured the general process of incorporation of lawyers into the public sphere and the new forms of political practice. But precisely, their liberal ideology would harm them in the later absolutist periods of the reign of Fernando VII, causing exiles, arrests and purifications which, on the other hand, would be of great value for those who survived after 1833. The public sphere of legal professionals (magistrates, lawyers and university professors) expanded during this period, but ideological incompatibilities and repression, which were the key factors of this historical moment, altered and distorted the evolution proposed throughout the reign of the last absolutist monarch.

Dressing code and professional prestige

From this crucial starting point, many aspects can be studied to approach the process of professionalization in the working environment of lawyers in the nineteenth century. Here, we will focus on three of them and we will point out a fourth that had an impact on the advocates' world since it differentiates them, together with other legal professionals, by establishing their dress code. This defined them as a professional group by regulating the path to access it; organize them hierarchically by attempting to establish a gradation of professional worth in a transcendental section such as oratory – although nowadays it might seem accessory; and, finally, it took them to the apex of power through the participation in the political game of its most prominent members.

Perhaps a necessary first step was to differentiate the lawyer from other groups of men of letters in the most symbolic place of their professional activity: the trial. And there is no other way to interpret a very early provision, dated 28 November 1833, which in its first article stated 'the ceremonial attire of the ministers and public prosecutors … henceforth in the same robe they now wear, and in a black hat'. The decree makes a subtle difference between the ministers of the higher courts and the rest of the staff with legal knowledge who would be allowed to wear this garment ('judges of first instance, lawyers, *relatores*, agents and public prosecutors') as the latter 'shall wear the same garment, with the difference that the sleeves of the robe must be without frills, and short so as must not extend beyond the elbow' (article 4), while magistrates and judges exclusively 'shall wear, both with the ceremonial and common garment, a silver medal, hanging from a blue ribbon around the neck' (article 5).[11]

11 Joaquín Escriche, *Suplemento al Diccionario razonado de Legislación y Jurisprudencia* (Madrid: Establecimiento Tipográfico-Literario Universal La Ilustración, 1847), 680. Article 2 describes it in detail: 'Art. 2. The sleeves of the robe shall be wide, tapering to the wrist, above which they shall end with the frills. The hat shall be of circular shape, the upper part of which shall be covered with an inlay that makes it protrude one inch at the top and around the circumference, with a silk tassel in the middle.'

Although throughout the rule it is fair to recognize differences between those who judge (magistrates and judges) and the rest of the judicial personnel, and between the magistrates and the prosecutors and the simple judges, a visual difference – and this is what interest us – is established between the experts in law and unprofessional men since the former did wear the robe. On the other hand, the reasons given by the Queen Regent also are remarkable, since she significantly refers to 'garment' and not to 'uniform'. Moreover, the purpose of regulating the attire is to 'separate from the attire worn in court all that is uncomfortable and not in accordance with the elegance and simplicity of modern taste … without diminishing the modest decorum, proper to judicial dignity'. But we have removed the most important part of the quotation for our own interests: 'maintaining the corresponding feature'.

But the differentiation and hierarchy of clothing (and also of the position occupied in the courtroom) are accentuated ten years later in another regulation. The decree of 29 August 1843,[12] signed as a minister by one of the most famous lawyers of the century, Joaquín María López, returned to the issue of clothing. It would further restrict the use of the symbolic robe, which would no longer visually differentiate those with legal knowledge in the courtrooms. It could now only be used by magistrates, judges, public prosecutors and lawyers, while the obligatory use of 'tailcoats and completely black attire' was specified for notaries of chambers, proctors and porters (articles 2 and 3). The privileged with robe also highlighted the value of their knowledge by replacing the 'black hat' of the previous decree with the more university-like 'ancient six-sided birretta' (article 2, section 1).

The decree also provides clues to subtle group differences in its description of the position of the different participants in the judicial sessions between articles 4 and 8. Thus, the judge o judges, 'under a canopy', would lead the sessions at the back of the courtroom, while the lawyers 'on upholstered benches with backrests', would be placed 'at the sides of chambers', 'on the same floor as the judges' seats, spatially symbolizing the union between justice and the people ('so that they come to be situated between the ministers and the public, without turning their backs to the latter').

12 Published in *Gaceta de Madrid* (31 August 1843).

Relatores, notaries of chambers and proctors, however, would be located on 'slightly lower flooring' and on benches with backrests, but not upholstered.

The praise of the legal profession is completed with the privileged position of the only group differentiated by the rule from the public attending the trial: the deans of the bars. They 'shall have a position in the public functions they attend with the courts, equal to that of the ministers and after the prosecutors' (article 11). Even symbolic, it does not seem a bad starting point for the development of the legal profession throughout the nineteenth century.

The control of the access to profession

We had left those who aspired to the legal profession with the obligation, among other requirements, to pass a double examination in front of the royal courts and the bars. With the arrival of the liberal regime and the reform of the administration of justice in 1834, there was an increase in the numbers of tribunals, both through the creation of courts of first instance and provincial courts. The abolition of most of the special jurisdictions and the homogenization that this reform brought about in the civil and criminal fields also helped to raise the number of practising lawyers in a society that in its process of modernization was increasingly using the administration of justice.

In the field of advocacy, the new general regulation would take place with the approval of the *Estatutos para el régimen de los colegios de abogados del reino [Statutes for the regime of the Bar Associations of the Kingdom]* in 1838.[13] Without further reading, article 1 establishes the importance given to the bars for the practice of the profession:

13 *Estatutos para el régimen de los colegios de abogados del reino, con los decretos y reales órdenes que los aclaran, modifican o derogan; precedidos de una reseña histórica sobre el Colegio de Madrid, su antiguo Monte-Pío y la Sociedad de socorros mútuos de los jurisconsultos; y seguidos de una reseña histórica y de las constituciones de la Academia Matritense de Jurisprudencia y Legislación*, 2nd edn (Madrid: Imprenta de la Revista de Legislación, 1859).

> Lawyers may freely practise their profession provided that they are residents and have an open office in the town in which they reside, and that they also pay the taxes imposed on them as lawyers. In towns where there is a Bar Association, they shall also need to be incorporated in its register.

The scope of the measure can be understood if the information is completed with article 2, which spread the bars to 'all cities and towns where the Tribunales Supremos [Supreme Courts] and Audiencias [Royal Audiences] reside', 'all provincial capitals', 'other towns where there are at least twenty lawyers with a permanent residence' and 'all judicial districts where there are twenty lawyers, even if they reside in different towns of the same district'.

Thus, it was necessary to be a member of a bar to practise as a lawyer, but it is also true that the general requirements for practising had been greatly simplified. In the entry 'Abogado' [Lawyer] of the first volume of the unfinished *Enciclopedia española de derecho y administración* [*Spanish Encyclopaedia of Law and Administration*] there are four minimum requirements to practise law: seven years of legal studies (following the 1845 syllabus), to be over 17 years of age, to take the oath before the corresponding authority and the aforementioned incorporation to a bar.[14]

This incorporation is regulated in the *Statutes* in a rather lax manner, especially if compared with the regulations of the Old Regime. The candidate had to apply to the pertinent bar, attaching the 'lawyer diploma'. With the prior approval of the examining board in which the diploma was issued, the bar would grant admission except for 'fair cause', which could only include 'doubts about the certainty or legitimacy of the lawyer diploma' or 'any legal impediment to practise law'.[15]

This was a major change from the Old Regime. In the new times, the training exam and even the apprenticeship were eliminated, and it was

14 Lorenzo Arrazola et al., *Enciclopedia española de derecho y administración, ó Nuevo Teatro Universal de la Legislación de España è Indias* (Madrid: Tipografía General de D. Antonio Rius y Rossell, 1848), I, 82–152.

15 Regulated by article 9 of the *Statutes*. A third, more discretionary reason would be added in the decree of 6 June 1844, which linked acceptance to moral behaviour, as admission could be refused due to 'lack of moral qualities in the opinion of the Junta de Gobierno [Governing Board] of the bar'.

assumed that the knowledge acquired at university qualified the applicant. Although denying membership in the event of possible doubts about the legality of the diploma is rather strange, as this procedure should have already been verified in the act of taking the oath before the corresponding authority, the powers granted to the bar regarding the admission of new members are undoubtedly more limited than in the eighteenth century. But it is precisely this laxity that can lead us – and not only us, as this question was also raised in the nineteenth century – to consider the very existence of the bars. The advocates of the bars found four reasons to justify it.

Firstly, the bars had a welfare function, the ultimate reason for their birth in the sixteenth century, which they retained during the nineteenth century and which, in general terms, was regulated in the *Statutes* (articles 35 and 36).

Secondly, the *Statutes* refer to the task of controlling the practice of law. Thus, in article 10, the bars were empowered to reprimand any member if they 'commit faults that make them detract from the honourable position they hold'. And, in the most serious cases, 'the Junta general de abogados [General Board of Lawyers] shall be informed so that it may determine what is most convenient for the decorum of the profession and of the Bar'. In addition, they also bound the professionals to their bar by regulating their possible intervention at other courts, limiting their geographical activity under the excuse of the problems caused by the transfer of cases (article 4).

Thirdly, we must remember that the bars carried out beneficial tasks for the administration of justice. The defence of the poor and the issuing of reports among them. The former was particularly important for the proper development of the legal apparatus.

The last, and most important point for our purpose, would be the defining nature of the bar itself. Thus, membership defined the profession because only by joining the bar could one be a lawyer. So, although the mechanisms of access had been lowered, membership allowed the creation of a group – or a body, if we use the language of corporate society. This was of vital importance for the lawyers, who, through the bar, defined themselves as such and presented and represented themselves in society. This would prove vital when, three years later, legislative changes brought about by political upheavals jeopardized the very existence of the bars.

By the royal order of 28 November 1841, under a progressive government, an order of the regent was passed, suppressing the first article of the *Statutes*. This was inspired by two provisions approved by the Courts in 1823[16] and 1837,[17] a time of intense liberal exaltation, which meant that they had no real chance of becoming effective. The subject matter of the three provisions is identical:

> This provision [the first article of the *Statutes*] has been the subject of several complaints on the grounds that it contradicts art. 1. of the decree issued by the Courts on 11 July 1837, which re-establishes another decree issued on 8 June 1823, concerning the fact that lawyers, doctors and other approved professionals may practise their profession in all parts of the monarchy, without the need to join any particular corporation or association, and only with the obligation to present their credentials to the local authority. Having heard the opinion of the supreme court of justice on the matter and in accordance with it, H.R.H. the Regent of the kingdom has resolved that while this ministry, in compliance with art. 2 of the decree of 11 July, gathers enough information to arrange the regimen of the associations in the most favourable manner to their object, and most compatible with freedom in the exercise of the profession, lawyers may practise their profession in all parts of the monarchy without being affiliated to any particular corporation or association, and only with the obligation of presenting their credentials to the local authority. They must perform by sharing the duties to which the members of the associations are obliged *ex officio* and concerning the destitute, but not in those involving establishments or corporations that are considered poor by privilege.[18]

The reaction of the bars to the provisions of 1837 and 1841 – the political instability concerning that of 1823 meant that its actual application was non-existent – is quite meaningful since they focused on considering that these regulations called into question the existence of the bars but,

16 Reproduced in *Diario de Barcelona* (21 September 1823).

17 Reproduced in *Colección de las leyes, decretos y declaraciones de las Cortes, y de los reales decretos, órdenes, resoluciones y reglamentos generales expedidos por las secretarias del despacho desde 1º de julio hasta fin de diciembre de 1837* (Madrid: Imprenta Nacional, 1838), XXIII, 70–1.

18 *Colección de las leyes, decretos y declaraciones de las Cortes, y de los reales decretos, órdenes, resoluciones y reglamentos generales expedidos por las secretarias del despacho desde 1º de enero hasta fin de diciembre de 1841* (Madrid: Imprenta Nacional, 1842), XXVII, 817–18.

curiously, they did not use arguments to defend their survival. In the Courts, in the session of 27 April 1837, the proposal to restore the provision of 1823, presented by the progressives and defended by the deputy Cristóbal Pascual Romero, was discussed. The deputy Felipe Gómez Acebo, member of the Junta de Gobierno of the Colegio de Abogados de Madrid, was responsible for defending the prerogatives of the bar. Without justifying the idea, Gómez Acebo tied in his speech the disappearance of the bars with the freedom to practise law outside them. ('Mr Pascual is well aware that there is a big difference between the current ordinances and regulations that strip schools of everything that could be detrimental and there being no schools in the Kingdom.')[19]

Such an opinion was expressed by the Junta de Gobierno of the Colegio de Abogados de Madrid at its meeting of 3 December 1841 as a result of the provision of 28 November. The aforementioned Felipe Gómez Acebo, at that time dean of the Colegio de Abogados de Madrid, resigned from his post as a consequence of the publication of the decree and, in agreement with the other three members of the Junta de Gobierno present at the meeting, Joaquín de la Torre Bossuet, José Ibarra and the secretary Juan García de Quirós,

> stated that they agreed with Mr Gómez Acebo because, although the order of the Regent of the Kingdom did not abolish the bars, they were in fact suppressed since everyone was authorized to practise their profession without the need to join any association. They were only obliged to present their credentials to the local authority, so no one wanted to join, since the members of the bar had no advantage over other lawyers. These being the effects of the aforementioned royal orden, and with the bars having been effectively extinguished, it was deemed that both the dean and the Junta

19 *Diario de sesiones de las Córtes Constituyentes. Dieron principio el 17 de octubre de 1836, y terminaron el 4 de noviembre de 1837* (Madrid: Imprenta de J. A. García, 1872), V, Session of 27 April 1837, 3044–5. This argument was also used by the deputies Gómez Acebo and Francisco Javier Ferro Montaos in their request that the reinstatement of the 1823 decree 'should be without prejudice to the regulations that the Government considers necessary for the good order and appropriate decorum and lustre of the legal profession'. But in the report submitted on 19 May, the Comisión de Legislación de las Cortes [Legislation Committee of the Courts] did not see this direct link between the freedom to practise the profession and the suppression of the associations (*Diario de sesiones de las Córtes Constituyentes*, 3601).

> de Gobierno had ceased in their respective functions. Consequently, neither the former was in a position to continue managing the affairs of the poor, nor should the latter henceforth exercise the attributions that corresponded to it by the Statutes.[20]

Beyond the illustrative description of the grim future of the bar, the absence of any justification reveals the link that the members of the Junta de Gobierno made between the bar and the definition of a lawyer, and the rupture that the free exercise of the profession would imply to that relationship. It was thus clear that the very existence of the bar, at least for its members, was intimately related to the very existence of the legal profession, regardless of whether this assertion was true or not.

Although the Colegio de Abogados de Madrid threatened in its response not to collaborate in the defence of the poor, it did not go any further, and at the beginning of the following year, both the handling of this type of business and the Colegio de Abogados continued.

However, the exemption from bar membership did not last long, as it was one of the first measures taken by Narváez when the moderates regained power in 1844. However, the royal decree of 6 June 1844 went beyond the re-establishment of compulsory membership.[21] It contained a series of changes that would allow the bars to survive but, in exchange, greater control by the administration and an internal hierarchy were established.

Firstly, the organization of the bars was updated to reflect the development of the profession. Thus, in article 5, the number of members of the governing boards of the largest bars augmented, as these required a greater amount of work. This also reflects that the number of lawyers was increasing significantly.

More difficult to justify would be the institutional interference approved with the active participation of public and government prosecutors in the performance of the bars, a clear sign of the direct control imposed by the administration. Hence, the bars were obliged to have a public

20 *Actas de la Junta de Gobierno (1838–1846)*, f. 162v. AHICAM., 2.1.1.9.

21 *Colección de las leyes, decretos y declaraciones de las Cortes, y de los reales decretos, órdenes, resoluciones y reglamentos generales expedidos por los respectivos ministerios desde 1º de enero hasta fin de junio de 1844* (Madrid: Imprenta Nacional, 1844), XXXII, 744–7.

or government prosecutor attend and act as honorary president at the governing meetings where the bars' positions were renewed and where the lawyers with powers of attorney were appointed (articles 7 to 10), a business that had been shown to be the most sensitive in the relations between the bars and the administration of justice. Furthermore, according to the last article of the royal decree, the prosecutors 'shall oversee the exact compliance with the statutes of the bars and this memo', thus imposing an external and state supervision on the theoretically private and professional body. Bar independence disappeared.

Among the control measures imposed by the moderate government, any body of the bar was prohibited from issuing any type of document 'on matters outside the private interest of the corporation or of its individuals as members' (article 14) and the grounds for refusal of admission of applicants were broadened to include a possible 'lack of moral qualities in the opinion of the Junta de Gobierno' (article 4). As part of this governmental control, the governing board and the dean are delegated to 'oversee the conduct of lawyers in the performance of their noble profession', which extends to their 'behaviour and habits' (article 11).

This delegation would ultimately lead to the need to establish the aforementioned hierarchy, requiring ten years of seniority in the institution to be appointed dean and five years to be a member of the governing board (article 6).

This new relationship between the bars and the administration, which was to prevail for the rest of the nineteenth century, could be seen as an intrusion of central power into a theoretically private and independent body, and such an interpretation would be correct. But there is also another possible view, that of an agreement within a new framework of relations in which a series of privileges, not all of them, were granted to the bars in exchange for their agreement to defend the doctrinal state that the moderates were establishing at all levels. Moreover, most of the legal elite to whom this solution was being offered defended it ideologically. If we change our perspective from one of confrontation and imposition to one in which common and collaborative elements predominate for mutual benefit, we will understand the scope and stability that was achieved in the medium and long term.[22]

After these ups and downs in the first half of the nineteenth century, when the new liberal regime was established, the bars had managed to bind the legal profession to enrolment in their associations. However, beyond the increasing number of lawyers inherent to the new times, this compulsory membership was less demanding than that achieved in the eighteenth century. After obtaining the law degree, it depended exclusively on the economic availability of the future advocates, which represented a class difference based on money. Finally, but not least, the leaders of the bars had in their hands the control over their members' actions and moral and social behaviour in a mixture of the public and private spheres characteristic of Spanish moderate liberalism.

Forensic oratory as an element of distinction

Once the profession was defined around the bar, it became stratified. As the number of lawyers augmented, it was necessary to build up a leading elite, as evidenced by the restrictions on the number of seats on the governing boards and the positions of deans mentioned above. In this second stage, it was essential that the hierarchization process did not rely exclusively on objectifiable parameters such as success in the profession or economic profit, as this would allow members from outside the ruling elite, who had obvious political links, to reach positions of power within the bars. Relational capital, the performance of political activities or the group and social consideration of such ethereal elements as cultural level

22 An account of the legislation on this subject subsequent to what has been discussed here is provided by Clara Álvarez Alonso in the last solid general contribution on the legal profession in the nineteenth century (Clara Álvarez Alonso, 'El abogado en la época isabelina (1834–1868)', in Muñoz Machado, ed., *Historia de la abogacía Española*, II, 1219).

made it possible to establish this ruling elite on which the practice of the profession would depend.

For our purposes, it is within this framework that the development of forensic eloquence should be introduced. The masterly studies of Professor Carlos Petit, from another perspective, have drawn attention to the importance of orality in the legal profession during this period, in case the transcendence of works such as those of Joaquín María López was not enough. The number of works on forensic oratory that were published during the nineteenth century is the best confirmation of their own importance.[23]

Clearly, the usefulness of this type of studies – it should not be forgotten that they were part of the syllabus – in the daily work of the legal profession and their implications for the intellectual world were more than enough reasons for the publication of the works. However, this second motive leads to new paths of interpretation in two ways that are ultimately complementary.

Initially, focusing on the works written in the first half of the century – and above all on that of Joaquín María López – these studies allow

23 From the texts used by Petit in his study, we can deduce a temporal evolution that would go from the first work, not completed in its original idea, by the pen of Pedro Sainz de Andino, *Elementos de elocuencia forense*, 2 vols (Madrid: Julián Viana Razola, 1828), to a collection of works in the 1840s: Ramón Sauri y Lleopart, *Elocuencia forense* (Barcelona: Herederos de la Viuda Pla, 1847); Francisco Pérez de Anaya, *Lecciones y modelos de elocuencia forense, estractadas las primeras de los mejores autores, ordenadas y reducidas á un tratado completo*, 4 vols (Madrid: Imprenta de Baltasar González, 1848–1849) and Joaquín María López, *Lecciones de elocuencia en general, de elocuencia forense, de elocuencia parlamentaria y de improvisación*, 2 vols (Madrid: Imprenta que fue de la Sociedad de Operarios, ahora de D.M. Gabeirós, 1849–1850); followed later by more reflective works on the phenomenon of forensic oratory: Fernando de León y Olarieta, *Consideraciones filosóficas sobre la elocuencia forense* (Valencia: Imprenta de El Valenciano, 1862); Enrique Ucelay, *Estudios críticos de oratoria forense. El foro y su elocuencia en Francia. Conferencias dadas en la Institución Libre de Enseñanza y su clase de Historia y modelos de la oratoria forense, seguidas de algunas de las principales defensas de los más célebres abogados franceses, traducidas por el mismo* (Madrid: Imprenta de la Revista de Legislación, 1880) and Enrique Ucelay, *Estudios sobre el foro moderno. Conferencias dadas en la Real Academia de Jurisprudencia en el curso de 1882 á 1883 seguidas de biografías y defensas de abogados célebres españoles* (Madrid: Viuda de J. M. Pérez, 1883).

not only the acquisition of an adequate eloquence in the development of the profession but also the appreciation of this discipline as particularly valuable. They also established the criteria to be followed to create a canon, thus making it possible to establish an evaluation of the professional work of the practising lawyer in terms of the art of oratory. As a result, an evaluation and ranking of such work among the growing number of practising lawyers can be established.

But the proposed canon presenting these ideal models of forensic oratory – and this is the second path to be explored – presents certain peculiarities. For the subject at hand, the most important thing is that the proposed oratorical rules are utterly subjective, based on the eclecticism of official romanticism and creators of an elite of orators among whom would be found, or would pretend to be found, the authors of the studies and the great lawyers who would supposedly set the standards of the ways of doing and saying in the forum.

The truly significant feature of this type of hierarchization derived precisely from the supposed objectification of something that could not fail to be subjective. A reading of the manuals and studies of oratory leads us to see how they were made up of a series of analyses of the main rhetorical figures, the parts of the speeches, the modes of declamation … All based, as it could not be otherwise, on the influences of classical oratory, the French authors of Classicism, some Hispanic figures and the occasional English one. This, as has already been said, was all within the eclecticism of official Romanticism, which in no artistic discipline was able to detach itself from the classical referent. In terms of literary theory, we would find ourselves with the final synthesis of the supposed confrontation between the neoclassical postulates of Charles Batteux and the supposedly pre-Romantic ones of Hugh Blair, defended in the Spanish case by Moratín and Quintana respectively, which could, in practice, coexist in the official salons of cultural institutions.

The main objective of this type of publications on forensic oratory was not the creation of a ruling elite among lawyers, which would be constituted by those who were recognized as having extraordinary gifts in the art of oratory. However, from the point of view that concerns us here, this type of literature and the elitist considerations that derived from it allowed the members of such an elite to count on, in Bourdieu's hackneyed terms, a 'symbolic capital' that secured them a foothold in the prestigious cultural world and because of its subjective character, unassailable and, very usefully, with margins of integration against new literary theories that might appear thanks to the flexibility provided by its theoretical character.

Oratory exercises, as is even reflected in the title of Joaquín María López's work, were also useful for the political battle within the framework of parliamentary activity. And it will be precisely in the political activity where the legal profession, through its highest representatives, who tend to be eminent politicians such as Joaquín Francisco Pacheco or the recently mentioned López – each on his own side of the two classical liberal parties – will take the final step to rise to a pre-eminent position. The whole building was crowned (or was based?) with the existence of these great political figures who, from relatively humble origins, managed to climb, with special emphasis on their forensic virtues, to the highest political offices of the incipient state. At the same time, they were the reference figures for new generations of advocates who were vying for the same positions. But the history of this process, beyond the numerous biographies of the main political lawyers of Spanish liberalism, is yet to be made.

PART II

Professionals of Warfare

PABLO ORTEGA-DEL-CERRO

Profession with Honour

Modernization and Legitimation of the Naval Officer Corps (c. 1800–1870)

ABSTRACT

This work focuses on the nineteenth-century Spanish naval officers. This socio-professional group, which had been so important throughout the eighteenth century, experienced a double challenge over the course of the following one. On the one hand, it had to adapt to new labour standards and undertake a new professionalization. On the other hand, the officers also had to face the social changes that took place throughout the century; they had to be integrated into the new social order, which implied a new form of legitimation and representation in society. The hypothesis of this chapter is that the professionalization and the search for respectability of the nineteenth-century naval officers were intertwined.

> From your pride I hope
> May you acquire a reputation for honest,
> Fine and well-educated,
> Courteous gentlemen;
> In matters of money
> Be decent and generous,
> You do not have to be ostentatious
> To be a respectable man
> And never humiliate your forehead
> With the reputation of cheating.[1]

1 Emilio Butrón, *Carta familiar de D. José Butron y Cortés dirigida a su hijo el guardiamarina D. Rafael Butron y Pareja: Décimas que D. Emilio José Butron y de la Serna dedica a su hijo el alférez de navío D. Emilio Manuel Butron y Linares* (Madrid: Librería de Fernando Fe, 1897), 61.

Introduction

The image of the nineteenth-century navy as a decadent and dying institution is quite widespread. According to this perspective, the history of the Spanish Navy in this moment could be summarized in the disasters with which the century began and ended: Trafalgar, in 1805, and the Spanish-American War of 1898. The crisis would have been chronic and constant. However – although there is still research to be done[2] – it is no longer possible to maintain this idea of a decrepit and outdated institution. Throughout the nineteenth century, Spain had an unquestionable maritime dimension, and its navy was a fundamental axis of its foreign policy. Thus, this image of decadence must be replaced by a more mutable one.[3] In fact, the very history of the nineteenth-century army was fluctuating. Although it is true that the institution underwent a deep deterioration, it managed to readapt itself to the new times and was able to acquire a respectable position. Although far from the British and French Navies, it barely differed from the Russian or American, and was similar in size to the Dutch.[4]

2 A good overview can be found in José Cepeda Gómez, 'La historiografía sobre la Marina en los siglos XVIII y XIX', *Cuadernos Monográficos del Instituto de Historia y Cultura Naval* 56 (2008), 143–5. The research of Fernando Bordejé y Morencos, *Crónica de la Marina Española en el Siglo XIX, 1800–1868* (Madrid: Ministerio de Defensa, 1993); *Crónica de la Marina Española en el Siglo XIX, 1868–1898* (Madrid: Ministerio de Defensa, 1994); José Cervera Pery, *Marina y política en la España del XIX* (Madrid: San Martín, 1979) continues to be a reference, although we currently have the synthesis of Agustín Rodríguez González, 'La armada', in Miguel Artola Gallego, ed., *Historia militar de España. Edad Contemporánea. El siglo XIX* (Madrid: Ministerio de Defensa, 2015), 183–222. Throughout this chapter we will cite more recent works on specific issues.

3 David Rubio Márquez, *Regeneracionismo en la Armada: la política naval española y los proyectos de creación de una nueva Escuadra (1899–1909)* (Madrid: Universidad Nacional de Educación a Distancia, 2014) and Agustín Rodríguez González, *Política naval de la Restauración (1875–1898)* (Madrid: San Martín, 1998).

4 According to Glete, in 1869, the British and French Navies had 825 and 461 ships respectively. Russia had a total of 160 and the United States, 150. The next maritime powers, in a distinctly inferior position, were the Netherlands and Spain, with

The nineteenth century was an age of change in many areas.[5] The profound political alterations and economic transformations went hand in hand with complex social mutations. From an unequal and discriminatory structure, which divided society into privileged and non-privileged – what could be termed 'Old Regime' – a new system with different foundations was slowly being built. The references were no longer the great nobles, the aristocracy, blood and inheritance, but legal equality, freedom, property, personal merit and respectability.[6] Throughout the nineteenth century, a new ideal was being shaped built on effort, work, respect, honest actions ... a model that could be summarized in the prototypical image of the 'hombre de bien' [honest man].[7]

Among the aforementioned phenomena – the evolution of the Spanish Navy and the social changes of the nineteenth century – were naval officers. This socio-professional group, which had been so important throughout the eighteenth century, experienced a double challenge over the course of the following one. On the one hand, it had to adapt to new labour standards, the modernization of the naval forces and a new organization.[8] The

---

69 and 65 warships respectively. Behind them were Denmark, Sweden, Norway, Naples, Austria, the Ottoman Empire and Brazil. See Jan Glete, *Navies and Nations: Warships, Navies and State Building in Europe and America, 1500–1860* (Estocolmo: Almqvist and Wiksell, 1993), 465.

5 Jürgen Osterhammel, *La transformación del mundo. Una historia global del siglo XIX* (Barcelona: Planeta, 2015).

6 Jesús Cruz, *El surgimiento de la cultura burguesa. Personas, hogares y ciudades en la España del siglo XIX* (Madrid: Biblioteca Nueva, 2014); 'El hombre fino: Bourgeois Conduct Ideals in 19th Century Spain', *The Bulletin of Hispanic Studies* 89/4 (2012), 347–62; F. M. L. Thompson, *The Rise of Respectable Society: A Social History of Victorian Britain, 1830–1900* (Cambridge, MA: Harvard University Press, 1988); and Guy Palmade, *La época de la burguesía* (Madrid: Siglo XXI, 1985).

7 James Bowman, *Honor: A History* (New York: Encounter Books, 2007); Albert Esteruelas i Teixidó, 'Los hombres de bien en la España del siglo XIX: Influencias y propuestas', in Enrique J. Belenguer Calpe, coord., *Educación popular: VIII Coloquio Nacional Historia de la Educación* (Santa Cruz de Tenerife: Universidad de La Laguna 1998), 191–200; Pilar Faus Sevilla, *La sociedad española del siglo XIX en la obra de Galdós* (Valencia: D.L., 1972).

8 Masson Battesti, *La Révolution maritime du XIXe siècle* (Paris: Service Historique de la Marine, 1987); Richard Harding, *Modern Naval History: Debates and Prospects* (London: Bloomsbury Publishing, 2015). As a sociological reference, see Brengt

Naval Officer Corps – name given to the navy officers – had to undertake a new professionalization. On the other hand, the officers also had to face the social changes that took place throughout the century; they had to be integrated into the new social order, which implied a new form of legitimation and representation in society.[9] Although they may seem to be processes of a different nature, both were closely related.[10]

The hypothesis of this chapter is that the professionalization and the search for respectability of the nineteenth-century naval officers were intertwined. The officers sought to underpin their military-scientific profile through their adaptation to the new professional parameters, but they also inevitably required to be integrated into the new dominant anthropological model, that is, to be seen as honest individuals and, therefore, a distinguished corps. In short, the society of the nineteenth century would not understand trigonometry, hydrography, steam mechanics or naval tactics, but it did know how to recognize prodigious, respectable, irreproachable and honest men. The aim of this chapter is to analyse this double process, which was not only essential for naval officers, but was also representative and indicative of this period. Our purpose is to study the strategies used by the navy to renew and modernize the corps to the challenges of the nineteenth century and the ways in which the group was portrayed in Spanish public opinion.

To this end, two major phases should be differentiated. The first third of the nineteenth century was a period of severe crisis for the navy. The old eighteenth-century model collapsed, and the institution was practically

---

Abrahamsson, *Military Professionalization and Political Power* (Beverly Hills: Sage Publications, 1972) and Josep Rodríguez and Mauro F. Guillén, 'Organizaciones y profesiones en la sociedad contemporánea', *Revista Española de Investigaciones Sociológicas* 59 (1992), 9–18.

9 Ricardo González Leandri, *Las profesiones: entre la vocación y el interés corporativo: fundamentos para su estudio histórico* (Madrid: Catriel, 1999).

10 Raquel Sánchez, 'Honor de periodistas: Libertad de prensa y reputación pública en la España liberal', in Raquel Sánchez and José Antonio Guillén Berrendero, eds, *La cultura de la espada: De honor, duelos y otros lances* (Madrid: Dykinson, 2019), 305–32 and Angel Smith, 'The Rise and Fall of Respectable Spanish Liberalism, 1808–1923: An Explanatory Framework', *Journal of Iberian and Latin American Studies* 22/1 (2016), 55–73.

dismantled. There were times when the navy barely had any warships or materials. This chronological period coincides with a time of great change for Spanish society. The structure of the Old Regime was gradually being dismantled and, in its place, a new social system was emerging, although it was not entirely shaped. The second period spans the central third of the century and, therefore, the reign of Isabel II. For the navy it was a time of recovery and empowerment. The institution was materially renewed and a new organizational chart was established. The construction of new ships allowed it to take on a leading role. This coincided with the forging of a new social model, with the consolidation of new social values that ended up becoming the guiding principles. It was a period dominated by the respectability and honourability of men.[11]

It is necessary to observe these processes in a broader framework. It is well known that the nineteenth century saw the professionalization of various trades, jobs and sectors. Whether in the scientific, educational, health, administrative, financial, commercial, or even ecclesiastical field, everyone sought to adapt to the new professionalizing scenario. In the military sector, the problem was particularly evident in the heated debates on academies, promotion systems, hierarchies and the functions assigned to each rank.[12] Less well known, but equally important, was the common

11 Fernando de Bordejé, *Crónica de la Marina Española*; Miguel A. Serrano Monteavaro, 'El poder naval en la España de entre siglos, 1890–1907', *Militaria. Revista de Cultura Militar* 2 (1990), 117–33; José L. Peset, *Ciencias y enseñanza en la revolución burguesa* (Madrid: Siglo XXI, 1978).

12 Enrique Silvela Díaz-Criado, *El proceso de profesionalización del Ejército en España: el Cuerpo de Estado Mayor, 1810–1932* (Madrid: Universidad Nacional de Educación a Distancia, 2015) and Geoffrey Best, *Guerra y sociedad en la Europa revolucionaria: 1770–1870* (Madrid: Ministerio de Defensa, 1990). For the case of the nineteenth-century army, see María del Carmen Martínez Utesa, *Ciencia y milicia en el s. XIX: el general Ibáñez e Ibáñez de Ibero* (Madrid: Universidad Complutense de Madrid, 2001); Blanca Buldain Jaca, 'Reformas administrativas y sociales del Ejército en la transición política de 1820', *Revista de Historia Militar* XXXII/64 (1988), 169–86; Rafael Bañón and José Antonio Olmeda, *La institución militar en el estado contemporáneo* (Madrid: Alianza Editorial, 1985); Julio Busquets, *El militar de carrera en España* (Barcelona: Ariel, 1984); Gabriel Cardona, *El poder militar en la España contemporánea hasta la guerra civil* (Madrid: Siglo XXI, 1983); Javier Barcelona Llop, 'Profesionalismo, militarismo e ideología militar',

quest for respectability of all these groups.[13] In fact, the present collective monograph will constitute a qualitative advance in this area, since it will allow us to verify that the modernization of many labour sectors went hand in hand with the social legitimation of each socio-professional group.

As far as naval officers are concerned, it is interesting to approach the problem from a comparative perspective. The British case is the main reference, since the Royal Navy was the first to undertake a new professionalization drive during the nineteenth century.[14] Furthermore, British officers have always played a major role in society,[15] which was considerably accentuated during this century. The officers were seen not only as heroes,

---

Revista de Estudios Políticos 51 (1986), 127–61; Fernando Fernández Bastarreche, *El Ejército español en el siglo XIX* (Madrid: Siglo XXI, 1978); 'El Ejército español en el siglo XIX. Aspectos sociales y económicos', *Revista de Historia Militar* XXV/ 50 (1981), 69–88; Stanley G. Payne, *Ejército y sociedad en la España liberal, 1808–1936* (Madrid: Akal, 1977); José L. Herrero Sierra, *El Ejército español en el siglo XIX* (Madrid: Cuadernos para el Diálogo, 1975).

13 Juan Pro, 'Las élites de la España liberal: clases y redes en la definición del espacio social (1808–1931)', *Historia Social* 21 (1995), 47–69; 'La formación de la clase política liberal en España (1833–1868)', *Historia Contemporánea* 23 (2001), 445–81; Pedro Carasa, 'Una mirada cultural a las élites políticas en los primeros pasos del Estado Constitucional', *Trocadero* 19 (2007), 31–54.

14 Charles I. Hamilton, *The Making of the Modern Admiralty: British Naval Policy-Making, 1805–1927* (Cambridge: Cambridge University Press, 2011); *Anglo-French Naval Rivalry, 1840–1870* (New York: Oxford University Press, 1993); John Beeler, *British Naval Policy in the Gladstone-Disraeli Era, 1866–1880* (Stanford: Stanford University Press, 1997). The French Navy, although less studied, also has a fundamental reference: Masson Battesti, *La Marine de Napoléon III, Una Politique Navale* (Paris: Service Historique de la Marine, 1997).

15 D. A. B. Ronald, *Youth, Heroism and War Propaganda. Britain and the Young Maritime Hero, 1745–1820* (London: Bloomsbury, 2015); Adam Nicolson, *Men of Honour: Trafalgar and the Making of the English Hero* (London: Harper Collins, 2009); Timothy Jenks, *Naval Engagements: Patriotism, Cultural Politics, and the Royal Navy, 1793–1815* (Oxford: Oxford University Press, 2006); Gerald Jordan and Nicholas Roger, 'Admirals as Heroes: Patriotism and Liberty in Hanoverian England', *Journal of British Studies* 28 (1989), 201–24; Miguel Alonso Baquer, 'La selección de la élite militar española en el siglo XIX', *Revista de Historia Militar* XXIV/49 (1980), 105–38; 'La reforma militar del siglo XIX', *Militaria. Revista de Cultura Militar* 1 (1989), 15–26.

but also as exemplary men who represented the emerging values: effort, sacrifice, responsibility, austerity, rigidity, prudence.[16] The case of the United States is also very suggestive. The development of its navy throughout the nineteenth century also involved an enormous effort to reinforce the honourability of the profession and the distinction of the corps.[17] In fact, for a long time USA naval officers were the most recognized and exclusive military group in the armed forces.[18]

Among the ruins of the Old Regime

At the beginning of the nineteenth century the navy was the Crown jewel. Blessed by kings and admired by people, the navy was a gigantic war and logistics machine, deployed throughout the seas of the globe. It consumed enormous economic and material resources, owned hundreds of ships and had thousands of personnel. But despite this brilliant image, shadows began to fall on the naval institution in the 1790s.[19] Three decades later there were barely a dozen active ships and a few hundred officers. The navy that had become the second largest and most powerful

16 Christopher Bell, 'The King's English and the Security of the Empire: Class, Social Mobility and Democratization in the British Naval Officer Corps, 1918–1939', *Journal British Studies* 48/3 (2009), 695–716 and C. I. Hamilton, 'Naval Hagiography and the Victorian Hero', *The Historical Journal* 23/2 (1980), 381–98.

17 Mark C. Hunter, *A Society of Gentlemen: Midshipmen at the U.S. Naval Academy, 1845–1861* (Annapolis: Naval Institute Press, 2010); Christopher McKee, *A Gentlemanly and Honorable Profession: The Creation of the U.S. Naval Officer Corps, 1794–1815* (Annapolis: Naval Institute Press, 1991); Peter Karsten, *The Naval Aristocracy: The Golden Age of Annapolis and the Emergence of Modern American Navalism* (New York: Free Press, 1992).

18 Charles W. Mills, *La élite de poder* (México, DF: Fondo de Cultura Económica, 2013).

19 Allan J. Kuethe, 'La crisis naval en tiempos de Carlos IV', *Minervae Baeticae. Boletín de la Real Academia Sevillana de Buenas Letras* 42 (2014), 269–81; Enrique Martínez Ruiz, 'La marina española en torno a 1802', in Antonio Morales Moya, ed., *1802. España entre dos siglos, Monarquía, Estado, Nación* (Madrid: Sociedad Española de Conmemoraciones Culturales, 2003), 263–76.

in the world was now a distant memory, almost a dream in the minds of older officers.[20]

> Cádiz, Ferrol, Cartagena, places once admired for their magnificent and sumptuous arsenals [...] where Spain displayed an accurate picture of its power and wealth, are today where it can properly be said that the cruel desolation and dreadful misery have set their dismal home.[21]

Despite this spectacular decline, the first third of the century was a very intense period for the navy. The years from 1793 to 1820 was a time of almost uninterrupted conflict. Squadrons fought on fronts that were spread throughout Europe, America and Asia. The navy had to be at full strength during the War of the Pyrenees of 1793–1795 and the Anglo-Spanish Wars of 1796–1802 and 1804–1809. The famous defeats of Cape St Vincent and Trafalgar took place in this war context. During the Peninsular War, the navy faced an eminently peninsular and European conflict, but also an American and global one.[22] The Naval Infantry was used to stop the French advance and the warships were subordinated to the land warfare. After the return of Fernando VII, the weakened navy that was left had to deal with the many conflicts that broke out in the American territories.[23]

During the first decade of the nineteenth century, the image projected by the navy oscillated between admiration and melancholy. It continued to be an essential institution for a monarchy whose territories extended across the globe, but, nevertheless, the successive defeats and progressive degeneration meant that the navy was seen as a slowly melting candle. In

20 According to data provided by Merino, in 1795 there were 163 warships, counting only ships, frigates, corvettes, brigs, xebecs and urchins, and 1690 officers. In contrast, in 1835 there were only 11 warships and 321 officers. See Merino, *La Armada Española*, 41.

21 José Vázquez Figueroa, *Exposición sobre el estado de la Marina Expuesta por el ministro Vázquez Figueroa* (Madrid, 1812).

22 María Luisa Lebrón García, 'La Armada española en la Guerra de Independencia', *Aportes* 70 (2009), 23–39; Carlos Martínez Valverde, *La Marina en la Guerra de Independencia* (Madrid: Editorial Nacional, 1974).

23 José Cervera Pery, *La Marina española en la emancipación de Hispanoamérica* (Madrid: Mapfre, 1992).

1806 Rosa María Gálvez[24] published *Oda en elogio de la Marina española* [*Ode in praise of the Spanish Navy*], a brief piece that perfectly summarized this scenario.[25] The mourning for the defeat at Trafalgar was blended with the praise for an institution unparalleled in the monarchy.

> While from the raging south
> The stirring breeze
> Announce the storm, a hoarse roar
> The pole throws, a sign of mourning and death,
> A terrible sign of future glory,
> Due to the brave champions
> That of the honour of Spain
> They set the illustrious fate
> With one and another inimitable feat.[26]

In this context, the navy itself tried to respond to the growing discredit of the institution with a wide range of actions.[27] José Vargas Ponce, prototypical intellectual of the Enlightenment and a naval officer,[28] published a book in 1807 entitled *Importancia de la Historia de la Marina*

24 Rosa María de Gálvez (Málaga 1768–Madrid, 1806) was a renowned writer who lived between the Enlightenment and Neoclassicism. Her role as poet and playwright allowed her to settle in the Court, where she managed to carve out a niche for herself among the most powerful circles. She was even protected by Minister Godoy during the last years of her life.

25 José Cepeda Gómez, 'Servir al Rey y servir a la Nación. Ilustrados, liberales y el deber militar', *Cuadernos de Historia Moderna* 16 (1995), 139–56.

26 R. M. Gálvez, *Oda en elogio de la Marina española* (Madrid: Imprenta Repullés, 1806), 3.

27 Guadalupe Chocano Higueras, 'La Armada, política exterior y prensa en el XIX', *Cuadernos de Pensamiento Naval* 25 (2018), 81–94.

28 José Vargas Ponce (Cádiz, 1760–Madrid, 1821). He entered the *Academia de Guardias Marinas* [Royal Academy of Midshipmen] in 1782 and, although he continued his naval career, he succeeded in establishing himself as a renowned historian, politician, poet and scholar of the late eighteenth and early nineteenth centuries. In 1786 he joined the *Real Academia de la Historia* [Royal Academy of History] and in 1813 the *Real Academia Española* [Royal Spanish Academy]. He published numerous treatises throughout his life, of literary, historical and political nature.

española: precisión de que se confíe a un marino [*Importance of the History of the Spanish Navy: precision of being entrusted to a seafarer*]. This was a desperate effort to demonstrate the importance of the navy in the Spanish monarchy, while emphasizing the scientific level and prestige of the naval officers. The latter was also developed through the biography genre. During these years, José Vargas Ponce himself published the collection *Varones ilustres de la Marina Española* [*Illustrious men of the Spanish Navy*], a series of biographies of important sailors that only had three issues.[29] A few years earlier, in 1803, the young and erudite officer of the navy Martínez Fernández de Navarrete published *Noticia biográfica del general de Marina D. Blas de Lezo* [*Biographical Note on Navy General Mr Blas de Lezo*] – a work re-edited in 1829. However, the most significant example of this apologetic effort made during the first years of the nineteenth century was the depiction of General Federico Gravina. Gone as a hero at Trafalgar, he was admired and venerated as if he were the twilight of the great navy.[30]

> Or instead of the purple command
> Which used to adorn his gentle figure,
> All covered with the dismal mourning,
> Pale and dejected
> The funeral tribute
> the sad Spain pays its General!

29 The first one was *Vida de don Pedro Niño* [*Life of mister Pedro Niño*], the first Count of Buelna, in 1807. It was followed by *Vida de D. Juan Josef Navarro, primer marques de la Victoria* [*Life of Mr Juan Josef Navarro, First Marquis of La Victoria*], in 1808; *Vida de Pedro Navarro, conde de Oliveto* [*Life of Pedro Navarro, Count of Oliveto*] and *Vida de Hugo de Moncada* [*Life of Hugo de Moncada*], in 1810.

30 Antonio Calvo Maturana, 'La oficialidad del ejército y la marina borbónicos: reformismo, fidelidad e identidad (1750–1808)', *Cuadernos de Historia Moderna* 41/2 (2016), 467–95. Several pieces were published in honour of Gravina, such as *Oración fúnebre que en las solmenes exequias del Exmo. Sr. D. Federico Gravina* [*Funeral oration for the Memorial Service of Mr Federico Gravina*]; *En elogio del excelentísimo señor don Federico Gravina, capitán general de Marina, oda por D.M.B.G.S* [*Eulogy of the Most Excellent Mr Federico Gravina, Captain General of the Navy, ode by D.M.B.G.S*]; and *Elogio del Exmo. Señor Don Federico Gravina, Capitán General de la Armada* [*Eulogy of His Excellency Mr Federico Gravina, Captain General of the Navy].*

In her deadly sorrow and in her bitterness
She sighs in pain,
Looks back, groans,
And the acerbic crying bathes her cheeks.
Around her, her loving children
Muted and silent
Contemplate her dismay
And affectionate try to mitigate it …
Lies the immortal hero, in whose name
The empire of the sea was shaking.
He was the son of courage from the cradle.[31]

However, the navy's crisis cannot be explained by one, two, or even three defeats. It was a more complex process. Rather than a crisis, we should speak of disintegration, which began in the last decade of the eighteenth century. Some structural deficits – such as the lack of sailors – were added to the drastic reduction in budgets from 1795 onwards. Almost overnight, the navy stopped receiving the millions of *reales* that were so necessary to keep operating ships and naval installations. Without funds, the warehouses were empty of supplies and provisions, salaries could not be paid and the ships began to rot. Added to this was the chronic discussion about the navy's organizational and management model. During the eighteenth century, the tandem formed by the Secretary of the Navy and the Directorate-General of the Navy was established. However, during the first third of the nineteenth century there were many changes with the intermittent incorporation of the Admiralty and its Council.[32]

Throughout these decades, a real turnaround was experienced within the Naval Officer Corps. In addition to the drastic reduction in personnel – from over 1,500 officers to barely 300 – the professionalization parameters that had been established during the eighteenth century were undermined. The enormous effort that had been made to create technical, intelligent and qualified officers vanished. A disastrous image of the corps became

31 D.M.B.G.S., *En elogio del excelentísimo señor don Federico Gravina, capitán general de Marina, oda* (Madrid: Imprenta de Álvarez, 1806).

32 Sigfrido Vázquez Cienfuegos, 'El Almirantazgo español de 1807: la última reforma de Manuel Godoy', *Hispania* LXXII/214 (2012), 475–500.

widespread, associating officials with corruption, inefficiency and ineptitude. The case of the midshipmen is a good example. From being models for the monarchy, in terms of service, merit and training, they became a paradigm of defects and vices.

> The young man who one day embarks on the difficult career of the Navy, perhaps leaving the sight of his parents always attentive to direct his heart, to fix his habits and to contemplate his passions, looks at himself as a foreign country, open to all paths of corruption, without finding a superior who prescribes any other obligation than a short study and many companions who instruct him in the vices he ignores.[33]

The radical change that took place in the navy is not without significance. From the greatest praise, flattery and admiration, naval officers became the perfect archetype of decadence. One of the most talked-about discussions was promotions. During the second half of the eighteenth century, promotions were made on the basis of confidential reports sent by each officer, a sort of secret evaluation made by superiors in which aspects such as piloting, manoeuvring, tactics, artillery, discipline, equipment, ordinance, languages, science, courage, talent, zeal, conduct and character were examined.[34] Unlike the Army, venality and seniority were not decisive elements in the promotions. In fact, within the navy it was said that 'seniority in a corps does not entitle one to promotion when more modern officers have served with distinction'.[35]

From 1808 onwards, this system was overshadowed by the demands of war and the international context. Since then, promotions were based on increasingly ambiguous criteria, without taking into account the demands of the profession. It was then that satires and mockeries began to become widespread within the Naval Officer Corps. Antonio de Escaño

33 Archivo del Museo Naval (hereafter, AMN), caja 253, manuscrito 473, folio 97, 'Reflexiones de un oficial aplicado sobre el estado de la Marina y mejorar que es necesario hacer en ella', 1803.

34 These are the features to be evaluated in the *Ordenanzas de la Armada* [Ordinances of the Navy] of 1793. The reports were later reformed by José Mazarredo through a systematization of the features and the notes.

35 Archivo General de la Marina Álvaro de Bazán (hereafter, AGMAB), Cuerpo General, legajo 491.

said that it was not possible to promote officers who 'were content to be in the Department with a warehouse key or doing a guard every eight days'. Nor could those be promoted who 'spend eternity in the American naval station for their own convenience [or] who use frequent temporary leaves'. The debate was not settled and, in fact, went beyond the bounds of the corps itself. In 1814 an anonymous piece entitled *Juicio crítico sobre la Marina militar, dispuesto en forma de cartas de un amigo a otro* [*Critical trial of the military navy, arranged in the form of letters from one friend to another*] was published. The book, actually written by Luis María Salazar – naval officer, General Intendant and minister on several occasions – was devastating.[36]

> The method for promoting, or upward mobility in the navy, has been the subject of continual conversation, or better said, of incessant murmuring; cause in reality the matter was rich and proper to it. … It is the case (let it be known to those who ignore it) that every two or three years, in fact, whenever it seemed convenient to them or to those who ruled the helm of our navy, one of these phenomena was prepared in the navy. And after much talking and writing, the long lists of the lucky ones came out to the public like a summer downpour … in which, as a trawl net, all sorts of subjects, medium, good and bad, and even the dead, used to appear confusingly mixed together … These enduring litanies were first prepared between the majority and the general management of the navy, and were then completed in the Secretary of the State of the Navy; not without certain and numerous arrangements being made for their establishment, in which all those who could have some transversal or direct influence worked effectively to place their relatives, friends and *protégés*.[37]

The author himself recognized that this system had created 'monstruosidades' [monstrosities] by giving promotions to 'hombres sin ningún verdadero mérito' [men without any real merit]. But the problems

36 The publication caused considerable commotion both inside and outside the navy. In fact, in 1817 the Minister of the Navy Vázquez de Figueroa wrote a counter-offensive work entitled *Anales de los servicios de la Marina de guerra Española* [*Annals of Spanish Navy Services*]. This book was intended to clear the name of the navy and justify its many problems due to the severe decline of the institution. See José Vázquez Figueroa, *Anales de los servicios de la Marina de guerra española* (Madrid: Miguel de Burgos, 1817).

37 Luis M. Salazar, *Juicio Crítico sobre la Marina Militar de España. Dispuesto en formas de cartas de un amigo a otro* (Ferrol: Ricardo Pita, 1888), 251.

lay not only in this organizational structure, but in the general social system that only allowed the noble class to enter the corps. Numerous voices, even within the institution, began to question the requirement of nobility, thus showing that the social order was immersed in a deep process of change.[38] One officer went so far as to say that 'it has been believed that, in order to have a young officer, it was enough to present his documents of noblility and *hidalguía*, just to teach him mathematics; that those who have thought this way can be disillusioned, that it is necessary to work on instilling in him ideas of honour and equity; to inspire a taste for study, to get used to being continually occupied'.[39] This same officer asked himself: 'What advantage does the nation take away from an ignorant and cowardly nobleman when a commoner, a virtuous man, of many services and talents, can give lustre to a homeland that is willing to favour him with justice?' The most interesting aspect of this debate is that the old noble values began to be replaced by other ideals that were still in formation:

> two are the qualities that help to bend a man to do well and to distinguish himself from others in heroic deeds of justice and patriotism: one is the civility given by his primogenitors; the other is the impression made on his heart by the maxims that have inspired him in his education. A young man who indulges himself in vice, even if he is the noblest, suffers from a frenzy that occasionally precipitates him into the most unseemly crimes; forgetting entirely the distinguished place in which nature has placed him … therefore, let it not be said that it is not necessary to teach good manners to the young men who are destined to be part of the distinguished corps of the navy; on the contrary, let us confess that this is the foundation without which a good naval officer will not be born, a men in whom the healthy principles of morals and good manners have been inculcated and acknowledged.[40]

The crisis of the navy did not cease to be accentuated in the years to come. The Minister of the Navy himself said that 'Your Majesty's Royal Navy today looks like a magnificent old building that has been completely

38 Enrique Martínez Ruiz 'Nobleza y milicia: tendencias de una nueva relación (1780–1868)', in Carmen Iglesias Cano, ed., *Nobleza y Sociedad en la España Moderna* (Oviedo: Ediciones Nobel, 1996), 153–73.

39 AMN, caja 253, manuscrito 473, folio 92.

40 AMN, caja 253, manuscrito 473, folio 92.

destroyed'.[41] It is not surprising, therefore, that during the 1820s the navy was not an alluring destination for families, becoming an almost residual institution:

> What advantages are there in the sight of honest parents to prepare and deliver their children for such profession? None: on the contrary, mothers weep over their sacrificed children, as they often say, and call their fathers executioners, asking for the same fate for them. Thus, the Midshipmen are usually the children of poor officers of the same corps, who, having nothing to support them with, nor any other choice due to the lack of resources, hand them over to maintain the whole family.[42]

Despite attempts at reform, the results were disastrous.[43] During the Liberal Triennium, the *Decreto Orgánico de la Armada* [*Organic Act of the Navy*] (1821) was approved, a document intended to solve the main and most urgent problems. For the first time the law established a differentiation between officers in active and passive positions. The former would be in charge of ships, arsenals and strictly military functions. Passive assignments, for officers who were not in a position to perform the previous tasks, were divided between the *matrículas de mar* [register of seamen] and the *capitanías* [captaincies-general]. The act also established that promotions should be provided according to seniority as main criterion, which was an important change from the eighteenth-century navy.

We have to wait for the long ministry of Luis María Salazar (1823–1832) to see noteworthy changes. This minister's purpose was to definitively dismantle the old eighteenth-century navy and lay the foundations for a new naval institution. In 1825, the *Real y Militar Colegio de Caballeros Guardias Marinas* [Royal Academy of Midshipmen] (1825–1828) was created, a new naval school that aimed to accentuate the technical and scientific character

41 AGMAB, Cuerpo General, legajo 499.

42 Anonymous, *Carta de un marino a otro en contestación a varias preguntas sobre la reforma que debía de hacerse en la Marina Nacional (carta quinta)* (Cádiz: Imprenta de Niel hijo, 1820), 4. Biblioteca Museo Naval, 516.

43 Juan R. Coronas González, 'La reforma de la Secretaría de la Guerra de 1820', *Revista de Historia Militar* 67 (1989), 120–43.

of the cadets.[44] The promotions of those years were provided by strict seniority, without regard to other types of merit or distinction. In fact, from 1830 onwards, it was strictly forbidden for officers to request promotion by means of petitions or memorandums, as had been customary during the eighteenth century. For the Ministry of the Navy, it became common to grant promotion based on 'mérito en general' [general merit], without specifying. Professional criteria, such as nautical and scientific knowledge, application or command ability, were assimilated with seniority.

Even in those years, the old noble values were definitely being relegated by the new ideals.[45] For example, the naval cadets were to have as their maxims 'el amor al rey, el pundonor, el decoro y la subordinación militar' [love of the king, punditry, decorum and military subordination].[46] In contrast, the model of the naval officer had to be based on two principles: honour and sufficiency. The latter was the result of 'a long apprenticeship in the Midshipman rank before any of these achieved officers [and] … on this good foundation each individual's personal dispositions will then progressively grow or develop by reason of his greater experience, genius, application'.[47] But besides application in the profession, the officer was nothing without honour. 'It is necessary to consider it as an idea, or a virtue, which is also acquired by instruction and example. Therefore, the means of spreading and making general the noble sentiments of good education and military pride must not be abandoned in the navy corps.'[48] Even in the confidential reports made to evaluate the officers, notes and adjectives appeared that were hitherto unknown. For example, in 1825 Fernando Bustillo's report noted that he was an officer 'de suma honradez' [of the utmost honesty].[49]

44 *Reglamento provisional aprobado por el Rey Nuestro Señor, para el establecimiento y gobierno del Colegio Real Militar de Caballeros Guardias Marinas* (Madrid: Imprenta Real, 1825).

45 Enrique Martínez Ruiz, 'El largo ocaso del ejército español de la Ilustración: reflexiones en torno a una secuencia temporal', *Revista de Historia Moderna* 22 (2004), 7–57.

46 AGMAB, Cuerpo General, legajo 499.

47 AGMAB, Cuerpo General, legajo 499.

48 AGMAB, Cuerpo General, legajo 499.

49 AGMAB, Cuerpo General, legajo 499.

The forge of the respectable navy

The second third of the nineteenth century was a key period for the Spanish Navy. The institution managed to adopt a new position within the monarchy thanks to the renewal of its structure and the transformation of its projection. It was no longer an imperial navy that sought to protect the extensive coasts of the American and Asian continents, but a national navy focused on the defence of the Peninsula's coasts and the safeguard of Cuba, Puerto Rico and the Philippines. This immaterial restoration was accompanied by a material reconstruction and a significant increase in the budget. The arsenals were repaired, the shipyards were reactivated and the workers returned to the workshops.[50] But this revival required a qualitative leap, and a real modernization of the institution was promoted, especially in naval engineering and in the officer corps. It can be said that, by the middle of the century, the Naval Officer Corps was immersed in a second professionalization – the first being implemented during the eighteenth century. Finally, and beyond the military and technical aspects, the navy embarked on a campaign of social legitimation that offered a new image of the institution and the officers.

If in 1830 the navy seemed to have practically disappeared, a real turnaround took place during the 1840s and 1850s. The reconstruction of the naval forces made it possible to have the fourth largest squadron in Europe, with a size and operability very similar to the Dutch one. In order to understand this process, it is necessary to mention the ministries of Francisco Armero Peñaranda (1844–1847, 1851–1852), Mariano Roca de Togores (1847–1851, 1853–1854), Antonio de Santa Cruz (1854–1856), José MacCrohon Blake (1858–1860) and Juan Zabala de la Puente (1860–1863, 1865–1866).[51] The main achievement of these ministers was to obtain better funding. They managed to increase the navy's budget, as well as to secure

50 Cristina Roda Alcantud, *Historia e ingeniería en el siglo XIX. Vanguardia de la industria naval en el Mediterráneo Occidental: el arsenal de Cartagena* (Cartagena: Ayuntamiento de Cartagena, 2008).

51 Carlos Alfaro, 'Trafalgar, el marqués de Molins y el renacimiento de la Armada en 1850', *Revista de Historia Naval* 97 (2007), 43–56; 'The Moderado Party and the

several large loans. As a result, a profound transformation was initiated. In 1838, for example, the navy was almost a residual institution. This year it received 30 million *reales*, while the Ministry of War received 545 million. During the reign of Isabel II, the budget of the Ministry of the Navy represented around 6 per cent of the State's budget. The maximum was 9 per cent in 1851–1852 and 1861–1866,[52] although there were years when it was reduced to 3 per cent. In any case, the percentages differed widely from those of the Ministry of War, which received about 20 per cent of the total budget.[53]

After all this effort, the Isabelline navy managed to reach a fairly respectable size. In 1867 there were a total of 114 warships divided into five types: first class, second class, third class, minor forces and others.[54] That same year there was a total of 566 officers, divided into one captain general, five lieutenant generals, fifteen squadron leaders, seventeen brigadiers, forty-six ship's captains, eighty frigate captains, 196 frigate lieutenants and 206 frigate ensigns. These were years of considerable activity for the navy, since in addition to the defence of the coasts and the protection of maritime trade, the warships participated in the First and Second Carlist Wars (1833–1840, 1846–1849), the Hispano-Moroccan War (1859–1860), the

Introduction of Steam Power in the Spanish Navy, 1844–1854', *War in History* 13/4 (2006), 451–67.

52 During the first half of the 1860s the Navy received an extraordinary loan as part of the Salaverría budget, a total of 142 million pesetas, which was intended for an ambitious naval reconstruction plan. See Fernando Comín, *El presupuesto del estado y la economía española, 1845–1935* (Alcalá de Henares: Universidad de Alcalá, 1987), 608.

53 Fernando Puell de la Villa, 'El Ejército y la España de Isabel II', in *Aproximación a la historia militar de España* (Madrid: Ministerio de Defensa, 2006), 433–52.

54 Among the first-class ships, there were six armoured frigates, eleven steam frigates and three paddle steamers. The second-class ships were comprised of one steam ship, ten paddle steamers and five sailing ships. The third-class ships constituted a larger group: twenty-five steam ships, ten paddle steamers, one sailing ship, ten steamer vessels and seven sailing vessels. The minor forces comprise seventeen paddle gunboats.

Dominican Restoration War (1863–1865), the Cochinchina Campaign (1858–1862) and especially the so-called War of the Pacific (1865–1866).[55]

These were also crucial years for the Naval Officer Corps. From 1840 onwards, scientific, technical and military innovations imposed a new process of professionalization. Steam revolutionized the navies, since in addition to changing the construction of ships, their command and management were drastically transformed. This required a comprehensive restructuring of the naval career, of the training, functions and skills of officers, thus reforms had to be undertaken in several areas. An essential step was the foundation of the *Colegio Naval Militar* [Military Naval School], a new educational centre that opened its doors in 1845 and closed them in 1868:[56] 'This School should be for the teaching of all sciences related to the navy, adding to navigation, naval architecture, hydraulics, artillery and astronomy.'[57] The new naval cadets had two training phases: a theoretical one, at the school, comprising six semesters and a final exam;[58] and a practical one, on board several ships over a period of six years.[59]

55 Agustín Rodríguez González, *La Armada Española, la campaña del Pacífico, 1862–1871: España frente a Chile y Perú* (Madrid: Agualarga, 1999); and Jesús Salgado Alba, 'La estrategia marítima española bajo Isabel II y Alfonso XII (1820–1885)', *Cuadernos monográficos del Instituto de Historia y Cultura Naval* 5 (1989), 7–22.

56 *Reglamento del Colegio Naval Militar* (Madrid: Román Matute, 1848); *Reglamento para el régimen, dirección y gobierno del Colegio Naval Militar* (Madrid: Imprenta Nacional, 1858).

57 AGMAB, Guardias Marinas, legajo 724.

58 The subjects were arranged as follows: first semester, arithmetic, sacred and profane history, morals and religion, drawing, gymnastics, military exercises and dance; second semester, elementary algebra, French, drawing, fencing, gymnastics, military exercises and dance; third semester, elementary geometry, French, drawing, fencing, gymnastics, military exercises and dance; fourth semester, analytical geometry, plane and spherical trigonometry, applications to the art of technical drawing, French, drawing, fencing, gymnastics, military exercises and dance; fifth semester, mechanics, experimental physics and chemistry, English, principles of artillery and weapons training, drawing, fencing, gymnastics, military exercises and dance; and sixth semester, cosmography and piloting, geography, English, manoeuvring and notions of shipbuilding.

59 During these years the midshipman had to be instructed in the pre-emption of supplies and water, in the increase or decrease of forces and crew, in the preparation of

This important measure was followed by others that directly affected officers. In 1849 a new naval hierarchy was approved – admiral, vice admiral, commodore, first- and second-class captain, frigate captain, lieutenant and ensign – and a maximum number of officers was set at around 450.[60] Confidential reports regained importance again, since they were the key instrument for gauging this new professionalization impulse within the officer corps. These evaluations examined piloting, manoeuvring, knowledge of steam engines, naval tactics, artillery, military discipline and exercises, conservation and consumption of supplies, pre-emption of ordinances, languages, knowledge about the other navy corps, courage, talent, character, zeal, conduct and subordination.[61] Reporting was a crucial issue within the Naval Officer Corps, and the utmost scrupulousness was always sought to ensure a genuinely fair assessment. It was standard practice for the instruction of such reports to recall that they must be 'the result of good faith, conscience and moral respectability'.[62]

In this reform process there were also important changes in the promotion strategy. Through different laws, enacted in 1841, 1844 and 1854, new criteria for promotions were established. As a general rule, two thirds of the vacancies were to be filled by rigorous seniority and the remaining third by selection on the basis of 'qualified merits'. Within the latter, a distinction was made between 'scientific', 'practical' and 'war service' merits.[63] The 1854 reform transformed this system, adducing that 'the promotion strategy among seafarers should not be governed by the simple fact of seniority, because it would not be fair, equitable or prudent'.[64] According

ships, in general and specific combat plans, as well as piloting, manoeuvring, naval tactics and steam engines.

60 AGMAB, Cuerpo General, legajo 505, 506 and 507.

61 AGMAB, Cuerpo General, legajo 626.

62 AGMAB, Cuerpo General, legajo 554.

63 The first involved 'maritime science and its various branches, as well as its own ancillaries, on mountains and woodlands; exploitation of mineral fuel or any other science, art or industry related to shipbuilding, and the handling, management and training of ships'. The 'practical merits' were intended to reflect the promotions that were due when an officer 'distinguished himself outstandingly', that is, 'the construction of any hydraulic naval work or some artillery work'. Finally, merits for war service were intended to reward extraordinary 'military service'.

64 AMN, caja 613, manuscrito 1935, folios 42–3.

to this system, promotions were to be provided on the basis of the merits and abilities of individual officers, and so a collegial board was created to qualify the proposals.

All this professionalization effort went hand in hand with another no less important process. Throughout the reign of Isabel II, the Naval Officer Corps embarked on a campaign of social legitimation that sought to present the naval officers as a respectable and honourable corps. The aim was to identify the group with the guiding values of the period so that they would be regarded as a distinguished segment of society. This problem had been present in all its magnitude since the 1830s.[65] In 1836 proof of nobility was forbidden as a means to access military schools, so new mechanisms of social differentiation had to be implemented. Henceforth, the entrance of 'young men of pure lineage, children of distinguished parents, full of talent and hope'[66] was allowed. Within the navy, it was said that applicants should be 'children of parents of good manners'.[67] 'It is advisable that the requested reports include the manners and morals of the parents, from which it can be deduced what education they have given their children.' In sum, as an internal instruction said, 'the first thing to look for is that they are from good families'.[68]

This new model was sanctioned with the opening of the *Colegio Naval Militar* [Military Naval School] in 1845.[69] The cadets had to 'arrange their behaviour according to the principles of honour, application and conduct', and more specifically, 'they must base their honour on their behaviour and chosen education, they will always bear in mind that a large part of this comprises modesty and composure in religious acts, as well as decency

65 Pablo Ortega-del-Cerro, 'El ocaso de la distinción estamental: retratos familiares e imágenes nobiliarias entre los guardiamarinas (1820–1844)', in Juan Hernández Franco and Francisco Precioso Izquierdo, eds, *Entornos sociales de cambio y ruptura de jerarquías en la nobleza española* (siglos XVIII–XIX) (Madrid: Sílex, 2020), 247–94.

66 AGMAB, Guardias Marinas, legajo 724.

67 AGMAB, Guardias Marinas, legajo 771.

68 AGMAB, Colegio Naval, legajo 822.

69 José Blanca Carlier, 'La Escuela Naval Militar: su origen histórico', *Revista Historia Naval* 32 (1991), 11–44.

and good manners in all others'.[70] In fact, it was mandatory that before entering the school, the applicants had to submit documents that proved 'that all the family of the applicant in both lines is considered to be honest in the public eye, without any incident that could tarnish or disgrace it, according to the current laws, adding to these the acknowledged manners of the applicant'.[71] Along with the honesty of the family, the condition of the young man and his father as Spanish citizens and the profession, practice or way of life of his father had to be certified. These evaluations were valid until 1865, when they were prohibited.[72]

Despite the importance of this evidence, the greatest effort to legitimize the corps was conducted through the public representation of the officers. Throughout the 1840s, 1850s and 1860s there was a genuine campaign to associate naval officers, and the navy in general, with the values of respectability and honour. Within this effort to exhibit honesty, three strategies can be distinguished: first, the development of naval journalism through the publication of several wide-ranging magazines; second, the printing of many and varied pieces demonstrating the achievements of the navy and justifying its actions; and finally, the writing and dissemination of biographies of navy officers that embodied the model of 'hombre de bien' [honest men]. Although it is true that there were hundreds of testimonies of this three-pronged strategy, the most relevant ones will be highlighted below.

During the Isabelline period, numerous magazines on maritime subjects were published.[73] Many of them were born under the direct auspices of the navy, and they ended up becoming a privileged channel of propaganda and circulation. Among them, *La España Marítima* (1838–1841), *Revista Militar* (1838–1840), *El Militar Español* (1846–1848), *El Fanal* (1842),

70 *Reglamento del Colegio Naval Militar*, 28.

71 *Reglamento del Colegio Naval Militar*, 13.

72 Pablo Ortega-del-Cerro, 'Pruebas de distinción en una sociedad en cambio: las informaciones de limpieza de sangre en la armada (1845–1865)', *Historia Social* 85 (2016), 63–82.

73 Fernando Pinto Cebrián, *Ejército e historia. El pensamiento profesional militar español a través de la literatura castrense decimonónica* (Madrid: Ministerio de Defensa, 2013).

Crónica Naval de España (1855–1860), *La Marina* (1867–1868), *El Marino Español* (1868?) or *El Lloyd Español* (1861–1868). A common denominator in almost all of these magazines was the participation or direction of Jorge Pérez Lasso de la Vega, an outstanding naval officer who became the *de facto* director of communication and representation of the institution.[74] Another important figure in these strategies was José Marcelino Travieso, a navy auditor and author of various works and publications.

The first of these magazines was *La España Marítima*, a pioneer in naval journalism and an example to be followed by successive publications.[75] Its objective would be twofold, since in addition to offering articles on various issues related to the navy – naval sciences, military art, commerce, administration, history, anecdotes – its true purpose was 'to correct the ideas currently held in Spain regarding the importance and necessity of its navy, considered as one of the means to ensure its power and prosperity' – subtitle of the journal. Therefore, the magazine would act as the first channel to legitimize the naval institution and begin to carve a new image within Isabelline society.[76] Fifteen years later, *Crónica naval de España: revista científica, militar, administrativa, histórica, literaria y de comercio* was founded. Its structure was the same: to offer articles on different topics related to the navy – sailing, news, budgets, hygiene, rescue,

74 Jorge Pérez Lasso de la Vega (San Fernando, 1792–Madrid, 1871) joined the navy during the War of Independence and was promoted in the naval hierarchy throughout the first third of the nineteenth century. As a brigadier, in 1837, he became an officer of the Secretary of the Navy. He was interim minister in 1846 and became director of the *Depósito Hidrográfico de la Marina* [Hydrographic Depot of the Navy] (1850–1852). He is particularly known for his prolific literary and journalistic work.

75 Itsaso Ibáñez, Luis M. Fernández-Martínez, '*La España Marítima* (1838–1841). Noticia sobre la primera revista española de marina', *Revista General de Información y Documentación* 28/2 (2018), 555–78.

76 '[…] is a noble arena destined to vindicate the glories of the navy, to air, to sustain its interests and rights, as well as those of commerce, its natural support and ally; it is a popular voice that we have wanted to give to a branch of the State, neglected, mute until now and generally unknown. The honour of advocating such a just cause, the example of other nations, here is what, with no other interest, has put the pen in our hands', in Ibáñez and Fernández-Martínez, 'La España Marítima', 569.

seafaring – and to develop a reiterative discourse on the importance and honourability of the institution. Throughout its five years of life, it was common to see a melancholic tone on the situation of the navy, but at the same time, there were strong claims for the respectability of the officers.

At a later stage, and once the navy had been renewed and modernized, *La Marina Española, periódico de ciencia e intereses marítimos* (1867–1868) was born. Although the structure of this publication was similar to the previous ones, it has a particular value: it embodied all the legitimizing efforts of the 1840s, 1850s and 1860s. There were frequent mentions, and even literal transcriptions, of articles previously published in *Crónica naval de España* and other magazines. In almost every issue, critical articles were introduced to explain the situation of the navy:

> It is perhaps Spain who owes the most glories, the most heroic traits, the most profits and the most power to the navy. The Spanish navy has a history without equal and worthy of another outcome; but the independent, brave and proud Spaniards, lacking sufficient malice and perspicacity, allowed themselves to be deceived by foreign interests, and their naval power perished, and with it the love of the navy. … Those nations in which there is no fondness and conviction of the necessity of the navy, all their official efforts crash against the general indifference, against the repugnance to things of the sea … The naval officer is the least fond of sailing, and almost the only one in Spain who supports the navy, even though from experience he knows how rough and how painful his job is, and if he were to be born again, as is often said, he would not be a *voluntary* midshipmen; and yet his children are seafarers. This exalts this worthy corporation, which serves with enthusiasm and exceeds its duties in everything.[77]

But in addition to the periodical publications, the social legitimacy of the institution and the officers was promoted through monographic publications. During the minority reign of Isabel II, several pieces of a vindictive nature were published, following the pattern of *Juicio crítico* [*Critical trial*] of Luis María Salazar. In 1835 Jorge Pérez Lasso de la Vega wrote *Desahogo crítico sobre cosas que atañen a la Marina de España, su estado decadente y medios intentados para su restauración* [*Critical appraisal of matters concerning the Spanish Navy, its decadent state and the means attempted for its*

77 *La Marina española. Periódico de ciencias e intereses marítimos*, 12 (12 January 1868).

restoration], and in 1841 *Los marinos displicentes. Correspondencia crítica epistolar* [*Dismissive sailors. Critical epistolary correspondence*].[78] Both publications were an attempt to demonstrate the importance of the navy in the monarchy and a justification of the deplorable state it was at the time. During the same period two other works were published, also relevant to the social legitimation of the institution, although they had a different perspective. Martín Fernández de Navarrete published his last works, presenting the important role that the navy had played in the science and progress of Spain, not without introducing certain heroic and romantic overtones.[79] Between 1825 and 1837, five volumes were published under the title *Colección de los viajes y descubrimientos que hicieron por mar los españoles desde fines del siglo XV, con varios documentos inéditos concernientes a la historia de la Marina Castellana y de los Establecimientos Españoles de Indias* [*Collection of the travels and discoveries made by sea by the Spanish since the end of the fifteenth century, with several unpublished documents concerning the history of the Castilian Navy and the Spanish Settlements of the Indies*]. Some years later, in 1851, the great work of Fernández de Navarrete came to light: *Biblioteca marítima Española* [*Spanish Maritime Library*], a compilation of all the existing publications on the navy.[80]

78 Jose Pérez Lasso de la Vega, *Desahogo crítico sobre cosas que atañen a la Marina de España, su estado decadente y medios intentados para su restauración* (San Fernando: Juan Franco, 1835); *Los marinos displicentes. Correspondencia crítica epistolar* (Madrid: Imprenta Ignacio Boix, 1841).

79 Martín Fernández de Navarrete y Jiménez de Tejada (Ábalos, 1765–Madrid, 1844), was a Navy Captain, a knight of the Order of San Juan and of the Royal American Order of Isabel the Catholic. He was Procer and Senator of the Kingdom, as well as director of the Depósito Hidrográfico de la Marina [Hydrographic Depot oh the Navy]. He stood out as one of the most important scholars of the navy at the end of the eighteenth and beginning of the nineteenth century. He was the author of numerous scientific and historical volumes.

80 Martín Fernández Navarrete, *Colección de los viajes y descubrimientos que hicieron por mar los españoles desde fines del siglo XV, con varios documentos inéditos concernientes a la historia de la Marina Castellana y de los Establecimientos Españoles de Indias* (Madrid: Imprenta Real, 5 volúmenes, 1825–1837); Biblioteca marítima española, *Obra póstuma del señor Martín Fernández de Navarrete* (Madrid: Viuda de Calero, 1841); *Colección de opúsculos del Exmo. Sr. Martínez Fernández de Navarrete* (Madrid: Viuda de Calero, 1848).

The 1850s witnessed a turnaround in this situation. Apologetic stories of the navy were written to demonstrate the importance of the institution, and at the same time the most unfortunate episodes of the navy were exalted.[81] In 1849, José Ferrer Couto wrote the first volume of *Historia de la marina real española, desde el descubrimiento de las Américas* [*History of the Spanish Royal Navy, since the discovery of the Americas*],[82] and in 1851, *Historia del combate naval de Trafalgar: precedida de la del Renacimiento de la marina española durante el siglo XVIII* [*History of the Naval Battle of Trafalgar: Preceded by History of the Renaissance of the Spanish Navy during the Eighteenth Century*].[83] Manuel Marliani also wrote about the Battle of Trafalgar in 1850. The book was entitled *Combate de Trafalgar: vindicación de la Armada española contra las aserciones injuriosas vertidas por Mr. Thiers en su Historia del Consulado y el Imperio* [*Battle of Trafalgar: Vindication of the Spanish Navy against the Injurious Assertions Made by Mr Thiers in his History of the Consulate and the Empire*].[84] The aim of these pieces was always the same: to exempt the naval officers from the defeats and decline of the navy during the first third of the nineteenth century. The Naval Officer Corps was portrayed as a respectable group of hard-working and honest servants, who only obeyed higher orders. With the same intention, Jorge Pérez Lasso de la Vega published in 1856 *La Marina Real de España a finales del siglo XVIII y principios del XIX. Memorias de familia, tipos, escenas y cuadros de costumbres, apuntes y materiales para la Historia de la Marina española* [*The Spanish Royal Navy at the End of the Eighteenth and Beginning of the Nineteenth Century. Family Memories, Models, Scenes and Pictures of Customs, Notes and Materials for the History of the Spanish Navy*].[85] The

81 Ana Sánchez Prieto, 'Historiadores militares españoles del siglo XIX', *Medievalismo* I/1 (1991), 99–105.

82 José Ferrer Couto and José March, *Historia de la marina real española, desde el descubrimiento de las Américas* (Madrid: Ducazal, 1849–1854).

83 José Ferrer Couto, J., *Historia del combate naval de Trafalgar: precedida de la del Renacimiento de la marina española durante el siglo XVIII* (Madrid: Izco, 1851).

84 Manuel Marliani, *Combate de Trafalgar: vindicación de la Armada española contra las aserciones injuriosas vertidas por Mr. Thiers en su Historia del Consulado y el Imperio* (Madrid: Matute, 1850).

85 Jorge Pérez Lasso de la Vega, *La Marina Real de España a finales del siglo XVIII y principios del XIX. Memorias de familia, tipos, escenas y cuadros de costumbres,*

last publication of this nature was written by the naval officer Francisco de Salas Rodríguez with the title *Marina española: discurso histórico reseña de la vida de mar y memoria en contestación a un proyecto sobre el ramo escrita de real orden* [*Spanish Navy: Historical discourse on the Life on the Sea and Memory in Response to a Project on the Written Branch of Royal Order*].[86]

Despite the importance of these strategies, the main instrument for legitimizing the institution and the officer corps was the biography genre. Throughout the reign of Isabel II there was a burst of biographies of officers from the eighteenth and nineteenth centuries. The purpose was simple, but essential: to identify the officers of the navy with the role model of respectable, honest and distinguished man. Social quality, family or even military merits were relegated to the background by pride, modesty or religiosity. In almost all the above-mentioned magazines there was a section devoted exclusively to the biographies of seafarers, generally senior navy officers who had recently deceased. For example, in 1867 the biography of Francisco Armero Peñaranda (Fuentes de Andalucía, 1804–Sevilla, 1866), a Captain General of the Navy and several times Minister of the Navy, was published in *La Marina española*. Amongst his many virtues were:

> The rightness of his conscience, the inflexibility of his will, the energy of his spirit and the good temper of his heart led him, with admirable speed, to the high position of adviser of the monarch; the loyalty of his noble behaviour drove him to confine himself in his small village, and the terrible political upheavals that continually agitated our country led him to a miserable dungeon from which he emerged innocent of all charges and with its reputation unscathed.[87]

The author of this passage was Cesáreo Fernández Duro, who during those years also wrote the biography of José Montojo Albizu and of García de Quesada.[88] Navarrete, Lasso de la Vega, Travieso and Hoyos also

---

apuntes y materiales para la Historia de la Marina española (Madrid: Viuda de Calero, 1856).

86 Francisco J. Salas Rodríguez, *Marina española: discurso histórico reseña de la vida de mar y memoria en contestación a un proyecto sobre el ramo escrita de real orden* (Madrid: Fortanet, 1865).

87 *La Marina Española, periódico de ciencia e intereses marítimos* 2 (12 November 1867).

88 The obituary of the latter said 'general of engineers … a person of great and vast instruction, of affable treatment, of kindly character, he was very much appreciated

published several works in this genre. But in addition to these small articles, a monograph was also published. In 1852 the captain and history scholar Francisco de Paula Quadrado published *Elogio histórico del excelentísimo señor don Antonio de Escaño, teniente general de Marina, regente de España e Indias en 1810, comendador de Carrizosa e individuo honorario de la Real Academia de la Historia* [*Historical Eulogy of His Excellency Mr Antonio de Escaño, Lieutenant General of the Navy, Regent of Spain and the Indies in 1810, Commander of Carrizosa and Honorary Member of the Royal Academy of History*].[89] A few years later, Marcelino Travieso wrote the biography of General Alejo Gutiérrez de Rubalcaba (Cartagena, 1768–Madrid, 1847), a book that immediately became a reference. In this work, General Rubalcaba was introduced with all the virtues of the time:

> He was born in Cartagena on the 23 May 1768, the son of an illustrious family, constantly dedicated to the service of the State in the noble and then highly considered naval profession … His long career was an uninterrupted series of useful services in which he showed the greatest zeal, disinterest and love for the throne and the public good, having achieved a high and enviable status for his vast instruction, for his consummate prudence and good sense in the handling of business, for his rectitude and purity and for the constant practice of all the virtues. With his death, the nation lost one of its loyal and honest servants, the throne a noble, determined and generous defender, and the navy a skilful and experienced chief who fought with glory and stood with honour in the days of his greatness.[90]

This strategy of legitimation undoubtedly culminated in 1873, when Francisco de Paula Pavía published *Galería biográfica de los generales de*

---

by his countless friends and by the high society in which he had always stood. … son of an officer and brother of officers. The rapid achievements of this general were won by his constant study and active laboriousness. Unmarried, sober and needless, he employed the surplus of his salary, following the tradition initiated by the midshipman, on objects of art.'

89 Francisco P. Quadrado y de Roo, *Elogio histórico del excelentísimo señor don Antonio de Escaño, teniente general de Marina, regente de España e Indias en 1810, comendador de Carrizosa e individuo honorario de la Real Academia de la Historia* (Madrid: Imprenta Real Academia de la Historia, 1852).

90 José M. Travieso, Biografía del excelentísimo señor D. Alejo Gutiérrez de Rubalcava (Madrid: Imprenta Fortanet, 1858), 22.

Marina, jefes y personas notables que figuraron en la misma corporación desde 1700 a 1868 [*Biographical Gallery of Navy Generals, Chiefs and Notable Men Who Were in the Same Corps from 1700 to 1868*].[91] This was a colossal compilation of more than 400 biographies in three volumes and one appendix.[92] In each of the entries, Pavía detailed the career of these officers, always with an introduction and a conclusion highlighting the social virtues of the corps. This discursive strategy is repeated throughout the entire publication.[93] Pavía added to all the biographies a series of adjectives that constituted the corpus of values of the society of the moment: honesty, rectitude, probity, pride, effort, loyalty. The most interesting aspect of the compilation is the association of early eighteenth-century officers with those of the mid-nineteenth century, as if they formed a coherent and homogeneous group. The eighteenth-century officers had a halo of distinction and glory that was combined with the respectability and honesty characteristic of the nineteenth century. For example, it was said of Federico Gravina (Palermo, 1756–Cádiz, 1806) that:

> He was always extremely cultured and eloquent in his manners and words, blameless in his habits and absolutely detached from all petty interests. Splendid with his friends, and generous with the needy. Kind and affable to even the last sailor, gentle and familiar with his subordinates, he captivated the hearts of those who were under his command. His mastery of the profession, his vigilant and judicious activity in

91 Francisco de Paula Pavía (Cádiz, 1812–Madrid, 1890), officer and general of the navy, was three times minister during the Restoration. He wrote numerous works, but he especially developed the genre of biography. Before the *Galería Biográfica* [*Biographical Gallery*] collection, he had published Francisco de Paula Pavía, *Biografía del brigadier de la Armada, Don Cosme Damián de Churruca, que murió gloriosamente en el combate naval de Trafalgar, mandando el navío San Juan Nepomuceno, de 74 cañones* (Madrid: Estado General de la Armada, 1850); *Biografía del Brigadier de la Armada Saturnino Montojo y Díaz* (Cádiz, 1856).

92 There is a precedent for this project in the navy, carried out by Martín Fernández Navarrete, *Colección de opúsculos del Exmo. Sr. Martínez Fernández de Navarrete* (Madrid: Viuda de Calero, 1848). This officer devoted himself to collecting biographies of officers and sailors, although his work was published posthumously.

93 Pablo Ortega-del-Cerro, 'Retratos del héroe naval: representación de la oficialidad naval en la sociedad de la honradez', *Cuadernos de Ilustración y Romanticismo* 26 (2020), 225–50.

> all kinds of enterprises, his impetuous courage in the advance, his uncompromising tenacity in the endeavour and above all his unalterable serenity, make him a perfect example of one of our most enlightened captains.[94]

Certainly, Gravina's portrait was anachronistic. Son of Spanish *grandees* and brother of a cardinal and nuncio, his mentality and behaviour should have been understood in the context of the Old Regime. However, by granting the same type of respectability to all the officers, whether of the eighteenth or nineteenth centuries, it was possible to ensure a much more homogeneous group framework. This is evident in biographies such as the one of Roque Guruceta Aguado (Cádiz, 1771–Madrid, 1854), who was presented as

> … of regular height and strong, robust build, his severe and even slightly dour appearance contrasted with his honesty and openness. Chivalrous in his bearing, rigid in his customs and religious without affectation, General Guruceta was as respectable in his private life as he was in his public office. He was a good husband, a tender father, a sincere friend and an honest and virtuous citizen. With the death of Roque Guruceta, Spain lost an enlightened patrician, the army a respectable and distinguished general, and his family a man who had always honoured it with his civic and military virtues.[95]

Conclusions

It is clear that naval officers faced a double challenge during the first third of the nineteenth century. The crisis of the institution and its subsequent renewal since 1840 onwards demanded new work arrangements; a new process of professionalization within the corps – in terms of training, duties, skills, knowledge, tactics – had to be undertaken. But while these same officers had to learn to operate the steam engines or implement new

94 Francisco de Paula Pavía, *Galería biográfica de los generales de Marina, jefes y personajes notables que figuraron en la misma corporación desde 1700 a 1868* (Madrid: Imprenta J. López, 1873), 138.

95 Pavía, *Galería biográfica*, 102.

naval tactics, they also had to accommodate and assume new values that were being shaped. The officers had to appear as a respectable, honest and exemplary corps in their professional and social behaviour. All this was a slow, complex process, especially for the navy, which during the nineteenth century was relegated to a secondary role. Nevertheless, professionalization and social legitimation were two sides of the same coin.

In strictly professional terms, the Naval Officer Corps experienced a critical moment during the first third of the nineteenth century. In addition to the severe institutional crisis, many of the achievements made in the second half of the eighteenth century vanished. The officers became one of the most technified and advanced corps, a small group of military men who were guided by such abstract principles as 'el mérito en general' [general merit]. A good example of this was the change in the criteria for promotion. If in the past the abilities, services, merits and skills of the officer were assessed through confidential reports, from the nineteenth century onwards seniority was imposed, without taking any other factor into account. Around 1820 it became clear that the navy had to dismantle the old pillars of the eighteenth-century navy and lay the foundations of a new model. Not without problems and fluctuations, this modernization accelerated after 1840. A navy adapted to the real needs of Spain was created and a new professionalization was undertaken: a new naval school, a new hierarchy, new laws and promotions shaped the Isabelline Navy, which reached its zenith in the 1860s.

This labour modernization went together with the new social portrait presented by the corps itself. At the beginning of the nineteenth century, the dominant image oscillated between concern about an institution that showed clear signs of decadence and admiration for the heroic, technical, scientific and distinguished naval officers. Throughout the 1810s, 1820s and 1830s, both inside and outside the navy, an ominous image was projected. Corruption, crisis and ruin. But with the renewal of the Isabelline period, a new picture of the institution and the corps was also built. Most importantly, beyond ensuring the significance of the navy, it was necessary to identify the naval officers as honest and respectable men. The purpose was to assimilate the image of the corps with the anthropological archetype of the period, so that they were seen as distinguished individuals. Several strategies were used to achieve this goal – regulations, press, monographs and biographies – which had a common denominator: to highlight the private and public virtues of the officers, essentially dominated by respectability and honourability. This was the key element in building a truly respectable navy.

DIEGO CAMENO MAYO AND JAIME TRIBALDOS MILLA

The Nineteenth-Century Soldier

The Professionalization of the Army

ABSTRACT
This chapter analyses the career and position of Spanish soldiers from a threefold perspective: first, it examines the relationship between the professionalization of the Army in its different branches and the construction of a liberal state. Second, it examines this process of professionalization through a case study: officers of the Artillery. Finally, it uses contemporary sources to examine the public image of the profession of soldier, with reference to the existing duality of a specialized officer unit and rank and file that carried out compulsory military service.

Introduction[1]

Despite the clichés about the politicization of officers in nineteenth-century Spain, most soldiers kept away from political issues and tried to carry out their trade in a strictly professional manner. The aim of these pages is to reveal something about these soldiers' working lives and the role they played in forming the Spanish State in the nineteenth century. The role played in this process by the armed forces, a fundamental pillar in any state, cannot be denied. As we will see, the Army exercised a decisive influence on the state in a number of ways, not only as its armed branch, but as an agent that transformed cities, forged the idea of society and supplied professionals who contributed to the creation of a modern and effective government. In turn, the Army received the necessary boost

1 This chapter is part of the research project 'Cultura del honor, política y esfera pública en la España liberal (1833–1890)' funded by the Ministry of Science, Innovation and Universities (PGC2018-093698-B-I00).

from government to succeed in its transition from a royal army, inherent to the Old Regime, to a national army formed by and for the citizens.

Given the diversity of situations that could result from an examination of this professional sector, we have chosen the officers in the Artillery as a case study, as it is a body that is different from the rest of the Army and only similar to the Engineers and the General Staff. As an example of these differences, we could note that its system of promotion and advancement differed considerably from the rest of the Army branches. In addition, the level of scientific and technical expertise required from Artillery officers was very high. Moreover, their behaviour and the tasks they were charged with also differed from those of the traditional soldier. Social origin was a key element for entering the artillery. It was very closely related to the *esprit de corps* which was such a feature of the nineteenth-century Spanish Artillery.

The Army and the State in nineteenth-century Spain

The construction of the Spanish State in the nineteenth century was supported by two key pillars: the Army and the Treasury. The monopoly of violence was one of the keys to the success of the building of the State. It was something that could only be provided by a professional army which, in turn, was not viable without the financial resources needed to maintain it; in other words, without the means that could be provided by the agents related to collecting public revenues, which explains the importance of these two institutions.[2] Thus, one of the keys to success in constructing the State in the nineteenth century was to have an effective and solvent treasury and army. Here will analyse the role played by the military institution in this process, as well as how the State worked to create a standing national and professional army.

It appears a commonplace in historiography to consider the Peninsular War (1808–1814) as the milestone that marked the transformation of the

2 This is one of the theories of Juan Pro, *La construcción del Estado en España. Una historia del siglo XIX* (Madrid: Alianza Editorial, 2019).

Spanish army. During the course of the conflict, the royal army of the old order, in which the officer class was composed of nobles, was transformed into a national army formed by citizens. This was true in general lines, but some qualifications should be added. After the Peninsular War (or War of Independence as it was called in Spain), King Fernando VII wanted a return to the pre-war situation; in other words, he wanted a return to the state of things in 1808, including in the armed forces. Despite everything, some reforms introduced during the war changed the way the Army was seen. They demonstrated the importance of having competent people in charge, who were trained and experienced in the field of battle, regardless of their social origins.[3] The death of King Fernando VII in 1833 and the Civil War triggered by the dispute over his succession (1833–1840) convinced the Spanish authorities of the need for a standing army, composed of citizens committed to the liberal regime, who would take up arms to defend their rights and freedoms. This is the idea that moved the government in 1835 to decree the levy of 100,000 men, 'the real starting point of the modern army in Spain'.[4] However, the problem this involved was that to mobilize this number of men the Army needed to be completely restructured. This was the reason behind the creation of, for example, the Cuerpo de Estado Mayor [General Staff Corps] (1838), which was charged with the organization and coordination of the different Army Corps and Branches.[5] This levy soon resulted in the implementation of compulsory military service

3 Pro, *La construcción del Estado*, 246. Conflicts of this nature tend to speed up processes of change in armies. Perhaps the most obvious example is the transformation of the old royal army during the French Revolution. See: Richard Cobb, *The People's Armies. The Armées Révolutionnaires, Instrument of the Terror in the Departments, April 1793 to Floreal Year II* (New Haven: Yale University Press, 1987); Jean-Paul Bertaud, *La Révolution armée: les soldats-citoyens et la Révolution Française* (Paris: R. Laffont, 1979); Rafe Blaufarb, *The French Army, 1750–1820. Careers, Talent, Merit* (Manchester: Manchester University Press, 2002); Julia Osman, *Citizen Soldiers and the Key to the Bastille* (Basingstoke: Palgrave Macmillan, 2015).

4 Pro, *La construcción del Estado*, 247.

5 Enrique Silvela Díaz-Criado, *El proceso de profesionalización del Ejército en España: El Cuerpo de Estado Mayor, 1810–1932* (Doctoral Thesis, Universidad Nacional de Educación a Distancia, Instituto Universitario General Gutiérrez Mellado, 2015).

in 1837.[6] The idea behind this system was to construct a standing professional Spanish National Army made up of Spanish citizens, regardless of their origin or condition, and reflecting faithfully the liberal ideas of the citizenry, without distinctions in compliance of their duty to the country.

Although the government propaganda talked a lot about the levy of 100,000 men, the reality was somewhat different. The number of recruits was much lower (though this was within the expectations of the authorities) and the measure did not enjoy popular support. The introduction of compulsory military services ended up being seen by the Spanish people as 'a contribution of blood' as payment of yet another tax to the State. In fact, the system established the possibility (one that already existed in Europe) of avoiding military service by a monetary payment.[7] This gave the impecunious state some help with its financial problems. The measure lasted for some time, with the amount being increased, making access by the poor to this benefit difficult. This broke with the principle of equality before the law, one of the criteria that had been the basis of the liberal state.[8] It generated unease and led to resistance and protests by the lower classes. Thus, starting in the mid-nineteenth century, popular disturbances and uprisings tended to be accompanied by slogans against the recruitment system, such as '¡Abajo las quintas!' [Down with the draft!]. First, the policy of using substitutes and the exemptions from military service led to a gradual de-professionalization of the lowest ranks in the Army, as the substitutes were 'people hardly appropriate for military service'. Moreover,

6 For the evolution of the system of recruitment in Spain, see Fernando Puell de la Villa, *El soldado desconocido, de la leva a la 'mili' (1700–1912)* (Madrid: Biblioteca Nueva, 1996); or the most recent study linked to nineteenth-century politics by Guillermo Rivilla Marugán, *Élites y quintas: el debate parlamentario sobre el reclutamiento militar durante el siglo XIX* (Doctoral Thesis, Universidad de Valladolid, 2014).

7 Valentina Fernández Vargas, *Sangre o dinero. El mito del ejército nacional* (Madrid: Alianza, 2004).

8 However, there were other ways of escaping from the hated military service. The local councils were in charge of the recruitment process. This allowed all those with sufficient influence in local government or related to the networks of client politics and local caciques to elude conscription.

it became a source of corruption and fraud, 'with the appearance of companies insuring against the drafts … in which notable political figures appeared to be involved'.[9]

The Army also influenced the construction of the State in other ways, for example, by modifying the urban landscape of Spanish cities. Initially, the new military forces were quartered in former convents, but it soon became clear that these facilities were not the most appropriate for army life. In the second half of the century, Spanish soldiers began to set up in newly constructed barracks. They tended to be located near major cities, very close to the main access and exit routes. In this way, the Army surrounded the cities, controlled access and established itself in places that were easy to defend, far from any possible epicentres of disturbances.[10] This strengthened the role of the 'Gendarme Army' dedicated to the control of public order, as a defensive body of the State against threats from the interior.[11] In the opinion of Juan Pro, the barracks played a key role in the construction of the State; and more than this, in the 'interiorization of State power' by the citizens. First of all, they transformed the urban landscape by being located in buildings previously occupied by the Church. The barracks controlled the population in two ways, as from them the troops could move quickly to put down rebellions or disturbances; and moreover, they were centres for the military education of young people of the lowest classes from all parts of the country, who went there to carry out their military service. There they were taught the basic military values of love of the motherland, discipline and order. Second, military service helped create the perception among the young and their families that they were actually contributing to the support of the State, not only with their taxes, but with their very lives.[12]

9 The conservative governments of general Narváez tried to change this. See Pro, *La construcción del Estado*, 278–9.

10 Pro, *La construcción del Estado*, 279–80.

11 Carlos Arenas Posadas, *Por el bien de la patria. Guerras y ejércitos en la construcción de España* (Barcelona: Pasado&Presente, 2019), 147.

12 Pro, *La construcción del Estado*, 250. For a comparison of this phenomenon in other countries, see Annie Crépin, 'De la nation armée au service militaire obligatoire: la consription au XIXe siècle. Perspectives et méthodologie d'un champ historiographique', *Annales Historiques de la Révolution Française* 316

The senior command and officers in general were aware of all the above, including the growing rejection by Spanish families of this system that tore their children from them at an early age, depriving them of manpower to work in the fields. This aversion was becoming hatred of the Army and all those who formed part of it. The publication of articles such as that signed by the commander of the General Staff, Joaquín Manso de Zúñiga, is therefore no surprise. In a text entitled *Educación intelectual que debe darse al Ejército* [*The Intellectual Education that the Army Should Receive*] he called for a more polished training for the military classes. Zúñiga thought that by improving training and turning the Spanish Army into a 'continuous school', perhaps the parents would no longer see it with 'repugnance', as their children would return from military service with a sound training that allowed them to access qualified jobs.[13]

Another question is the participation of the military in politics, about which much has been written.[14] We are not going to deal with this matter here. It only appears necessary to reflect on the overlapping of the military and political worlds, seen from the purely professional point of view. A summary analysis leads us directly to the issue of leadership as one of

(1999), 373–81; Thomas Hippler, *Soldats et citoyens. Naissance du service militaire en France et en Prusse* (Paris: Presses Universitaires de France, 2006); Dorit Geva, *Conscription, Family and the Modern State. A Comparative Study of France and the United States* (Cambridge/New York: Cambridge University Press, 2013); D. Colin Jaundrill, *Samurai to Soldier. Remaking Military Service in Nineteenth-Century Japan* (Ithaca/London: Cornell University Press, 2016).

13 *La Asamblea del Ejército y de la Armada* XII (1866), 241–76.

14 See José Luis Comellas, *Los primeros pronunciamientos en España (1814–1820)* (Madrid: CSIC, 1958); Stanley G. Payne, *Los militares y la política en la España contemporánea* (Paris: Ruedo Ibérico, 1968); C. Christiansen, *Los orígenes del poder militar en España (1800–1854)* (Madrid: Aguilar, 1974); Daniel R. Headrick and Jaime Melgar Botasis, *Ejercito y política en España (1866–1898)* (Madrid: Tecnos, 1981); Julio Busquets, *Pronunciamientos y golpes de Estado en España* (Barcelona: Planeta, 1982); Carlos Seco Serrano, *Militarismo y civilismo en la España contemporánea* (Madrid: Instituto de Estudios Económicos, 1984); José Cepeda Gómez, *El ejército español en la política española (1787–1843). Conspiraciones y pronunciamientos en los comienzos de la España liberal* (Madrid: Fundación Universitaria Española, 1990); Javier Fernández López, *Militares contra el Estado. España, siglos XIX y XX* (Madrid: Taurus, 2003).

the basic features of politics, which in turn leads us to ask what features of leadership in the professional military sphere, transferred to the field of politics, achieved a particularly significant prestige in it. This will help us understand the abundant presence of the military in European nineteenth-century politics.[15] It would raise significant sociological, cultural and political questions which we cannot enter into now. The comments of the Catholic thinker Jaime Balmes are particularly informative on this point:

> Much has been said in recent times about the need to destroy the preponderance of the military and strengthen civil power; we consider that the question has been raised the wrong way round ... : we do not believe that civil power is weak because military power is strong; but that, on the contrary, military power is strong because civil power is weak.[16]

Once the close relationship between State and army in the nineteenth century has been established, it is time to understand the process of selection, entry into and professionalization of the Army through a specific case (as we have already mentioned): that of the Artillery.

The Artillery: Between privilege and science

Traditionally, the highest ranks of military officers were occupied by the aristocracy. In Spain, the close links between the nobility and the military go back to the Middle Ages. The relationship was broadly speaking maintained until 1811. Until then, a military career was closed to all those who were not nobles. It is true that starting in the Middle Ages, one could become a noble by way of service in the Army, but this only reinforced the

15 Raymond Horricks, *Military Politics from Bonaparte to the Bourbons. The Life and Death of Michel Ney (1769–1815)* (New Brunswick, NJ: Transaction Publishers, 1995); Nick Mansfield, *Soldiers as Citizens: Popular Politics and the Nineteenth-Century British Military* (Liverpool: Liverpool University Press, 2019).

16 Jaime Balmes, *Escritos políticos* (Madrid: Imprenta de la Sociedad de Operarios del mismo Arte, 1847), 643.

overwhelming presence of nobles among officers and senior positions in the Army.[17] It was a reflection of the scheme of a class-based society, where the nobility occupied the important positions.[18]

In the eighteenth century, the Artillery Corps exemplified this model well, given that to enter the Academy as a cadet you had to comply with a number of requirements along the lines mentioned above. Applicants to the Artillery College had to demonstrate their status as nobles, meaning at least '*Hijodalgo notorio* [known noble], under the laws of Castile'.[19] An applicant who could not prove sufficiently clearly the nobility of his father and mother was rarely admitted. Priority was always given to those who were children of Artillery officers, with the minimum requirement being that the father was a lieutenant colonel. Following this in order of preference were children of soldiers in other corps. These criteria entered into the logic of academies such as those of the Artillery, Engineers or the Navy, whose aim was to house 'exclusively' nobles, hidalgos and descendants of soldiers.[20] Automatic recruitment obviously contributed to the creation of castes and families within the officers of the Army, which little by little clashed with the increasingly influential criterion of professional training as a mechanism of promotion. However, automatic recruitment has been considered very positively by some specialists, because it simplified the candidates' learning process. The example of the decision of King Fernando VI (1755) tends to be cited. He gave preference to descendants of officers because he knew that the parents would educate their children

17 Antonio Morales Moya, 'Milicia y nobleza en el siglo XVIII', *Cuadernos de Historia Moderna* 9 (1988), 123–4. For an overview of this, see Christopher Storrs and H. M. Scott, 'The Military Revolution and the European Nobility, c. 1600–1800', *War in History* 5/1 (1996), 1–41.

18 Julio Busquets, *El militar de carrera en España* (Barcelona: Ariel, 1984), 48–9.

19 José Cotrina Ferrer, 'El Colegio de Artillería en Menorca', *Revista de Menorca* 16 (1917), 320–1. On this subject, see: Santiago Fajardo Gómez de Tracevedo, *Pruebas de hidalguía o nobleza para ingresar en el Real Colegio de Artillería de Segovia* (Madrid: Patronato de Huérfanos de Oficiales del Ejército, 1977).

20 Busquets, *El militar de carrera*, 51–2. A chart on the decrees regulating access to officer rank in the Artillery between 1755 and 1830 in Morales Moya, 'Milicia y nobleza', 125–6.

in advance to allow them to enter the Academy and perfect their training in it without any problems.[21]

Thus, there is a period that extends from the second half of the eighteenth century to the Peninsular War, in which the only requirements demanded from men wishing to be cadets in the Artillery were first, to be a member of the nobility; and second, to know how to read and write, as well being physically fit. In this respect, the Artillery was no different from other elite military corps, which also gave great importance to the social origin of the cadets, and where belonging to the nobility was an essential condition.[22] If the applicant also brought with him a recommendation, his path opened up swiftly. The problem raised by access requirements such as those mentioned is that young people with a very elementary education could enter the corps without the training needed to deal with the complex subjects taught in the Artillery College. If the cadet did not pass the exams, he would never become an officer, so the pressure was immense.[23]

The Peninsular War disrupted the military system detailed above. Although, as will be seen below, the artillery soldiers tried to maintain the educational demands on their cadets, they could do nothing against the spirit of the times. During the period of war, and when King Fernando VII was absent, the liberal Parliament (1810–1814) assumed control of the country, taking advantage of the opportunity to implement reforms, including that of the Army. For the liberals, two points had to characterize the new armed forces: maintenance of discipline and the implementation of the principles of 'equality', that is, access by all the qualified citizens to the ranks of military command.[24] The positions of responsibility had to be

21 Jorge Vigón, *Historia de la Artillería española*, 3 vols (Madrid: Instituto Jerónimo Zurita, 1947), vol. 1, 301–2.

22 One example that has been studied in some detail is that of the marine guards. To understand the change in the access requirements for officers in the Navy, see Pablo Ortega-del-Cerro, 'Del honor a la honradez: un recorrido por el cambio de valores sociales en la España de los siglos XVIII y XIX', *Cuadernos de la Ilustración y Romanticismo* 24 (2018), 597–618.

23 Ricardo Pieltain de la Peña, 'II Centenario de la fundación del Colegio de Artillería en el Alcázar de Segovia', *Revista de Historia Militar* 16 (1964), 111–13.

24 Carlos Seco Serrano, *Militarismo y civilismo*, 32. In italics in the original.

performed by those who had the necessary qualifications, and this was not given by birth.[25] Thus the Decree of 17 August, 1811 and subsequently on 9 March, 1813, did away with the tests of nobility for eligibility to become a cadet in the military academies.[26] The illustrious origin of the artillery soldiers, and more than this, the family sagas that made up the corps, had given results, so they felt very proud of being one of the most consistent corps in the Spanish army and with the greatest collective spirit. Although starting in 1811 any individual was eligible, whatever his origin, if he demonstrated a superior intellectual level and capacities, this spirit would not last.[27]

In 1814, once the war ended and the liberal period had concluded, the absolute monarch Fernando VII did away with all the legislation of the Cádiz Parliament. A royal decree of 17 June 1814 re-established the tests of nobility, and thus initiated a somewhat turbulent period in which political change, shifting between absolutism and liberalism, led to modifications of the access requirements to the Artillery corps. The tests of nobility were not finally eliminated until 1836 (Royal Decrees of 21 and 28 September), once Fernando VII had died.[28] This did not mean that after that, any person would be accepted as an officer in the Spanish Army. Once the nobility

25 Pablo Ortega-del-Cerro had already demonstrated how personal qualities and merits eased out social origin in the Navy. See Pablo Ortega-del-Cerro, *El devenir de la élite naval. Experiencias de los oficiales de la Armada en tiempos de cambio (inicios del XVIII-finales del XIX)* (Madrid: Sílex, 2018).

26 *Colección de los decretos y órdenes que han expedido las Cortes Generales y Extraordinarias*, 4 vols (Madrid: Imp. Nacional, 1813–1814), vol. 1, 188–9 and vol. 4, 6–7.

27 The 1804 regulation already took into account not only social origin but certain personal qualities and requirements. Candidates for cadets had to 'know how to read, write and have the right talent to make the most of the studies'. *Reglamento de nueva constitución en el Colegio Militar de Caballeros Cadetes del Real Cuerpo de Artillería* (Madrid: Imp. Real, 1804), 59.

28 Although they continued unofficially in the Royal Guard and the Guard de Corps until these corps were abolished by General Baldomero Espartero in 1841. There is a good summary of these suppressions and re-establishments of the nobility tests in Enrique de Ocerín, *Índice de los expedientes matrimoniales de militares y marinos que se conservan en el Archivo General Militar (1761–1865)*, 2 vols (Madrid: Instituto Jerónimo Zurita, 1959–1967), vol. 1, XXI; Busquets, *El militar de carrera*, 61–2; Morales Moya, 'Milicia y nobleza', 127–8.

tests were removed, others were created, known as the 'tests of clean blood and legitimacy'. The new requirements were to be Catholic, certify legitimate birth (presenting the parents' marriage certificate) and to have 'clean blood' (being an 'old Christian' and not having ancestors dedicated to 'vile trades' such as hangman or butcher). These conditions remained in force until 16 May 1865.[29] They were not difficult to meet in what was a largely Catholic country. Starting in 1865 the demand that the fiancée should certify her nobility to authorize her wedding with an artillery officer. So, this first half of the century saw the abolition of the limits that had made it difficult for the emerging classes to become officers.[30]

Finally, it should be noted that even if the legal obstacles had been removed, applicants still had to surmount the financial hurdles. Anyone wishing to become an officer in the Artillery had to have sufficient liquidity to pay the costs involved in his studies. No candidate as officer could enter the College if the latter did not have a precise knowledge of his family's finances. According to María Dolores Herrero Fernández-Quedasa, in the early 1860s, until an Artillery cadet was promoted to sub-lieutenant, he cost his parents around 16,055 *reales*, a sum only exceeded by the amount for cadets in the Cavalry, who needed 16,175 *reales* (which included keeping the horse).[31] In line with the times, equality was only legal, as with the abolition of the nobility tests, the requirements of social origin were replaced by those of an economic nature.[32]

29 Law of 16 May 1865, *Gaceta de Madrid* (18 May1865).

30 Busquets, *El militar de carrera*, 62.

31 María Dolores Herrero Fernández-Quesada, *Cañones y probetas en el Alcázar. Un siglo de la historia del Real Colegio de Artillería de Segovia* (Segovia: Patronato del Alcázar de Segovia, 1993), 51–2.

32 Fernando Fernández Bastarreche, *El Ejército español en el siglo XIX* (Madrid: Siglo XXI, 1978), 108.

Entry into service and training: The Real Colegio de Artillería de Segovia

The Real Colegio de Artillería de Segovia [Royal Artillery College of Segovia] was created on 16 May 1764 in the reign of the reformist Carlos III. Established as an example of his military policy, it has been classified as a 'symbol and paradigm of the Spanish Enlightenment' and one of the 'clearest examples of an outstanding and brilliant Military Enlightenment'.[33] Also of note was the high level of scientific education received there by the Artillery officers, who were real pioneers of science in Spain. In any event, the education and instruction of soldiers was not something inherent only to those known as the technical corps (Artillery and Engineering). The authorities and even the working soldiers valued army education greatly and called attention to the need to extend it to all the corps and classes.[34] However, from the start, the artillerymen and engineers claimed the need for specific education, which marked a clear criterion of distinction with respect to the other military corps. The Artillery and Engineers protested strongly when in February 1824 King Fernando VII called a meeting of the Army Council, and its deliberations concluded with the creation of a Colegio General Militar [General Military College] in which the Infantry, Cavalry, Artillery and Engineers were to study together. Their arguments were based on the harm that the unification would bring for their specialization and overall education. The officers of the Engineering and Artillery corps argued for the importance and superior technical qualifications needed to exercise

33 In the prologue to María Dolores Herrero Fernández-Quesada, *La enseñanza militar ilustrada. El Real Colegio de Artillería de Segovia* (Segovia: Academia de Artillería de Segovia, 1990), 16.

34 The specialized military press wrote extensively on this matter. The following is a selection of the articles published at the start of the reign of Isabel II: *La Asamblea del Ejército* (1856), 14–20; *El Archivo Militar. Sección Militar* (17 June 1842), 1–3; *El Archivo Militar. Sección Militar* (7 March 1842), 1–3; *El Boletín del Ejército* 262 (5 February 1845), 3–4; *El Boletín del Ejército* 289 (11 April 1845), 2–3; *El Boletín del Ejército* 339 (6 August 1845), 2–7; *El Grito del Ejército* (1 June 1841), 14–18.

their respective professions, which could not be reduced to standardize them with the rest of the soldiers.[35]

The first artillery officers of the nineteenth century studied under the rules dating back to Carlos III. They received a complete education that ranged from various branches of mathematics (algebra, arithmetic, geometry) to languages, orthography and dance, with a special focus on the subjects related to their area, such as fortification, drawing and artillery. The subject of statics, often part of artillery or tactics, was very important, as was chemistry, which began to gain increasing importance in the curriculum. Of course, military training was not left out, with military exercises, fencing and parade drills.[36] In 1804 a new regulation for the College was published. After that year the number of subjects increased. The cadets were taught new disciplines such as surveying, history, religion and rifle exercises. From this time the duration of the studies was specified as four years. After four years the most outstanding students were sent to Madrid to take two more years of the 'noble studies' (chemistry and metallurgy).[37]

Specialists have highlighted two important aspects. First, there was the access to information available to the cadets. The outstanding (both in terms of quality and quantity) library of the College had more than 3,000 volumes in 1807. It helped add to the prestige of the institution, which in the early nineteenth century was already 'one of the most prestigious teaching centres in Spain and Europe'.[38] Second, there were the tough conditions of life in the school. The cold winter temperatures in the city of Segovia and the lack of comforts offered by an old fortress which was barely refurbished to house students, were combined with a very demanding study plan with very tough working hours (from six in the morning to ten at night, the courses running from September to July), to say nothing of the

35 In fact, it would be demonstrated that their protests were well founded, as in March 1829, the Artillery College in Alcalá de Henares was re-opened. Pieltain de la Peña, 'II Centenario de la fundación', 124–5.

36 The list of subjects studied in this period is given in Herrero Fernández-Quesada, *Cañones y probetas*, 25; and Pieltain de la Peña, 'II Centenario de la fundación', 101–3.

37 *Reglamento de nueva constitución*, 105–17.

38 Herrero Fernández-Quesada, *Cañones y probetas*, 23 and 34. The quotation is from Herrero Fernández-Quesada, *La enseñanza militar*, 147–8.

rigorous examinations that students were faced with at the end of each year. The discipline was as to be expected in the Army, severe and rigid. Good conduct, attitude and application were rewarded, but infractions were punished rigorously.[39]

This is not the place to discuss the various changes in location of the College in Spain during the Peninsular War, in response to the advances and retreats of the allied troops.[40] However, it is worth noting the strong desire to maintain the institution operating despite the difficulties and to sustain the prestige enjoyed by the College across the continent. As far as possible, an attempt was made to continue with normal practice in the College: timetables, subjects, exams (with oral tests before a jury), educational methodology (with study manuals, including that of Tomás de Morla) and the same rewards and punishments.[41] After the commotion of the war, the subject of chemistry became increasingly important in the curriculum, and a chemistry laboratory and a mineralogical studio was set up.[42] The also hectic times of the Civil War of 1833 to 1840 forced the College to further moves, although once more an attempt was made to update the training curriculum of the artillerymen through a new regulation in 1830.[43] Once the war ended, the cadets asked for their home to be restored to Segovia. Their wish was granted in 1839. This period began with

39 For the infractions, punishments and rewards, see Herrero Fernández-Quesada, *La enseñanza militar*, 217–20.

40 On this period see María Dolores Herrero Fernández-Quesada, 'El Real Colegio de Artillería de Segovia en la Guerra de la Independencia', *MILITARIA. Revista de Cultura Militar* 7 (1995), 287–96; and Guillermo Frontela Carreras, 'El Éxodo del Real Colegio en la Guerra de la Independencia', *Revista de Historia Militar*, Extraordinary Issue 1 (2014), 135–84.

41 Herrero Fernández-Quesada, *La enseñanza militar*, 136–8 and 169–70. This author has researched specifically on this brilliant artilleryman: María Dolores Herrero Fernández-Quesada, *Ciencia y milicia en el siglo XVIII: Tomás de Morla, artillero ilustrado* (Doctoral Thesis, Madrid: Universidad Complutense de Madrid, 1989).

42 Herrero Fernández-Quesada, *Cañones y probetas*, 45.

43 *Reglamento del Real Colegio de Artillería* (Madrid: Imprenta Real, 1830); Diego Quirós Montero, 'Segovia y la Artillería: 250 años de convivencia', *Revista de Historia Militar*, Extraordinary Issue 1 (2014), 247–9; and Herrero Fernández-Quesada, *Cañones y probetas*, 46–7.

another regulation (1838), which increased the relevance of the subjects of chemistry, physics and mineralogy. The curriculum was also extended with a final course of 'noble studies' for some, while others went to the so-called 'application school', with more practical contents. The Artillery College was among the most prestigious teaching centres in Europe. From it came Artillery officers but also the first Spanish industrial engineers. However, the fire that swept through it in 1862 put an end to it all. It consumed much of the material housed in the College (instruments, books, etc.) and interrupted the brilliant history of this centre.[44] After a number of vicissitudes linked to the restructuring of the Artillery corps, the College re-opened its doors in September 1873 as the Artillery Academy.

The professional life of the artilleryman

Once we have established the process establishing the training requirements that constituted the basis of the professional corps of artillerymen, we have to move on to the system of promotion followed in the career of officers of the Artillery in the nineteenth century. Through it we will see how little by little the meritocratic criterion, together with the traditional seniority, came to become more important in a corps that had its own characteristics within the Army.

Since the reform by Carlos III in 1762, the Artillery corps promoted men by a rigorous process of seniority, without taking into account other criteria such as merit or service record (which were the basis for promotion in other branches of service).[45] This question generated much debate and conflict in the following two centuries, particularly because the other corps did not look kindly on the fact that the artillerymen (and then the corps of Engineers and the General Staff) should be promoted through the

44 Pieltain de la Peña, 'II Centenario de la fundación', 120–30.

45 Luis Miguel Balduque Marcos, *El Ejército de Carlos III. Extracción social, origen geográfico y formas de vida de los oficiales de S.M.* (Doctoral Thesis, Universidad Complutense de Madrid, 1993), 137–40.

ranks by a different method. The authorities tried to reform this system, but the deep-rooted resistance of the artillerymen prevented any semblance of reform.[46] When soldiers from other corps expressed the problems with this system, they pointed to the special features of their trade. To the criticisms of their detractors, the artillerymen answered that their model was the least damaging, given that despite the problem of having generals of an advanced age, and much longer careers than in other corps, vices such as favouritism or arbitrariness in promotions were eliminated. These were very harmful for the Army, as they fostered injustice and lack of discipline and undermined internal unity. The Artillery Corps always had the most experienced men in the positions of greatest responsibility, thus legitimizing the positions of authority among the youngest, who could trust in their own promotion with the passage of years.[47] As can be seen, the feeling of belonging to the corps and the distinction granted to their professional activity with respect to other military occupations was an extremely important element that bound the corps together.

This does not mean that there were no internal tensions in the Artillery Corps, sometimes created by the system of promotion and sometimes by the entry system. As has been noted, to become an officer of the Artillery a soldier had to enter the Academy and pass a series of demanding exams that demonstrated the candidate had the necessary knowledge to perform any task he was entrusted with, whether scientific or military. As well as the officers (the elite in the corps), there were the warrant officers. The warrant officers were a secondary rank, who had a separate system of promotion and despite being in charge of small units, they did not have the theoretical knowledge to exercise the functions of the full officers.[48] The sub-officers could also not be promoted to full officers, as in the other corps, for the same reasons as the warrant officers. Obviously, the difficulties established within the system itself to access officer status for the secondary levels generated discontent among the latter, which led to an armed confrontations between officers and subordinates on 22 June 1866

46 Vigón, *Historia de la Artillería*, vol. 2, 23–6.
47 *Memorial de Artillería* 41 (31 October 1847), 1–16.
48 *Memorial de Artillería* 18 (30 November 1845), 830–7.

in what was known as the uprising of the San Gil Barracks.[49] This confrontation, together with the outright refusal of the officers to introduce some flexibility into access to the higher ranks, would arise later, contributing to the political climate of instability which led to the abdication of King Amadeo I (February 1873) and provoking the dissolution of the Artillery Corps that same month.[50]

Finally, the system of promotion by seniority also raised a problem that was extremely important for the soldiers: rewards for actions of merit. One of the reasons for not adopting a system of promotion by merit resided in the multiple functions carried out by artillerymen. How could the merit of two different officers be recognized or calibrated: one a brave soldier who had contributed to an important victory in the field of battle; and the other, whose scientific knowledge had considerably improved the fire-power and resistance of the canons available in the factory? It was a difficult question. What was clear is that no action could be left without reward, which is why a form of 'dualism' emerged. It was a phenomenon that was characteristic of this time and current until 1889, generating great confusion among the ranks.[51] In addition, it was also common for rewards to be given to officers with crosses and other decorations (both civil and military), which explains their profusion among the officer ranks of the Artillery in the nineteenth century.

The professional career of the Artillery officers was not always linked to war. There are even examples of artillerymen who never participated in an armed conflict. However, their army careers were much more varied than those of the soldiers in other corps, particularly the Infantry and Cavalry. The artillerymen were in charge of factories of arms and munitions, arsenals and the training of future officers. They also had their own representative

49 On San Gil and the technical rank: Vigón, *Historia de la Artillería*, vol. 2, 98–101; and Seco Serrano, *Militarismo y civilismo*, 125.

50 Arenas Posadas, *Por el bien de la patria*, 215–16; Pablo González-Pola de la Granja, 'Las disoluciones del Cuerpo y su repercusión sobre el Colegio/Academia de Artillería', *Revista de Historia Militar*, Extraordinary Issue 1 (2014), 185–234.

51 On this dualism see Eladio Baldovín Ruiz, *Las Ordenanzas militares en España. 250 aniversario de la publicación de las Ordenanzas de Carlos III en 1768* (Madrid: Foro para el Estudio de la Historia Militar de España, 2018), 303–9.

bodies such as the Junta Superior Facultativa [High Technical Council], the Junta Superior Económica [High Economic Council], the Directorate-General and the sub-inspectorates and general command of the Artillery departments.[52] Moreover, when Isabel II took the throne, trips abroad by commissions of officers from the professional corps were boosted 'so that whatever was considered useful and appropriate could be applied to the Spanish army'.[53] The success of these enterprises is beyond any doubt if we read the chronicles published in the main press outlet of the corps, the *Memorial de Artillería* [*Artillery Journal*].[54]

Many artillerymen also linked their futures to the Artillery Academy, where they acted as professors, directors or heads of studies, and also performed other functions related to their profession, such as surveying. Intellectual and scientific work was essential in this Corps, as can be seen from their destinations in the Artillery College. It contributed not only to the training of new officers, but to carrying out essential work for the State. In fact, the Artillerymen, together with military engineers, performed an important mapmaking role for the State in extending knowledge and structuring of the physical space. They were responsible for the creation of a modern and up-to-date general map of Spain, which helped to improve the administrative work of government.[55]

52 For more on these, see Vigón, *Historia de la Artillería*, vol. 3, 232–48.

53 *Diario de Sesiones: Congreso de los Diputados* (10 October 1844), 1–3.

54 *Memorial de Artillería* 28 (30 September 1846), 359–65. This periodical was one of the most important ways of keeping the artillerymen up to date in terms of technique and professionally.

55 See Miguel Alonso Baquer, *Aportación militar a la cartografía española en la historia contemporánea. Siglo XIX* (Madrid: Patronato Alonso de Herrera-Instituto de Geografía Aplicada, CSIC, 1972).

Soldiers in literature: Everyday life and representations of their work

We will now deal, albeit briefly, with the public image of professional soldiers, as it is largely based on perceptions about the good or bad service they provided to society. The most notable element we can mention in this concise analysis is the duality between officers and the rank and file. It is a commonplace in the press and literature of the time to assess the rank-and-file soldiers positively (soldiers, sailors and sub-officers) and the higher ranks unfavourably (officers and generals). The former, because they provided services selflessly with no other aim than to comply faithfully with their service. The latter, because they were dominated by personal ambitions that they could only satisfy by continuous interference in the public sphere.

To carry out this analysis, we will use the examples offered by works in the genre of literature based on local customs (*costumbrismo*), which were very popular at the time, as well as other very interesting texts for the subject we are dealing with. The scenes (or 'tableaux') of local customs, like any literary category, suffer from exaggerations and manipulations, generally of a comical or satirical nature, and deliberately positive or negative projections. However, they are very eloquent when it comes to appreciating the different sensibilities and an attitude with respect to what is represented, not only from a historical, but also sociological point of view. This form of literature is also a very valuable instrument for studying the genesis, reproduction and dissemination of social stereotypes.

However, it is noteworthy that despite the relevance of the martial element in political, social and cultural life of nineteenth-century Spain, there are few representations of soldiers in a literary genre as important as that of *costumbrismo*. The explanation appears to lie in the 'respect and fear' which, together with groups as relevant as the aristocracy and the Catholic Church, inspired the armed forces, even at the end of the century.[56] The figure of 'soldier' appears tangentially in the very well-known

56 María de los Ángeles Ayala Aracil, 'Las colecciones costumbristas en la segunda mitad del siglo XIX: *Los españoles de ogaño*', *Anales de Literatura Española* 3 (1984), 70.

Los españoles pintados por sí mismos [*The Spanish Painted by Themselves*] and in its self-defined successor *Los españoles de ogaño* [*The Spanish of Today*],[57] with a gap of thirty years between them.[58] The first of these nearly always talks about soldiers by means of feminine types. They are soldiers who are normally involved in sexual or courting situations. In 'La lavandera' ['The Washerwoman'] written by the playwright Manuel Bretón de los Herreros, apart from presenting the woman pejoratively, comments that:

> Despite their ugliness and old age, there are very few local washerwomen who do not have a lover … The garrison of Madrid is large, the stomach of the soldier is 'without scruples',[59] and when there are no extras, what does a grenadier not put up with? What does he lose by letting himself be loved by someone close to him … ?[60]

Something similar occurs with 'La cantinera' ['The Barmaid'], where the soldier appears represented as a lover or lady-killer of a primary and violent nature:

> But there tend to be soldiers … who manage to inspire her with a maternal love or a real passion, according to their age, and … there is no prosperity or future that is not exposed to the follies of the lucky lover or adopted son who, in general, and due to the effect of human failures, pays with disappointments and even with merciless blows her generous self-denial and constancy.[61]

57 *Los españoles pintados por sí mismos*, 2 vols (Madrid: Establecimiento Tipográfico de Ignacio Boix, 1843–1844); *Los españoles de ogaño. Colección de tipos de costumbres dibujados a pluma* (Madrid: Librería de Victoriano Suárez, 1872). Publisher's prologue: 'All the types that could not be included in the latter work [meaning *Los españoles pintados por sí mismos*] occupy a notable place in the present, so that without any further thought, the authors of *Los españoles de ogaño* have simply written a second part' (5–6).

58 This work uses the edition of *Los españoles pintados por sí mismos* published in 1851. Nearly three decades passed between the first edition of this work (1843–1844) and *Los españoles de ogaño*, published in 1872, without either of them dealing specifically with the military.

59 A colloquial expression meaning not having scruples and being capable of the most terrible things.

60 Manuel Bretón de los Herreros, 'La lavandera', in *Los españoles pintados*, 93.

61 José de Grijalba, 'La cantinera', in *Los españoles pintados*, 105.

The exception is in the type called 'El retirado' ['The Veteran']. In it, the writer and journalist Gabino Tejado gives us a small biography of a veteran who has been involved in the most recent episodes of Spanish history. The leading figure shows his value and dedication as a soldier. He has always avoiding getting mixed up in politics, considering himself to be only a soldier and remaining faithful to the institutions that he would serve as a soldier. He proves this with his refusal to join the liberal military rebellion of 1820, which meant for him 'his licence releasing him from service', condemned 'to die of hunger in the name of freedom'. The author of this scene depicting local customs describes how the main character, who continues trying to remain out of politics despite his difficulties in life, is humiliated by the locals of his hometown when he once more refuses to participate in another uprising of an absolutist nature. After these ups and downs, the solder ends up having to find his sustenance in the best way possible by living with a barmaid. It is not rare to find in the books of local customs that retired soldiers ended up married to women with a trade or business, in an explicit sign of the precarity in which they lived and the need to find a source of support.[62] Begging, of course, was also common among the soldiers who were no longer in service or retired without an alternative trade.[63] The author of 'La cantinera' ends his story saying that his main character, the retired soldier, died in absolute poverty without any recognition.[64] With a great deal of drama, the author comments the lack of interest and consideration of governments and parliaments ('an ungrateful motherland') to him, and many others, men of arms who went

62 Thus, for example, 'La cantinera' says that it was not uncommon for these women to be married to soldiers (104), as in 'La casera de un corral' (175). With respect to the male characters, there is also the change in profession of the soldiers, such as the soldier who ends up as an innkeeper ('El ventero' [The Innkeeper], 242), one who aims to be in parliament ('El diputado a Cortes' (The Member of Parliament), 362–5) and who ends up as a porter ('El portero' [The Porter], 366). *Los españoles pintados*.

63 The testimony offered by Mesonero Romanos in his scenes of local customs is heartbreaking, such as in 'Una visita a San Bernardino' (A Visit to San Bernardino), a charity home. Ramón de Mesonero Romanos, *Escenas matritenses por 'El curioso parlante'* (Madrid: Gaspar y Roig Editores, 1851), 113–16.

64 Gabino Tejado, 'El retirado', in *Los españoles pintados*, 378–82.

'to their graves without more company than their scars, earned in the field of honour'.[65]

In the other work reflecting local customs that we will deal with here, *Los españoles de ogaño*, there are also few explicitly military figures, but the brief references to them are very eloquent. One example is the character described in 'El hombre importante' ['The Important Man'], which represents any person who has achieved high responsibilities and consideration without any merit.[66] Among them, according to the author, the senior military hierarchy, which is described as a group plagued by ignoramuses and frauds:

> If the important man belongs to the honourable profession of the military, he will always occupy the highest ranks; he will have all the known crosses and bands, whether national or foreign, in order to stand out in major and even in minor occasions; he will dispense almost absurd favours to anyone who he is devoted to; and finally, it is very probable, by way of example, that everything he knows about the military life of who is now Prince of Vergara is limited to the fact that he is a captain general in the Army.[67]

The 'important man' who has reached the highest ranks in the armed forces has done so by means of 'skilful intrigues', to 'the rhythm of a rigadoon', among 'hypocritical smiles' or 'opportunistic wave of the censor'. The most positive qualifications are in this case dedicated to the professional and discreet soldier who does not look for more recognition than that which is legitimate due to his merits in battle or by seniority, being 'the last in the jumble-sale of pseudo-reputations, until the time comes to be the first in the positions of honourable danger'.[68]

Although, as has been said, there are not too many works on local customs involving soldiers, there is a work dedicated exclusively to them: *La milicia y sus excesos* [*The Army and Its Excesses*], written by Mario de Iveja.

65 Tejado, 'El retirado', 382.

66 Pedro María Barrera, 'El hombre importante', in *Los españoles de ogaño*, 200. The author defines men of this type as follows: 'Their most outstanding characteristics are: audaciousness, ignorance and the absolute lack of shame.'

67 Barrera, 'El hombre importante', 201.

68 Barrera, 'El hombre importante', 203–4.

The book is in favour of a reform of the armed forces and its regulations, and appraises the state of the institution negatively. It is an extremely rich journey into the everyday life of a captain of the guards Emilio Guerra and the daily life in his units, personal and professional relations with his superiors and subordinates, the distribution of his means of subsistence, opportunities for promotion, and considerations on legislation. The criticisms in this text of the organization and operation of the Army are organized around these core elements: the precarious material situation of the soldiers; the rigidity and obsolescence of the regulations and the passivity of the governments and ministers of war in undertaking necessary changes. To illustrate the lack of resources for the subsistence of the soldiers, the author gives details in a table of the difference between the remuneration of the main character and his expenses, which offers interesting details on the everyday life of an officer in the middle level of the ranks. A captain received '50 *duros* per month in pay' (250 *pesetas*), but between paying rent for his house, paying for servants, daily expenses on food and tobacco ('0.34 *pesetas* for a packet of tobacco that lasted two days') and a contribution to an military benefits association, his expenses came to a total of 269.93 *pesetas* per month. Given this, the soldier survived 'by a miracle' with 'horrific debts'. Moreover, the opportunities for promotion were fairly difficult due to the problems resulting from the irregularity in promotions. According to Captain Guerra, at his 54 years of age, and according to the expected system of promotion, he should have had 'a guaranteed job and retirement of lieutenant colonel'. In the situation in which he saw himself at his age, with no hopes of promotion, he complained of the difference between being paid the 200 *pesetas* corresponding to him as a retired captain, instead of the 360 he would collect as a lieutenant colonel, which is the rank he deserved due to his service record.[69]

La milicia y sus excesos also offers information on how the interpersonal relations were perceived within the Army. It comments, for example, the rigidity of some of those in charge with respect to their subordinates. In a conversation between Captain Guerra and his superior, the reader notes

69 Mario de Iveja, *La milicia y sus excesos. Cuadros de costumbres militares contemporáneas* (Valladolid: Imprenta de Hijos de J. Pastor, 1889), 63–4, 22–3.

how Commander León treats his inferior very harshly because he found a number of individuals playing cards in a room. León blames Captain Guerra for their lack of discipline, although he was not even present in the barracks, and threatens to apply severe measures against him without the possibility of appealing to any other official. However, the author does not oversimplify by equating all the officers in his criticisms, as he shows us a wide range of characters among the middle ranks of officers (those closest to the troops). Among them are, for example, Lieutenant Mesoneros, who had 'of good character, although [he was] a little frivolous'; Lieutenant Colonel Marcial, the most loved of the unit, 'the father of all the subordinates, the soul of the regiment'; the assistant captain Valentín, the son of Marcial, who had the 'same' character; and Commander Vázquez Urra, who was 'a man of extraordinary courage, hard-working, and more than anything a friend of the motherland'. For the author of the story, the differences in the conduct of the middle-ranking officers could be explained in part by their social origins and professional careers within the Army, showing to what extent the frustrated expectations or successes achieved conditioned the internal life of the barracks. Thus, the bad-tempered Commander León 'came from the rank and file and had obtained his promotions little by little'; the colonel of the regiment, Pedro Lobo, of 36 years of age, did not have 'any brilliant qualifications for the military', but ascended quickly in the Cuban campaign (1868–1878), as did Lieutenant Mesoneros; and Commander Vázquez Urra, despite his 'brilliant service record' was obliged to withdraw as commander 'when it was his turn to be promoted to Lieutenant Colonel'.[70]

Finally, a key aspect that is continuously present in this book is the need to address seriously the reform of the regulations and military law. In fiction, Commander Vázquez Urra, a neighbour and friend of Captain Guerra, 'of liberal ideas that were logical for the time' and 'crazy about the military', comes to be a member of Parliament for Oviedo, elected as an independent although with a programme that is 'democratic, and clearly reformist'. In a speech he makes in the Lower House, he presents the main complaints of the armed forces, among them the inconsistency of the

70 Iveja, *La milicia y sus excesos*, 15–18, 26–8, 49.

reforms carried out during the century, defined as an 'immense total of bits and pieces brought together without unity'. For example, those relating to the territorial and administrative division of the Army, on the unjust payments to avoid military service, promotions as a offered as favours, the very low wages and the incompetence of the ministers of war, make up the detailed analysis presented by the member to Parliament, which reflects the internal concerns of the armed forces.[71]

If Mario de Iveja offers us a critical view of the professional army from a progressive vision, the journalist Juan Rico y Amat analyses the same issue from a monarchist and conservative perspective. His *Diccionario de los politicos* [*Dictionary of Politicians*], published in the mid-nineteenth century, is a set of satirical commentaries of various aspects of the reality of his time. The entry dedicated to the 'Ejército Permanente' [Standing Army] is not less critical than the commentaries we have just seen in the work of Iveja. For him, the Army is: '[a] Giant of innumerable mouths that cause the ruin of nations; if he had never known the need to maintain it, peace and abundance would reign in society and mankind would not have been drowned in blood on many occasions'.[72] Calling the Army a 'thermometer of freedom', he relates in an inversely proportional way the dimensions of this institution with the quality of the liberal institutions of a country.[73] For him, political instability and the important role played by the Army in Spanish society is due to the loss of traditional Christian virtues and values, which had been capable of holding society together without the need for artificial mechanisms. The lack of 'religious principles, justice in laws and morality in customs' leads to tyrannical governments and societies that are materially ruined and politically disgraced.

71 Iveja, *La milicia y sus excesos*, 49, 216–34.

72 Juan Rico y Amat, *Diccionario de los políticos ó verdadero sentido de las voces y frases más usuales entre los mismos escrito para divertimiento de los que ya lo han sido y enseñanza de los que aún quieren serlo* (Madrid: Imprenta de F. Andrés y Compañía, 1855), 170.

73 'Where the giant has colossal dimensions, there freedom is stunted and petty; and conversely, where the giant is weak, freedom is strong and vigorous' (Rico y Amat, *Diccionario de los políticos*, 171).

Conclusion

The leading role of the Army in Spanish politics in the nineteenth century has led to a shift in the focus of interest for historians to the balance between militarism and civil society, covering other key aspects of analysis to understand the role played by the military in the new liberal society. The Army was completely transformed by the liberal revolution, which coincided with a time of armed conflict (the Peninsular War and the Carlist War), fostering the creation of a national Army. Although reality imposed itself on theory and an unfair system of recruitment remained in place, in which military service was perceived as a 'tax in blood' by those who could not free themselves from it, the Army became a decisive element in the construction of a liberal state that wished to ensure its monopoly over violence.

At the same time, the Army had to mould itself to the changes after the fall of the old regime, such as the dismantlement of the society of corporate classes. The case of the Artillery corps, access to which was denied to all those who were not nobles, illustrates this wide-ranging mutation. It is no coincidence that the Parliament of Cádiz (1810–1814) suppressed the tests of noble birth for entry to the military academies, and thus began a process of opening up the officer class in which the old criterion of class was replaced by an economic one, more in line with the new class society. The entry into the Artillery Academy ensured a solid scientific foundation, as well as a professional career peculiar to this corps, in which the system of promotion was based on seniority, and not merit or war record as in other Corps.

At the same time as these changes, soldiers were subject to criticism and satire in literary works on customs. Beyond the deformation or reality of these works, the genre included the popular perceptions about military life, in which writers established a clear difference between an ambitious officer class and the rank and file who represented selflessness in compliance with their duties. Economic precariousness, the rigid interpersonal relations in the hierarchy, the old regulations and the lack of interest by governments to carry out changes, are some of the evils most referred to.

All this leads us to consider the need for more in-depth examination of the process of professionalization of the Army and its political and socio-cultural repercussions. In view of this, some hackneyed historiographic ideas on the military should be revisited in the light of the transformations of the broad and complex military universe. In particular, everything referring to its interrelation with the new political actors, such as the State and the parties, would have to be considered from these points of view. This is a history that still has to be written, with many analytical possibilities, some of which we have tried to sketch out here.

PART III

Healthcare Professionals

VÍCTOR M. NÚÑEZ-GARCÍA

A Physician and a Gentleman

Individual Dimension of the Collective Pursuit of Social Standing

ABSTRACT
In the context of nineteenth-century political and professional transformations, physicians and surgeons strove to improve their social standing and get acknowledged by the society and by the ruling elites as supreme authority in the field of healthcare. They developed a series of collective and individual strategies to achieve this double aim. This chapter explores the interaction between the individual and collective dimensions of this pursuit, the focus being on court physicians, a privileged group among medical professions, who, nonetheless, played a key role as individuals in shaping both institutional framework and public image of medicine in mid-nineteenth-century Spain.

Introduction: Towards a new social history of medical professions in nineteenth-century Spain[1]

Physicians, as well as lawyers, have existed as consolidated professions for centuries. Such a high degree of professionalization was based on three pillars. First and foremost, medical education was institutionalized at universities since the very foundation of these establishments of higher education. While there were many other ways to access medical practice, the link with universities helped consolidate the image of medicine as compatible with high social status of practitioners.[2] Second, the physicians

1 This chapter is part of the research project 'Culture of honour, politics and public sphere in liberal Spain (1833–1890)' [PGC2018–093698–B–I00]. I thank Darina Martykánová for her extremely useful comments and suggestions.

2 Besides the well-established practice of teaching medicine in establishments of higher learning in the medieval Muslim world, the first universities founded in

were highly recognizable figures in both popular and elite culture. Last, but not least, for centuries, their professional practice was acknowledged as useful by both society and governing elites. As for the latter, physicians had their place at the courts of Europe, Middle East and China in the Medieval and Early Modern Eras.[3] Moreover, surgeons' status rose and well-paid post proliferated in the eighteenth century due to the growing acknowledgement by the State of their usefulness in the expanding military and naval structures.

The eighteenth and the nineteenth centuries represent an important milestone in the professionalization of medicine, in the boost to the public image of physicians and in their social standing. Medical professionals actively themselves engaged as individuals and as professional group(s) in the processes that transformed medical practice in this period. They were five. First of all, the institutionalization of medicine was taken to a new level through the creation of public posts for expert physicians and of large institutions (i.e. hospitals) in the framework of the discourse of public health, endorsed by both public authorities and individual philanthropists.[4] The second process was the effort by physicians to establish a monopoly at the health market or at least to become acknowledged and referred to as supreme authority. The professionals of the art of healing operated on a competitive market, fighting for patients, their trust and their money. Physicians and surgeons ended up merging into a single profession, which – together with the legal and institutional backing of the State – enabled them to win the fight and expel to the margins of healthcare the men

Europe in the twelfth century (Paris, Bologna and Oxford) and in the first half of the thirteenth century (Toulouse, Montpellier, Naples, Padua, Vienna, Cambridge, Salamanca …) tended to have four faculties: theology, law, medicine and arts.

3 Concerning Early Modern Spain: María del Mar Rey and María Esther Alegre, 'La ordenación normativa de la asistencia sanitaria en la corte de los Habsburgos españoles (1515–1700)', *Dynamis* 18 (1998), 341–75; Soledad Campos, 'La organización administrativa sanitaria en el palacio de los últimos Austrias (I). Médicos', *Anuario de Historia del Derecho Español* 68 (1998), 171–238.

4 The transformation of royal colleges of surgery into faculties of medicine was a major milestone. For a long-term development of hospitals in Spain, see Margarita Vilar–Rodríguez and Jerònia Pons–Pons, eds, *Un siglo de hospitales entre lo público y lo privado (1886–1986)* (Madrid: Marcial Pons, 2018).

and women who engaged in healing practices without official credentials and whom they labelled as intruders and charlatans.[5]

The following two processes were closely intertwined with the second one: the professionalization of healthcare further increased due to the physicians' effort to control the access to medical practice, the third process I have identified. This was to be achieved by strengthening the link between medical practice and official medical training and by tightening the control over this medical training. This included subordinating medical practice such as midwifery to the authority and supervision of physicians, by introducing inspections of the midwives' practice and/or mandatory credentials granted by physicians.[6] The fourth process, the fight for professional

5 On the issue of charlatanry in the professional discourse of nineteenth-century Spanish physicians, see Víctor M. Núñez-García and Darina Martykánová, 'Charlatanes versus médicos honorables: El discurso profesional sobre la virtud y la buena praxis (1820–1860)' *Dynamis* (in press). A selection of international historiography on this topic Kohn, Alexander, *False Prophets. Fraud and Error in Science and Medicine* (Oxford: Basil Blackwell, 1986); Roy Porter, *Quacks: Fakers and Charlatans in English Medicine* (London: Tempus, 2001); David Gentilcore, *Medical Charlatanism in Early Modern Italy* (Oxford: Oxford University Press, 2006); Nicole Edelman, 'Médecins et charlatans au XIXe siècle en France', *Tribune de la santé* 55/2 (2017), 21–7; Toby Gelfand, 'Medical Professionals and Charlatans. The Comité de Salubrité Enquête of 1790–91', *Social History* 11 (1978), 62–97.

6 Josep Danón, 'Sobre los inicios de la medicina clínica en España, 1801–1850', *Medicina e Historia* 12/3rd series (1986), 3–26; Josep Danón, ed., *La enseñanza de la Medicina en la Universidad Española* (Barcelona: Fundación Uriach, 1998); Alejandro Ridruejo, *La enseñanza de la Medicina en España. Planes de estudio (1843–1931)* (PhD. Thesis, Universidad de Valladolid, 1979). Concerning midwives and their training, see: Dolores Ruiz–Berdún, 'La primera enseñanza reglada de las matronas en España: el Real Colegio de Cirugía de San Carlos de Madrid', *Llul. Revista de la Sociedad Española de Historia de las Ciencias y de las Técnicas* 36/78 (2013), 387–410; Dolores Ruiz–Berdún, 'La inauguración de la Casa de Salud Santa Cristina de Madrid y su escuela de Matronas', *Matronas Prof* 17/2 (2016), 30–8; Rosario Martín Alcaide and Dolores Ruiz–Berdún, 'Un hospital para mujeres promovido por mujeres: la Casa de Salud Santa Cristina de Madrid', *Temperamentvm. Revista Internacional de Historia y Pensamiento Enfermero* 15 (2019), e12642; María Luisa Calero–Delgado and Encarnación Bernal–Borrego, 'La implantación de la enseñanza de matronas en la Universidad de Sevilla (1861)', *Arenal* 23/2 (2016), 403–30.

autonomy, was linked to the third one by the drive to control access to professional practice, but also had to do with striving for self-regulation and control over the public image of the profession. It was embodied in the creation of medical chambers (*colegios médicos*) and medical societies as well as by proliferation of medical press. The nineteenth century was a period when medical press experienced a true boom in Spain, serving as a space for professional discussion and for shaping and voicing collective demands.

The fifth process was the development and dissemination of a set of formal and informal rules concerning appearance and behaviour. These codes of behaviour, including the notion of professional ethics, were supposed to have a positive impact on the image of medical profession as a whole. In Spain it took longer for these codes of professional ethics to become fixed and official than in many other European countries. The five processes can be observed in Europe and America and beyond, synchronically and diachronically, and with local varieties. All these dynamics shaped the effort by the physicians to consolidate their social standing as gentlemen in the new context of bourgeois societies.[7]

With a varying degree of depth and success, social history of medicine has dealt with all the above-mentioned issues.[8] Studies on quackery, medical ethics, professional fraud, honour or science and masculinity abound in

7 For Spain, this issue has recently been addressed in Víctor M. Núñez-García and Darina Martykánová, 'Charlatanes', in press; Darina Martykánová and Víctor M. Núñez-García, 'Ciencia, patria y honor: los médicos e ingenieros y la masculinidad romántica en España (1820–1860)', *Studia Historica* 38 (2020), 45–75; Darina Martykánová and Víctor M. Núñez-García, 'Vaccines, Spas and Yellow Fever: Expert Physicians, Profesional Honour and the State in the Mid-Nineteenth Century', *Theatrum Historiae* 25, 2021 (in press).

8 Maria Malatesta, *Professionisti e gentiluomini: storia delle professioni nell'Europa contemporánea* (Torino: Ed. Einaudi, 2006); Jean-Paul Barrière and Hervé Leywers, *La construction des professions juridiques et médicales. Europe occidentale, XVIIIe–XXe siècle* (París: Presses Universitaires du Septentrion, 2020); Darina Martykánová, 'La profession, la masculinité et le travail. La représentation sociale des ingénieurs en Espagne pendant la deuxième moitié du XIXe siècle', in Antoine Deroquet, Simon Paye and Christelle Frapier, eds, *Les ingénieurs. La production d'un groupe social* (París: Garnier Classiques, 2018), 79–102.

international historiography.[9] Scholarly production on Spain boasts with valuable works on the so-called assistance pluralism (*pluralismo assistencial*) concerning all kinds of people involved in healing practices.[10] Little has been published, however, on the effort made by physicians as a group to establish their exclusive expert authority vis à vis both public institutions and society (including their patients), and to consolidate their social standing among the elites in the context of emerging constitutional regime, as a group and as individuals.[11]

As I have already mentioned, one of the most important institutional changes in the Spanish medicine during the late eighteenth and the great part of the nineteenth century was the complex process of unification of medicine and surgery, which involved a major transformation of university education in medicine and stimulated the trend towards a growing specialization in the framework of the unified medical profession. The self-representation of Spanish medical professionals in the first half of the nineteenth century was shaped by the romantic ideal of physician as

9 Robert A. Nye, 'Honor Codes and Medical Ethics in Modern France', *Bulletin of the History of Medicine* 69 (1995), 91–111; Robert A. Nye, 'Medicine and Science as Masculine "Fields of Honor"', *Osiris* 12/2nd Series (1997), 60–79; Andreas Maehle, *Doctors, Honour and the Law: Medical Ethics in Imperial Germany* (London: Palgrave, 2009); Andreas Maehle, 'Doctors in Court, Honour, and Professional Ethics: Two Scandals in Imperial Germany', *Gesnerus* 68/1 (2011), 61–79.

10 Agustín Albarracín Teulón, 'Intrusos, charlatanes, secretistas y curanderos. Aproximación sociológica al estudio de la asistencia médica extracientífica en la España del siglo XIX', *Asclepio* 24 (1972), 323–66; José Valenzuela, 'El espejismo del ejercicio libre. La ordenación de la asistencia médica en la España decimonónica', *Dynamis* 14 (1994), 269–304. For the concept of assistance pluralism, see: Álvaro Martínez, Rosa Ballester and María Luz López, 'La realidad de la práctica médica, el pluralismo asistencial en la monarquía hispánica (ss. XVI–XVIII). Introducción', *Dynamis* 22 (2002), 21–8; Enrique Perdiguero, 'El fenómeno del pluralismo asistencial, una realidad por investigar', *Gaceta Sanitaria* 18/4 (2004), 140–5.

11 Darina Martykánová and Víctor M. Núñez-García, 'Sacerdotes en el mercado, héroes del progreso: los médicos e ingenieros y las transformaciones de la masculinidad liberal (1820–1900)', in Darina Martykánová and Marie Walin, eds, *Las masculinidades en la España del siglo XIX* (Sevilla: Universidad de Sevilla, in press).

a self-effacing sacerdotal figure, full of altruistic love of the Humankind.[12] This canonical vision of physician as a generous and philanthropist man[13] who served the common good was highly functional and compatible with demanding 'fair' payment for his work. As Martykánová and Núñez-García have pointed out, there was a patriotic dimension to this ideal, too. The physicians argued that the progress of medical science was part of the effort that was to be made to place Spain among the 'cultivated' nations of Europe, in a context of international geopolitical competition, which included a growing scientific nationalism.[14] This canon underwent a major transformation towards the end of the nineteenth century, and in the first decades of the twentieth century a new, rather different image is discernible, shaped by scientific positivism, of physician as a tireless fighter against the disease, less expressive and emotional, but also less understanding towards the ignorance of the patients.

Physicians as a group developed a series of strategies to project this ideal self-representation and use it to consolidate their social standing among the elites of the time. A physician had to appear spotless as for his individual behaviour before the society and public institutions. If a physician transgressed these formal and informal rules, his transgression harmed the reputation of the whole professional group. This could be the case even if the problem consisted of a physician not being able to embody the figure of a respectable, well-off gentleman, due to poverty. It was therefore necessary to act collectively on behalf of the physicians who were systematically threatened by poverty, particularly rural physicians paid by municipal governments. Even the most privileged royal and urban physicians had their stake in this fight, as for medicine to be perceived as

12 Martykánová and Núñez-García, 'Ciencia, patria y honor', 45–75.

13 The gender hierarchy was strengthened in the nineteenth century, result of the processes of expulsion of healers without official titles and subordination of female practitioners such as midwives to the authority of physicians who remained mostly male despite the fact that, in some countries, medicine was one of the first degrees in modern universities from which women graduated in significant numbers. See Montserrat Cabré and Teresa Ortiz–Gómez, Dosier 'Mujeres y Salud: Prácticas y Saberes', *Dynamis* 19 (1990), 17–400.

14 Martykánová and Núñez-García, 'Ciencia, patria y honor', 45–75.

a gentlemanly occupation, all the physicians had to be paid enough to be able to live as gentlemen.[15] This explains that the salary of rural physicians remained a hot topic in medical press throughout the nineteenth and early twentieth centuries.

The interaction between the collective and individual dimensions of the fight for a privileged social standing was bi-directional. The physicians as a group were happy to rely on outstanding individuals in their midst to act as very visible embodiments of physicians' collective social aspirations and to spearhead professional demands. Some of these men were active politicians and promoted measures related to public health, such as José Pedralbes and Ignacio de Luzuriaga who were deputies at the Cortes of the Constitutional Triennium (1820–1823).[16] Others stood out for their contribution to medical science and practice,[17] such as Federico Rubio y

15 This dynamic has been analysed in Martykánová and Núñez-García, 'Sacerdotes', in press.

16 See Darina Martykánová and Víctor M. Núñez-García, 'Luces de España: las ciencias útiles durante el Trienio Constitucional', *Ayer*, in press; Álvaro Cardona, 'Los debates sobre salud pública en España durante el Trienio Liberal (1820–1823)', *Asclepio* 52/2 (2005), 173–202.

17 López Piñero argued that the nineteenth century is a period that lies between two glorious moments of Spanish medicine, the Enlightenment and the boom of a scientific–positivist, experimental, laboratory medicine that emerged in the end of the nineteenth and the first decades of the twentieth century. José María López Piñero, 'Las ciencias médicas en la España del siglo XIX', *Ayer* 7 (1992), 193–240. The emphasis on the usefulness of medicine that characterized the professional discourse of Spanish physicians and surgeons in the nineteenth century could not hide that their contribution to the progress of medicine worldwide was rather limited. This harsh assessment shall be put into a context. Firstly, the first half of the nineteenth century was not a period of great developments in medicine elsewhere in Europe and America, either. Thus, Spain did not stand out as particularly weak, although there was clearly a perception of weakness and Spanish physicians emphasized this when engaging in the practice that was common everywhere in Europe and America, that is, to look at what was going on in other countries (particularly France, the German world, Great Britain and, occasionally, the USA) in terms of medical science and medical institutions. Secondly, there were indeed some major contributions by Spain and Spaniards (though sometimes working abroad) to medicine, such as the vaccination expedition led by F. J. Balmis, Mateo Orfila's work in the field of chemistry or Jaime Ferrán's cholera vaccine.

Galí. Rubio introduced innovative surgery techniques: he was the first in Spain to carry out a hysterectomy (1861), an extirpation of an ovary (1863), of a kidney (1874) and of the whole larynx (1878). He promoted the creation of new medical institutions: Escuela Libre de Medicina y Cirugía de Sevilla (1868), Instituto de Terapéutica Operatoria in Madrid (1880) and the Escuela de Enfermeras Santa Isabel de Hungría in Madrid (1896). In fact, his capacity to spearhead such initiatives led to him enjoying an overall positive image among Spanish physicians, independently of his active engagement in radical politics, as a federalist republican.[18] Physicians could also be admired by their peers for their prestigious professional standing, such as royal physicians, possibly the most privileged group among medical professionals in terms of payment and prestige in mid-nineteenth-century Spain. Serving royal family made them enjoy public acknowledgement in Madrid and beyond, and socialize with political and economic elites of the time. There was also a link between serving as court physicians and holding posts in nation-wide professional associations and public institutions such as universities and academies. I will now focus on this privileged group within medical profession and, in particular, on two court physicians, Pedro Castelló and Tomás del Corral, who stood out for their capacity to lead Spanish physicians in voicing their professional demands. Their professional leadership benefited greatly from their socio-political influence, which they achieved by exploiting the close proximity to the monarchs granted them by their posts as personal physicians to Fernando VII and Isabel II, respectively.[19]

18 Juan Luis Carrillo, ed., *Medicina y Sociedad en la España de la segunda mitad del s. XIX. Una aproximación a la obra de Federico Rubio y Galí (1827–1902)* (El Puerto de Santa María: Ayuntamiento de El Puerto de Santa María, 2003); Encarnación Bernal–Borrego, Víctor M. Núñez-García and María–Luisa Calero–Delgado, 'El regreso de los estudios médicos a Sevilla. Un centenario dentro de más de 500 años de Historia', *Andalucía en la Historia* 58 (2017), 70–73.

19 For an analysis of court physicians as a group in mid-nineteenth-century Spain, see: Víctor M. Núñez-García, María–Luisa Calero–Delgado and Encarnación Bernal–Borrego (2019). 'Médicos en la corte española del siglo XIX. Influencias, sociabilidad y práctica profesional', *Asclepio* 71/2 (2019), 278.

Court physicians: A professional and a social elite

> I am very worried about Castelló. He has had a terrible cough, very dry, for a long time; it got worse in Tarragona; it improved in Valencia; when he returned to Tarragona it got worse, and here too, it is made worse by a great fatigue in the chest which gives him very bad nights; he says the sea air does not agree with him; that the same thing happened to him when he was in Mallorca, and that when he returned to the mainland he recovered; he has been in bed with a slight fever; he was living at the Palace but this afternoon he has got out of bed to move to a house in Barcelona itself but right on the other side of the sea; if he does not get better he is thinking of going to Igualada, where he has a house; let's hope he recovers or it will be a great loss.[20]

Spanish King Fernando VII sent this letter to his private secretary, Juan de Grijalba, from his trip to Catalonia, the Balearics and the Spanish Levant. He wrote about the poor health of his personal physician, Pedro Castelló y Ginestá, who was, at the time, the first *médico de cámara* (*médécin de chamber, Kammerarzt*) at the Spanish Court.

When the king and his entourage stayed in Barcelona, Pedro Castelló did indeed move to a house in the Sarriá area where he was visited by Fernando VII himself, who continued to provide detailed information on his physician's progress: 'Castelló is getting better and seems to be a different man since he has been living in a house far away from the sea.'[21] To the extent that his state of health allowed, Castelló closely monitored Fernando VII's attacks of gout during the rest of the journey, to which end the physician to the royal family Marcelo Rebot, and Castello's son, Juan Castelló y Roca, joined the royal entourage.[22]

The relationship between the physician and his patient went well beyond the professional realm; it came close to a friendship. Fernando VII trusted his personal physician Pedro Castelló, and relied on him. This

20 Letter from Fernando VII to Grijalba, 17 December 1827, quoted in Juan Arzadun, *Fernando VII y su tiempo* (Madrid: Imp. Galo Sáez, 1942), 328.

21 Letter from Fernando VII to Grijalba, 19 December 1827, quoted in Arzadun, *Fernando VII*, 328.

22 Arzadun, *Fernando VII*, 243.

closeness granted the doctor a prominent position in the social circles of the Court, where personal networks of interdependence and influence were forged. Xavier Mauduit shows similar dynamics were in play in France, such as when personal and political affinities proved more important than a prestigious professional career in appointing Napoleon III's personal physicians: 'Since the physicians serve per ward their presence by the side of the sovereign is intermittent and those closest to the Emperor are there for other reasons than their medical capabilities. Conneau, First Physician, is above all a companion in adventure of the pretender to the imperial throne. Acar, first pharmacist of the Emperor, had taught chemistry to Louis-Napoléon Bonaparte in Ham in 1840.'[23]

23 Xavier Mauduit, *Le ministére du faste. La Maison de l'empereur Napoléon III* (Paris: Fayard, 2016), 168. There is a large number of works on medical professionals and healthcare at European courts of the Early Modern and Modern Eras: Vivian Nutton, ed., *Medicine at the Courts of Europe, 1500–1837* (London and New York: Routledge, 1990); Raymond Lamont Brown, *Royal Poxes and Potions: The Lives of Court Physicians, Surgeons and Apothecaries* (Phoenix Mill: Sutton Publishing, 2001); Marilyn Nicoud and Andretta Elisa, eds, *Être médecin à la cour (France, Italie, Espagne, XIIIe–XVIIe siècle)* (Florence: Sismel, 2013). On the Court physicians and their contributions to the medical profession and issues related to professional ethics, see, for instance, Leon Bernard, 'Medicine at the court of Louis XIV', *Medical History* 6/3 (1962), 201–13; Lunel Alexandre, *La Maison médicale du roi. XVIe–XVIIIe siècles, le pouvoir royal et les professions de santé* (Seyssel: Champ Vallon, 2008); Xavier Mauduit, 'Le ministére du faste. La Maison de l'empereur Napoléon III', *Parlement [s], Revue D'Histoire Politique* 3/4 (2008), 69–83; Mauduit, *Le ministére*, 168 and 353–4; G. A. Russell, 'Physicians at the Ottoman Court', *Medical History* 34/3 (1990): 243–67; A. L. Wyman, 'Samuel Barrow, M.D. Physician of Charles II and Admirer of John Milton', *Medical History* 18/4 (1974), 335–48; Maehle, 'Doctors in Court', 61–79; Chiara Crisciani and Gabriella Zuccolin, eds, *Michele Savona: medicina e cultura di Corte* (Florence: Sismel, 2011). The work on the medical staff at the Court of Queen Victoria has focused mainly on the structure and organization of healthcare and on professional experience of the physicians and other staff: Brown, *Royal Poxes*; Elizabeth Longford, 'Queen Victoria's Doctors', in Martin Gilber, ed., *A Century of Conflict 1850–1950. Essays for A.J.P. Taylor* (London: Hamish Hamilton, 1966), 75–87; A. M. Cooke, 'Queen Victorian's Medical Household', *Medical History* 26/3 (1982), 307–20. With regard to France, see 'La médicine à la cour de France' and the database 'Le monde médical à la cour de France. Base de données biographique'

Pedro Castelló,[24] and later also Tomás del Corral,[25] exploited well their posts of personal physician to the reigning monarch. They used this proximity to the Crown and their therapeutic successes to promote their personal and professional agendas. Pedro Castelló was successful in treating

on the web page 'Cour de France', <https://cour-de-france.fr/?lang=fr>, accessed 5 January 2021.

24 Pedro Castelló Ginestá (1770–1850) was a key figure in Spanish medicine in the first half of the nineteenth century. He had been army surgeon before his appointment as surgeon to the royal family in 1801 and he served as court physician until 1850. Towards the end of the reign of Fernando VII, Castelló was appointed as first royal physician and he kept this post during the reign of Isabel II. He promoted the reform and unification of the studies of Surgery and Medicine (1827), the creation of the Military Medical Corps and the Corporation of Spa Physicians and the construction on the Atocha Street in Madrid of the headquarters of what was originally the San Carlos Royal College of Surgery and later the Faculty of Medical Sciences. The posts he held included Member of the Royal Governmental Committee of Medicine and Surgery, an institution that played a decisive role in the reforms he promoted, Professor in Santiago and Barcelona, Professor of the Chair of Childbirth, Women's and Children's Diseases and Syphilitic Diseases at the San Carlos Royal College of Surgery, Director of the Royal National Academy of Medicine and member of the General Inspectorate of Public Education. Archivo General de Palacio (AGP), Personal, box 16.772, file 27; Luis Granjel, 'Legislación sanitaria española del siglo XIX', *Cuadernos de Historia de la Medicina Española* 11 (1994), 255–308; Luis Granjel, *Historia de la Real Academia Nacional de Medicina* (Madrid: Real Academia Nacional de Medicina, 2006); Dolores Ruiz–Berdún, 'La enseñanza de la Obstetricia en el Real Colegio de Cirugía de San Carlos: la Cátedra de partos', *Medicina e Historia* 1/5th series (2014), 22–35; Josep Massons, *Un catalá a Madrid. Biografía del Dr. Pedro Castelló Ginestá* (Guissona, Girona: J. Santeularia, 1990); Francisco Alonso Rubio. 'Biografía del Doctor D. Pedro Castelló y Ginestá', in *Discursos pronunciados en la inauguración de las sesiones del año 1862 en la Real Academia de Medicina de Madrid* (Madrid: Imp. de Rojas, 1862), 15–38.

25 Tomás de Corral (1807–1882) held posts which included that of court physician from 1849 to 1882, army doctor to Alfonso XII during the Third Carlist War, Professor of Obstetrics (Chair of Childbirth) and Women's and Children's Diseases and librarian at the San Carlos Royal College of Surgery in Madrid, Rector of the Central University of Madrid from 1854 to 1862, member and president on several occasions of the Royal National Academy of Medicine in Madrid, honorary president of the Spanish Gynaecology and Obstetrics Society, member of the Royal Spanish Academy, Senator and Counsellor for Public Education and Health.

the gout that plagued Fernando VII later in his life.[26] Tomás del Corral was in charge of assisting Queen Isabel II in the birth of her son, future Alfonso XII. This apparently gained him Queen's favour and he was her personal physician until her dethroning in 1868. Both physicians used their privileged position and influence to take a leading role in reform efforts concerning medical profession.

Political environment in Spain during the central decades of the nineteenth century was marked by the conflict between absolutism, in decline, and the rising liberal constitutionalism, conflict that, in its most extreme, took the form of the First Carlist War (1833–1839). Moreover, there were major divisions among the liberals, too, the tensions between the conservatives and the progressives shaping the politics once the liberal constitutionalism had triumphed. For the Spanish court, similar to other European courts, the nineteenth century is the time of a gradual and conflict-laden transition from an Ancien Régime court with aristocratic features, to a court adapted to the new political culture of constitutional liberalism.

The physicians who served at the court in Madrid were a small, select professional group and their working conditions differed greatly not only from the downtrodden rural physicians, but also from their colleagues who worked in different institutions or offered their services as liberal professionals in the cities. Hardly any systematic study exists on the court physicians of nineteenth-century Spain. I argue that focusing on these privileged men makes it possible to ascertain their contribution to the transformations of Spanish medicine in this period of dramatic political,

---

AGP, Personal, box 16.806, file 3; Francisco Alonso Rubio, *Juicio crítico del Exmo. E Ilmo. Dr. Don Tomás del Corral y Oña* (Madrid: Imp. de Alejandro Gómez, 1883); Valentín Matilla Gómez, *Galería de Presidentes de la Real Academia Nacional de Medicina* (Madrid: Real Academia Nacional de Medicina, 1982); Ruiz–Berdún, 'La enseñanza', 33; Germán Rueda, *Isabel II* (Madrid: Arlanza Ediciones, 2001), 251–2; Granjel, *Historia de la Real Academia*,171–5, 199, 200–4, 211 and 368.

26 In general terms, historiographic accounts about this figure agree that Castelló was lucky when it came to Fernando VII's recovery from the attack of gout he suffered but do not mention his hypothetical professional skill in the treatment of the monarch. For example, Luis Granjel describes his conduct as 'a fortunate professional intervention which gained him the favour of Fernando VII'. Granjel, *Historia de la Real Academia*, 164.

scientific and institutional changes. Castelló and Del Corral played an important role in the court circles, networks of informal power and influence surrounding the Crown. These physicians lived in the Palace and checked daily King Fernando VII and Queen Isabel II, respectively.

Overall, there was a change of paradigm in the organization of healthcare in the Palace. A model based on a great number of salaried medical staff was replaced with another one, based on external assistance, relying on renowned physicians that were called to the Palace when needed, to attend to a health problem or concern.[27] This shift was not related to specific political changes that took place during the nineteenth century, but rather to the long-term change of mentality and institutional practice, from the Ancien Régime court to the court of Spain as a constitutional monarchy. By the mid-nineteenth century, the Spanish court was undergoing such transformation, engaging in practices such as rationalization and restraint in spending.

In other European monarchies, the presence of a group of medical professionals at the court was common, too. In the United Kingdom, when Queen Victoria came to the throne, she had thirty professionals at her disposal, twenty-five in England and five in Scotland.[28] At the court of the French Emperor Napoleon III the medical staff was divided into *médecins ordinaires, consultans* and *médecins par quartier*, besides ordinary and honorary surgeons and an *accoucheur* (a male obstetrician). There were also specialists such as assistant-surgeon and surgeon-dentist.[29] Portuguese royal household at the end of the nineteenth century relied on physicians of the Royal Chamber, on the one hand, and consultant physicians, on the other. From 1907 on, the number of medical staff decreased, replaced with honorary physicians.[30]

In Spain, like in other countries, the healthcare professionals all practiced medicine at the Palace as the culmination of remarkable professional

27 AGP, Ordenanzas Generales, box 942; AGP, Reglamentos, box 943; AGP, Reinados, Isabel II, box 8654, file 89 and box 8685, file 12.

28 Cooke, 'Queen Victorian 's Medical', 308–10.

29 Mauduit, *Le ministére*, 353–4; Mauduit, 'Le ministére', 74–6.

30 Pedro Urbano, *Nos bastidores da Corte: O Rei a Casa Real na crise da monarquía, 1889–1908* (PhD Thesis, Universidade Nova de Lisboa, 2013), 93–5.

and academic careers, especially when they achieved the rank of practicing royal physicians. To work at the service of the royal family and the Palace was considered a major professional accomplishment which situated these men at centre stage within the Spanish medical profession.[31] In the United Kingdom, honorary physicians and surgeons could be appointed in recognition of their professional distinction or for services rendered in the Royal Navy, Army, India or Public Health. This scheme would remain in place for the rest of the nineteenth century with no major changes.[32]

Pedro Castelló and Tomás del Corral had already had well-established careers as scholars and university lectures when they entered the healthcare service of the Palace. In Spain, court physicians generally held a PhD and had a teaching career within Madrid higher education structure, at San Carlos Royal College of Surgery and at the Central University's Faculty of Medicine. In 1832, Tomás del Corral y Oña, for example, defended his thesis *Dissertatio in qua VI aphorismus Sectionis secunda Oráculi et Cos comentatur* at the San Carlos Royal College of Surgery and Medicine.[33] Pedro Castelló was Professor of Obstetrics (the so-called 'Chair of Childbirth'), Women's and Children's Diseases and Syphilitic Diseases;[34] and Tomás del Corral was Professor at the Clinic for Childbirth, Women's and Children's Diseases and Rector of the Central University of Madrid.[35]

The academic careers of court physicians included publishing activity. The lectures, reports and treatises they published had, nonetheless, a limited scientific value. Pedro Castelló and Tomás del Corral were particularly prolific. The most notable works of the former include *Report*

31 In her study on the organization of healthcare at the Court of the last Monarchs of the House of Austria in Spain, Soledad Campos argues that to practice medicine at the Palace was the greatest honour for the professionals and the culmination of an already outstanding career. Campos, 'La organización', 173.

32 Cooke, 'Queen Victorian's Medical', 308–10.

33 Rubio, *Juicio crítico*, 9–10.

34 AGP, Personal, box 16.772, file 27; Ruiz–Berdún, 'La enseñanza', 31–3.

35 Del Corral took over from Pedro Castelló in the Chair of Obstetrics. AGP, Personal, box 16.806, file 3; Rubio, *Juicio crítico*, 5–8; Ruiz–Berdún, 'La enseñanza', 33; *Guía de Forasteros en Madrid, para el año 1845* (Madrid: Imprenta Nacional, 1845), 273. He was appointed Dean of the Universidad Central de Madrid in February 1854. *El Siglo Médico* (26 February 1854), 71.

on the Arrangement of the Science of Curing (Memoria sobre el arreglo de la ciencia de curar) from 1826, in which he proposed to unify academic curricula and qualifications of medicine and surgery,[36] or his *Treatise on Women's Diseases* from 1817.[37] The work of Tomás del Corral is multi-faceted as he wrote about both scientific and medical matters and philosophical and linguistic issues. His most outstanding scientific works were *De la obliteración del orificio uterino en el acto del parto, and de la histerotomía vaginal* (1845), *La homeopatía o farmacología análogo-infinitesimal ante el criterio y el sentido común* (1850) and *Historia de la Filosofía Médica* (1869). He also contributed with comments and additions to the Spanish edition of the French work *Tratado completo de enfermedades de las mujeres* (1845) and published his admission speech to the Royal Academy of the Spanish Language in 1879 under the title *The Logical Concordance of Thought with its Expression*.[38] Neither Castelló nor Del Corral contributed much to the Spanish medical press. They did not pen articles addressing the issues medical professionals had to deal with, either. Rather, they chose other platforms and means to intervene as privileged public figures and shape medical profession in Spain.

Pedro Castelló and his role in the institutional renewal of Spanish medicine

At the beginning of the nineteenth century, medicine and surgery were two discrete professions, with different training. However, in Spain and elsewhere in Europe, there was a strong drive towards the unification of medicine and surgery in that period. Pedro Castelló, first royal physician

36 This report presented to the Directorate of Studies of the Realm, was published at the Aguado Press in 1836.

37 Some of his works and manuscripts are freely accessible on the Galería de Metges Catalans website: <http://www.galeriametges.cat/galeria–obrapublicada.php?icod=II>, accesed 25 October 2020.

38 Rubio, *Juicio crítico*, 9–10.

of Fernando VII, played an important role in the institutional development of Spanish medicine in general, and in the unification of medicine with surgery in particular. In 1827 he was behind a major reorganization of Spanish medicine, when his plan to unify medical professions in one, outlined in his *Memoria sobre el arreglo de la ciencia de curar*, served as a basis for a new law aimed at bringing together the theoretical and philosophical elements of medicine and the 'art' of surgery, based on practical skills and know-how.[39] Nevertheless, heterogeneousness and diversity of medical professions persisted well into the nineteenth century.

Castelló's reform pioneered the unification of medical training at the level of higher education. It served as a basis for the future regulations concerning medical education, such as, for instance, the creation of *colegios de prácticos en el arte de curar* (colleges for the practitioners of the art of healing) by the so-called Plan Mata in 1843 or the 1845 reform introduced in the Plan Pidal.[40] When the above-mentioned 1827 reform changed the name of *Real Colegio de Cirugía de San Carlos* [San Carlos Royal College of Surgery] to *Colegio Nacional de Medicina y Cirugía* [National College of Medicine and Surgery], Castelló arranged for the construction of a new main building of the college, opened in 1834 at the Atocha Street. Eventually, the institution was renamed as *Facultad de Medicina de la Universidad Central de Madrid* [Faculty of Medicine of the Central University of Madrid] in 1845, in culmination of an institutional development in which Castelló, the head of the college and the first royal physician played a key role.

The joint degree in medicine and surgery finally became a standard in Spain in the last third of the nineteenth century, after disputes and active resistance among medical professionals. The process of its creation and implementation brought with important changes, such as the introduction of

39 Spanish ruling elites in the eighteenth century heavily promoted surgery, creating royal colleges of surgery (*reales colegios de cirugía*), as this 'art of healing' was considered useful for the country, particularly for military reasons. These colleges became very prestigious and existed in parallel with the well-established faculties of medicine attached to the universities. See, for example, Burke, Michael E., *The Royal College of San Carlos* (Durham: Duke University Press, 1977).

40 Danon, ed., *La enseñanza*.

clinical practice in faculties of medicine that stimulated the establishment of stable links with specific hospitals.[41] As I have mentioned in the introduction to this chapter, the unification of medicine and surgery, to which Castelló contributed due to his influence as King's personal physician, was extremely important for the physicians' fight to monopolize authority in the art of healing and achieve a privileged access to expert public posts and to the dynamic and competitive market of patients.

The high profile of Isabel's court physicians as prominent personalities of the medical profession at the national level was also reflected in their elite sociability and involvement in prestigious professional associations. The best example of this was the Royal National Academy of Medicine. The post of its President, according to its original regulations from 1733, was to be held by the first royal physician.[42] For many years, the institution was headed by Pedro Castelló, who took his turn with other professionals linked to the Palace such as Ignacio Jáuregui, Hilario Torres and Vicente Martínez;[43] Juan Drumen and Tomás del Corral.[44]

The reform initiatives of Pedro Castelló during the last years of absolutist regime, when he enjoyed great influence due to his closeness to King Fernando VII, seem to be an expression of his liberal political ideas. Identified as pro-liberal, he fell victim to the purge of liberals from the Palace at the beginning of the second restoration of Fernando VII and was even imprisoned in 1824. He was summoned back the following year when Fernando VII suffered from gout and, thanks to the success of his treatment of the king and a good personal relationship with the monarch, he became

41 Víctor M. Núñez-García, 'Los hospitales docentes en la España contemporánea: el caso de los hospitales clínicos universitarios' *Dynamis* (in press).

42 Granjel, *Historia de la Real Academia*, 148 and 164.

43 Granjel, *Historia de la Real Academia*, 156–8.

44 Rubio, *Juicio crítico*, 8.

In Great Britain, A. M. Cooke points out that at least forty-seven physicians of the royal household during the Victorian era were presidents for a time of the Royal Colleges and forty-two were members of the Royal Society, including two presidents, which is similar to the case of Spain. Cooke, 'Queen Victorian's Medical', 308. In France Henri Conneau, *médecin personnel* and *premier médecin* of the emperor Napoleon III, was a member of the academies of medicine of France and of Ferrara and of the academy of statistics of Milan. Mauduit, *Le ministére* (2016), 168.

an influential figure at Court in the final stage of Ferdinand's reign. His close personal relationship with Fernando VII has been interpreted as a decisive factor in the success of the reform of medical education and qualifications for medical practice which Castelló outlined in 1826 and, especially, in the reinstatement of teachers and professors at the San Carlos College who had been removed from their posts in the purges against pro-liberal professionals during the second restoration of Ferdinand. While Pedro Castelló, who undoubtedly wielded power at Court in the final stage of Fernando VII's reign, might have been behind the implementation of important reforms, his influence also had its limits. He defended the reopening of, and the return of scientific activities to, the Royal National Academy of Medicine in 1828, which had ceased its activity in 1824 in the context of the above-mentioned anti-liberal purge; the institution was closed and its members were to be purged until they had given an account of their activities since 1808. However, although the first royal physician achieved the reopening of the academy, he did not succeed in overturning the debarment of the academics who had been appointed during the Constitutional Triennium.[45] There is no doubt that Pedro Castelló played an important role in reforming medicine and its institutions in the first third of the nineteenth century. In the 1850s–1860s it was Tomás del Corral who became the prominent physician who exercised great influence due to his post at the Spanish court, a constitutional one by then.

Tomás del Corral and the collective demands as medical professionals in mid-nineteenth-century Spain

The effort to modernize medical institutions and the defence of professional interests were other important professional issues during this period in which royal physicians took part, albeit not in a particularly decisive way. The following strategies were deployed at institutional

45 Granjel, *Historia de la Real Academia*, 158 and 164.

level: promoting medical associations (colegios),[46] attempting to establish a national medical association headed by the first royal physician of Isabel II (Tomás del Corral), granting more power to the healthcare deputy delegates.[47] This association was supposed to be a federation of provincial associations represented by delegates in a national assembly. Tomás del Corral presided the first assembly. It is clear that appointing a prestigious and well-connected royal physician, such as Del Corral as the president was a way of showcasing the association's ambition to represent Spanish physicians as a whole. Nonetheless, this initiative eventually failed. In general, outstanding physicians were encouraged by medical press to exercise influence in medical issues through public education committees and through political institutions such as the Parliament, but royal physicians avoided representative political institutions.[48]

These actions strove to address a series of issues that plagued Spanish medicine, such as professional malpractice and corruption and the shaky economic situation and social standing of medical professionals, particularly rural physicians. Illegal medical practice and 'charlatans' (quacks, faith healers, people who practiced medicine lacking certified training, remedy sellers) were constantly denounced in medical press. The use of 'fake titles' as well as physicians and surgeons exceeding their authority

46 Medical professionals petitioned the Queen to reopen the medical college of Madrid; several court physicians were among those who signed: Tomás del Corral, José Roviralta, José Figuer, Juan Castelló y Tagel, Tomás Santero and Gabriel Usera. *El Siglo Médico* (26 March 1854).

47 The aim was to render them capable of fighting infringements against sanitary legislation and illegal professional practice more efficiently. *El Siglo Médico* (18 June1854).

48 In the 1850s medical press campaigned for medical professionals as candidates in general elections, independently of their political allegiance. The aim was to use the presence of physicians as elected representatives in the Parliament (*Congreso de los Diputados*) to promote of the profession and push for specific reforms. The impact of such a campaign is unknown, but physicians tended to be well represented among the deputies: in the 1854 elections sixteen seats in the Parliament went to medical professionals. *El Siglo Médico* (12 October 1856). Nonetheless, there were hardly any court physicians among the deputies; in fact, only Tomás del Corral served as senator in 1877–1884.

and 'invading' one another's professional field were deemed harmful for medical professionals in the context of competition for patients/clients in the free market. Professional press considered this a situation 'terrible for the medical classes' and damaging for the 'good name of the government of an enlightened nation'.[49]

Medical professionals also considered that, as a group, their social and economic standing was precarious due to low remuneration. In this aspect, court physicians were clearly a privileged segment of the profession, their salaries being the highest among all salaried physicians in Spain, as I will show below. Economic precariousness had been denounced by medical professionals since the beginning of the nineteenth century. Only 'university chairs and posts in the Palace' were deemed lucrative enough, besides exceptional cases of prestigious physicians practicing in wealthy urban areas, who, 'due to their opinion or sheer luck, have been able to earn a good living', while the rest of medical professionals depended on 'the gratitude and good will of the patients'.[50] These complaints were particularly bitter in the case of rural physicians: 'What about the fees of a physician? … We are *profesores*[51] who practice an art, and for this, as everyone else, we want [our] reward in the general market … Nonetheless, our economic field is abandoned, in the state of anarchy!'[52] These exclamations were framed in a debate about the 'organization of public contracts for physicians' (*arreglo de los partidos médicos*), an issue that was particularly important for rural physicians who demanded reforms to combat 'the deplorable state of medical professions in Spain'.[53]

Economic situation of physicians in Spain varied greatly. Those who depended on municipal salaries often struggled to maintain a middle-class lifestyle.[54] Their dependence on the whims of municipal councils and the

49 *El Siglo Médico* (1 January 1854).

50 *Décadas Médico-Quirúrgicas* 1 (1820).

51 In the language employed by the medical press of the period the word *profesor* referred to physician who held a university diploma in Medicine.

52 *El Siglo Médico* (15 January 1854).

53 *El Siglo Médico* (2 April 1854).

54 The decree *Arreglo de partidos* of 1854 aimed at regulating the practice of municipal physicians, set at minimum salary at 2,000 *reales* per year for physicians serving in small municipalities and at 4,000 for these working in more populous

low salaries of those who lived in smaller municipalities threatened the fight for authority and gentlemanly status of the profession as a whole. If the physicians were unable to impress their patients with their outfit and behaviour befitting a gentleman, use a suitable vehicle of transport and have a 'decent' residence,[55] the physicians' effort to be part of social elites was under threat. While the economic difficulties and dependence on local authorities of rural physicians was particularly problematic for the profession's public image, physicians who practised in urban areas also struggled to impose and actually get fees high enough for them to live as gentlemen. Those who worked for public institutions were not beyond such concerns, either, as this complaint (dated to 1847) of doctors working at charity hospital attests to:

> They get paid 5000 rs [*reales*] in Madrid, 4000 in the province capitals where there is a court (audiencia) and 3000 in the others. Such mediocrity is even more striking if compared to the payments granted to some posts in other classes of the Administration, even when, in order to carry them out, one does not need more than to know how to read and write ... The consequence of this habit turned into law is this mediocre retribution given in the great part of hospitals to those in charge of the most essential thing, visiting the patients. ... the highest salaries reach seven or eight thousand *reales*, but we find, and there are not few, those of four, three, two thousand *reales* and even lower. It is shameful to say: we have seen expert hospital staff being paid less than the concierges.[56]

At the other end of the range, there was the most privileged – and highly influential – group of court physicians, a true economic elite within the profession. The surgeon physicians at the service of the Royal Household would come to enjoy a considerable salary for that time; in the middle of the century royal physicians were being paid between 20,000 and 50,000

---

municipalities, with the option to increase the salary according to the size of the population be serviced. *El Siglo Médico* (12 April 1854).

55 In mid-nineteenth century, physicians mostly visited their patients in their homes. Only later it became common for the doctors to receive patients in their office or associate in order to establish small clinics. These spaces under the physicians' control, together with the use of a white coat, contributed to strengthen their authority over the patients.

56 *La Verdad* (18 August 1847).

reales de vellón and supernumeraries between 20,000 and 30,000 *reales de vellón*,[57] amounts comparable, for example, with those paid to senior officials of the judiciary.[58] Pedro Castelló combined his Palace salary as first royal physician with income of 14,000 *reales* per year as retired professor of the San Carlos College of Medicine and Surgery.[59] Tomás del Corral was paid 40,000 *reales* per year as court physician (in 1854).[60]

Physicians' collective battle for social and economic improvements continued throughout the nineteenth century. Particularly, the issue of rural physicians and the districts they were supposed to attend to remained a hot topic for decades. It became linked to the overall critique of the 'excessive' influence of local elites, the famous debate on the *caciquismo* [caciquism] as a hindrance to the progress of Spain. As I have already mentioned, municipal physicians in rural areas had low salaries, which they were often paid late and they depended on the goodwill of local elites not only to get this meagre income, but also to be able to complement it with fees from private patients. Tomás del Corral supported the demands of rural physicians and was chosen by his peers to spearhead initiatives of reform. However, the results of his effort were modest, particularly if compared

57 AGP, Personal, box 00.922, file 45, box 2.668, file 5. Furthermore, the royal bloodletting surgeon was paid 18,000 *reales* per year. AGP, Reglamentos, box 943.

58 In the middle of the century, the prosecutors at the Supreme Court of Justice were paid an annual salary of 60,000 *reales de vellón* and the members of the Legislative Committee 50,000 *reales*. See Díaz, Braulio, *La politización de la justicia. El Tribunal Supremo (1836–1881)* (PhD, Thesis: Universidad Complutense of Madrid, 2004).

59 AGP, Reinados, Isabel II, box 352, file 13.

60 AGP, Personal, box 00.922, file 45, box 2.668, file 5. See also Núñez-García, 'Médicos en la corte'. Besides his salary as court physician, Del Corral also enjoyed a salary as lecturer at the Universidad Central de Madrid. After his retirement as Chair in 1868, he was paid 3,200 escudos per year. Archivo del Senado (AS), Personal File, HIS–0410–03. In the United Kingdom, the physicians of the Court of Queen Victoria were paid a salary of 300 pounds per year, in addition to other remunerations for specific services rendered. In Scotland and Ireland these stipends amounted to between 50 and 100 pounds per year. The highest salaries were paid to the surgeons to the Household (400 pounds) and those in charge of the Royal Apothecary (550 pounds) as their professional tasks were considered the most arduous. Cooke, 'Queen Victorian 's Medical', 311–12.

to the major contribution of his predecessor Pedro Castelló to the reform of medical professions a few decades before.

In his later years, Tomás del Corral served as senator in 1877–1884. He was Senator elect for the Central University of Madrid from 1877 until 1882, being first elected in 1877 and re-elected in 1879 and again in 1881.[61] He was member of the Senate's public health committee on several occasions, but he did not intervene in the debates concerning healthcare. Neither did he bring up in the Upper Chamber any of the professional issues that were of concern for Spanish physicians.

Conclusion

In the nineteenth century, physicians and surgeons strove to consolidate their expert authority *vis à vis* the society and the State, and also improve their social standing. As I have argued, the strategies deployed have both collective and individual dimensions, as individual outlook and behaviour of a physician had impact on the image of the profession as a whole. I have used two outstanding public, court physicians Pedro Castelló and Tomás del Corral, to show how men whose standing was rather exceptional within the medical profession as a whole, could serve as leaders to promote professional demands, but also as embodiments of a model professional to which all physicians aspired. This pattern can be observed elsewhere in Europe, too. Court physicians (and not only those in old monarchies; Dr Conneau, personal physician to Napoleon III, is the example of a similar figure in the French empire)[62] enjoyed a privileged position in terms of status, remuneration and proximity to power, which they sometimes used to voice the demands of medical profession as a whole.

Benefitting from their privileged position close to the Crown in the times when this institution still exercised great influence, Pedro Castelló and Tomás del Corral, became emblematic figures in the Spanish medical

61 AS, Personal File, HIS-0410-03.

62 Mauduit, *Le ministére*, 168.

profession. They accepted the call to exercise influence and voice professional demands in the 'right places'. Their actions helped enhance professional cohesion and social standing of physicians and surgeons in the new context of a liberal, post-revolutionary society. There is no doubt about the role Pedro Castelló in particular played in promoting the unification of education of physicians and surgeons in Spain, following the model of revolutionary France. This unification was an important milestone in the physicians' fight for monopoly on expert authority and for control of the access to the healthcare market. We must not forget, though, that Castelló's initiative of 1827, under the absolutist monarchy, was only one of the first stages of a long and contested process. Thus, in 1857 Spanish medical press still discussed the 'ordering of the medical classes'. The influential journal *El Siglo Médico* [*The Medical Century*] argued that 'if the desired reform is presented, social standing of the *profesores*, protected as they would be by the government … they would have a guaranty of a honest and decorous subsistence, in a just retribution of the great importance of their services and of the hardship of their work'.[63]

Regarding symbolic aspects, Pedro Castelló and Tomás del Corral embodied many of the treats of the model physician and were able to perform as gentlemen among liberal elites, as they enjoyed the means and prestige to do so in a credible way. It must be stressed that the two physicians were, at the same time, highly exposed to public scrutiny. If they proved successful in their treatments – and if they failed, this reflected not only on their personal credibility as medical practitioners, but also on the profession as a whole. Del Corral's successful handling of the birth of infanta María Cristina was praised in medical press, linking the profession and the Nation: 'It has not taken much for the experience to prove that those sentiments and desires were inspired by our Spanish patriotism (*españolismo*) and by our love of the profession!'[64] Little mattered that the *infanta* died two days after she was born.

63 'Cuatro palabras sobre el arreglo de las clases médicas', *El Siglo Médico* (4 January 1857).

64 'Feliz alumbramiento de S. M. La Reina', *El Siglo Médico* (8 Junuary 1854).

As it is nowadays, in the nineteenth century the death of a great figure tended to be a moment when legacy of the deceased was praised, often supressing all criticisms. In their necrologies, Spanish medical press lavished praise on both court physicians, exaggerating their achievements. Pedro Castelló was described as 'illustrious regenerator of Spanish medicine'. Patriarchal metaphors were employed to this effect: 'rest, … virtuous elder, in the affection of your tender children, of honourable/respectable (*pundonorosos*) physicians, of those who did not let themselves become corrupted'.[65] He was acknowledged as a key actor of the renewal of Spanish medical profession.

When Del Corral died, however, the necrologies dwelled less on his contribution to medical science and profession. Rather they focused on his loyalty and proximity to the monarchy, stressing that, despite being showered with honours, he remained humble, virtuous and honourable:

> Few who share his condition of physician and without ever wishing to leave the area of science, obtained from their kings so many distinctions and honours, or proofs of consideration and friendship, which is the least common and the most difficult [thing] among the sovereigns, like her first royal physician Don Tomás Corral y Oña constantly received![66]

65 'Al Excmo. Sr. D. Pedro Castelló', *El Eco de la Medicina* (5 October 1848).

66 'A la memoria del Excelentísimo Sr. D. Tomás Corral y Oña. Marqués de San Gregorio', *El Genio Médico–Quirúrgico* (22 December 1882), 603–4.

CARMEN GONZÁLEZ CANALEJO AND
RUBÉN MIRÓN-GONZÁLEZ

The Healthcare Middle Class

Female Professions and Patriarchy (1856–1931)

ABSTRACT
In this chapter we analyse the origins of what the contemporaries called the 'healthcare middle class' from the second half of the nineteenth century to early twentieth century. This model evidenced the social inequalities and the discourses of the politics which defended the male groups' interests. Methodologically, the object of the study has been approached from a gender perspective. The aim of this chapter is to reconstruct the historical process from trade to profession of midwives, nurses and female practitioners and its institutionalization in Spain.

Introduction

The origin of the 'healthcare middle class' would be difficult to understand without prior knowledge about the Spanish Liberal State and its relation to the social and healthcare system created under four fundamental laws: *Ley de Beneficencia* [Charity Law] (1848), *Ley General de Sanidad* [General Health Law] (1855), *Ley de Desamortización de Madoz* [Madoz Law of Confiscation] (1855) and *Ley de Instrucción Pública* [Law of Public Instruction] (1857).

The period from the enactment of the first of these laws (1848), which regulated healthcare, to the first decade of the twentieth century was a turning point to what contemporaries called 'the auxiliary healthcare classes'.[1]

1 *Colegio de Auxiliares de Medicina y Cirugía. Periódico científico-profesional*, 1917; *La Cirugía Menor. La revista de los auxiliares de Medicina y Cirugía*, 1905–1908.

First of all, it is important to say that these new professional groups comprising practitioners, midwives and, a few years later, nurses were not new on the social and professional scene, as they had their roots in the trades that the Old Regime had called '*ministrantes* [surgical practitioners], nurses and midwives'.

A second issue that allows us to understand the increasingly visible presence of these professionals in public and institutional scenarios is the need for a broader and more secularized healthcare than what had been provided until then. From the mid-nineteenth century onwards, it was the liberal state, and not the Church, who would gradually provide secular, professionalized healthcare based on the rational and scientific principles of the time, rather than on charity or Christian faith, as had hitherto been the practice of the everlasting religious orders. Some of these, both locally and foreign founded, were constituted by a large group of nuns and friars who had formed the basis of healthcare since time immemorial but were progressively being displaced by the new healthcare classes.

A final noteworthy issue is the emergence, from the second half of the nineteenth century onwards, of new groups, mostly from the working class, who became social agents with technical university studies or training at professionalized schools. Over time, both practitioners and midwives, and later certified nurses, developed a vindictive social conscience. This materialized in the longing for independence that demanded non-subordination to the dominant healthcare class. At the same time, women in healthcare were developing a gender awareness that demanded the recognition of their work as a scientific practice, which they could perform with the same capacity as men. They asked for greater equality in the labour and social spheres, a demand that became even more visible in the second decade of the twentieth century.

Through newspaper and archive sources, we will try to reconstruct on these pages how these professions originated and developed from what had been trades in the Ancien Régime to the 'new' professions of the intercentury period, which in time led to a movement upward on the social class ladder of those who chose to pursue these careers.

A gender analysis through the discourses of female health professionals reveals the prevailing inequality of opportunities in the field of healthcare as a reflection of a profoundly patriarchal society.

Analysing the 'healthcare ancillary classes' in general, but paying particular attention to how the women who chose these careers were trained, involves going beyond reconstructing a history concerned with the experience and contribution of the 'social subject' of the middle and popular classes (Guizot's *moyenne* class). It entails discussing their access to professionalized education, work aspirations, social inequalities, desires and interpretation of the reality in which they lived. It is about giving voice to those of 'lower status' to understand class consciousness and seeing how sexual differences were ideologically manipulated to legitimize unequal opportunities in the working world. Our focus will be on women who left the domestic sphere to enter, through education, into a masculinized professional environment while examining how they became aware of inequalities inside and outside their work.[2]

The origin of the healthcare middle class: Midwives and nurses

In September 1857, during Claudio Moyano's term as Minister, university degrees of 'practitioner' and 'childbirth teacher' were approved. These studies were designed and conceived exclusively to assist medical professionals by introducing technical innovations in the programmes for the exercise of a delegated practice. The immediate effect of this law was that the modernizing impulse necessary for the development and autonomy of the newly legitimized professional competences was not implemented. This is one of the unresolved issues that, during the second period of the Restoration (1902–1923), would favour the struggle of those who

2 *El Practicante Almeriense* (May 1920) and following issues.

practised these professions, aimed at insistently demanding their independence and professional development.

As we have already mentioned, alongside the Moyano Law, the Madoz Law of Confiscations was passed, which obliged the Church to transfer all healthcare establishments, both hospitals and asylums, to the provincial and municipal administrations. This entailed a new organization in the healthcare field and the management of these establishments.[3] The ecclesiastical administrators were replaced by doctors, who took control of most of the hospitals and had considerable power in the new corporations.

The Church was strongly opposed both to the transfer of competences and to the liberal conception of healthcare. As a consequence, its religious communities, especially Hijas de la Caridad [Daughters of Charity] and Siervas de María [Servants of Mary], slowed down the incorporation of the new professionals, since the religious sisters had handled many of the duties of the new nurses. This led to a hindering process of professional incorporation and development, particularly evident in the case of nurses.[4]

Despite the Church's restraint and the political crises of the nineteenth century, the educational impulse of the Sexenio Democrático [The six democratic years] and the social hygiene movement was consolidated, resulting in a favourable and visible change in the inter-century period.[5] Liberal positions and progressive groups were more concerned with improving public healthcare, which resulted in a stimulus for these professions. Among these projects, it is worth analysing the obligatory nature of public healthcare for the most disadvantaged strata of society – which was already included in the new spirit of the Charity – a factor that had a positive influence on the need to recruit professionalized female staff. In the period from 1850 to 1860, the number of health establishments increased from 10 per cent to 14 per cent, and by 30 per cent at the end of

3 Marcelo Martínez Alcubilla, *Diccionario de la Administración Española*, 4th edn, vol. I (Madrid: Administración, 1886), 568. See section 4 of the Royal Order of 30 September 1848 on the official qualifications of practitioners and midwives.

4 Carmen Domínguez Alcón, *Los cuidados y la profesión enfermera en España* (Madrid: Pirámide, 1986).

5 Mariano Esteban de Vega, 'La asistencia liberal en la España de la Restauración', *Revista de la historia de la economía y de la empresa* 4 (2010), 49–61.

the century.[6] It seems clear that the liberal project of extending healthcare coverage both in hospitals and at home highlighted the need to integrate these professions into the welfare organization.

The advances of liberalism favoured a process that would become the seed of the working class, which from this half of the century onwards would gradually evolve into the middle class.[7] From the beginning, the new healthcare class was created for technical tasks that doctors delegated under their strict orders and supervision. It was a type of health care that involved more direct contact with patients and women in labour.

At first, the more conservative physicians opposed the social advancement of midwives,[8] but this resistance was overcome once they realized how few midwives had enrolled in the programme. This small number did not threaten the economic interests of medical professionals. Nor did this pose any danger to their social or professional status, as they were only ancillary jobs. The activities that female midwives, practitioners and nurses carried out were always under medical prescription and control. Both the training, both by the doctors and the syllabus prepared to obtain these diplomas strongly emphasized the nuance of subordination, especially concerning midwives and nurses.[9]

Furthermore, doctors also benefited from the creation of these professions due to the possibility of adding the diploma of practitioner and midwife to their medical degree, as established by the Moyano Law. The result was a usurpation of the competencies of midwives since their field of work had focused on everything related to childbirth since ancient times. Rural midwives were the ones who suffered the most, both economically and professionally, since not only doctors but also practitioners performed midwifery in municipalities with less than 10,000 inhabitants.

6 Pedro Carasa Soto, *El sistema hospitalario español en el siglo XIX. De la asistencia benéfica al modelo sanitario actual* (Valladolid: Universidad de Valladolid, 1985), 121.

7 María Isabel Ruiz García, *El obrerismo consciente. Almería 1900–1923* (Almería: Universidad de Almería, 2015).

8 María del Carmen Álvarez Ricart, *La mujer como profesional de la medicina en la España del siglo XIX* (Barcelona: Anthropos, 1988), 181.

9 Manuel Jesús García Martínez, 'Las carreras auxiliares médicas', *Híades. Revista de historia de la enfermería* 5–6 (1999), 56–61.

From the early years of the twentieth century, when the number of practitioners became significant, they also disputed the right to attend births. The conflict between midwives, practitioners and rural doctors lasted for several decades.

From then on, midwives began to show a clear awareness of being a discriminated professional group against doctors. Both practitioners and midwives had established a federal network by founding professional associations in all provincial capitals. They had their own news media and began to assert their interests.

In the early years of the twentieth century, the first promotions of professional nurses had already graduated. By the end of the 1920s, despite the tripling of the number of practitioners, midwives and nurses, they were still tenuously involved in the trade union association. This explains the continuous complaints and statements they wrote in their newspapers, such as *El Practicante* [*The Practitioner*] or *El Eco de las Matronas* [*The Echo of Midwives*].[10]

It should be highlighted that female access to these professions was designed to consolidate the sexual division of work and to provide women with 'appropriate' training for what the patriarchal mentality of the time considered should be their traditional role as wives and mothers. The idea of female emancipation through education was not considered in the liberal ideology as a key factor for social progress. In other words, although the Law of Public Instruction gave women access to education, it was not equal. In this case, the training of midwives, nurses and also of female practitioners ensured, over time, their subordination to doctors and even to male practitioners.[11]

The work carried out by the women who entered these professional paths was based on the cult of domesticity and the stereotype of the 'Modern Woman'.[12] Candidates were required to have the qualities of affability,

10 *El Eco de las matronas*,1889; *El Practicante Moderno*, 1903–1904.

11 Carmen González Canalejo, *Las cuidadoras. Historia de las practicantas, matronas y enfermeras* (Almería: Instituto de Estudios Almerienses, 2006).

12 Historiography argues that 'the modern nurse' ceased to be 'the angel in the house' and became 'the angel in the hospital'. When modern women or the new woman entered the labour world, the archetype had domestic and traditional elements attached to it. This is clearly seen in their clothing – apron, muffs, bonnet, etc. These

observational skills, obedience and unquestioning medical subordination. In addition to this, they had to have solidly developed family affections.[13] The domestic role traditionally assigned to women was extrapolated to the space where female health workers developed their professional activity. This projected a negative image of their training, setting aside the scientific recognition of their practices, which made women's distinction and equal work opportunities unfeasible.[14]

The process of professionalization: A long and difficult road

If the history of women in healthcare is characterized by its most significant events, there is no doubt that, among them, the aforementioned liberal educational impulse of the mid-nineteenth century – consolidated through the Sexenio Democrático – should be included.[15] In the most conservative mentality, especially for the Church, women's access to education in the health sector was a threat to the existing socio-family structure. It was widely believed that the incorporation of women into the labour market once they had finished their studies would not only lead to the decline of the health system itself, but also of the families, whose functioning was based on the mother figure.

---

clothes reminded women that, despite having a professional education, they should not forget what their contemporaries called their 'feminine condition'. And this imposition has remained unresolved to this day.

13 Joaquín Pi y Arsuaga, *Cuidados que merece un enfermo* (Madrid: Imprenta y librería de Nicolás Moya, 1903), 4.

14 Carmen González Canalejo, 'Mujeres sanitarias y derechos de ciudadanía en la España Contemporánea', in Carmen González Canalejo and Fernando Martínez López, eds, *La transformación de la enfermería. Nuevas miradas para la historia* (Granada: Comares, 2010), 163–82; José Luis Medina Moya, *La pedagogía del cuidado: saberes y prácticas en la formación universitaria en enfermería* (Barcelona: Alertes, 1998).

15 Mercedes Suárez Pazos, *A educación en España durante o Sexenio Revolucionario (1868–1874)* (Vigo: Universidad de Vigo, 2002).

An important aspect of the late nineteenth-century debate on the so-called 'women's question'[16] was whether by entering the labour world women would forget what were considered to be 'the duties of their sex'. Domestic work and family care – including care for the elderly members of the group and the education of children – should also be the main obligations for those women who chose wage labour. This premise implied that women would enter the productive sphere as long as they did not forget the domestic and maternal role that had been assigned to them by the social order.

As specialists in the field of education state regarding women's academic access,[17] besides the pessimistic outlook in the classrooms of medical schools, which was a privilege to which only a minority of men had access, university admission was a privilege rarely granted to women.[18] And not only did they face subtle ideological obstacles, but also legal ones, since the doors of universities and schools were not opened for midwives until the democratic impulse of 1868 and for female practitioners until 1904.

A common characteristic of the female practitioners, midwives and nurses was the enormous number of strategies they had to implement for their access to professionalized education and their incorporation into the labour market. All of this reflects the enormous social obstacles that had to be overcome to ensure that, over time, their incorporation into hospitals and public spaces was not problematic.

Once the educational barrier was overcome, the social discourse focused on whether women had the same capacity to practice with the same scientific rigour as male doctors, surgeons, hygienists, pharmacists or practitioners who were socially and institutionally designated as 'facultatives'.

But female education was a process that could not be reversed, and access to professionalized training for the first midwives, nurses and practitioners, although it was a slow process, nevertheless meant their economic

16 A. Blanco et al., eds, *Nuevas visiones de la maternidad* (León: Publicaciones de la Universidad de León, 2002).

17 Pilar Ballarín and Ana Iglesias, 'Feminismo y educación. Recorrido de un camino común', *Historia de la educación. Revista interuniversitaria* 37 (2018), 37–67.

18 Rosa María Capel, *El trabajo y la educación de la mujer en España* (Madrid: Ministerio de Cultura, 1982).

independence and the power to choose whether or not to marry. We should remember that legitimizing the teaching of these old professions fulfilled the institutional purpose of providing health coverage to an increasingly large sector of the citizenry, such as the maternal and infant groups, following the reformist directives of the new liberal order.[19]

As can be seen, the educational factor was decisive. But there was still a long road ahead for the full integration of women in the healthcare system, not only in terms of equal employment opportunities but also in being accepted without undermining their intellectual capacities and recognition as experts.

Studies focusing on the education of the first women in healthcare have pointed to female doctors as the first university women in Spain. However, it is possible to verify through the aforementioned Law of 1857 that a small group of women obtained the midwifery degree at the Faculty of Medicine in Madrid before these studies were cancelled between 1860 and 1866. Although, altogether, only six women completed their studies due to the continuous letters and protests launched by the conservative medical sector. Initially, the official teaching established the obligation to distribute the theoretical and practical subjects over two academic years. This design was intended to allow female students to combine two theoretical courses in medical schools with two years of training in hospitals.

Female candidates were instructed in subordination and dependence since the theoretical studies were only designed to train 'doctor's assistants' and the training to be subordinated to what the manuals called 'facultative orders'.[20] As we have already pointed out, the studies were suspended due to opposition from conservative doctors and were resumed after the Sexenio Democrático, once the male health professionals considered that midwives did not pose any danger to them.

19 Carmen Blasco, 'La incorporación de practicantes y matronas al sistema sanitario español (1901–1950)', *Index de enfermería. Información bibliográfica, investigación y humanidades* 4–5 (1993), 7–10.

20 Francisco Alonso y Rubio, *Manual del arte de obstetricia, para uso de las matronas* (Madrid: Imp. Nacional, 1866).

> As for midwives, we say nothing, because even in Madrid, where we believe most of them are enrolled, no year there are more than six. Our Spanish women are not like English or German women, and therefore we should not fear that they will harm us in our careers and professional destinies.[21]

In some schools, practical teaching was tutored by experienced midwives. This was the case of Pilar Jáuregui de Lasbennes, a teacher of childbirth, who in 1875 opened a School for Midwives located next to the Anthropological Museum in Madrid. It was directed by the renowned hygienist Ángel Pulido, who delivered theoretical lessons at the school.[22] The fact that Ángel Pulido held the position of Director was not exceptional. The same situation was replicated in all the nursing schools that were founded during the first third of the twentieth century, as in Spain women were not allowed to become school directors.

Thus, in no case were women able to manage the centres where these studies were taught. Moreover, the female promoters of these educational projects were aware of the obstacles that the society of their time imposed on women, so ceding the leading role to men was the only viable solution for women to gain access to these degrees and to build a modern society.

Despite the obstacles and difficulties that entailed the studies of midwives in medical schools, at the end of the nineteenth century, coinciding with an increasing number of media, midwives were the first to publish their own newspapers and magazines. In the aforementioned *El Eco de las Matronas*, in addition to scientific and technical sections on obstetrics and childcare, articles on their expectations, experiences and work stories were published.

The liberal governments between 1888 and 1904 reorganized the careers of midwives and practitioners since, until 1904, the latter was only reserved for men. Although women in medical schools undertook the same studies and acquired the same skills as men to obtain the official diploma known as 'Auxiliar en Medicina y Cirugía' [Assistant in Medicine and

21 Álvarez Ricart, *La mujer como profesional de la medicina*, 180.

22 Teresa Ortiz Gómez, 'Las matronas y la transmisión de saberes científicos sobre el parto en la España del siglo XIX', in Emilia Moreno Sánchez, ed., *Orientaciones para una educación no sexiste* (Oviedo: Septem, 2010), 33–52.

Surgery], popularly known as Practitioner, discrimination against women was present from the very beginning of the enrolment process. In this sense, women could not enter before the age of 23, as opposed to 16 for men, because it was considered that women had a maturational delay that prevented them from assimilating the studies with solvency.

The idea of the female lower intellectual capacity of women is key to understanding why the Moyano Law did not contemplate access of women to the practitioner studies. Bearing in mind the importance of sexual roles in mid-nineteenth-century Spain, the most generalized position was to consider these studies to be beyond what was assigned to the female condition. Contrary to what happened with midwifery and nursing, considered as 'appropriate' for women by the patriarchal mentality.

In addition to the father's or husband's authorization for access the faculties and professional schools, female candidates for healthcare programmes, including the practitioner studies, needed an ecclesiastical report certifying their good morals. Theoretical tests for female students were held every six months, with the final exam being conducted 'behind closed doors'. The students were examined by a board of three medical professors who ensured that the candidates, besides having the necessary knowledge, had developed the requirements of obedience and unquestioning medical subordination. This type of examination behind closed doors was reserved exclusively for women, while men were test in public and were only demanded to have the theoretical and practical knowledge required in the syllabus.[23]

As gender historiography has described, the effort carried out during the first third of the twentieth century did not reorganize work equally between men and women. There was a part of the social mentality that defend that the supposed weakness and fragility of the female body would determine its predisposition for certain jobs.[24] By the same biological principle, the strong constitution and greater capacity of men made them more suitable for manipulating the bodies of anaesthetized patients, opening,

23 González Canalejo, *Las cuidadoras*, 32–3.

24 Mercedes Arbaiza Vilallonga, 'La "cuestión social" como cuestión de género. Feminidad y trabajo en España (1860–1930)', *Historia Contemporánea* 21 (2000), 395–458.

dissecting, amputating and resisting interventions in the surgical scenario. This perception led to a sexualized design in the programme of the practitioner degree, which remained in place even after these studies were reorganized in 1904. Women now had access to these studies, but they were still considered exclusively male.

According to Capel, in 1900 there were eight female students enrolled in the 'practitioner' degree.[25] They were not officially admitted to the faculties, since legally, as we have just mentioned, women could not access these studies until 1904. In other words, before the law, there were at least two promotions in which some women enrolled this degree. One can therefore suspect that the actual number of female pupils enrolled was higher than is described in the above-mentioned source. The fact that women gained access at least two years earlier than was permitted by law means that during the half-century of male monopoly there were female requests that laid the foundations for this instruction. Requests that did not reach their destination or at least did not receive a reply from the official spheres, despite the impulse of the Sexenio and the liberal and progressive aspirations of the last quarter of the century.[26]

In spite of the late access of women to this profession and their scarce presence, the number of female applicants to the 'practicant' degree increased throughout the first third of the twentieth century. According to Domínguez-Alcón, the first eight female students mentioned in 1900 increased to thirty a decade later.[27] In the final years of the Restoration, the increase is even more evident, with ninety-four female students. However, despite the efforts carried out to this date, the number of female students was a minority compared to the number of male students, as the latter was four times higher.

It is particularly noteworthy, as it is unprecedented in gender historiography, that after obtaining their first degree, women who we have called 'middle-class health professionals' continued studying to obtain a second

25 Capel, *El trabajo y la educación de la mujer*, 441.

26 Carmen González Canalejo, 'El acceso educativo de las primeras practicantas (1900–1931)', in *Mujeres y educación: saberes, prácticas y discursos en la historia* (Sevilla and Buenos Aires: Diputación Provincial de Sevilla, 2005), 119–33.

27 Domínguez Alcón, *Los cuidados y la profesión enfermera*, 120.

and even a third degree. This phenomenon is exclusive to these female groups and is found in the collegiate documentation more frequently from the second decade of the twentieth century onwards. By this time, most of the midwives had already obtained the practitioner diploma and the female practitioners, the midwifery degree. In some cases, the latter also qualified as nurses.[28]

At the end of the 1920s, the professional figure of midwives and nurses with double degrees appeared frequently. This illustrates the high demands placed on women in waged labour, as a single qualification was not enough for professional development. This phenomenon may have been more common than might be imagined at first, since it has been a constant for midwives and nurses who, since the Transition period, have been moving upwards on the academic ladder.

Private practice was also a strategy used by dually qualified female practitioners and midwives to compete in the difficult labour arena with doctors and practitioners, as many women opted to attend in their practices as well as in the homes of patients or women in labour. We interpret this phenomenon as a desire for greater job autonomy that relieved women of institutional pressure, more obvious in the intra-hospital space. Here, the subordination to medical power and the control of the Hijas de la Caridad were greater. Ultimately, most midwives and female practitioners chose self-employment because it allowed them to distance themselves from an androcentric world, which prevailed in healthcare spaces with an organizational structure that followed deeply patriarchal cultural principles.

28 *El Practicante Almeriense* (November 1922). Some cases are known thanks to this newspaper. From the 1920s onwards, it was common to send a welcome note to the midwife who had already obtained the diploma of practitioner, and this was recorded in the aforementioned newspaper.

The 'New Woman', the 'New Nurse'

The context in which the professionalization and upward social mobility of nurses in Spain emerged coincided with the educational impulse of the Institución Libre de Enseñanza [The Free Institution of Education], which is related to the paradigm of what in the early years of the twentieth century was known as the 'New Woman' or the 'Modern Woman'.[29] Federico Rubio Galí, a doctor from Cádiz connected to Pi y Margall's Republican group, was the founder of the first school in Spain. He was one of the men closest to Giner de los Ríos, with whom he had been friends since their student days in Cádiz.[30] As an intellectual of the last quarter of the nineteenth century, he combined his medical work with extensive political activity. As a young republican, he had participated very actively in the democratic impulse of the Sexenio. In the last years of the nineteenth century, the years of his physical and intellectual maturity, he moved to Madrid where he worked in the training and pedagogy of young people who wanted to be educated in the health field. Like many republican and free-thinking intellectuals of the time, he had drawn from Krauso-institutionalist sources. He brought this philosophy to the school he established in his clinic, located near Moncloa, where dozens of young surgeons and nurses were trained. In 1880, he founded the Instituto de Terapéutica Operatoria [Surgical Therapeutics Institute]. This centre had sixty beds and functioned for eighteen years as a surgical school. In 1896, the educational offer was broadened with the establishment of the first nursing school, located in one of the wings of the hospital. All the teaching principles were secular.[31] The whole complex was

29 Mary Nash, 'Dos décadas de historia de las mujeres en España: una reconsideración', *Historia Social* 9 (1991), 137–61.

30 Antonio Orozco Acuaviva, 'Médicos gaditanos y la obra de Gines de los Ríos', in *La Institución Libre de Enseñanza: su influencia en la cultura española* (Ronda, Málaga: Diputación de Málaga, 1998), 197–212.

31 Concha Germán, Yolanda Martínez and Marta Mas, *Las primeras enfermeras laicas españolas. Aurora Mas y los orígenes de una profesión en el siglo XX* (Zaragoza: Prensas de la Universidad de Zaragoza, 2020).

a clinical-pedagogical laboratory supported by the motto *Enseñanza mutua, libre examen y ausencia de amor propio* [*Mutual instruction, free thought and absence of ego*],[32] where the principles of *science* or *art* were removed from the religious sphere.

Federico Rubio saw the need for education for the progress and health of the community. Like many republicans of his time, he was convinced that the combination of education and healthcare could result in a happier society, which made him one of the regenerationists who most strongly defended a social and health reform based on the idea that educated people were healthy people. He advocated for democratization and plurality in the field of healthcare, arguing that medicine, surgery and nursing were sciences to be studied in books, hospitals, laboratories and patient wards. He stated without a shadow of a doubt that the usefulness of these sciences emanated from an eminently practical approach. The professors who taught at this centre excluded from scientific training any teaching other than freedom in method and choice of interventions based on science. For they understood that there was no subject, divine or human, that could not be freely examined and analysed. The philosophy that permeated the teaching of the new nurses wore the unmistakable institutionalist stamp. As the years went by, the centre acquired greater prestige. The students acquired a thorough scientific preparation and were in a position to solve any problem posed by clinical practice.[33]

Domínguez-Alcón notes that in 1896 the first thirty-two nursing students were enrolled in this school, of which eight were internal and twenty-four external.[34] The teaching programme combined very intense activities, conducted in eight to twelve-hour periods in patients wards and surgical areas of the hospital, with theoretical lessons. After two years, the students

32 *Revista Ibero-Americana de Ciencias Médicas* (1903), 53. Textual quotation.

33 Rubén Mirón and Carmen Gonzáles Canalejo, 'Los profesionales de la sanidad andaluza: masonería, discurso y represión (1868–1945)', in José Miguel Delgado and Antonio Morales, eds, *Gibraltar, Cádiz, América y la masonería. Constitucionalismo y libertad de prensa, 1812–2012*, vol. 1 (Zaragoza: Centro de Estudios Históricos de la Masonería Española, 2014), 313–51.

34 Domínguez Alcón, *Los cuidados y la profesión enfermera*, 106.

completed their training after the corresponding theoretical tests and were awarded a diploma entitling them to practise health care in hospitals.

After the death of Federico Rubio in 1902, coinciding with women's difficult educational beginnings, Joaquín Pi y Arsuaga, son of Francisco Pi y Margal, became director of the school. Federico Rubio, teacher and mentor of this young surgeon, left him in charge of the future of this reformist and secularist project for professional nurses in Spain.

However, despite the weight of the scientific rationality of Krausist philosophy and the secular context that permeated the teaching, nurses were relegated as ancillary to doctors and male practitioners. The recognition of women's rights to education was not enough because it was based on already existing social inequalities, which became very evident when nurses entered the professional world, as was the case with female practitioners and, previously, midwives.

Around this question, academic feminism has posited the existence of a phenomenon that comes from two different realities.[35] On the one hand, one that emerged from liberal politicians and regenerationist intellectuals who advocated for an improvement in productivity by incorporating women into the working world, while demanding an urgent social reform in healthcare capable of healing an ailing society. In this sense, regenerationist intellectuals such as Federico Rubio, hygienists such as Ángel Pulido and also reformist women such as Concepción Arenal, to cite a few examples, facilitated the incorporation of nurses and women in general into all areas of waged work. But, on the other hand, there was also another reality whose ideological aspects were supported by the Church and an ultra-conservative-minded social sector, who were in the majority radically opposed to the emancipation of women. As a consequence, ultra-conservative inertia revalued women's domestic, educational and reproductive work. And this cult of 'domesticity' was extrapolated, both to the teaching of female health workers and to the public spaces where they worked once they had obtained their qualifications.

35 Viginia Guichot-Reina, 'La educación de la mujer d fines del siglo XIX a través de la prensa femenina. La madre de familia', in *La constitución de Cádiz. Genealogía y desarrollo del sistema educativo liberal* (Cádiz: Universidad de Cádiz, 2013), 647–56.

Profiles, aspirations and discourses of female health workers

The working class was not the only one who wanted a female profession for their daughters. Their aspirations were mixed with those of the middle bourgeoisie and the rural bourgeoisie who, to maintain or improve their position, sent their daughters to undertake these studies. These careers were considered by the mentality of the time to be 'female jobs', as a professional salary would be a financial aid to the family. In the case of some professionalized schools, such as the Federico Rubio School, the profile of the first applicants was very varied. While some were over the age of majority, others were 23 or even 20 years old, as the age at which they could enter these studies was lowered as the aspirations of Spanish women became more in line with those of other European countries. According to the aforementioned Joaquín Pi y Arsuaga,[36] while some barely fulfilled the minimum educational requirements, there were other applicants with a wider range of studies and even those who spoke several languages, which confirms the enormous variability among them.[37]

In some schools, such as the one in Madrid created by Federico Rubio, and, years later, the Montepío School in Barcelona, education for the daughters of the working class was free of charge to give them preference. In the case of midwives and female practitioners, the cost of enrolment in medical schools was 912 reals in the mid-nineteenth century and this expense was higher in private facilities, which indicates that the purchasing power of female midwifery candidates was higher.[38]

In any of the three cases, the requirement for access to these degrees was to have passed elementary education and to be between twenty and forty years. Whether or not they were married was a different matter, but it was compulsory to have the authorization of their father or husband. In addition to this list of requirements, a certificate from their priest-parish

36 Pi y Arsuaga, *Cuidados que merece un enfermo*, 6.
37 Pi y Arsuaga, *Cuidados que merece un enfermo*.
38 *La Gaceta de Madrid* (28 November 1861).

or priest certifying that they were of *buena vida y costumbres* [*good life and right conduct*] was also mandatory.[39]

With a few exceptions, most of the women who pursued these careers did it to gain economic and marital independence. In short, those who chose the professional training of midwife, practitioner or nurse came from a varied spectrum of social origins, but access to these professions served to fulfil the aspirations of a middle and working class, compatible with greater preparation, economic independence and improved social opportunities. These aspirations were in tune with the 'New Woman' of the new century, a motivation that was growing in Spain in the first third of the twentieth century. From 1915 onwards, women had clear access to hospital schools and medical faculties, which translated into an increasing female presence in healthcare spaces, traditionally occupied by doctors and female religious congregations. But in the conservationist discourse and the patriarchal mentality, the matter of employment and marriage came together. The few university women used to call this phenomenon 'the modern problem', because many of them, when they got married, abandoned their studies or jobs because of the difficulties to maintain full dedication in both areas according to patriarchal demands. This generated a gender consciousness that was capable of recognizing discrimination, sentiments and ideas that were permeating the incipient Spanish and European feminist movements.

By the end of 1919, some women clearly described these feelings in the Smith College *Weekly* editorial:

> We cannot believe that it is in the nature of things that a woman must choose between a home and her job when a man can have both. There must be a solution, and the challenge of our generation is precisely to find it.[40]

From the analytical perspective in which we stand, one of the categories that is specific to the origin and profile of the women who joined these

39 Paloma Salvadores, Susana Limia and María Elena Pileño, 'Los reglamentos de las escuelas de enfermeras durante la primera mitad del siglo XX', in *La enfermería profesional. VI Congreso Nacional y I Internacional de Historia de la Enfermería* (Alcalá de Henares: Universidad de Alcalá, 2003), 208–9.

40 Georges Duby and Michelle Perrot, *Historia de las mujeres*, vol. 5 (Madrid: Taurus, 1993), 116.

professions is the apostolic mission and religiosity generally attributed to the female population and, frequently, to the professions exercised mainly by women. Some authors have erroneously considered that, in particular, the profile of Spanish nurses was the heritage of upper-middle-class and even aristocratic conservative women, whose ideological roots came from the field of social action.

Advocates of this thesis have argued that women were trained in this profession to exercise the values of charity towards the sick, rather than to become part of the modernizing sphere of the new social competencies. Although in some specific areas of Spain many young upper-middle-class women could enter this profession to be in perfect harmony with the spirit of sacrifice that their moral qualities demanded of them when it came down to it, this minority sector would never have thought of access a career to work hard twelve and twenty-four-hour shifts in a hospital.

A detailed study of the primary sources confirms that this was not the general trend. Examples of those who fulfilled these aspirations are some nurses of the 1920s who are described as prototypical middle-class women.[41] But this profile is not broadly applicable to the case in point, because the upper-middle class and aristocratic nurses in the Church's social action movement were confined to a small and restricted educational sphere of private nursing schools, which emerged under the protection of the Church and conservative nationalism in the most industrialized areas.

From our perspective of analysis, these canons reflect the prototype of bourgeois women who – as occurred in the project of political Catalanism or in the Basque Country – symbolized traditional values. However, this was not the model of the women who accepted this process of modern professionalization, present in the schools directed by intellectuals and in the official teachings with a clear secular position.[42] Therefore, the prototype

41 Miren Llona, *Entre señorita y garçonne. Historia oral de las mujeres bilbaínas d clase media (1919–1939)* (Málaga: Universidad de Málaga, 2002).

42 Germán, Martínez and Mas, *Las primeras enfermeras laicas españolas*; Cristina Dupláa, 'La figura femenina como elemento legitimador del poder hegemónico de una cultura nacional', in *Mujeres y hombres en la formación del pensamiento occidental*, vol. 2 (Madrid: Universidad Autónoma de Madrid, 1989), 333–41.

nurse or midwife that was promoted where nationalisms took root cannot be generalized.

The incorporation of female nurses into the working world encountered a series of difficulties that hindered their access with full rights in the healthcare scenario. Both midwifery and nursing, although traditional professions, were renewed by educational reforms and came to be presented, as mentioned above, as 'new professions', destined for the 'Modern Woman' of the new century. The presence of women transformed the healthcare scenario hitherto reserved exclusively for men. It meant recognizing attitudes and aptitudes that until then had been forbidden to them due to a naturalization of domestic skills and a 'lower mental capacity of women' that was being increasingly questioned. However, despite the qualitative leap that came with the possession of a degree, in practice, patriarchal values relegated female labour to an ancillary position.

There was a rigid control of the care functions of female groups. And not only by doctors and male practitioners but also by the Church, who exercised real control over the possible consequences that could be discordant with the imposed morality. It was the midwives, female practitioners and nurses themselves who, over time, sought strategies for greater autonomy and who were responsible for implementing specific actions, either within the collegiate associations or through the professional press or trade union activity.

As was the case for women in other sectors who entered the labour market, a wide range of causes contributed to an unequal relationship in terms of salaries, job performance or sacrifices, such as obtaining two degrees, combining domestic duties with hospital work and, in short, demanding a bigger effort in 'voluntary' work than men.

Over time, this process enhanced gender awareness among those who came from a lower social status. Women progressively rebelled against the hard twenty-four-hour work with barely any breaks to eat or sleep, the rigid uniform, the cleaning of instruments ... Nor was there any scientific recognition of their practice and, besides, they received unjustifiably unequal pay, as female nurses in the provinces in the early years of the twentieth century were earning up to a third of the salary earned by male nurses, and female practitioners and midwives, 50 per cent less than male practitioners. This prompted a form of protest little studied by historians: the publication of numerous articles, notes and writings in both social and health newspapers in which women raise their voices against the wrongful situation.

Women and the press: Identity discourses

The first articles were published by midwives. From an early date, and even before the foundation of their own magazines, midwives began to express their discontent in social publications such as *El Globo* [*The Globe*] and *La Tribuna* [*The Tribune*]. Their articles also appeared in *El Siglo Médico* [*The Medical Century*], the most prestigious medical magazine at the time. In the mid-1970s, one of these texts was signed by the midwife Pilar Jáuregui, who made a clear statement on the role of women in health sciences studies:

> It is a good time for a woman to study obstetrics and the many phenomena that can occur in its practice; thus, endowed with a good spirit of observation, she acquires enough security to face with firm courage the complications of an extremely laborious delivery or the disastrous outcome that some of them quickly present, because only when she is confident enough she will take the measures that will temporarily contain the disease, thus giving enough time for the doctor to arrive, whose duty in law and in fact is to dictate the definitive measures to avoid the catastrophe.
>
> Study also everything concerning the practitioner, because endowed with greater patience and resignation than man, a corps of female nurses could be formed who, after hearing the doctor's orders, would strictly follow them, and possessing the necessary knowledge, would effectively help the doctor's plan, which is often rendered useless due to the imperfection or negligence of those who take care of the sick, especially if there are acute illnesses that demand exquisite care, and in this lies the salvation or loss of the sufferer.
>
> Finally, the woman should know the principle of the ailments of the womb, since it is less embarrassing for the woman to be examined by another woman than by a male doctor, although the moment she recognizes that there is a condition beyond the limits of her observations she should frankly tell the patient, so that the medicine does not delay its remedies, gaining precious moments for a prompt cure.

> And if she can devote a few hours of study and many hours of observation to the hygiene and care of children, she will be able to avoid many cases of scrofula, which affects children so much, and which causes so much havoc.[43]

The period between 1898 and 1929 saw a veritable explosion of newspapers created as a platform for the defence of midwives. The first to be founded were *El Eco de las Matronas* (1898) and *El defensor de la Matrona* [*The Defender of Midwives*] (1921), both published in Barcelona. A few years later was *La Unión Matronal* [*The Midwives' Union*] (1927), a similar newspaper published in Madrid. These publications served as a model for those founded during these years in Zaragoza, Madrid, Barcelona and Seville, such as *La Comadrona* [*The Midwife*], *La Matrona* [*The Midwife*], *La Matrona Moderna* [*The Modern Midwife*], *La Voz Matronal* [*The Midwifery Voice*] or *La Matrona Hispalense* [*The Sevillian Midwife*].[44]

These magazines were usually structured in several sections: a literary section, which included social criticism; a section on legislation, which dealt with labour issues and included the protests and aspirations of midwives; and a third section dedicated to intrusiveness, as well as other articles devoted to current socio-health issues, especially focused on the promotion of maternal and child health.

From the very beginning, women realized the power that the written press granted them. Particularly noteworthy are the articles full of desire for personal and professional autonomy, the denouncements launched against the despotism of mayors and doctors who allowed intrusiveness that was so harmful to society and put public health at risk, and their conflicts with doctors and practitioners over the usurpation of their functions.

43 Álvarez Ricart, *La mujer como profesional de la medicina*, 187–8.

44 All these magazines are located in the Hemeroteca Municipal de Madrid, Biblioteca Nacional and Hemeroteca Municipal de Barcelona, except for *La Matrona Hispalense*, which belongs to a private collection of which we have a digitalized copy thanks to the researchers who located this source: Jesús Manuel García Martínez and Antonio Claret García Martínez. The characteristics and description of this magazine can be found in the article of Manuel Jesús García Martínez and María Dolores Espina Gutiérrez, 'La revista sevillana *La Matrona Hispalense* (1922–1933). A la búsqueda de una identidad profesional', *Híades. Revista de historia de la enfermería* 5–6 (1999), 285–396.

In this regard, the epigraph written by the midwife Rosalía Robles Cerdán in *La Matrona Hispalense* is very illustrative:[45] 'If science is done in the hospital ward, or the classroom of the faculty, it is also done, and surely with more benefit for the patriotic credit, in the printed sheets called newspapers and magazines.'[46]

One of the aspects that women opposed the most was the discourse of 'women's mental inferiority'. The first third of the twentieth century had already accepted the presence of women in medical faculties and professional schools, but the misogynistic idea of women's intellectual inferiority still prevailed in society.

In particular, physiologists and psychiatrists of the alienist school of thought still maintained in the first decade of the century that women were less able to learn:

> In all countries where women persist in pursuing higher studies, it is universally acknowledged that they are excellent pupils, and the shorter the teacher's comprehension, the more willingly he will cultivate the careful determination of his female pupils; determination that is reduced to learning by heart the subjects they are taught.
>
> Therefore, if despite this, the vast mass of the female sex learns very little and soon forget what they have learned, this should not be attributed to poor ability, but lack of goodwill.
>
> The middle-class woman is exclusively self-interested, and if she does not see in education a personal advantage in the near future, she is generally averse to education. Very rarely is there a case of real interest in education.[47]

In contrast to this kind of discourse that predominated until well into the twentieth century, the voices of midwives and female practitioners began to be printed in a multitude of articles and bibliographies, unravelling the cultural error based on the idea of the intellectual incapacity of women and their discrediting in healthcare. At the same time, they demanded greater access to further knowledge in health sciences. They were

45 *La Matrona Hispalense* (April 1929).

46 *La Matrona Hispalense* (April 1929).

47 Paul Julius Moebius, *La inferioridad mental de la mujer* (Valencia: F.ª Sampere y C.ª Editores, n. d. [estimated year of publication: 1904]), 48–51. This book has been found in the Archivo Municipal de Almería.

convinced that training was the only way to achieve the same professional recognition as men. In the 1920s, coinciding with the consolidation of their magazines and professional press, they wrote numerous reflections on the error of some doctors and male practitioners in considering women to be unjustly insecure and impotent for the practice of healthcare. In 1927, the practitioner Flora Senosiain wrote the following letter addressed to the collegiate union of practitioners:

> Some years ago, it seemed that the medical professions (doctors and practitioners) were exclusively for men, and women were considered impotent for it, finding it immoral and shameful for a woman to practice, especially if she was unmarried.
>
> Since women have been authorized to follow the same career as men, there have been many women who have pursued the careers of Doctor and Practitioner, some of whom have reached very important positions in Spain, without there being any evidence that women's delicacy is incompatible with the exercise of this profession, because it is well known that they do not look at the sick with other eyes than those of mother science.
>
> Women, given the faculties with which they are endowed, are very well suited to these careers and can perform them as well as men without anyone finding any fault.
>
> The woman who studies and practises as a Doctor, Practitioner or Midwife is not free as some unjustly believe: on the contrary, she is as delicate and timid as she used to be, but she acquires a certain poise and serenity that comes from the study and practice indispensable to professional activity. She is never too delicate for this, but let it be understood, remaining strong on the rough edges that we can all be presented with.
>
> For the record, it is not my intention to superimpose women over men in any matter, but to demonstrate to anyone who is against it that women do not lose their feelings of modesty in exercising a profession that dignifies and honours those who practices it, but that they place themselves in such conditions of security that they are invincible in the struggles of life amid an environment such as the one that surrounds us today.[48]

Since 1915, when the liberals granted official status to the nursing degree, male practitioners began to show their disagreement and dissatisfaction. The androcentrism prevailing in the more conservative society and the falsely scientific treatises published mainly by psychiatric doctors

48 Flora Senosiain, 'El error de algunos', *El Practicante almeriense* (5 June 1927).

had a strong influence on the idea held, also by the male practitioners, that the new female nurses would harm their competences:

> There is no doubt that the required duties show that nurses are inferior to male practitioners, and it must be determined beforehand, and so it will be a lesser evil.
>
> If we do not succeed in annulling the nurse and reducing her to her true mission as a mechanical assistant, the death of the career of the male practitioner is doomed in the not-too-distant future.[49]

In the late 1920s, the corps of practitioners was still almost entirely male, and its members already had a strong organizational base. The members of the Agrupación Federal [Federal Association] were unwilling to allow nurses to compete on the level of what its members thought belonged exclusively to men. Through their newspaper, *El Practicante*, they launched a fierce campaign between 1927 and 1934 to discredit nurses in light of the imminent extension of the nursing curriculum from two to three years. In the months before this extension, in January and February 1927, the Agrupación Federal mobilized the 7,000 practitioners throughout the country in protest against what they called 'the nurses' lawsuit'. This was stated in one of the numerous written complaints in their newspaper:

> The foundation of the corps of Nurses was a matter of common knowledge and that this, when achieved, would be more than sufficient reason to provoke a great advocacy movement among the Practitioners Class, since the creation of the Corps of Nurses would be very harmful to the Auxiliaries of Medicine and Surgery ... We consider this to be a great detriment to the tired and long-suffering Practitioners Class: because it will evolve in a very detrimental direction for them; because, although it is true that at first they would be little noticed, in time they would be the enemy that would take over our field: and it is necessary, but also urgent, that we all, absolutely all, protest to the Presidency of H.M.'s Government with all due respect.[50]

The conflict between practitioners and nurses was not confined exclusively to one area of competence. Practitioners constantly hindered the professional development of nurses until the arrival of the liberal government

49 *El Practicante salmantino* (March 1927), 3–5.
50 'Ya se sabía', *El Practicante almeriense* (March 1927).

of Romanones in 1915, when they were granted the official diploma. Until then, nurses only worked with the certificates they obtained in the different schools. Practitioners, as had happened previously with conservative doctors and the first qualified midwives, were afraid that nurses could compete with them in the labour market, so they widely disseminated discourses of exclusion and discredit towards them. In 1927 the extension of the nurses' curriculum from two to three years was blocked by the continuous protests and denunciations of practitioners. The conflict was not resolved favourably for nurses until the constitution of the Second Republic.

Conclusions

At the beginning of these pages, we discussed the emergence of the professions known as 'ancillary health classes', analysing the access to education of women who chose the careers of midwife, nurse or practitioner, whose practices were very different to that of medicine and of the practitioners.

The study of the profiles of the first female applicants and their incorporation into the labour market leads us to unravel their aspirations, which were to achieve scientific recognition and independence in their practice, within what was at that time a sexualized and mainly male environment. Their life aspirations coincided with the desires for women's emancipation proclaimed by the first feminist movements in neighbouring countries.

Although it might be thought, even expected, that such female collectives developed medical practices, it is clear that this was not the case. The core of their practice was based on the development of care, the essential feature of which, maintained over the centuries, had focused on life support, communication with the sick and popular health education, rather than healing per se. This practice was renewed in the educational reforms that followed from 1857 until the dawn of the Second Republic, constituting what contemporaries called the 'new professions', 'ancillary health classes' or 'lower hierarchy' groups.

The women who chose these professions were part of the liberal project to reform the care of the sick within the sphere of Charity, once the health establishments had passed from the hands of the Church to the State. In this context, female healthcare professionals encountered numerous obstacles both in terms of access to the corresponding studies and in terms of their professional development. Women's access to the 'New Professions' in the healthcare field transformed the health scenario, motivating women to work in jobs with greater prestige, as they could be promoted as civil servants in the health sector.

From the end of the nineteenth century onwards, especially at the beginning of the twentieth century, a discourse of identity, gender and working-class consciousness took root in these women, strongly asserting their desire for work independence, equal pay and, above all, recognition of their worth in professional practice. These discourses were reflected in the social and professional press that they published and that we have categorized as protests in favour of social equality.

In terms of work, they developed a wide range of care activities, different from those carried out by doctors and practitioners who focused their praxis on the curative and technical aspects of health. The role of women in healthcare was decisive in improving the living conditions of the most disadvantaged strata and the general health of the population, providing new categories of care which are the basis for the nursing and midwifery practice of today.

To conclude these pages, it should be emphasized that the incorporation of those who entered the middle-class health professions encountered a series of difficulties that prevented them from joining the sector with full rights. Although these were old professions, reforms in the field of education made it possible to renew them and present them as 'new professions', destined for the 'Modern Woman' of the new century. The presence of women in these professions meant recognizing attitudes and aptitudes that until then had been 'forbidden' to them due to a 'naturalization' of domestic skills and 'women's inferior mental capacity', something that was increasingly being questioned.

PART IV

Literary and Artistic Professionals

JOAQUÍN ÁLVAREZ BARRIENTOS

Towards Respectability

Ejercicio cómico and the Acting Profession

ABSTRACT
Although for centuries comedy was most commonly referred to as 'exercise', it was recognized as profession (with salaries, contracts and retirement pensions), even though it was not well regarded. In the general imaginary, actors belonged to the marginal. But from being called 'exercise' it was renamed 'profession' and from being 'comics' or 'comedians' they became 'actors', as can be seen in the definitions of the *Diccionario de Autoridades de la Real Academia Española* [*Dictionary of Authorities of the Royal Spanish Academy*], in which until the 1791 edition, the usual word to designate the one who acts in the theatre is 'comedian', while from the 1803 edition onwards this observation disappeared, as the other is imposed as more dignified.

I can also say about them that they earn their bread by the sweat of their brow, with unbearable labour, constantly committing their roles to memory, turned into perpetual Gypsies going from place to place and from tavern to inn, concerned with pleasing others, because their own well-being depends on the pleasure of others. What is more, with their occupation they deceive no one, because they continuously show their wares on the public square to be judged and seen by everyone. The work of the directors is incredible, and the care they take is extraordinary, and they have to earn a great deal so that at the end of the year they are not so deep in debt they are obliged to begin bankruptcy proceedings. And even so, they are as necessary to society as woods, tree-lined walks, watching entertainment, and the things that provide us with decent amusement.[1]

1 Miguel de Cervantes, *El licenciado Vidriera*, English version quoted in Roberto González Echevarría, ed., *Miguel de Cervantes. Exemplary Novels*, trans. by Edith Grossman (New Haven: Yale University Press, 2016), 190.

Achieving citizenship

Between the eighteenth and nineteenth century, many activities underwent processes of dignification and reformulation in order to acquire a modern and professional consideration. This process was in line with the changes that society introduced in the ways of relating to others and in the coordinates of prestige and usefulness required for the trades. Providing them with academic institutions and curricula was part of these processes. The engineers were an exemplary corps in this respect, for they made good use of the political circumstances to establish their school and to portray an image of themselves as essentially competent and useful, fundamentally liberal – although, as in all professions, there were different ideologies. But their image was identified with progress and modernity. In contrast, architects, who also struggled at the turn of the century to improve their training and catch up with the image demanded by the new society – they created their School of Architecture in 1844 – were seen as conservative, absolutist and not as useful as engineers. The confrontation between the two professional groups, which lasted several decades, displays how they struggled to win over public opinion and gain power in a changing landscape.[2]

What they exemplified as the updating of their professions can be found in the military, doctors, etc., in any activity. Bullfighters, for example – in 1796, 'Pepe Hillo' already referred to 'professional bullfighters' – were also familiar with this process. They maintained their structure, the 'cuadrilla', which although based on the guilds, gave way a more modern understanding of the profession, based on the growing society of the spectacle. There was no lack of textbooks – for example, those of 'Pepe Hillo' (1982) and 'Paquiro' (1983) – or the school, founded in Seville in 1830 on the initiative of the Count of La Estrella.[3]

2 Antonio Bonet Correa, Fátima Miranda and Soledad Lorenzo, *La polémica ingenieros-arquitectos en España. Siglo XIX* (Madrid: Colegio de Ingenieros de Caminos, Canales y Puertos/ Ediciones Turner, 1985).

3 Pedro Romero de Solís, ed., *La Real Escuela de Tauromaquia de Sevilla (1830–1834)* (Sevilla: Fundación Real Maestranza de Caballería de Sevilla/ Universidad de Sevilla, 2005).

Comedians experienced a similar process. On the one hand, quite a few of them sought recognition of their activity and to be considered useful citizens, with a strong campaign developed since the mid-eighteenth century continuing with their demands for the use of the word 'citizen' as a term to designate themselves. They sought the abolition of the medieval laws that considered them unworthy. Others also sought recognition and reform of the activity from the establishment of centres that regulated the teaching of the profession. Schools were requested and some were founded in Seville and Madrid,[4] but they operated only until the creation in 1831 of the Escuela de Declamación Española [School of Spanish Declamation]. These educational-professional attempts were accompanied by campaigns aimed at reforming the collective imaginary regarding social consideration, in which actors such as Isidoro Máiquez, Rafael Pérez and Antonio Prieto, the latter two disciples of the former and teachers at the School of Declamation, played a prominent role. In order for the new regulations to be complete, textbooks were published, often translations. The manuals and schools were not always accepted by those comedians who were established in the tradition of learning from their colleagues and on the stage. Those elements brought a new way of acting, corresponding to the new literary, aesthetic and social tastes of the public, once the French model had been rejected.

In addition, to stop learning in the traditional way – orally, through experience and by inheriting a knowledge that was kept as a secret within the companies, in the same way as happened with artisan and manual trades such as quantity surveyors, bricklayers, stonemasons and builders – implied a change in the notion of knowledge. Now there was another idea that involved valuing theory more than practice when it came to learning, leaving experience in a subordinate role, which had to be adjusted to this theoretical model. It took time for these changes to be accepted, but they were another manifestation of the transformations that were taking place at the time, at the turn of the nineteenth century, regarding the teaching of the different trades.

4 Joaquín Álvarez Barrientos, *El actor borbónico (1700–1831)* (Madrid: Asociación de Directores de Escena de España, 2019), 316–49.

Actors were aware that, in order for their profession to be appreciated, they had to change their social habits and social customs. They had to acquire bourgeois manners and be exemplary in their conduct so that they would not be accused of immorality, vileness, etc., all appellatives that had been used in European laws since the Middle Ages. This awareness had been there before, but Andrés Prieto reflected it in the textbook he wrote for the students of the School of Spanish Declamation in the Royal Conservatory [Real Conservatorio] of María Cristina in 1835. In other words, these ideas had become part of the curriculum, they were not longer mere reflections exposed by diverse intellectuals when discussing acting. The chapter that reflects on the value of the stage professional is precisely entitled 'On the dramatic profession', and begins by acknowledging a reality that is fairly widespread, but not sufficiently so, with language that owes much to the lexicon of the Enlightenment: 'The dramatic profession enjoys nowadays political consideration and is part of the fine arts; the stupid preoccupation has disappeared and the comic talent has taken a new direction with the torrents of light that are spreading over all peoples.'[5] The acting profession is respectable because it is useful, the theatre being the most powerful means of 'knowing and spreading national feelings and love for the arts and sciences'.[6]

To illustrate these ideas, which are obvious to him, he then examines the conduct of comedians and the consideration they enjoyed in different times and places, although what interests him is to highlight the opinions that preserved the actor as a common being, like any other citizen: 'the comedians, although they may have vices, as is inherent to the human species, also practice virtues, and the civic virtues to a high degree', and he then goes on to recall the position taken by the actors in Cádiz against the French[7] and recalls that he himself, Dionisio Solís and the Máiquez brothers defended Ferdinand VII from 'the fury of the anthropophagi who comprised

5 For the struggles, strategies and procedures followed until that time, both to consider declamation as a fine art and to dispel prejudices, see Álvarez Barrientos, *El actor borbónico (1700–1831)*, 135–96.

6 Andrés Prieto, *Teoría del arte dramático*, ed., J. Vellón Lahoz (Madrid: Fundamentos/RESAD, 2001) 59.

7 Álvarez Barrientos, *El actor borbónico (1700–1831)*, 157–84.

the greater part of the Napoleon's army'.[8] The usefulness and honour of the comedians is endorsed by other actions in the years after the war, such as the performances 'in favour of the emergencies of the treasury',[9] or in aid of the victims of misfortunes such as the recent earthquake of 1829 in Spanish Levante. All to conclude that they are political subjects: 'The comedians pay their contribution at the same rate as other citizens, they are called up and serve in the army like other citizens … and could it not be said that they do something else? They dedicate part of the proceeds of their work to the relief and consolation of the indigent, for there is no theatre in Spain from which some amount is not taken for orphans, hospitals and other pious works. You see here, then, true citizens, instituted with all the sacred characters of the law.'[10] Naturally, without forgetting their condition as good Christians. For the reputation of comedians to change definitively and for positive opinion to spread, Andrés Prieto saw the need for comedians to be exemplary, since more than any other professional they are exposed to the judgement of public opinion. Thus,

> … it is very essential that the comedian should be penetrated with one great truth, and that is, that being more visible and more in contact with the public that any other person in society, he must necessarily have more circumspection and reserve in his private conduct. Disorder and low inclinations are what most oppose the perfection of the arts, and there is no profession that demands more enthusiasm and elevation in manners and feelings than that of the comedian.
>
> The reputation of the comedian does not lie essentially in his talent alone, but in the considerations relating to his person, his character and his conduct in certain circumstances, for everything is weighed on the scale of opinion. The comedian must observe himself and take great care of his exterior, his composure, and always bear in mind that he will be judged in the theatre according to how he has behaved in society.[11]

Prieto's ideas are similar to those published by Larra in his famous article 'Yo quiero ser cómico' ['I want to be a comedian'][12] and to many of

8 Prieto, *Teoría del arte dramático*, 65–6.
9 Prieto, *Teoría del arte dramático*, 67.
10 Prieto, *Teoría del arte dramático*, 67.
11 Prieto, *Teoría del arte dramático*, 237.
12 *La Revista Española* (1 March 1833).

those published by Bretón de los Herreros in different reviews. All this has its origins in the eighteenth century and an effective and multitudinous formulation in the *Diario Literario-Mercantil* of 26 April 1825, which summarizes almost in the form of a decalogue the opinion regarding the comic shortcomings and possible solutions, always favouring the moral perspective over the profession. The anonymous article entitled '¿Qué haría yo si fuera cómico?' ['What would I do if I were a comedian?'] is addressed first to comedians and then to actresses, indicating artistic aspects, bad habits and customs, and ways of solving them. Once again it is a desiderata, the expression of the desire for an ideal actor, both professionally and morally. A perfect prototype of a human being. The italics are the author's:

> What would I do if I were a comedian?
>
> I would like to possess all the external features that increase the illusion caused by skill without ever being able to replace it; I would like to have a sonorous and pleasant voice, a pure pronunciation, an interesting figure, a ready intelligence and a happy memory.
>
> If I were a comedian, I would spend the whole morning studying my roles, reading poets, historians, travellers, and I would achieve the essential instruction that most of those who pursue a career in the theatre lack.
>
> If I were a comedian, I would punctually attend the reading of the plays to be performed, I would listen without being distracted, I would judge a new play by the impression it made on me as a whole, and without paying attention exclusively to the part I was to play; no respect, no particular recommendation would influence my voice. At rehearsals, which I would never fail to attend, I would sometimes ask the author's advice on how to express his thoughts, and I would not always think I knew more than he did what he intended to say. I would carry modesty so far that I would resign myself to treat him as an equal, and I might even persuade myself that the genius that invents has a kind of superiority over the art that executes.
>
> If I were a comedian, I would have a great respect for the public, and would rather give up an amusement, than be the cause of an announced comedy not being performed on my account. I do not say that I would never be ill, but when the public were told that I was ill, they would see me nowhere else but in bed. Furthermore, my deep respect for the public would not go so far as to submit to their whims and sacrifice to them my dignity as a man and the interest of art.
>
> If I were a comedian, I would teach what I know to young men who were beginning their careers, and I would have the vanity in training artists who might succeed me.

> Nor would I ever refuse to play minor parts, if only to teach those who commonly play the advantage that can be obtained from even the most inferior of them.
>
> If I were a comedian, I would reflect much on my art, and every evening I would take notes of the of the observations I had made on my role, on the effect it had produced on the public, writing them down so that they would not be forgotten, or to compose a memoir at the end of my career, in which I might determine the theory of an art entrusted too long ago to the worries of routine and the uncertainty of tradition.[13]

The writer highlights long-standing faults, above all the lack of professional awareness, while denouncing the attachment to acting traditions and routines, the lack of respect for the public and for oneself. But he also refers to the actresses. As in the previous case, he mixes general and old reflections with concrete and current issues, although he insists more on moral aspects:

> What would I do if I were a comedienne?
>
> When I was in the presence of the public, I would think that there was no less talk in the galleries and stalls of my conduct than of my ability, and that for comediennes there are two reputations, one that they must earn, and one that they may lose.
>
> If I were a comedienne, I would see the theatre as a place where I should seek more to acquire fame than to make a fortune, as a picture designed to show my wit rather than my grace.
>
> If I were a comedienne, I would not confuse the cult of Venus with that of Thalia, and when I had received the apple of Paris, I would not believe that I held in my hand the laurel of Apollo.
>
> If I were a comedienne, I would not think of the costume I was to wear to play a role until I had made myself well aware of its true meaning and character; I would not think I was a queen because I wore a crown, an innocent because I wore white, nor a villager because I wore a necklace of patens.
>
> If I were a comedienne, I would not be intimate with common people, fearing that some of their manners might imperceptibly rub off on me, and I would endeavour to deal with people known for their talent and refinement, from whom I would learn without their knowing it, a portion of the little things which are the mark of good manners, and that perhaps no other kind of friends could teach me.

13 '¿Qué haría yo si fuera cómico?', *Diario Literario-Mercantil* (26 April 1825), 102–3.

If I were a comedienne, I would not want to be able to point out the vices only as I had observed them in others and, on the contrary, I would want to express all the delicate feelings as I experienced them myself.

If I were a comedienne, I would want to be observed, but I would not look at the audience instead of being in the scene and paying attention to the actor who speaks to me and to the action in which I have participate.

If I were a comedienne, I would not engage in any gossip while I was at rehearsal, I would not refuse a pretty piece if my competitor had an interesting part in it, and I would see to it that there were not many spelling mistakes in the note on which I wrote to excuse myself from work on account of being indisposed.

If I were a comedienne, I would know that instinct is not enough to supply skill, and that I ought to have a little more instruction than other women; I would seek it in good books and in the conversation of enlightened people, which I should prefer to the chatter of my passionate ignorant.

If I were a comedienne, I would not want to be one except in the theatre, and I would not want the people who had relations with me to think that I was just trying to play the role that suited me.

If I were a comedienne, I would not pout at a diarist when he gave sound advice, nor at an author because he would not give me at forty the role of a fifteen-year-old girl.

If I were a comedienne, I would think when I played the innocent and the flirtatious that one day I would have to play the role of the mothers and the matchmakers.

If I were a comedienne, I would try to ennoble my profession by the brightness of my triumphs, by my disinterestedness, by my fidelity; I would keep away from me all the gossip, all the intrigues to show myself off and depress others, and I would have more vanity in being a little esteemed by the public than in getting the greatest applause.

If I were a comedienne, I would want to be charitable, kind and good person outside the theatre, so that my retirement from it would not seem a renunciation of all the pleasures of the world.

Finally, if I were a comedienne, I would like to be a Mars in terms of skill, and a Rita Luna in terms of judgement.[14]

14 '¿Qué haría yo si fuera cómico?', *Diario Literario-Mercantil* (26 April 1825), 103. Rita Luna, rival of Mª Rosario Fernández 'La Tirana', left the stage in 1806; Mademoiselle Mars was a French comedian contemporary of Talma, admired by Napoleon Bonaparte (Álvarez Barrientos, *El actor borbónico (1700–1831)*, 302–8).

As when dealing with comedians, the indications are addressed towards both the interpretative aspects and the consideration in which the profession must be held in order to achieve the labour and social dignity required, as Andrés Prieto would later said, both on and off the stage. The anonymous writer proposes a model based on the technical, artistic and moral qualities that the comedian must possess, as well as on the intellectual attitude that he must have, as the manager of a profession in which one is continually learning, but also continually exposed to the critical or prejudiced gaze of others. That is why, more than anyone else, he must be exemplary in his conduct. Reflection on his qualities is a moral reflection on the type of professional desired, on the conditions he lacks and the mistakes he makes, but also on how he is seen, considered and valued by society, as in Larra's 'I want to be a comedian' ['Yo quiero ser cómico']. The reflection was still valid in the twentieth century, when the great actor José Mª Rodero pointed out: 'It is necessary that we actors earn, with our behaviour, with our study, with our dedications, the respect of the public.'[15]

The aim is to achieve the status of citizens, as other professionals already have. Andrés Prieto, in his *Teoría del arte dramático* [*Theory of Dramatic Art*], always considered them as such, as did many eighteenth-century theorists, who used the term to refer to actors. They are citizens because they are useful to the State, because, like everyone else, they collaborate in the good running of society by paying their taxes, enlisting when it is necessary to defend the nation, etc. They also have a School of Spanish Declamation since 1831,[16] sponsored by the queen, which legitimized their profession and displayed them as valid subjects, who have an institution for learning, similar to those for other professions.

15 Andrés Amorós, *Maestros y amigos. Semblanzas y recuerdos* (Madrid: Fórcola Ediciones, 2020), 251.

16 Guadalupe Soria Tomás, *La formación actoral. La Real Escuela de Arte Dramático (1831–1857)* (Madrid: Fundamentos/RESAD, 2010).

The treatment of 'don'

During the formation of the companies in the 1815 season, the musicians referred to the actors as 'debased frauds', which triggered their protest. Isidoro Máiquez led the protest and also asked the authorities to allow them to use the don that the musicians employed. It was not a whim but a reflection that would show whether or not they were worthy professionals, whether or not they were citizens. The lawsuit gave rise to a *Expediente formado a consecuencia de orden del Consejo sobre que la Sala informe en razón de la representación hecha a S. M. por Isidoro Máiquez, a nombre de los cómicos de esta Corte, en solicitud de que se declare que su profesión no es infame, ni ellos, por consiguiente, viles* [*Dossier formed as a result of an order of the Council that the Chamber should report on the representation made to His Majesty by Isidoro Máiquez, on behalf of the comedians of this Court, requesting a declaration that their profession was not infamous, and that they were therefore not vile*].[17] A long consultation began which only in 1819 was resolved in favour of the comedians, although it was indicated that there were old laws that had not been repealed that said the opposite of what had been sentenced. The different reports show the doubts in this respect, as an expression of the diverse attitudes towards the disappearance of the Old Regime and the changes and alterations that entailed. Society was ahead of the law, which protected those who were resistant to change. The verdict, in March 1819, considered that negative ideas about actors were typical of earlier times, and that in the nineteenth century they had to be considered a lawful and honourable profession. It concluded, therefore, that they were honest, citizens like everyone else and they could receive the treatment of don.[18]

However, despite the ruling, routine and custom were not displaced. It is possible that it was not published or did not come into force because in the following years actors did not receive this treatment and only those who were part of the faculty of the School of Declamation from 1831 onwards

17 Archivo Histórico Nacional, Sala de Alcaldes, libro 1408, folios 1312–25.

18 Álvarez Barrientos, *El actor borbónico (1700–1831)*, 188.

received it received. So, they had the right as teachers, not as actors.[19] It is strange that, on the eve of the Liberal Triennium (1820–1823), which used Isidoro Máiquez as a propaganda tool to spread his criticism of absolutism and promote his ideology, this sentence was not implemented. But the truth is that the situation continued in the more or less familiar terms, although some things changed.

There is a well-known anecdote about the actor José Valero, who appeared at the 1832 Carnival ball organized by a society to which 'the most distinguished and vital classes of the population' belonged, as Mesonero Romanos recalls, and who, despite the aforementioned sentence, was expelled from the party. The actor addressed to the king and the latter ordered that he had to be invited the following day by means of 'a personal ticket', as was done. Mesonero reflects on 'the unjust disdain or contempt in which the stage profession was held until recent times, and what was then meant by a comedian, who was denied even the petty don'.[20] Later in the nineteenth century respectful treatment of comedians became widespread, actresses even married aristocrats and Spanish grandees, such as María Guerrero and Fernando Díaz de Mendoza.

Myth and respectability

Besides institutional and administrative strategies to ensure respect for their profession, comedians used other resources common to all trades. One of them was to create a pantheon of illustrious actors to vindicate the value of their activity, in the same way that artists, intellectuals and politicians did in their respective fields. In this they were no exception, for the same happened in other countries. As many professions had their patron saint, they also had one, in this case a layman: Roscius, an actor praised by Cicero who achieved great prestige in Rome, symbolizing all the values

19 Soria Tomás, *La formación actoral*, 419.

20 Ramón Mesonero Romanos, *Memorias de un setentón* (Madrid: Castalia, 1994), 443.

and aspects desired to shape his image: social integration, artistic respect, usefulness, prestige and economic power.

Among all Spanish actors, the one who stood out as a true myth was Isidoro Máiquez, as he embodied all the elements to become a reference figure, both for his successes and his work on behalf of the acting profession, and for what he suffered at the hands of absolutism. The liberals of 1820 appropriated his figure, controversial for different reasons, ambiguous at certain points in his career, and made him a central element of Liberalism and its cultural and political demands. Thus, having become a valid point of reference for the new times, the figure of the actor Isidoro Máiquez gave artistic, moral and political prestige to comedians,[21] as well as to the liberals themselves, who consequently had a martyr to their cause. And so it was seen at the time of his death in 1820, when poems and articles were dedicated to him but, above all, they vindicated his work to modernize the acting profession (and Spain, by extension), facing the supposed difficulties that the Old Regime placed in the way of this process. The article writers wanted a broad and lasting recognition of the figure: tributes, busts, etc., to immortalize his memory, and for the government to protect his orphan daughter, as a means of distinguishing themselves from an earlier absolutist political action that was rejected. The death of Máiquez was an opportunity for liberals to display their political project, to exemplify the difference.

Several obituaries were then published about the actor. On the one hand, they mythologized him, on the other, they were a praise of melancholy, as a lost opportunity for regeneration, as so often happens in Spain. Along with the one appeared in El Universal [The Universal] and some other already discussed,[22] is especially interesting the one appeared in *El Cetro Constitucional. Semanario Político* [*The Constitutional Sceptre. Political Weekly*], in issues two and three. In this, the actor is synonymous with 'the good and useful' in Spain and, proving the efficacy of the romantic

21 Emilio Cotarelo y Mori, *Isidoro Máiquez y su época*, ed., J. Álvarez Barrientos (Madrid: Asociación de Directores de Escena de España, 2009); Álvarez Barrientos, *El actor borbónico (1700–1831)*, 135–96.

22 Joaquín Álvarez Barrientos, 'Emilio Cotarelo, Isidoro Máiquez y la melancolía', in Emilio Cotarelo Mori, *Isidoro Máiquez y su época* (Madrid: Asociación de Directores de Escena, 2009), 58–66 (9–90).

constructions that are so popular, he is presented as a hero, someone lacking resources and education, but with great genius for overcoming the adverse circumstances that hinder his intuition. Máiquez is a lay genius, and individualist, unique because he possesses qualities not found in others:

> Gifted with an elegant figure, an expressive physiognomy, a sensitive heart, a lively imagination and an energetic character, he also had (when he reached the age of reason) such an observant spirit that he acquired such a fine and delicate touch that allowed him to express properly what he knew how to feel and distinguish, before learning it. [23]

The romantic-liberal construction continues by indicating that he could barely read in his youth and that he learned to write at advanced age; that he 'reflected and observed' and came to the conclusion that he should 'seek in the study of nature the infallible means of imitating with true the various affections which he had to express'. Thus, the author comes to show him as someone who has almost had a project, with a visionary plan to reform the theatres, that is to say, to regenerate Spain through art, for which Máiquez clamours, even if he has to confront popular taste. He did not hesitate to carry out his plan because his mission was to correct the faults and mistakes of both the comedians and the public: 'He was also convinced that in order to bring about the reform he planned, and to become a true comedian himself, it was essential to begin by shocking public opinion, sowing rebuffs in order to reap applause and a deserved reputation in due course.' So, the hero does not hesitate to immolate himself, even if the public does not understand him, because his understanding of the facts goes further by having a historical vision/mission that the vulgar lacks.

The construction of the referential myth, both for professionals and politicians, continued in the next issue of the weekly. The actor is famous, arrogant because he is independent, knows what he wants and that he is right, convinced of his decision and his purpose, he knows what his destiny is and that he is able to bend the audience. Sacrifice took him to Paris, where, without knowing French, he was helped by the Countess-Duchess

23 All the following references in 'Necrología', *El Cetro Constitucional. Semanario Político* 2 (1820), 32–6.

of Benavente; there he rubbed shoulders with great actors such as Talma and with writers, he 'rectified his ideas' and achieved a method which, without imitating the French, would be useful in Spain. 'He created a new acting system, more natural, more varied and the only one that suited the Spanish audience.' Giving the observations he makes, the person responsible for the obituary considers the profession of actor to be an essential one in the nation, showing the degree of civilization achieved, as well as the political implications of the activity, as governments have often made use of comedians, along with writers, to spread their plans and projects.

According to the liberal perspective, with his new method Máiquez portrayed society, he showed how the triumph of merit, even if it was individual, benefited everyone, because the actor gave himself to his audience. But the character of Isidoro and the liberal consideration of his profession, the very fact of professionalizing the activity, clashed with the absolutist governments. To make a biography/eulogy of the comedian was to criticize the previous political period. Since the eighteenth century, at least, there was a struggle for acting to be understood as a 'liberal art', so that quite a few artists of the time, Máiquez among them, tried to achieve the necessary independence to develop their abilities, which the court system of artistic production, based on protection and commissions, restricted because it also treated them as servants, not as equals, within the aristocracy of the intelligentsia. Although this court system was beneficial for many, it did not allow for the display of creative possibilities, subject to fashions and conventions. Máiquez fought against this, as well as against the excessive control exercised by authorities over comedians, and for all this he was punished and exiled, a time he used as an opportunity for strengthen himself emotionally. But by that time, he was already a public figure, of whom interested spectators were informed. The obituary ended claiming for the honours due to the genius, the recognition of the 'glory and national enlightenment' Isidoro is, the monument that will remind future generations of him and will save him from the indifference of the forgotten homeland, and ends with the sonnet that Leandro Fernández de Moratín – in exile – dedicated to him on his death.

Another 'Soneto en la muerte del inimitable actor español Isidoro Máiquez' ['Sonnet on the death of the inimitable Spanish actor Isidoro

Máiquez'] was published in *El Cetro Constitucional* [*The Constitutional Sceptre*] on 27 March 1820, alluding to one of the actor's greatest and most conflictive success, in order to highlight, in case it had not been clear, the appropriation and construction of the character. He had performed in 1813, and other occasions, the tragedy *Roma Libre* playing Brutus, always with a good reception, sometimes even with exalted responses from the public, who took the streets inflamed with the desire for freedom. Mesonero Romanos recalled in his memoirs that when the actor recited certain verses of the play 'the audience, electrified, rose en masse to applaud and cheer', so that 'the soldiers of the guard took up arms' to control the disorder.[24] That is why, in the sonnet, from among the 'illustrious shadows' that chorus and applaud him, one speaks to him like this: 'Take seat, he said, beside me,/ that Brutus I am, liberator of Tibre./ Split mine the laurel with thy brow/ that, although for Rome I was a bloody father,/ no greater than you, I was no freer'.[25] The author is Dionisio Solís, friend and collaborator of the comedian, political colleague and responsible for much of his fame and success. He had adapted the plays to his abilities and had taught him the new art of acting, leaving aside the repeated reference to Talma. The political reading of the figure, as can be seen, always prevails.

Around the same time, *El Constitucional* of 25 March 1820 also gave news of his death and, always in liberal terms, added a new perception. Spain was in a new era of justice for all and recognition of merit as opposed to caprice or cronyism. In this new era, it seemed that classes had disappeared, as genius could be praised, regardless of where one belonged:

> Spanish theatre has suffered an irreparable loss. The famous Isidoro Máiquez passed away in Granada (after a long and painful illness) on the 18 of this month at half past one in the morning, mourned by all those who loved national glory and, consequently, the fine arts. We gather as much news as may be connected with the events of his life, in order to give our readers an idea, if not of his regular merit, at least such as may be sufficient to qualify him; and we are persuaded that this homage will be pleasing to them, for the day has now come when we may with impunity pay due praise to true genius, whatever the class to which the individual belongs.[26]

24 Mesonero Romanos, *Memorias de un setentón*, 257.

25 'Necrología', *El Cetro Constitucional. Semanario Político* 3 (1820), 3–20.

26 *El Constitucional* 4 (25 Mars 1820), 323.

New times, old hopes. The mythification of the actor and his recognition as an outstanding member of the comedy profession continued in newspapers such as *El Universal* and *El Censor*, an example of the cult of personality of great men and the nascent concept of celebrity, which manifested itself through a theatrical tribute in September 1821 entitled *The apotheosis of Isidoro. An allegorical composition to be performed at the Prince's theatre on the night destined for the benefit in honour of his memory* [*El apoteosis de Isidoro. Composición alegórica para representarse en el teatro del Príncipe en la noche destinada para el beneficio en obsequio de su memoria*]. The earnings would be used to form a dowry for his daughter. The piece ended with these verses:

> Free Spain from infamous chains, to her children a thousand prizes are offered, and to her glory undoubtedly deserves the impulse that she actively gives them. With the arts the nation prospers: Spaniards, without them there is nothing; Appreciate them and Europe, in admiration, will give you the palm of enlightened[27]

As can be seen, the rise of the 'Spanish Roscius' is also the rise of civilization and arts, of which they are an expression and, in particular, of the comic art. This process continued with different acts, the most important milestone being probably the construction of a monument, funded by the brothers Julián and Florencio Romea and Matilde Díaz. It was in Granada, the city where the actor died, placed on 17 May 1839 with the motto 'Gloria al genio' [Glory to the genius] and an inscription with several of the titles in which he stood out: *Otelo*, *Óscar*, *Los hijos de Edipo*, *Fenelón*, *García del Castañar* and others.[28] It was made by José Contreras and it is surely the first monument erected to an actor, which should be understood as a gesture of legitimization and professional pride, as a sign of respect for one of the tutelary angels of the profession. Angels and myths that come and go, some forgotten when others are born, and who have different functions depending on the period: Máiquez, Julián Romea, Margarita Xirgu, Fernando Fernán Gómez, etc.

27 Cotarelo Mori, *Isidoro Máiquez y su época*, 475.

28 Antonio Reyes, *Julián Romea. El actor y su contorno (1813–1868)* (Murcia: Academia Alfonso X el Sabio, 1977).

The School of Spanish Declamation

The creation of the School of Spanish Declamation, first as a department chair within the María Cristina Conservatory in 1831, was a response to the establishment of cultural, entertainment and educational centres, whether private or not, typical of the liberal period, inherited form the Bourbon cultural policy of the eighteenth century. In addition to the organizations already existent in the eighteenth century and the Museum of Paintings [Museo de Pinturas] (1819), there were the Ateneo [Athenaeum] in 1822, the Conservatorio de Artes y Oficios [Conservatory of Arts and Crafts] (1824), the museums of Artillery and Engineering in 1827, a split of the Military Museum created in 1803, the Real Gabinete Topográfico [Royal Topographical Cabinet] (1831), the Liceo Literario y Artístico [Literary and Artistic Lyceum] (1837) and others, only to mention the Madrid centres. A policy which, in the professional order, was to contemplate the different laws and reforms of education until 1857, when the Law of Public Instruction, which gave declamation the category of higher education, was passed, taking into account the law of the minister Alejandro Mon in 1843.

The name Escuela de Declamación Española [School of Spanish Declamation] and not Escuela Española de Declamación [Spanish School of Declamation] emphasize that what was taught was the national mode or modality of acting, as opposed to the French, Italian and other models. From the eighteenth century onwards, people talked about a Spanish-style declamation, French-style declamation, etc., to differentiate between the various schools, in clear national evidence. A nationalism that reached all the arts.

Studying at the School gave professional and moral distinction and certain employment facilities that were not always fulfilled. The careers of several of these students were brilliant or quite brilliant, such as those of Julián Romea and his brother Florencio, the comedian Mariano Fernández, the Boldún brothers, the buffo Antonio Arderíus and others.[29] The analysis

29 Soria Tomás, *La formación actoral*, 156–81.

of the lists of actors hired shows that the School produced a good number of actors who established a network linked to theatre companies and sometimes important politicians, as in the case of Julián Romea. So, it partly fulfilled its objective of being an influence for the situation of actors in the labour market.

Moreover, if the School of Spanish Declamation aimed to improve the social and professional image of actors, it also sought to prepare comedians who exemplified the ideal, desired model of performer: respectful of religion and the king. Some of them, especially those involved in teaching, represented this idea well and were recognized with appointments and distinctions. Carlos Latorre, José García Luna and Julián Romea were made Supernumerary Knights of the Order of Charles III in 1847, and Antonio de Guzmán in 1856.[30]

However, while some prospered and achieved success thanks to their time at the School, there were other who criticized it for being useless in achieving the objectives for which it was created. This was the case of Gaspar Gómez Trigo, a pupil who devoted himself to composing zarzuelas and in 1850 made a harsh criticism, along the same lines as that published years after its foundation (on 1 March 1836 in *El Español*) by Mariano José de Larra, regarding the fact that the students only learned the method and the clichés of the teacher. He also denounced the lack of ambition of the institution and their faculty, content with their salary, their treatment as don and littler more.

> Two chairs of declamation were created; each was allocated six thousand *reales*, or something similar, by fees; two professors were appointed, individuals from the companies of Madrid; they were given 'don' in the offices of appointment [the fact that I emphasize this shows the novelty of it], and boys on the school seats, and they were told: 'Teach there as much as you know; you already have a house, uniform, don and six thousand *reales*; the theatre is already protected; you will see the actors that come out.' And we have already seen it, by the way.[31]

30 Soria Tomás, *La formación actoral*, 419.

31 Mariano José de Larra, 'Teatros', *El Español* (1 Mars 1836).

Gómez Trigo indicated that there was no teaching, except 'to read with some sense';[32] that, of the two hours set aside for declamation, one was lost and the other was used to recite fragments of comedies. He complained that there were no qualifications or requirements for entry and all applicants were accepted, even if they had no skills. Finally, it was a waste of time to attend classes because one only learnt vices and affectations. Moreover, having gone through it did not qualify one for employment.

However, the critical student went beyond his invective and offered solutions to improve the training of the comedian, whom he considered to be a professional with an important 'mission' in society. His recipe was to eliminate all those who were not qualified and to hire teachers who were not actors, so that the students would develop their abilities and not just learn their tics. A commission should be created to supervise classes, programmes and the selection of students, who should already have a basic knowledge of history and grammar. There had to be a good theatre to rehearse and perform, which would also serve to provide income, and a library. Finally, it was necessary to establish a curriculum that would set the length of the degree, hold exams and award a diploma at the end of the studies that would be useful for recruitment in theatres. All this would contribute to forgetting the discredit of the profession and to reducing the number of those who dedicated themselves to the theatre believing it to be an easy career, when it is not, and formed the 'not small battalion of comedians in Spain'.

In the middle of the century, Gaspar Gómez Trigo still demanded from the authorities much of what was demanded decades ago, and it gave the impression that nothing had changed, even though this was not true, but it is typical of those periods when something has not yet established and it is not possible to judge it clearly. Of course, the situation was not the same in Madrid as in the provinces, nor in a stable company as in one travelling; the latter continued to drag with them all the bad image and lack of professionalism that in other companies and other areas, if not disappeared, was greatly reduced. In the case of travelling companies, we can speak of

32 Following references in Gaspar Gómez Trigo, *La declamación: Opúsculo* (Madrid: Establecimiento tipográfico de D. Francisco García Padrós, 1850), 49–56.

'another' professionalism, since they had to perform with very scarce means and resources, in premises without possibilities, in geographies far for the aesthetic trends, amidst prejudices, etc.

In any case, the fact that actors had a school, which later existed in other capitals, marked a before and an after in the consideration of actors, whether social, artistic or professional. At the same time, for some of them it provided a solution or continuity of employment once their career on the stage was over. There were those who combined both activities, precisely in decades of profound professional changes. Being a teacher in the last stage of their lives, as happened, for example, to Carlos Latorre, Rafael Pérez, Joaquín Caprara, Julián Romea, to name just well-known actors, showed the transition they had undergone, the prestige achieved, their promotion in the social ladder. Being a teacher at the School symbolized recognition as a useful person, as a citizen, endorsed by the Crown itself.[33] This is the case of Romea.

Julián Romea or the triumph of the actor

Julián Romea was one of the first students at the School of Declamation. He came from a well-off family whose wealth declined. He began to work as an actor in 1833, using the naturalistic method employed by Máiquez, after having spent two years in the classes of Carlos Latorre. The narrative of his life is relatively similar to that of his Murcian fellow. Both share an already consolidated biographical and psychological model, the one of the hero turned myth: poverty, genius, arrogance, independence, solitude in the great talent and the awareness from very early on being destined to an unavoidable mission. For Isidoro is to renew declamation; for Romea, practically the same. Moreover, he takes the opportunity to link himself to this outstanding figure, who was a renovator of the stage and is considered unique: 'Since I was a boy – he wrote in 1866 in *Heroes at the*

33 Joaquín Álvarez Barrientos, 'Introducción', in Rafael Pérez, *Madrid en 1808. El relato de un actor* (Madrid: Ayuntamiento de Madrid, 2008), 13–67.

Theatre – an instinct has kept me away from this [acting] routine and I have anxiously sought something else, which I did not even know how to formulate, but which I felt I needed.'[34] With these words he presents himself as an enlightened man called to revolutionize performance. And, like Máiquez, he is alone in the world, but he has charisma, a new invention that is already well established, thanks to which he can face adversity and triumph.[35]

The often novelized biographies written about both of them coincide in their difficult beginnings, their generosity, their capacity for friendship despite their haughtiness, their unfortunate marriages. However, they differ when it comes to death. If the death of Isidoro was in exile and abandoned almost by everyone, buried in Granada almost in oblivion, the death of Romea was among friends, with a mass burial in the streets of Madrid, a carriage whose ribbons were carried by different personalities from politics and culture, stopping at different places such as the Spanish Theatre [Teatro Español]. From the balconies of the theatre, decorated with black hangings as a sign of respect and mourning, the actresses watched his passing and said goodbye from that coliseum and the Teatro de la Cruz [Theatre of the Cross]. It was the higher recognition, as the capital was brought to a standstill to pay tribute to the actor. If Máiquez was the 'Spanish Roscius', Romea is the 'Spanish Talma'; if for the former there were requests for distinctions and a bust to immortalize him, the famous Ernesto Rossi, from the Barcelona stage where he was working when he heard the news of his death, also asked for a monument to his memory.[36]

When he died in 1868, the notion of 'great man' was established among the population and in the routine of institutional recognition, so it was possible to make such great manifestations of affirmation and gratitude, along with the ritual that accompanied them. Something similar had happened in the eighteenth century when María Ladvenant died on 1 April 1787, to the extent that part of Atocha Street, other neighbouring streets

34 Julián Romea, *Manual de declamación para uso de los alumnos del Real Conservatorio de Madrid. Los héroes del teatro* (Madrid: Fundamentos/RESAD, 2009), 193.

35 Edward Berenson and Eva Giloi, eds, *Constructing Charisma. Celebrity, Fame, and Power in Nineteenth-Century Europe* (New York/Oxford: Berghahn, 2010).

36 Antonio Reyes, *Julián Romea*, 212–16.

and the Square of Antón Martín were filled with people eager to accompany her on her last journey; she lived in Fúcar Street. The news was so talked-about that the expulsion of the Jesuits, known on the same day, went unnoticed.[37] Unlike the Romea case, this demonstration was spontaneous, not organized by the administration. It took a hundred years for an actor to receive similar, albeit greater, treatment: actors, at least some of them, had entered the group of individuals and professionals entitled to this kind of distinction granted by the State. But it is important to keep in mind that Romea, besides being an actor, was a writer and an academic; a member of the order of Charles III, whose blue star-spangled mantle enveloped the coffin; and a gentleman of the king; he had achieved honours that no comedian had ever achieved before. But, even so, it is possible that the funeral did not so much recognize the distinguished man (academic, courtier, etc.) as the one better known as an actor, without forgetting, however, his contact with rulers, hardly explored by critics, as his two sisters married politicians: Cándido Nocedal and Luis González Bravo. It implied extending the network of relations and contacts.[38]

Romea was a self-made man, as were the two journalists and politicians, Máiquez, Matilde Díaz, the actor´s wife, an so many others in the profession. All of them are examples of the social mobility that happened in Madrid society at least since the eighteenth century. In the field of theatre, mobility has to do with the abandonment of the aforementioned old court system, with the forgetting of the old structure of theatrical production protected by institutions such as the Town Hall and with the assumption of a private business system, more risky that the previous one, in which ups and downs were frequent. An example of this happened to Romea himself in the Teatro Español, where he worked for twenty seasons,

37 Emilio Cotarelo Mori, *Actrices españolas en el siglo XVIII. María Ladvenant y Quirante y María del Rosario Fernández La Tirana*, ed., J. Álvarez Barrientos (Madrid: Asociación de Directores de Escena de España, 2007); Álvarez Barrientos, *El actor borbónico (1700–1831)*, 106–8.

38 José Cano Benavente, 'Romea. Nocedal. González Bravo (Vértices de un afecto fraternal)', *Julián Romea. Primer centenario (1813–1868)* (Murcia: Ayuntamiento de Murcia, 1968), 115–29.

thirteen of them as businessman.[39] Trade liberalization had begun around 1823 and two years later it was a reality against which those comedians who preferred the known security of the old system rebelled. The supporters of this new business vision were called 'speculators'.[40] They were led by Juan de Grimaldi, a soldier who arrived in Spain with the Hundred Thousand Sons of Saint Louis and made his fortune as a theatrical businessman.[41] The business model was abandoned until its revival in 1836. A definitive change that gave way to the wide range of theatrical manifestations of the eighteenth century, from opera to zarzuela, going through the género chico [little genre], buffo, high comedy, etc.

The increasing number of theatres, actors, singers and musicians in that century implied the definitive professionalization of the world of theatre, its entry into the economic structures of supply and demand that existed in other labour areas, as well as the creation of societies to defend the economic rights, especially of comedy writers and musicians, who were better organized than comedians, as Julio Nombela recalls in his memories.[42]

39 Jesús Rubio Jiménez, 'Introducción', in Julián Romea, *Manual de declamación para uso de los alumnos del Real Conservatorio de Madrid. Los héroes del teatro* (Madrid: Fundamentos/RESAD, 2009), 21–2.

40 Joaquín Álvarez Barrientos, 'Introducción' to Rafael Pérez, *Madrid en 1808*, 29.

41 David T. Gies, *Theatre and Politics in Nineteenth-Century Spain. Juan de Grimaldi as Empresario and Government Agent* (New York: Cambridge University Press, 1988).

42 Julio Nombela, *Impresiones y recuerdos* (Madrid: Tebas, 1976), 751–5.

AINHOA GILARRANZ-IBÁÑEZ

'Art Is Confused with Trade'

The Defence of the Painter as a Profession in the Spanish Fine Arts (1833–1868)

ABSTRACT
Starting from the inaccuracy of the notion of 'hegemonic masculinity', this chapter studies one of the masculine identities of Spanish liberalism. Specifically, I study the image and discursive tools used by male painters to defend their professional status during the reign of Isabel II (1833–1868). I have analysed the significance of the employment in the building of their identity. Also, I have compared if these discourses were similar in other professionals' groups as lawyers, engineers and physicians To do so, I study the construction of their identity through three main discursive approaches: their position against artisans, their defence of study against innate genius and their image as male artists against female ones.

Introduction[1]

This chapter studies one of the professional identities of Spanish liberalism, that of an artist. Specifically, I focus on the self-representation of artists and on the discursive tools used by male painters to defend their professional status during the reign of Isabel II (1833–1868). I analyse how they construed their identity through three main discursive approaches: differentiating themselves from artisans, defending training and hard work against innate genius and insisting on their image as male artists against female ones.

1 This work is part of the research project entitled 'Cultura del honor, política y esfera pública en la España Liberal (1833–1890)' (ref. number PGC2018-093698-B-I00) and financed by the Spanish Ministry of Science, Innovation and Universities.

The concept of 'hegemonic masculinity' has evolved since its creation in the 1980s to the present day. Formulated within the discussions of a group of researchers in Australia, it refers to a series of patterns that men and masculinity present in a given socio-cultural context.[2] According to this original notion, in any society there would be one hegemonic masculinity and several subordinate ones. That is, one that represents ideal behaviours and others that do not meet these standards. However, recent works in gender studies have criticized this concept, advocating the co-existence of several masculinities with no fixed hierarchy among them.[3] My chapter intends to be a contribution to this debate.

In the construction of masculine identities in the new political paradigm of liberal constitutionalism, property and activity played an essential role. Profession became one of the ways through which a man could inscribe himself into the ideal of an active citizen. The social status of different professions varied greatly, though. This plurality in terms of public acknowledgement, prestige and social standing, resulted in a variety of ways in which each profession was construed as masculine.[4] Since the eighteenth century, some figures – such as writers – were turning their activity into a profession, without being able to rely on the link to a specific education,

2 There is a broad framework of scholarship on the concept of 'hegemonic masculinity'. For its origin, formulation and practical application, see Mike Donaldson, 'What Is Hegemonic Masculinity?', *Theory and Society* 22/4 (1993), 643–57; Robert W. Connell and James W. Messerschmidt, 'Hegemonic Masculinity: Rethinking the Concept', *Gender and Society* 19/6 (2005), 829–59.

3 For a historiographical analysis of the latest lines of research, see Nerea Aresti, 'La historia de las masculinidades, la otra cara de la historia de género', *Ayer* 117 (2020), 333–47. For concrete studies, see Henar Gallego, ed., *Feminidades y masculinidades en la historia de género* (Granada: Comares, 2018); Nerea Aresti and Darina Martykánová, eds, *Masculinidades, nación y civilización en la España contemporánea*, special issue of *Cuadernos de Historia Contemporánea* 39 (2017).

4 For a recent study on physicians and engineers, see Darina Martykánová and Víctor M. Núñez-García, 'Ciencia, patria y honor: los médicos e ingenieros y la masculinidad romántica en España (1820–1860)', *Studia Historica* 38 (2020), 45–75. For artists, see María Victoria Alonso, *Representaciones de masculinidad y asociacionismo. El retrato de artista en la pintura española del siglo XIX* (PhD thesis, Universidad de Valladolid, 2018), 24–8.

on social practices and selection mechanisms of a guild or on the capital available in the industrial sphere.[5] Artist, such as painters, sculptor or engravers, were among these liberal professionals who fought for public respect for their work, thus defending also their social standing. They had to combat the stereotypes associated with their professional practice due to the limiting legislation derived from antiquated regulations. The artistic field was in the midst of a process of change. The old patrons – Church and Monarchy – were not as active in promoting artists as they had been during the Early Modern Period; above all, they did not dominate the field anymore. The art market was opening up to a new clientele. However, the rules and legislation that regulated the practice of the fine arts – the regulations of the academies themselves or the legislation concerning the sale and purchase of artistic works – hindered artistic production. The painters' fight also had a clear class dimension: they strove to clearly situate themselves above artisans, establishing a sharp division between a routine, mechanical trade (*oficio*) and their 'noble art' that could only be performed by a sensitive and creative man of distinction.

In this context, Eugenio de Ochoa published an article in defence of painting as a liberal profession. In a well-known publication specialized in the fine arts, he spoke of the confusion that the very concept of painter caused in society. He wondered why the Spanish vocabulary did not have a word to differentiate the painter who practised 'a mechanical trade' from the one who practised 'a noble art'.[6] The words of the author, a relative of the painters José and Federico de Madrazo, clearly show his concern for the social standing of artists. This was a centuries-old struggle, started in the Early Modern Period and raging during the nineteenth century, to differentiate an artist from a craftsman.

5 Raquel Sánchez, *Mediación y transferencias culturales en la España de Isabel II. Eugenio de Ochoa y las letras europeas* (Madrid: Iberoamericana Vervuert, 2017), 63.

6 Eugenio de Ochoa, 'Pintor-Pintura', *El Artista* (1 April 1835), 256.

'Art is confused with trade, the artist with the artisan'

A clear differentiation between design and intellect, on the one hand, and manual skill, on the other, in artistic creation appeared during the Early Modern Era, with a greater value ascribed to the former. Treatises defending the painting and the painter as a creative genius became popular from the seventeenth century onwards. Furthermore, other practices such as the author's signature highlighted the individual creation over the collective work carried out by the guild.[7] Despite these early attempts, the concept of art continued to encompass both mechanical and fine arts throughout the eighteenth century. Certainly, there were many attempts to monopolize the term 'artist' for an individual creative genius, situated above the artisan in terms of prestige and social standing. Specialized publications, such as Jacques Lacombe's *Dictionnaire portatif des Beaux Arts* [*Portable Dictionary of Fine Arts*] (1756) or the *Dictionnaire des Artistes* [*Dictionary of Artists*] (1776), written by the Abbé de Fonteneay, presented the artist in its modern conception.[8] However, the boundaries between craftsman and artist were still blurred in the nineteenth century. Eugenio de Ochoa wondered in 1835 how 'a language as rich as Castilian' could use the same word, *painter*, to designate the one 'who immortalized the surrender of Breda' (Velázquez) and 'the obtuse labourer who, with a brush in one hand and a bucket in the other, covers doors and windows with green or lilac'.[9] His conclusion was clear: 'art is confused with trade, the artist with the artisan'.

Artists defended their place among the educated – or, rather, cultured – social elite. Therefore, their self-fashioning as artists emphasized the intellectual nature of their work. This rhetorical tool was common in

7 Luis Arciniega, 'La consideración del artista en inscripciones, medallas y otras memorias ocultas', in María del Mar Albero and Manuel Pérez, eds, *'Yngenio y arte': elogio, fama y fortuna de la memoria del artista* (Madrid: Fundación Universitaria Española, 2018), 228–9.

8 Nathalie Heinich, 'De l'apparition de 'l'artist' à l'invention des 'beaux-arts'', *Revue d'histoire moderne et contemporaine* 37 (1990), 10–11.

9 Eugenio de Ochoa, 'Pintor–Pintura', *El Artista* (1 April 1835), 256.

other liberal professions, too. For example, physicians and engineers, whose work also required manual skills, stressed their scientific knowledge as essential not only for their professional practice, but also for the good of the society and the progress of the nation.[10] As for artists, this exaltation of intellectual and spiritual elements, including sensibility, is clearly visible in their portraits and engravings. In 1835, the magazine *El Artista* [*The Artist*] showed two opposing images entitled 'el pintor de antaño' [the painter of yesteryear] and 'el pintor de hogaño' [the painter of today].[11] The first illustration depicts a painter more closely linked to the practice of craftsmanship. The artisan appears in his studio surrounded by his working tools, such as an easel, oils, brushes, etc. In contrast, the other image shows the modern painter. The artist is now depicted pensive in front of his canvas. He is staring at his work, reflecting on its composition and surrounded by books of renowned authors such as Byron, Dante and Victor Hugo.

This exaltation of intellectual labour was also present in the representation of their workspaces. The artist's studio went from being a workshop where he appeared executing his pieces, as in Johannes Vermeer's *The Art of Painting* (1666), to becoming a social space where he demonstrated his sensibility and intellectual knowledge. The representations of their ateliers aimed to show the eighteenth- and nineteenth-century humanist ideal of the artist as creator and sensitive, cultivated man.[12] A clear example of this is the painting by Antonio María Esquivel, *Contemporary poets. A reading by Zorrilla in the painter's studio* (1846). The workspace became an important

10 Darina Martykánová and Víctor M. Núñez-García, 'Ciencia, patria y honor', 50–7; Darina Martykánová, 'La profession, la masculinité et le travail. La représentation sociale des ingénieurs en Espagne pendant la deuxième moitié du xixe siècle', in Antoine Derouet and Simon Paye, eds, *Les Ingénieurs, unité, expansion, fragmentation (XIXe et XXe siècles). Tome I. La production d'un groupe social* (Paris: Classiques Garnier, 2018), 79–102.

11 Federico de Madrazo, 'El pintor de antaño' and 'El pintor de hogaño', *El Artista* (1 April 1835).

12 For the representation of Spanish artists' studios in the nineteenth century, see Inés Antón, 'Artista sin taller es como pájaro sin nido: la imagen de los estudios de pintores españoles del siglo XIX a través de las artes plásticas: Algunos ejemplos representativos', in María del Mar Albero and Manuel Pérez, eds, *'Yngenio y arte'*, 595–616.

social factor in the artist's identification as a professional. On his trip to Rome in 1840, the painter Federico de Madrazo wrote to his father that he 'chose two other rooms better than the first ones he had selected'.[13] These were not only 'more suitable for painting', but also 'nobler and more convenient for receiving those who come to see me in the future'. Of course, the painter's studio was a working space. But it was also considered the main setting for socializing, attracting new clients and selling some of his work.

The Madrazos, one of the most influential family sagas in the Spanish cultural sphere during the reign of Isabel II, were among the leading defenders of the arts and artists. Federico de Madrazo founded the journal *El Artista* with his brother-in-law, Eugenio de Ochoa. They used it to denounce the low value that Spanish society placed on artists and the discredit that their comparison with guild work or craftsmanship entailed. For Pedro de Madrazo, another member of this artistic family, in Spain 'everyone ignores the difficulty and great study that the fine arts need, but also their nobility. They thus lack accuracy and grossly vilify the worthiest employment of a person, confusing the artist, the man of genius, … with the prosaic artisan'.[14]

The struggle for acknowledgement of the artist's intellectual work went beyond an issue of ego. It was a class issue and was closely linked to political identity, too. Social consideration was intrinsically connected to political participation. The constitutional regime in Spain established a range of economic and ability requirements for a man to actively participate in the system as a voter or political representative, that is, to be a full citizen. Specifically, in 1836, the debate on electoral law revolved around the terms 'quality' and 'capacity'. These concepts appeared continuously in questions about the profile of voters during Spanish liberalism.[15] On the one hand, liberal politicians defended that owning property or possessing

13 Federico de Madrazo to his father José de Madrazo (17 April 1840), in Federico Madrazo, *Epistolario* (Madrid: Museo del Prado, 1994), 305–7.

14 Pedro de Madrazo, 'Protección debida a las Bellas Artes', *El Artista* (1 April 1835), 50–2.

15 María Sierra, María Antonia Peña and Rafael Zurita, *Elegidos y elegibles: la representación parlamentaria en la cultura del liberalismo* (Madrid: Marcial Pons, 2010), 279–80.

a certain amount of wealth was a sign of quality. On the other hand, they considered capacity in terms of education and/or professional status as a characteristic that justified an exception from the property requirements and an inclusion of such men among the voters. According to these standards, artists had to define their profession within the intellectual sphere and defend a certain exclusivity of knowledge. All the professions that claimed high social status faced this problem, though the degree of their public and legal acknowledgement differed.[16] Thus, Antonio Alcalá Galiano argued in 1836:

> No to democracy, that is to say, to the Greeks' demos. No to the mob, no to popular power, for these classes that are generally understood as the people. However, yes to the true liberal spirit, to enlightened poverty, which must be independent to a certain extent. The Commission does not grant them the right to come and occupy these seats. For that purpose, they need other qualities. However, for the right to elect, a relative capacity is sufficient … Then there remain [among the possible electors] doctors and graduates, architects, sculptors and painters, who need an academic title to distinguish the artist from the one who dips a paintbrush in a bit of Verdigris and then puts it on a door.[17]

On the path to social recognition, the academies of fine arts played a crucial role. Thus, academic qualification became essential to define the artist as a professional. The institutionalization of the educational system marked access to expert knowledge and professional practice. In this way, artists gradually professionalized their art introducing procedures that the sociology of professions deems characteristic for this process. The construction of modern professions is understood to require the definition of education and training considered necessary to obtain expert knowledge, the limitation of access to the labour market and the configuration of discourses and practices to construct an identity as a professional group.[18]

16 Darina Martykánová and Víctor M. Núñez-García, 'Sacerdotes en el mercado, héroes del progreso: los médicos e ingenieros y las transformaciones de la masculinidad liberal (1820–1900)', in Darina Martykánová and Marie Walin, eds, *Masculinidades en la España decimonónica* (Sevilla: Universidad de Sevilla, 2022), in press.

17 *Diario de Sesiones. Estamento de Procuradores* (19 January 1836), 492.

18 Martykánová, 'La profession, la masculinité et le travail', 81.

From the second half of the eighteenth century, it was the acquisition of an academic title of 'master in painting' (or master in sculpture or master in architecture) which marked the separation between artisans and artists. Manuals and specialized journals frequently published biographies of renowned painters and sculptors emphasizing these official credentials. At times, artists manipulated their biographies to construct an academic lineage since childhood. For example, the Cordovan painter Diego Monroy falsified his history to conceal his links to the guild system.[19] Besides distinguishing themselves from artisans, academicism helped artists rise above two other figures in the art world: amateurs and women artists. This shaped the figure of a professional artist around a male identity influenced by the values of liberalism and romanticism.

Professional vs amateur attitudes

The construction of the modern professions was deeply influenced by the creation of the liberal state. Useful occupation was crucial in creating liberal masculinity, and, as Martykánová has argued, work was an important, though problematic feature of a respectable man.[20] This model was born at the end of the eighteenth century, when the new social elite strove for legitimacy as such appealing to personal merit rather than blood and family ties.[21] In this sense, from the Enlightenment to the mid-nineteenth

19 The life and work of this painter has been studied in José Antonio Vigara, 'La academia como paradigma del ascenso profesional: el caso del pintor Diego Monroy', *Espacio, tiempo y forma. Serie VII, Historia del Arte* 22–3 (2009–2010), 141–56.

20 This idea needs to be revisited. In liberal worldview, the respectable man was identified with a productive, hard-working person. However, the elites still stigmatized physical labour as something particular to the lower classes, as stressed by Martykánová, 'La profession, la masculinité et le travail', 92.

21 Álvaro Molina, *Mujeres y hombres en la España ilustrada: identidad, género y visualidad* (Madrid: Cátedra, 2013); María Victoria Alonso, 'El siglo XIX como campo de estudio de la masculinidad: el artista y su representación en el ámbito español', in Roca Casado et al., eds, *Aportaciones a la investigación sobre mujeres y género* (Sevilla: Universidad de Sevilla, 2015), 27.

century, artists portrayed themselves as working men. They appeared reflecting upon the composition or in a more active pose, holding their palette and brushes.[22] A clear example of this is José de Madrazo's self-portrait (1840), currently held in the Museo del Prado. Surrounded by all the tools of his craft, he expressed the ennoblement of the painter's profession as a result of hard work and personal effort.

These two values served the artists to distinguish themselves from whom they considered their antagonists, the amateurs. An indignant Pedro de Madrazo said that 'they dare to speak, to give their vote, to criticize and praise in front of the professors [a term that, during that period, could be used for titled practitioners and teachers at the academy] without no fear or shame'.[23] In short, amateurs were to him 'the woodworm of the arts, the uneducated professors'. Expert knowledge and constant effort not only distinguished the professionals of the fine arts from the amateurs. They also created hierarchies among academic painters. In order to make the criticism of amateurs sustainable, the painters had to constantly prove their laboriousness, and, therefore, lazy and idle students were sternly criticized. This attitude is also related to the construction of the liberal male identity. Ultimately, passivity was associated with femininity and contrasted with male productivity.[24] Thus, any artist who neglected his studies and did not practice assiduously was frowned upon by his peers. As Federico de Madrazo wrote,

> I do not think Carlos Ribera will be able to exhibit anything neither this year nor next. At the rate he is going, he will finish the painting on doomsday. And yet the painting is not very big. He works very little; it is evident that his father [the painter Juan Antonio Ribera] had him completely tied down. He has come to Paris, he has mixed with famished and stupid Spaniards and that alone has made him lose his little interest in studying. Since Perico [Pedro de Madrazo] has been here, he has done

22 For an exhaustive discussion of the artist's portraiture in the nineteenth century, see Alonso, *Representaciones de masculinidad*.

23 Pedro de Madrazo, 'Pintura', *El Artista* (1 April 1835), 14.

24 Nerea Aresti, 'La hombría perdida en el tiempo. Masculinidad y nación española a finales del siglo XIX', in Mauricio Zabalgoitia, ed., *Hombres en peligro: género, nación e imperio en la España de cambio de siglo (XIX-XX)* (Madrid: Iberoamericana Vervuert, 2017), 24.

> some work. The poor guy is a bit remorseful for the time he has lost. I think Aníbal Álvarez [architect] is another slacker, but I have not seen him yet.[25]

The insistence on hard and constant work was not only a way of defining individual merit, but also a collective one. One of the most praiseworthy traits of Spanish liberal masculinity was public activity; a man was to serve the nation. To be acknowledged as a valuable member of political community of Spaniards, a man had to either be part of the public institutions or contribute with his work to the general interest. Many liberal professions stressed their contribution to the common good and the usefulness of their work for the country when demanding public recognition and high remuneration. For example, physicians and engineers argued that through their professional practice, they contributed to place Spain at 'the vanguard of European civilization'.[26] Artists and their supporters promoted a similar discourse. As Eugenio de Ochoa stated,

> As long as an employee enjoys more public consideration in Spain than an artist or a *savant* , we shall have, as now, many employees and few artists and *savants*. In the modern social system, this is a big sign of backwardness in terms of civilization.[27]

Like other liberal professionals, artists showed a keen interest in public affairs and promoted several projects that, in their understanding, contributed to the nation's progress.[28] In doing so, they not only showcased their interest in the common good; they also legitimized their demands for a dignified position for their craft. They argued that the governments had to promote the arts, particularly by increasing scholarships to study

25 Federico de Madrazo to José de Madrazo (21 October 1837), Archivo Museo del Prado, AP: 4, file 35.

26 Martykánová and Núñez-García, 'Ciencia, patria y honor', 68.

27 Eugenio de Ochoa, 'De los artistas españoles', *Semanario Pintoresco Español* (17 April 1836).

28 A clear example was the proposals led by a group of professors from the Real Academia de Bellas Artes de San Fernando [Royal Academy of Fine Arts of San Fernando] to create a National Museum with the assets disentail between 1835 and 1836 or a Historical Museum of Contemporary Artists. See Ainhoa Gilarranz, *El Estado y el Arte: historia de una relación simbiótica durante la España liberal (1833–1875)* (Valencia: Prensas de la Universidad de Valencia, 2021).

abroad. In Eugenio de Ochoa's opinion, these aids were insufficient and even hurt 'national pride'.[29] In this way, he asked 'is this fair or decent?' He stated that 'all the civilized governments maintain a considerable number of youths studying fine arts in Rome'. So, 'if we want to be as good as the great European nations, the Spanish government must encourage the fine arts with all its might'.

Public demonstrations of the usefulness of their work also served to defend both their professional freedom and honour. The change in patronage had a significant influence on the nineteenth-century art system. In the twofold dynamic of expanding global capitalism and growing state intervention, the relative weight the Crown and the Church as patrons diminished. The private collector market was not robust in mid-nineteenth-century Spain. Thus, the State assumed the chief role of patron of the arts, commissioning and purchasing most of the works. As a result, many painters focused on subjects that satisfied an institutional taste, notably history painting. Some artists defended this relationship of dependence, demanding further institutional support for the fine arts. However, it also had its detractors, such as José Galofre, who was quite critical of the main public art institution, the Real Academia de las Artes de San Fernando, and argued for the creation of yearly national exhibitions to attract private buyers, foreign and local. He hoped this would increase the artists' creative freedom, leading to a greater diversity of appreciated genres and topics.[30]

In this context, a group of artists and academics drew up a petition to found a national museum. They requested a fixed salary for the teachers of painting, sculpture and engraving who would be part of the new museum and create works to be exhibited there. Another group of academics and professors criticized the proposal. They considered the limit on the number of salaried members to be unfair and argued that the museum should not refrain from buying works of other artists, either.[31] However, for its

29 *El Artista* (1 April 1835). Eugenio de Ochoa, 'Los pensionados en Roma', *El Artista* (1835), 181–3.

30 Tomás Pérez-Vejo, 'Géneros, mercado, artistas y críticos en la pintura española del siglo XIX', *Espacio, tiempo y forma. Serie V. Historia Contemporánea* 24 (2012), 34–6.

31 'Comunicado', *El Heraldo* (22 December 1847).

promoters, a fixed salary meant recognition major improvement in working conditions of the artists and acknowledgement of their labour. Traditionally, the artists were paid for their work after the delivery, which, they argued, hindered their intellectual work, as they had to work fast in order to earn the fee and adapt to the buyers' demands and tastes. While they argued for greater economic stability, it was important for them to highlight that 'they do not propose to create decent salaries to feed idleness. They are attached to relevant obligations'.[32] As they underlined,

> Unfortunately, the artist who has only the wealth of his productions must necessarily pay more attention to quantity than to quality. We all complain about this situation, which requires an urgent remedy. It must be avoided that, after a huge investment of his time, the artist would have to keep a remarkable work in his studio for four or five years or forever because buyers do not want to purchase it for its fair value. Therefore, by working for the new museum, artists can create with the security of being useful and harmonized with the interests of the fine arts and the state.

This debate points directly to one of the main challenges faced by the liberal professions, particularly relevant for professions linked to expert knowledge and intellectual production. Remuneration for the services rendered was a thorny issue. It was liked to class, political status and also masculinity. In the liberal discourse, a man's honour was related to his freedom and independence, also an economic one. At the same time, independence in intellectual terms meant the capacity to exercise their profession freely, following creative and expert criteria, not bowing to private interests and demands. Each profession had its peculiarities that marked the groups' course of action in this complex negotiation. For physicians, their professional honour was linked to professional autonomy and materialized in a collective struggle for decent wages or fees. For instance, there was a broad movement to improve the conditions of rural physicians, whose salary depended on the town councils. Well-off urban physicians endorsed this struggle, because the rural physicians' relative poverty and dependence endangered the image as gentlemen of the whole medical profession.[33] In

32 'Fundación de un Museo Nacional', *El Español* (28 December 1847).

33 Martykánová and Núñez-García, 'Sacerdotes en el mercado'; Martykánová and Núñez-García, 'Ciencia, patria y honor', 72.

the world of letters, professions such as writers and translators had to join the state administration to gain a certain degree of economic independence.[34] The same was true, at least before the 1860s, for engineers.[35] Public employment was the only way for them to fund a life of a middle-class man through the exercise of their profession.

Overall, it is problematic to define the man of letters within the parameters of professions such as lawyers, physicians, or engineers. However, there was a certain collective identity that endowed them with coherence. Academic artists were halfway between them. They defended their profession through public institutions, namely the control mechanisms introduced in the Real Academia de Bellas Artes de San Fernando.

The professional monopoly of the male artist

During the yearly exhibition of paintings of Royal Academy of Fine Arts of San Fernando in 1847, Pedro de Madrazo wrote an opinion piece in which he defended the schools of fine arts and their importance in training 'good painters'. 'Whatever genius one may have', he said, 'meditation on natural objects is futile for anyone who does not know how to observe them.'[36] For this reason, 'without a training school, without hard and conscientious study, without obedience and deference to the advice of those who know how to see and feel, no one will become a good painter, no matter how generous nature has been to him.'

The discourse of academic artists was strongly marked by elements of romantic masculinity.[37] That is to say, by an interest in the collective, the

34 Sánchez, *Mediación y transferencias culturales*, 65–7.

35 See the chapter of Darina Martykánová and Juan Luis Pan-Montojo in this book.

36 Pedro de Madrazo, 'Exposición de pinturas de 1847', *Semanario Pintoresco Español* (7 November 1847).

37 For romantic masculinity based on specific cases such as the politician Tassara and the writer Bretón de los Herreros, see María Sierra 'Política, romanticismo y masculinidad: Tassara (1817–1875)', *Historia y política* 27 (2012), 203–26,

stress on the common good and a male identity that was in no way lacking passions, but rather required the management of feelings. Precocious talent and distinguished sensitivity were among the characteristics attributed to artists during Romanticism. This fascination with the creative spirit often appeared in the biographies of painters, sculptors and writers published during the first half of the nineteenth century.[38] All of them used to point to the innate sensitivity manifested since childhood by famous artists. A particular emotionality was attributed to the artist. As Pedro de Madrazo pointed out, 'there are beings privileged by the nature, to make a *material man* feel the charms of divinity, of supernatural beauty. And these are called artists.'[39]

However, liberal discourse used emotional excess and the absence of rationality as an excuse to remove women from both the elite professions and the political sphere.[40] In this context, the conception of an artist as someone particularly sensitive enabled women to negotiate their place in the professional sphere of artists. This proved far more complicated and even impossible in the case of other liberal professions, though by the end of the nineteenth century, women in some countries were able to explore similar patterns and discursive tensions to gain access to university studies in medicine. Moreover, many art treatises often argued that women were artists because of their temperament. Women's aptitude for artistic practice was widely accepted and was also considered as resulting from an

and *Género y emociones en el Romanticismo: el teatro de Bretón de los Herreros* (Zaragoza: Institución Fernando el Católico, 2013).

38 Alonso, *Representaciones de masculinidad*, 42–3.

39 Pedro de Madrazo, 'Pintura', *El Artista* (1 April 1835).

40 Mónica Burguera, *Las damas del liberalismo respetable: los imaginarios sociales del feminismo liberal en España (1834–1850)* (Madrid: Cátedra, 2012) and 'Mujeres y revolución liberal en perspectiva esfera pública y ciudadanía femenina en la primera mitad del siglo XIX en España', in Encarna G. Monerris, Ivana Frasquet and Carmen G. Monerris, eds, *Cuando todo era posible: liberalismo y antiliberalismo en España e Hispanoamérica* (Madrid: Sílex, 2016), 257–96; María Cruz Romeo, 'Domesticidad y política. Las relaciones de género en la sociedad posrevolucionaria', in María Cruz Romeo and María Sierra, eds, *La España liberal, 1833–1874* (Madrid: Marcial Pons, 2014), 89–130.

individual innate talent in harmony with their nature.[41] Faced with this possibility of women achieving professional status, male artists began to strategically question or minimize the archetype of creative genius. Natural talent could manifest itself in childhood, as many biographies of renowned artists recounted. Even so, male artists stressed that it was only one of the features of an artist. The most important factor in becoming a true artist was study and constant dedication that allowed one to become a fine arts master. As José Manjarrés said, 'Genius is often regarded as productivity solely by sentiment. This fact denies the artist "artistic conscience" and the judgment he needs to make and correct his work. The artist needs to have genius. But this consists of neither a flighty spirit nor an unconscious productivity. Besides genius, the artist needs to have knowledge; he must be intelligent and highly educated.'[42] In my opinion, this apparently meritocratic discourse had both gender and class aspects, as such education and dedication were costly and most often relied on the cultural capital and financial support of young artists' family. In fact, some artists who were not born into well-off families started their training at a workshop and only entered the academy once they earned enough money though their art. This step legitimized a posteriori their professional capacity and help hide its 'practical', non-elite origins of their artistic success.

The academies of fine arts directed and coordinated this elite training that professional artists had to go through. The art institutions insisted on the insufficiency of creative genius and the importance of systematic and institutionalized training to become a real artist. In 1874, on the occasion of the reform of the Real Academia de Bellas Artes de San Fernando's internal regulations, the politician Joaquín Francisco Pacheco insisted on the existence in the world of 'something more than genius'.[43] In his opinion, 'criticism and reason lead to these results and prevent genius itself from wandering and going astray. There is the atmosphere that fills order and talent and which is, perhaps, more useful to nations than isolated or disorderly

41 Estrella De Diego, *La mujer y la pintura en el XIX español: cuatrocientas olvidadas y alguna más* (Madrid: Cátedra, 1987), 166.

42 José Manjarrés, 'Mamotreto artístico', *El Arte en España* 7 (1868), 141.

43 'Discurso del Excmo. Sr. D. Joaquín Francisco Pacheco', *El Arte en España* 3 (1864), 299.

genius.' Academies were thus the appropriate space for moulding these creative spirits. However, they were conceived and organized for a specific type of artist, the male one, and most often also proceeding from well-off families willing to support them throughout their studies, and designed to boost their professional and social status. Once the academy became the way to acquire special skills and professional consideration, women – and lower-class men – were in a disadvantaged position. There were female students in the fine arts academies, and some of them even stood out on the Spanish artistic scene.[44] However, there were major obstacles that made it impossible for women to compete on equal terms with male artists, and thus these women could be easily construed as exceptional individuals whose presence did not threaten the male – and gentlemanly – nature of the Spanish art establishment.

The first of these obstacles was the educational system itself. Women were admitted to schools but – due to the alleged threat to morals – could not attend classes in human anatomy, colouring and composition.[45] This situation continued until 1888, when the Escuela Especial de Escultura, Pintura y Grabado [Special School of Painting, Sculpture and Engraving] gave female pupils access to the subjects of drawing *au naturel*, colouring and composition.[46] The lack of such knowledge and training prevented (not only) Spanish women from standing out in the European art system, which was strongly marked by a thematic hierarchy. In painting, history

44 For an in-depth analysis of women's access to the study of fine arts in Spain, see De Diego, *La mujer y la pintura*. Some recent research on specific women artists can be found in Sheila Barker, 'The Female Artist in the Public Eye: Women Copyists at the Uffizi, 1770–1859', in Temma Belducci and Heather Belnap Jensen, eds, *Women, Femininity and Public Space in European Visual Culture, 1789–1914* (London: Routledge, 2014), 65–79; María Ángeles Pérez-Martín, 'Eulalia Gerona de Cabanes Pintora. Mujeres en el Academicismo ilustrado en España', *Dossiers feministes* 19 (2014), 189–204; Carlos G. Navarro, ed., *Invitadas: fragmentos sobre mujeres, ideología y artes plásticas en España (1833–1931)* (Madrid: Museo Nacional del Prado, 2020).

45 De Diego, *La mujer y la pintura*, 190.

46 Concha Lomba, *Bajo el eclipse. Pintoras en España, 1880–1939* (Madrid: CSIC, 2019), 61.

painting was the most respected artistic genres by academicism, being the only one in which an artist could develop their full potential.

In Spain, the Real Academia de Bellas Artes de San Fernando was the leading institution in artistic matters. It prioritized history painting over other artistic genres, particularly during the first half of the nineteenth century. Thus, historical subjects were a regular feature of the prizes and competitions organized by the institution.[47] In such paintings, the importance of human figures was key, and artists who had not received special training were in clear disadvantage.

Among the art examinations organized by the Academy of San Fernando was the one aimed at obtaining the title of Académico de Honor [honorary academician], regulated since 1757. It was a certificate of great value for artists because it gave them access to various privileges within and outside the art world. This distinction was usually awarded to personalities interested in fine arts as members of royalty, nobility and high-raking government officials and public employees, to gain their favour for the Academy of San Fernando.[48] This title granted them certain privileges, such as the involvement in art commissions, the management of the museums or the participation in ministerial departments.[49]

However, in the case of painters graduated from the academies, the importance of obtaining this title was due to different reasons. This title enabled the qualified artists to become teaching staff of the academies. From 1821 onwards, in the specific case of painting, anyone who wanted to be a professor at the royal academies of the fine arts had to be an Honorary Academic for history painting. The examination had two phases: 'de repente' [the instantly] and 'de pensado' [the thought-out]. In the first one, the candidate produced a compositional sketch on half a sheet of paper in less than fifteen uninterrupted hours. The second one consisted

47 Carlos Reyero, 'El reconocimiento de la nación en la historia: el uso espacio-temporal de pinturas y monumentos en España', *Arbor* 740 (2009), 1199.

48 It was common practice to award the title of Honorary Academic to the staff of the Fine Arts Department of the Ministry responsible for Public Works, even if they had no connection with art. This was the case, for example, of Joaquín Íñigo de la Fuente. See Gilarranz, *El Estado y el Arte*.

49 Vigara, 'La academia como paradigma', 152.

of capturing this first draft in oil.[50] The title could be obtained in other genres such as miniature, flower painting or perspective. However, only the subject of history ensured access to the teaching profession.

From the end of the eighteenth century and throughout the nineteenth century, several women received the title of Honorary Academic. None of them taught at the Real Academia de Bellas Artes de San Fernando.[51] The painter Rosario Weiss was one of these few honorary academics, one elected for her merit as artist, not for being a patroness of art as the other women who were granted such distinction as academics. Since 1840, she taught drawing to Queen Isabel II and her sister, Princess Luisa Fernanda, but she was never granted a teaching post at the Royal Academy.[52]

Another essential step in the artist's curriculum was to obtain a scholarship to further their artistic studies abroad, usually in Rome and Paris. Education abroad with French or Italian masters became a particularly valued stage in an artist's training, one that increased the artist's prestige, and was common also among painters from Central Europe and Great Britain. As Carlos Reyero pointed out, in many cases, it seems that the studies abroad served more for promoting one's career than to receive training from recognized masters in the fine arts.[53] Here, again, their lack of specific art education left women in a disadvantaged position when compared to their male colleagues. But there were also social and gender impediments: for instance, it was hard for a respectable Spanish woman, particularly one in reproductive age, to travel and live on their own far from her family. Women had to travel accompanied if they did not want to endanger their honour and reputation. Thus, their mobility was linked to and

50 Esperanza Navarrete, *La Academia de Bellas Artes de San Fernando y la pintura en la primera mitad del siglo XIX* (Madrid: Fundación Universitaria Española, 1999), 93–7.

51 A list of women Honorary Academic can be found in <https://www.realacademiabellasartessanfernando.com/es/archivo-biblioteca/archivo/relacion-general-de-academicos>, accessed 24 February 2021.

52 Raquel Sánchez, *Señoras fuera de casa. Mujeres del siglo XIX: la conquista del espacio público* (Madrid: Catarata, 2019), 96–7.

53 Carlos Reyero, 'Pintores españoles del siglo XIX en la escuela de Bellas Artes de París: entre el aprendizaje cosmopolita y el mérito curricular', *Academia: boletín de la Real Academia de Bellas Artes de San Fernando* 72 (1999), 377–96.

conditioned by the desires of men. This made it extremely difficult for a woman artist to move freely to a foreign country to study, and thus remedy the limited availability of suitable training in Spain. While international displacements for the purpose of training became an element of prestige and recognition for men, it symbolized quite the opposite for women and prevented them from achieving professional relevance. The difficulties concerning independent mobility also affected women in other professions, such as in the art of healing. For example, home visits at any time of the day or night were considered risky and socially compromising for women and thus hindered the professional practice of women in medicine.[54] There was a certain shift in attitudes towards the end of the nineteenth century, when female students' international mobility became a worldwide phenomenon (particularly Central and Eastern European women flocked to study in Paris): first government grants to female Spanish artists appeared at the end of the nineteenth century. They were usually painters from the provinces who try to improve their education in Madrid. Studying in Paris or Rome did not become common for Spanish women until the twentieth century, the first being Inocencia Arangoa. When she was awarded her scholarship in 1901, it generated an intense social debate because women could not participate in the competitive examination. Voices renowned in the art world had to defend her so that she would finally be allowed to compete with the rest of her male colleagues.[55]

All these obstacles were not limited to the academic sphere, but also concerned the (lack of) women's public acknowledgement as creators. The presence of women in exhibitions was commonplace, such as the art exhibitions organized by the Real Academia de Bellas Artes de San Fernando or the national exhibitions held from 1856 onwards. However, women painters were never considered and treated as professionals. As one newspaper noted at a painting exhibition in 1836, 'the small paintings of Mrs Weiss, Mrs Nicolau, and Mrs Montufar had a distinguished place among the amateur productions. The first has attracted attention for its beautiful copies of Velázquez's horses, the second for a beautiful miniature

54 Martykánová and Núñez-García, 'Ciencia, patria y honor', 70–1.

55 Lomba, *Bajo el eclipse*, 68–73.

and the third for two beautiful composite pencil drawings.'[56] The works submitted by women were labelled as amateur and commented on with a paternalistic attitude.[57] This fact also affected the awarding of prizes and medals in these competitions. History painting was by far the favourite of the main patron of the time, the State. Among the paintings presented at national exhibitions, historical themes accounted for about 20 per cent of the total. However, 100 per cent of the first-class medals went to historical compositions until 1892, when interest in these compositions began to wane.[58] Therefore, for most of the second half of the nineteenth century, history painting monopolized the artistic genres valued by the public, the critics and the most important patron, the State. Consequently, historical painters were honoured, lauded and rewarded. These awards gave the painters prestige, but also strengthened their position for a place in the art academies. Besides promoting their careers at national level, these medals were a boost to their international projection. The paintings entered for the International Exhibitions were almost entirely selected from those that had won prizes in the national competition.[59] The whole artistic system was set up in a way that prevented women from climbing to the top of the profession. The lack of special artistic training prevented them from achieving great results in genres such as history painting, and this led a chain of negative consequences – not winning awards in exhibitions, not being eligible for scholarships abroad – that prevented them from competing with their male peers.

56 'Exposición de pinturas en la Academia de San Fernando en el presente año de 1836', *El Eco del Comercio* (15 October 1836).

57 Sánchez, *Señoras fuera de casa*, 95.

58 Pérez-Vejo, 'Géneros, mercado, artistas', 28–30.

59 Pérez-Vejo, 'Géneros, mercado, artistas', 43.

Conclusions

Following the indicators defined by the sociology of professions, I argue that painters became increasingly professionalized in nineteenth-century Spain. The artist as a professional became defined by an institutional framework. First and foremost, the academies of fine arts designed a path of training for painters, and thus achieved, at least partially, to control the process of making of a professional painter. The possession of a title marked a clear separation from other painters: the lower-class artisans, who trained in a workshop though a master-apprentice system, and the amateurs, who might have been upper class, but exercised the same practice without such institutional endorsement. In this sense, the academic qualification was essential to the artists' corporate identity. It permitted their self-identification as painters, but it was also essential for their social standing, as clearly shown by the electoral law and their access to the vote. While the access to the profession was not clearly defined and was rather an accumulation of elements in the nineteenth century academicism strove to impose a range of requirements for one to be considered a professional painter.

Also, the artists' professional identity was clearly marked by gender. Romantic masculinity influenced the painters' self-definition as professionals through a discourse centred on the common good and on the mastery of their passions, not their negation. Adapted to the particularities of their occupation, artists used several discursive practices similar to those deployed by other liberal professions, such as physicians or engineers. Thus, professional painters constructed their identity within the parameters of the honourable man as conceptualized by liberalism. Social recognition no longer came from the family ties that characterized the Old Regime. Now, it came from work, training and involvement in a collective enterprise closely related to the ideal of the public man.

This process of identity construction implied the exclusion of women from the professional sphere. The institutionalization of the educational system prevented women artists from competing on equal terms with men. The growing power of academicism in the artistic field aggravated the situation. From its inception, the Spanish art system made it difficult for women to pursue a professional career. The limitations on their training imposed a basic distinction that prevented them from engaging in many practices that benefited the careers of their male peers. Moreover, on the few occasions when they achieved access to privileged spaces of the world of art, such as great exhibitions and competitions, they were treated as mere amateurs. For women, obtaining merits, awards and social recognition was almost impossible within an institutional circle founded on gender inequality.

RAQUEL SÁNCHEZ

Journalism

A Profession for Men of Letters (1820–1920)

ABSTRACT
The following pages will be studying the process of professionalization of the journalist starting with the premise that journalism, as a profession, was one of the many facets of the activity of the man of letters. This activity would take on its own identity and develop a set of differentiated practices within the literary field. From its roots in the Enlightenment, and throughout the nineteenth century, new-gathering profession would gradually acquire features that would mould it through challenges of a diverse nature: growth and diversification of the reading public, technological innovation and modernization of businesses in the publishing industry, consolidation of the journalism genre as a new form of writing, etc. Ultimately, it was a process based on the gradual autonomy and growing reputation of journalism with regard to the other functions performed by men of letters, in particular narrative writing, drama and poetry, which had traditionally enjoyed greater prestige in the Republic of Letters.

Not such a modern profession

It is very common to read that the professional journalist did not appear in Spain until the Bourbon Restoration of 1875, a time when newspaper publishing businesses began to take shape and live off their own resources, which came both from advertising and the sale of copies. However, it was already possible to find individuals who could be classified as journalists in the eighteenth century, as demonstrated by different studies.[1]

1 Among them: Joaquín Álvarez Barrientos, 'El periodista en la España del siglo XVIII y la profesionalización del escritor', *Estudios de historia social* 52–53 (1990), 29–39; Elisabel Larriba, 'Los periodistas y el derecho a la educación para todos', *Cuadernos de Historia Moderna. Anejos* 6 (2007), 119–45; Inmaculada Urzainqui, 'Periodismo/periodismos en la temprana Ilustración', *Edad de oro* 31 (2012),

Although they were described by different titles, these enlightened men of letters were aware that they performed a role – somewhere between information and education – that they believed to be essential in a changing society. Consequently, it was not a simple question of title, but of the existence of certain individuals devoted to meeting a social need at a time in which the public sphere was undergoing remodelling, as it was during the final decades of the eighteenth century.

Although the format of the newspaper was not new in the second half of the eighteenth century, it was adapted extraordinarily well to the transformations resulting from the changes made to the public sphere during this period. The flexibility of the medium turned it into a profitable instrument for communicating opinions, fashions and trends, which provided men of letters with income that was rarely obtained from their literary works.[2] Hence, there was only one further step required to turn this supplementary work into a profession, which was taken not only by the well-known Francisco Mariano Nifo, but by other contemporaries such as Cristóbal Cladera and Antonio Valladares de Sotomayor. According to Álvarez Barrientos, by the end of the eighteenth century, there could be said to exist an awareness of journalism as an activity distinct from that of aesthetic creation that was able to create or guide public opinion in a large number of subjects and offer the reader an interpretation of the real world. Moreover, journalism brought about a significant change in the actual literary endeavour as it made inroads as a free genre, unencumbered by the conventions of other forms of creation. The capacity of journalism to challenge literary norms and, to some extent, modify them with its style, would continue throughout the nineteenth century, as well as the following centuries. And it would not only modify the rules of writing in

---

323–49; Alba de la Cruz and Mª Victoria López-Cordón, 'Impresores que escriben, periodistas que editan en tiempos de crisis y revolución (España 1780–1823)', *El Argonauta español* 13 (2016) <https://doi.org/10.4000/argonauta.2395>, accessed 19 December 2020.

2 An analysis of the situation in Spain in Joaquín Álvarez Barrientos, 'El periodista en la España del siglo XVIII y la profesionalización del escritor' and Joaquín Álvarez Barrientos, ed., *Los hombres de letras en la España del siglo XVIII: apóstoles y arribistas* (Madrid: Castalia, 2006).

terms of style, but also in the sociological aspect by accommodating the figure of the critic, an agent who mediated between the literary work and the public, who would influence the reception of the former by the latter and whose weight would become increasingly important in the literary field.

The existence of journalism as a practice was unevenly matched by the evolution of the standard Spanish name for those who practised it, *periodista*. The titles they received included *gacetero* [gazetteer], *autor público* [public author] *jornalista* [cognate of the English term 'journalist'], *diarista* [diarist, derived from the Spanish word for both a diary and a daily newspaper, *diario*], *semanarista* [derived from the Spanish word for a weekly newspaper, *semanario*], *redactor* [newswriter, also sub-editor or copy editor], *articulista* [columnist] and *escritor público* [public writer]. The first record of the use of the word *periodista* (cognate of the English term 'periodical') dates from 1763 and it is credited to Juan Antonio Aragonés, who used it in a set of three speeches that were published in *El amigo del público*.[3] The Royal Spanish Academy would take its time to accept the term, and it only appeared in its 1884 version of the *Dictionary of the Spanish language*, where its entry came with the definition 'composer, author or news-editor of a newspaper [*periódico*]', a somewhat imprecise definition that covered both the material and intellectual tasks associated with the trade. It was not until 1925 that the term *periodista* would be defined as an individual 'who [has] the aim of writing in newspapers [*periódicos*]'. The 1884 version of the dictionary did include an entry for journalism, *periodismo*, defined as 'the exercise of the profession of a journalist [*periodista*]', the first time it would appear in this form in any of the Academy's publications. Somewhat belatedly, as can be observed. Its place was occupied by the term *diarista*, which since 1817 has remained an entry in the Academy's dictionaries with the definition 'a person who composes or publishes some sort of diary/newspaper [*diario*]'.[4] Entries in other dictionaries could be seen to be approaching the current usage, such as the dictionary published

3 Antonio López de Zuazo, 'Origen y evolución del término 'periodista', *Estudios sobre el mensaje periodístico* 2 (1995), 45–52.

4 See the Royal Spanish Academy's Mapa de Diccionarios Históricos [Map of Historical Dictionaries] <https://webfrl.rae.es/ntllet/>, accessed 20 December 2020.

by Pedro Labernia, which in 1848 put forward the definition that would later be used by the Academy to define *periodista*: 'composer, author or news-editor of a newspaper [*periódico*]'.[5] Likewise, the first edition of the highly popular *Diccionario nacional*, published in 1849 by Ramón Joaquín Domínguez, defines *periodista* as the 'author or news-editor, newswriter or collaborator of a newspaper [*periódico*]', also providing the synonym *escritor público*. There was also an entry for the word *periodismo*, defined as 'the profession of a journalist [*periodista*]' and as 'the set of journalists [*periodistas*]'. Domínguez also drew attention to the existence of the expression *prensa periódica* [periodical press] and indicated that 'the Academy does not accept this term'.[6] Use of the word *periodista* may even predate this. In his second volume of *Los españoles pintados por sí mismos* [*The Spanish Portrayed by Themselves*] Mesonero Romanos already refers to the *periodista* as one of the *tipos hallados* (found figures, a depiction of the types of figures emerging in the society of his time).[7] In short, *periodista*, although commonly used, took a long time to become the prevalent term. The word was interchanged with others to refer to the profession and the individuals who practised it, at least until the mid-nineteenth century. The most commonly used were *escritor público* and *redactor*.

In any case, journalism became for many aspiring men of letters a way to make a name for themselves or to survive. A very important proportion of the young men who joined newspaper offices in the 1830s and afterwards had no aspirations to become journalists, as some of them expressed in writing.[8] Their sights were set on artistic creation or becoming playwrights, which was a more profitable literary activity than writing poetry

5 Pedro Labernia, *Diccionario de la lengua castellana con las correspondencias catalana y latina* (Barcelona: Imprenta Grau, 1848), vol. II, 458.

6 Ramón José Domínguez Hervella, *Diccionario nacional o gran diccionario clásico de la lengua española* (Madrid: Establecimiento Tipográfico de Mellado, 1849), vol. II, 1362. According to the *Catálogo Colectivo del Patrimonio Bibliográfico Español* [Collective Catalogue of Spanish Library Heritage], up to fifteen editions of the *Diccionario nacional* were published in the nineteenth century.

7 Ramón Mesonero Romanos, 'Contrastes. Tipos hallados, tipos perdidos', in *Los Españoles pintados por sí mismos* (Madrid: I. Boix, 1844), vol. II, 486–87.

8 Julio Nombela, *Impresiones y recuerdos* (Madrid: Tebas, 1976), 342.

or novels. The same can be said of the individuals who used newspapers as a dais from which to gain the political visibility that they would otherwise never have achieved.[9] In fact, newspapers during the reign of Queen Isabel II were branded mere springboards for candidates wishing to become parliamentarians or businessmen seeking to influence the decisions of governments and legislative assemblies. Although this was true, it should also be said that this was not the only journalistic offering available to Spanish readers of the time, given that periodicals with an informative focus began to appear in the 1840s and 1850s. *La Correspondencia de España* and *Las Novedades* are examples of this.[10] The co-existence between the political and ideological press and the informative press was therefore intrinsic to the Spanish newspaper scene. The prevalence of the former in the historical studies conducted on the period must not conceal this other reality from us. Furthermore, the political press also created jobs, generally precarious in nature, for young writers.[11] In short, the process of professionalization that journalism experienced during the reign of Isabel II should not be underestimated. It can even be said that the fact that many publications were a response to a specific political tendency, that they were financed by the private fortunes of their instigators – in order, therefore, to further their interests – or that they had an ephemeral existence does not negate the fact that these men of letters or writers considered the profession of journalist as a stage in careers that may, or may not, have been aimed in other directions. One became a journalist to earn money, fame or influence, but one had to 'be a journalist'. This entailed the discipline of work inherent to the profession and a specific way of writing. These explanations, which

9 In Mediterranean Europe, the journalism of the nineteenth century was thus heir to a double tradition: literary and political (Thomas Ferenczi, *L'invention du journalism en France. Naissance de la presse moderne à la fin du XIXème siècle* (Paris: Plon, 1993), 13).

10 Juan Francisco Fuentes Aragonés and Javier Fernández Sebastián, *Historia del periodismo español: prensa, política y opinión pública en la España contemporánea* (Madrid: Síntesis, 1998), 99.

11 An example of how these political newspapers operated is given by Julio Nombela in *¡¡Los 300000 duros!!: historia de un pobre hombre* (Barcelona: Salvador Manero/ Madrid: Antonio San Martí, 1866), vol. 1, 697–743.

appear to be valid for men of letters, could also be applied to other professionals who entered into politics and, in addition, practised other trades. Among them were lawyers, many of whom engaged in the profession of journalism before and after becoming important political figures, while keeping up the practices where they served their clients. Juan Bravo Murillo and Manuel Cortina match this description. Men of letters, therefore, were incorporated into an economic system in which the practice of different activities associated with the world of culture had become the norm. These included the writing of plays and novels, translation, teaching, journalism and, occasionally, politics. Most writers, consequently, combined several of these activities for which they received varying levels of remuneration, depending on the prestige of the individual in question and the evolution of the publishing industry.[12]

The idea that major business projects did not exist in journalism under the reign of Isabel II must also be downplayed. Obviously, the creation of businesses on a larger scale took place in later periods, during the Bourbon Restoration more specifically, when the economic fabric of Spain was consolidated and allowed the so-called 'newspaper publishing business' to emerge. Also worthy of note is the fact that the newspaper publishing business also co-existed during the Bourbon Restoration with the forms of political journalism characteristic of previous periods. The presence of businessmen and fully professional journalists who were exclusively dedicated to the medium during the reign of Isabel II cannot be denied. The case of Andrés Borrego is probably the best known. He began his activity after the death of King Ferdinand VII and contributed to modernizing the news industry by incorporating machinery and methods of modern journalism that he had seen in France and Britain.[13] Both in *El Español*

12 Raquel Sánchez, 'How to Be a Man of Letters', in Andrew Ginger and Geraldine Lawless, eds, *Spain in the Nineteenth Century. New Essays on Experiences of Culture and Society* (Manchester: Manchester University Press, 2018), 216–32. A case study is given in Raquel Sánchez, *Mediación y transferencias culturales en la España de Isabel II. Eugenio de Ochoa y las letras europeas* (Madrid: Iberoamericana Vervuert, 2017).

13 Concepción Castro, *Romanticismo, Periodismo y Política. Andrés Borrego* (Madrid: Tecnos, 1975).

and in his subsequent businesses, Borrego appeared with the double facets of businessman and journalist. His interest in renewing the industry and creating a product for consumption by the rising middle classes showed his entrepreneurial character in an economic sector undergoing a process of change. Added to this was his facet as an *escritor público* or journalist that reveals, on the one hand, an individual in whom the educational motivation of the enlightened journalists was still present; and on the other, we glimpse in him the vocation of the modern journalist: becoming the main figure of scrutiny over the excesses of governments. In other words, Andrés Borrego understood the press to be an instrument for keeping power in check. As is known, he did not hold any public office and his political leanings – which existed and were very strongly held, as shown by his role of parliamentarian over several terms and his many writings in favour of conservative parties – did not include the intention of taking part in active politics. Ángel Fernández de los Ríos is another paradigmatic example of press baron and professional journalist. With more progressive ideological leanings than Borrego, Fernández de los Ríos created publications such as *Las Novedades* and ran *La Ilustración*, *Semanario Pintoresco Español* and *La Soberanía Nacional*, among others. He collaborated with the newspaper offices of *La Iberia*, *El Museo Nacional*, *El Imparcial* and *La Ilustración Española y Americana*, for which he acted as foreign correspondent in Paris. He also had a noteworthy facet as an essayist and translator. In other words, he was the supreme example of the nineteenth-century man of letters. His relations with the world of politics were sporadic and he did not hold any policy-making positions.[14] Therefore, his practice of political journalism did not invalidate his professionalization; rather, it was a stage in his process of specialization.[15] Furthermore, political journalism co-existed with other forms of journalism, such as those found in the publishing ventures undertaken by Ramón Mesonero Romanos, verging on entertainment

14 He only served several terms as a *diputado*, a member of the lower house of Spain's parliament, during the Sexenio Democrático, the six-year revolutionary period between 1868 and 1874.

15 Borrego offers his thoughts on political journalism in three articles he wrote as a commentary on the workings of the British press (*El Correo Nacional*, 31 July 1840; 1 and 2 August 1840).

through the Spanish literary genre of Costumbrismo, the depiction of local customs and manners.

The journalist's work: Between the newspaper office and the street

If there is something that materially embodies the daily work of a nineteenth-century journalist, it is the copy desk. This large desk, with its green, ink-stained blotter, appears in the descriptions from the time as a material and virtual space symbolizing the collaborative work at a newspaper office. Mesonero Romanos described this piece of furniture in *Semanario Pintoresco Español*; in it a form of work characterized by a set of practices that defined the journalist as a professional of letters is subsumed. This desk with its green blotter would endure over time, and we find it again and again in prints and photographs, such as the one in which the newswriters of *La Época* are gathered that was published in the book commemorating the newspaper's fiftieth anniversary,[16] and the ones taken by Franzen of the staff of *Blanco y Negro* and of *La Correspondencia de España* in 1891 and 1897, respectively. The copy desk dominated a room whose walls were covered with maps, books and shelves with back issues of newspapers and where it was possible to find ink pots, fountain pens and pounce pots. All of which was evidence of a model of group effort where privacy did not exist and in which there were continuous interruptions and movement in the room.[17] The daily work of the journalist took place in this frenetic environment. Moreover, aside from the comings and

16 León Roch, *75 años de periodismo: con motivo de las bodas de diamante de La Época: aportaciones para la historia del periodismo madrileño* (Madrid: R. Velasco, 1923), 152–3.

17 José Francos Rodríguez, *Discurso leído ante la Real Academia Española en la recepción pública del Excmo. Sr. D. José Francos Rodríguez el día 16 de noviembre de 1924* (Madrid: J. Morales Impresor, 1924), 23.

goings of the journalists, the newspaper office was visited by other individuals who were there for different reasons.[18]

Few changes could be observed in the way in which the news was prepared, which was closely related to the characteristics of the staff and the actual newspaper. Conditions were no longer the same owing to the technological and professional evolution of the newspaper business in this period of history. However, if we attempt to draw common patterns, we will find certain trends that were repeated between the 1830s and the end of the century. In general terms, newspaper offices did not tend to have a large number of staff, meaning that the work was usually quite intense, as Bretón de los Herreros satirically reflected in his 1836 comedy *La redacción de un periódico* [*The Newpaper Office*] or as described in the semi-autobiographical novel by Enrique Vera González, *Memorias de un periodista* [*Memoirs of a Journalist*], published in 1890. The core of the newspaper office comprised 'in-house' journalists, particularly with regard to informative newspapers, whose staff tended to have greater continuity than that of political newspapers. It was up to them to put together the newspaper through its specialist news sections, which did not imply that the journalist was an expert at the task or tasks entrusted to him. In his memoirs, Julio Nombela provides an example of the organization of the editorial work at one of the many newspapers with which he collaborated. The newspaper in question was *El Porvenir*, a short-lived publication based in Madrid, which he joined at the start of the Bienio Progresista, the two-year period from 1854 to 1856 of attempted political reform. Nombela tells us that at *El Porvenir*, the writers Carlos Navarro and Juan Antonio Viedma, together with the editor of the newspaper, Juan Belza, took care of writing the editorials.[19] Luis García Luna was entrusted with political briefs, perusing the *Gaceta* and other Madrid newspapers to scan for the

18 Memoirs and other documents from the time describe people who would go to newspaper offices to offer their services as collaborators, to place advertisements or to demand explanations from the editor of the newspaper regarding articles that, in their opinion, had attacked their reputation or that of the institution to which they belonged.

19 Julio Nombela (*Impresiones y recuerdos*, 395) referred to them as 'doctrinal articles' in which the political ideas supported by the owner of the company were defended.

most interesting news items, 'for which it was very important to know how to use scissors well'.[20] Gustavo Adolfo Bécquer did the same with French newspapers and wrote literary and theatre reviews. Finally, Nombela was in charge of checking provincial newspapers, the religious section, stock market prices and advertisements for shows.

As can be seen, specialization of work barely existed at the time, meaning that the young journalist passed through all the sections of the newspaper, which was considered part of the training process. A similar situation was experienced by somebody else who, owing to the status of his family, could have climbed directly to the highest ranks of the profession. The man in question was Alfredo Escobar, the son of Ignacio José Escobar, the Marquess of Valdeiglesias and editor of the royalist newspaper *La Época*, one of the most influential among the upper classes during the reign of Isabel II and the Bourbon Restoration. When Alfredo Escobar joined the newspaper office after training in the United States, he was entrusted with all manner of tasks: 'I would go to the ministries to gather news; I would frequent the conference rooms of the Congress and the Senate; I would also go to the magistrates' court; and I never ceased to attend most of the theatres.'[21] The first tasks given to Escobar at the newspaper headed by his father were those allocated to the *gacetillero* (writer of miscellaneous news, the Spanish equivalent of the cub reporter), a young journalist who would visit different public and private spaces in order to gather first-hand information to send to the newspaper office. *Gacetilleros* did not have a very good reputation owing to the indiscreet nature of their work. Both their inopportune questions and their presence in certain places were seen as

20 This expression (and its variants) was very common in the journalistic jargon of the nineteenth and early twentieth centuries. Rafael Mainar explained its meaning as follows: 'When there are few good things to say at home, between filling the gaps with rubbish and debris or doing so with your neighbour's things that deserve to be read and circulated, the scissors and cuttings win. Yes, scissors are a resource in both cases; but their use is only reliable when the cutting is honourably admitted to and there is no intention of passing off what has been taken from somewhere else as your own' (Rafael Mainar, *El arte del periodista* (Barcelona: Destino, 2005), 189).

21 Marqués de Valdeiglesias, *Setenta años de periodismo: Memorias* (Madrid: Biblioteca Nueva, 1950), vol. 2, 91.

a latent threat to privacy, one of the best-guarded, albeit fragile, treasures of public figures. The mere insinuation of suspicious conduct was in itself a threat to their reputation.

Escobar's words are a reference to other spaces that, together with the newspaper office, were also considered the journalist's places of work. Noteworthy among them were the public galleries of the lower house of parliament, the Congress. Practising their profession in the Congress and in the Senate obligated journalists not only to be able to recognize the politicians of the day and to have contacts that allowed access to them, but to master techniques that had become very useful to them, such as shorthand. Although the figure of the parliamentary commentator would subsequently develop as interpreters of political discussions, journalists sent to report from the parliament would initially have to spend long hours listening to the speakers and taking notes on their speeches. For this reason, they were pitied by others in the profession, as shown by the words of Mesonero Romanos regarding the stenographer, whom he considered the 'martyr of national representation'. Or in the words of Galdós, who described them as 'martyrs of the system'.[22] The transition from simple stenographer to parliamentary commentator came with the growing focus on political information in the press and the need to explain it to the public. Therefore, the press gallery became one of the most important spaces for journalists because it was where the news could be tapped directly. It gave rise to political news and the parliamentary commentator, which would become educational tools to facilitate understanding of the workings of the liberal political system to readers. Both, political news and, by extension, its writer, helped to familiarize the public with the constitutional formalities and political and economic language from the platforms provided by their

22 Mª Isabel Rovira, *Los aprendizajes de Benito Pérez Galdós: del periodista político al novelista en ciernes (1865–1876)* (Barcelona: Universidad de Barcelona, 2017), vol. I, 118. Andrés Borrego was the first to reproduce the *Diario de Sesiones de las Cortes*, the record of parliamentary proceedings, in the press, more specifically in *El Español*. For this purpose, he hired Ángel Ramón Martí, the son of Francisco de Paula Martí Mora, who was responsible for introducing shorthand into Spain (Augusto Martínez Olmedilla, *Periódicos de Madrid. Anecdotario* (Madrid: Editorial Aumarol, 1956), 103).

newspapers. Moreover, the press gallery turned into a meeting place for and a space shared by columnists of different ideological leanings, creating the most immediate forum for political discussion, aside from the actual assembly halls.[23] In a way, it can be said that the press gallery mirrored the various ways in which parliamentary debate was interpreted and later filtered to public opinion.

Aside from the work involved in searching for and writing about practical information, the articles of greatest political content fell to the writer of editorials and his collaborators, depending on the period and the newspaper. Often uncredited (particularly in the first decades of the reign of Isabel II), editorials allowed the ideological leanings of the publication to be identified.[24] The editorial, considered a text of reflection and analysis, provided the key to respectability in the profession. The journalists themselves placed great importance on the writing of this section of the newspaper as the most complete expression of their work as professionals because it allowed them to project their knowledge and guide public opinion. However, the conditions under which this work took place hindered the writing of work of higher quality. A very interesting article published in *El Imparcial* complained that the 'writers of editorials' were made to write an analytical article every day – whether on the subject of politics, diplomacy or economics – in addition to the other tasks they carried out at the newspaper office, without the time or tranquillity with which to familiarize themselves with the subject in any depth:

> In the academies and the public galleries of the houses of parliament we have applauded all the men who have for many years consummated that great effort of intelligence, who have written a daily article and twenty briefs, and have translated the drama, and have made the newsletter, and written up the newspaper in the absence of their colleagues, the people in charge of these sections.[25]

23 Modesto Fernández González, 'La tribuna de periodistas', in *Madrid por dentro y por fuera. Guía de forasteros incautos* (Madrid: Biblioteca Nueva, 2008), 419–31.

24 The anonymous nature of the articles and the role that can be attributed to them in the development of the profession of journalism deserves a more detailed analysis than can be given within the scope of this chapter.

25 *El Imparcial* (20 March 1869).

On many occasions, particularly in the final decades of the nineteenth century, editorials were commissioned from highly renowned firms that brought the newspaper prestige, although it was generally the chief editor (or lead editor, as he was sometimes known) and the editor of the newspaper who took care of them. In this respect, it is noteworthy that the figure of the editor of the newspaper was also undergoing professionalization and gaining prestige in the world of the press to the extent where his personal reputation was closely linked to that of his newspaper. Throughout the century, the newspaper editor who used the press as a political platform (José Luis Albareda, Práxedes Mateo Sagasta) co-existed with the editor who was purely focused on running the newspaper (Abelardo de Carlos Almansa). Torcuato Luca de Tena, founder and editor of *Blanco y Negro* and *ABC* would come to embody the figure of the modern newspaper editor.[26] Finally, in order to deal with the restrictions brought on by censorship, in the nineteenth century there existed the figure of the 'liable news-editor', an individual who, in exchange for remuneration, would be held liable before the authorities for violations committed by newswriters. The liable news-editor was, ultimately, in the words of the *costumbrista* Antonio Flores, 'the truly legal journalist; the only one to hold the legal status of *escritor público* before the courts'.[27]

While the entire office was involved in producing the newspaper (particularly the more modest ones), at crucial times (editorial deadline), the most important decisions were made by both the chief editor and/or the editor of the newspaper, and the person in charge of the actual printing of the newspaper.[28] In the journalistic world of the nineteenth century, this person received the title of *regente*. The *regente* or printing manager

26 A case study on newspaper offices and their editors at a local level (Asturias) in Gabriel Santullano, 'El oficio del periodista en el siglo XIX', Jorge Uría, ed., *Historia de la prensa en Asturias* (Oviedo: Asociación de la Prensa de Asturias, 2004), vol. 1, 455–92.

27 Antonio Flores, *La sociedad de 1850* (Madrid: Alianza Editorial, 1968), 232–3. During his youth, the politician Alejandro Lerroux was the 'front man' or liable news-editor for the Republican newspaper *El País*.

28 Without mentioning the staff required to administer the newspaper, who were responsible for, among others, ensuring its economic viability.

connected the manual tasks of printing the newspaper (typesetters, proof-readers, printers, etc.) with the intellectual work of the newspaper office, first with the layout man[29] (layout editor in contemporary terminology) and afterwards, if necessary, with whomever had to decide on more specific cases: the chief editor and the editor of the newspaper. It was up to the *regente* to provide information on the adjustments required for manuscripts presented by journalists depending on the final layout of the issue: either cutting down or enlarging the originals. The chief editor would quite often have mutilated the text before sending it to press, which was frowned upon by certain journalists whose sights were always set on their dreams of literary fame and held a fascination for creative genius, without interference from chief editors or any other news-editors.

Journalism: An open profession

Unlike other occupations of the modern bourgeois society, journalists did not enter the profession after completing officially regulated studies meant to provide them with proper skills for the job. They did not need to undergo validation at different stages of an education that led to a university degree in which they obtained the required knowledge and learnt the codes of conduct inherent to a closed group that other professionals aspired to enter, such as lawyers and doctors. In short, there were no specific study programmes to qualify as a journalist. One learnt to be a journalist by being one: by imitating one's colleagues in the newspaper office, dealing with a wide range of people in many different social settings, visiting authorities and informers, cultivating relations with the reading public, etc. Journalism was ultimately an open profession, but with internal rules that had to be learnt by any young man considering a career of writing for a newspaper office. Although journalism did not come to develop its own code of ethics, continuous reflection on the practice of the profession allows us to deduce the existence of a series of intrinsic

29 Antonio Flores, *La sociedad de 1850*, 237.

values that we can refer to as either 'good journalism' or 'good journalistic practice'.

This reflection began as early as the Trienio Liberal, the period of liberal government in Spain between 1820 and 1823. It was when *El Imparcial* (28 February 1822) recommended that newswriters 'before becoming men of letters, should be men and citizens' and as such should 'cultivate and practise the private and public virtues that constitute good men and virtuous citizens'.[30] In 1821, *El Censor* also commented on the qualities that journalists should have: 'the most absolute independence', 'the most severe impartiality', 'serious and profound studies', 'knowing their time and their people' and 'not slandering their fellows in the trade'.[31] Added to this was 'fine judgement' because, although 'it is never lawful to lie or to defend error', 'nor can or must one tell every truth'. The influence of the Enlightenment was very evident in *El Censor*, particularly in its educational concept of the work of a newspaper, which would explain the precautions it took as to what could or could not be published. Ultimately, *El Censor* was a newspaper produced by followers of French Enlightenment ideals with an educational and elitist view of its role as informer. However, this interesting article already raised the points that have been and continue to be the subject of debate, such as impartiality and independence, considered the two greatest aspirations of the world of newspapers. Throughout the nineteenth century and in the early decades of the twentieth century, there was ever-present concern for journalistic ethics, to the point where different committees were created to deal with it, and thought was even given to the establishment of a tribunal for possible wrongdoings that could be committed during the practice of the profession.[32]

Furthermore, *El Censor* also brought to the fore a point of prime importance in relation to the open nature of the profession of journalism. It

30 Elisabel Larriba, 'La Prensa', in Pedro Rújula and Ivana Frasquet, eds, *El Trienio Liberal (1820–1823). Una mirada política* (Granada: Comares, 2020), 195.

31 *El Censor* (18 August 1821).

32 Mª Luisa Humanes, 'Nacimiento de la conciencia profesional en los periodistas españoles (1833–1936)', in Carlos Barrera, ed., *Del gacetero al profesional del periodismo. Evolución histórica de los actores humanos del cuarto poder* (Madrid: Editorial Fragua, 1999), 49–50.

dealt with training for journalists, or the lack thereof, which was one of the most disparaging aspects in building up the public image of these professionals. If there is something on which sources coincide, it was to insist that the practice of journalism should require a compulsory minimum level of education. According to Francisco Pérez Mateos (under the pseudonym León Roch), there had to be a 'journalistic cultivation'; in other words, a cultivation that was 'varied, but not deep', one 'that allows everything to be known and spoken of, without delving deeply into anything'. The educational level of the average journalist throughout the nineteenth century was very inconsistent, precisely owing to the open nature of the profession. Co-existing with writers and intellectuals of the standing of Donoso Cortés and Peréz Galdós were individuals who greatly lacked erudition, which contributed to the discrediting of the profession. The concern for the quality of training journalists received was heightened during the Bourbon Restoration, which was a time when some of the professions that had emerged from or were redesigned by Spain's bourgeois society had already achieved great standing, which was reflected by good economic returns and broad social respectability. The first initiatives to found academic institutions to regulate the access to the practice of journalism were taken in the 1880s. In 1887, Fernando Araújo Gómez, a professor at the University of Salamanca, began to teach a course on journalism at that institution.[33] Araújo had experience in the world of the press owing to his collaborations with different publications both local (*El Eco del Tormes*) and national (*La Ilustración Española y Americana* and *La España Moderna*). In 1889, Gabriel Ricardo España Amenábar, parliamentarian and also journalist, sparked public debate on the need to create a journalism school in Madrid. The campaign led by España Amenábar bore fruit with the publishing in late 1899 of the regulations governing the operation of and subjects to be studied at the School of Journalism, founded under the auspices of the Press Association of Madrid.[34] Years later, coinciding with the holding of the First National Non-Daily Press Convention, it was proposed that

33 For further information on these projects, see Mª Luisa Humanes, *La formación de los periodistas en España* (Madrid: UCM, 1997), 105 ff.

34 *Revista Política y Parlamentaria* (30 December 1899).

the programme of journalism studies should be turned into a university degree course.[35] Although nothing practical came out of this, the question of training continued to linger in the air, as shown by the contacts held in 1919 between José del Prado Palacio, Minister for Public Instruction, and Miguel Moya, president of the Press Association of Madrid and editor of *El Liberal*. The most complete project was the school of journalism opened by the newspaper *El Debate*, whose editor was Ángel Herrera Oria. Founded in 1926, the *El Debate* school followed the approach of similar institutions that had emerged in the United States at the turn of the twentieth century.[36]

The idea of creating schools and teaching programmes for journalists, whether as a university degree or as a trade, was not shared by everybody in the profession. This has continued to be an important point of debate in the world of journalism both in Spain and abroad. On the one hand, given the breadth and diversity of tasks carried out at newspaper offices, it was the opinion of many that the best thing for the journalist, as previously stated, was to have a broad education that was neither academic or specialized, and to carve out a career through the daily grind. On the other hand, in keeping with the ideas expressed in the first part of this text, journalism maintained its close links to literary creation because the vocational nature of its practice had become its legacy. The comments made by León Roch in regard to Ignacio José Escobar highlighted this facet of its nature. The important thing, according to Roch, was not the studies held by the first Marquess of Valdeiglesias; what was important was that he 'had been born … into journalism' because 'the journalist, just as the artist and poet, are born and not made'.[37] The vocational nature of the profession, therefore, came to downplay the academic grounding of the journalist in order to focus on the intuitive appeal of an activity that was not always respected or well remunerated. Moreover, the sense of mission that a number of contemporaries attributed to the work of the journalist as a propagator 'of Truth and

35 First National Non-Daily Press Convention, held in Barcelona on 8–11 February 1915.

36 Juan Cantavella, *La Escuela de Periodismo de El Debate. Primeros pasos para la formación de periodistas en España* (Madrid: Fundación Universitaria San Pablo CEU, 2017).

37 León Roch, *75 años de periodismo*, 180.

Good' contributed to reinforcing this perception.[38] Nevertheless, according to the interpretation made by certain journalists, the characterization of journalism as a primarily vocational activity distorted its professional nature and justified the low salaries and poor working conditions experienced by many of them.[39] The journalist Rafael Mainar took this line. He believed the journalism of the late nineteenth century to be a 'product of modern industrialism' and, therefore, the journalist was a professional tied to his company, like any other employee. This meant, according to Mainar, that the journalist had to forget the literary whims of the 'romantic period of journalism'. Journalism was for him a trade that had to be learnt and not studied because the journalist needed 'activity, ingenuity and discernment, qualities that a degree did not [give], supposing that degree in journalism degree could be taken and until it was a degree'.[40]

The misunderstood reputation of the journalist

The specific nature of the profession of journalism as an open profession had a bearing on its public image. Several things contributed to this. First of these was the already mentioned lack of academic qualifications for its practice, which produced a workforce with great diversity of technical, intellectual and even ethical skills. As they had to be learnt through professional practice, technical skills were not always guaranteed. The lack of an intellectual education, on the other hand, limited the aspirations of many journalists to progress to specialist news sections. Finally, given that journalism for some was a means and not an end, the profession ran the risk of being used in a spurious manner. Secondly, the economic insecurity of many newspaper companies throughout the century meant that remuneration was non-existent or very low. Although this was a

38 Modesto Sánchez Ortiz, *El periodismo* (Madrid: M. Romero impresor, 1903), 9.

39 Mª Cruz Seoane and Dolores Saiz, *Historia del periodismo en España. 3. El siglo XX: 1898–1936* (Madrid: Alianza Editorial, 1996), 47.

40 Rafael Mainar, *El arte del periodista*, 110–11.

general reality, a few clarifications should be made. It should be noted that the grievances about poor returns from intellectual work were continuous in the world of letters in the nineteenth century and in the first decades of the twentieth century. The complaints made by men of letters should not conceal from us the fact that, in spite of this, there was great growth in the publishing sector at this time, allowing more people to dedicate themselves to writing in any of its multiple manifestations.[41] One of the keys that may explain this dissatisfaction can be found in the fact that many journalists felt they were being treated, in economic terms, as manual workers, which contrasted with the high reputation that, in their opinion, the practice of letters and the work of the journalist as an educator deserved. Furthermore, some of them, who came from higher social ranks that what their salaries reflected, perceived themselves to have been declassed. It is true that a large proportion of journalists did not receive high salaries for their work (or they received none at all), but gradual interest could be observed in the time of Larra from journalists that became attractive to readers and, therefore, gave prestige to a masthead. The salaries paid to Larra by *El Español* (20,000 reales a year), *El Mundo* and *El Observador* (40,000 reales a year) are renowned, and on contracts that allowed him to pen articles for other publications using a pseudonym.[42] While this was not the norm, Larra's was not an exceptional case.

As in most professions, differences in salary were the result of different factors. In the case of journalism, as previously explained, the prestige of the journalist's name was one of the most important. Among the implicit rules of the profession was, in fact, the importance of making a name for oneself, leading many young journalists to use a very common strategy that can be exemplified in the conduct of the chief editor of *El Nacional*,

41 Raquel Sánchez, *El autor en España, 1900–1936* (Madrid: Fundamentos, 2008); Jesús A. Martínez Martín, *Vivir de la pluma: La profesionalización del escritor, 1836–1936* (Madrid: Marcial Pons, 2009).

42 Leonardo Romero Tobar, 'Mariano José de Larra (1809–1837): el primer periodista moderno en España', in Enrique Rubio Cremades, Joaquín Álvarez Barrientos and José María Ferri Coll, eds, *Larra en el mundo: la misión de un escritor moderno* (Alicante: Universidad de Alicante, 2011), 133.

Salvador Canals. He published articles by budding journalists without paying them anything so that they could make their names known and open the doors to other, more solvent newspapers.[43] In the case of companies that were less well known or using young journalists, if these received any payment, it was intermittent or very scarce. This was Julio Nombela's experience during his time at *El Porvenir*. However, it opened the doors to working for *Las Cortes*, a more important daily newspaper run by Camilo Alonso Valdespino.[44] This practice was not out of the ordinary; rather, it was taken for granted by aspiring journalists as a step in their career development, a mechanism that was part of the unofficial *cursus honorum* in the profession of journalism.

Another thing that was partly responsible for lowering the respectability of journalism was the nature of how this profession was practised. In a bourgeois society whose moral guide was an orderly life as far as society, economy and family were concerned, the practice of journalism involved continuous movement and timetables that lacked a systematic distribution of time devoted to work and to leisure. As was seen earlier, despite the existence of certain, almost ritualistic habits and formalities in the way work was organized inside newspaper offices (checking the press and information from agencies, setting out responsibilities, etc.), a large part of the work of the journalist involved improvisation. News and unexpected events could disrupt the initial structure of the newspaper, increasing even more the sensation that the organization of work was provisional. The profession, therefore, lacked planning and defined timetables, and was often characterized by the pressure to meet deadlines. The speed at which articles were

43 León Roch, *75 años de periodismo*, 213.

44 Nombela's salary at *El Porvenir* was initially to be twenty duros a month (similar to that of his colleagues García Luna and Bécquer), but he finally only received half of this. He started out at *Las Cortes* earning sixteen duros a month (Nombela, *Impresiones y recuerdos*, 395–8). Information is available on the budget of *La Correspondencia de España* for the years at the turn of the twentieth century. It came to 78,000 pesetas in 1906. The part allocated to the newspaper office was only 5,000 pesetas. The salaries of in-house newswriters ranged between 50 and 100 pesetas a month. At this time, the most prestigious journalists could earn up to 200 pesetas (Jean-Michel Desvois, *La prensa en España (1900–1931)* (Madrid: Siglo Veintiuno, 1977), 6–8).

written greatly contrasted with the slow pace at which literary works were composed, a point that had obsessed journalists since the 1830s.[45] Aside from this matter, the fact that in the practice of their profession, journalists came into contact with a wide variety of people, some respectable and others not so, played an important part in their poor reputation. Particularly in the latter case, continuous relations with individuals of questionable morals even led to journalists being considered morally suspect.

The non-existence of set timetables, the need to frequent a wide range of people and places and job insecurity led to journalism being likened to the bohemian lifestyle typically associated with artists and writers. Because bohemia was considered the opposite of respectability, it invariably marked journalists, despite their insistence on presenting themselves as untiring, responsible and hard-working. This is evident in practically all the sources consulted for the writing of this chapter, and in their interest in letting readers know how they carried out their work because 'if the public had a precise idea of it, they would have a greater and better appreciation of the press'.[46]

However, what most clearly led to discrediting the image of the journalist and, consequently, smearing that of the profession was the relationship between politics and journalism. A description of this has already been given in this regard in the opening pages of this work, particularly in relation to partisanship, and therefore no further explanation will be given. What can be added, nonetheless, is an important point that overshadowed the image of the journalist where politics were concerned: venality. Accusations of bribery weighed like a millstone around the necks of journalists and journalism throughout the nineteenth century. They were called 'bell-ringers of the political churches' by Rico y Amat,[47] while José María Andueza would write: 'The journalist's conscience is a great auction,

45 Dorde Cuvardic García, 'Las relaciones de los escritores costumbristas y modernistas con las empresas periodísticas', *Reflexiones* 89/2 (2010), 85–97. The delivery of instalments of serialized novels were subject to the same time restraints as newspaper articles.

46 Mainar, *El arte del periodista*, 214.

47 Juan Rico Amat, *Diccionario de los políticos o verdadero sentido de las voces y frases mas usuales entre los mismos* (Madrid: F. Andrés y Compañía, 1855), 275.

where the buyer who pays the most takes home the goods.'[48] These were some of the qualifiers attached to this professional collective even by people close to it, such as these two authors, both of whom were men of letters. In summary, the journalist was by nature an immoral being always likely to be bought by anybody. The journalist's reputation in this respect did not improve during the Bourbon Restoration, when the newspaper publishing business was established, from which it can be deduced that venality was seen as a stain on the reputation of the press throughout the century.[49]

Added to this was the ability of journalists to ruin the reputations of others. This was an extremely important matter that left the core of social standing of men and women in the nineteenth century – their honour – in the hands of people who did not always conform to the standards of respectability required in bourgeois society.[50] Mesonero Romanos, himself a journalist, realized this very early on when he wrote the following:

> Modern civilization has instead gifted us with this new figure whose influence can be contrasted with that described in the preceding lines [the member of a religious order] … the *Periodista* is a social power who makes and removes laws, who causes peoples to rise up at will, who varies the social order on the spot. What enigma is this of modern society that lets itself be led by the first parvenu, that trembles and is shaken to its foundations by the simple opinion of an audacious man, that entrusts its powers to a callow youth in order to represent it, lead it, turn it upside down and raise it again?[51]

48 José Mª Andueza, 'El escritor público', in *Los Españoles pintados por sí mismos* (Madrid, I. Boix, 1843), vol. I, 211.

49 There was constant suspicion all over Europe that ministerial budgets contained funds to finance the press for propaganda purposes (the notorious 'slush funds'), which were heightened during this period. For the case of Spain, see Jesús Timoteo Álvarez, 'La estructura subterránea de la prensa en la Restauración', in Luis Otero and Angel Bahamonde, eds, *Madrid en la sociedad del siglo XIX* (Madrid: Alfoz, 1986), vol. 1, 228–48; for the case of France, see Christian Delporte, *Les journalistes en France, 1880–1950. Naissance et construction d'une profession* (Paris: Seuil, 1999), 140–8.

50 For further information, see Raquel Sánchez, 'Derechos en conflicto. Honor, libertad de expresión y vida cotidiana en la España del siglo XIX', *Historia constitucional: Revista Electrónica de Historia Constitucional* 21 (2020), 510–32.

51 Mesonero Romanos, 'Contrastes. Tipos hallados, tipos perdidos', in *Los Españoles pintados por sí mismos*, vol. II, 486–7.

This immense power wielded by journalists could first be made out in the world of show business, where the theatre critic had the ability to make or destroy the reputation of artists and business initiatives at a time when theatre was the main leisure activity and a highly profitable industry.[52] It would later be transferred to politics, where numerous commentaries by journalists about leading political and military figures would drive these individuals to defend their honour from what they considered to be attacks against their public reputation. In certain cases, such feelings were channelled through primitive means such as physical violence. This is exemplified by the blows delivered by the future General Prim upon Modesto Lafuente after being mocked by the latter in his political satire *Fray Gerundio* (1841). Prim thus showed his offender the little regard he deserved, treating him as an individual without entitlement to the least social respect among gentlemen and demonstrating his disdain for journalism.[53] In other cases, resorting to a duel – a sophisticated strategy for reasserting one's honour – evidenced the significance of the accusations received, the professional status journalists began to acquire and the growing importance of the press in building up the reputation of public figures.

Seeking professional respect

Certain writers and journalists encouraged the derogatory connotations associated with the profession, such as Larra, who ironically commented on his work: 'I am a journalist. I spend most of my time, like any *escritor público*, writing what I do not think and making others believe what

52 Flores, *La sociedad de 1850*, 236. A good example of this is the famous duel between the actor Julián Romea and Ignacio José Escobar, a newswriter and critic from *El Corresponsal*, which took place in 1843 (Pedro Gómez Aparicio, *Historia del Periodismo Español* (Madrid: Editora Nacional, 1968), vol. 1, 279–82).

53 Lafuente interpreted the Prim's violence against him as an 'attack against the freedom of the press and personal safety' (Gómez Aparicio, *Historia del Periodismo Español*, vol. 1, 252).

I do not believe.'[54] Others, however, aware that this facet of the activity of men of letters had positive repercussions for themselves, developed – consciously or unconsciously – a series of strategies and initiatives for the purpose of countering the most denigrating accusations.

A matter of special importance was the awareness of belonging to a profession, which was evident in the reflections that had been made on the subject since the eighteenth century. These reflections were directed inside the profession, at the journalists themselves, as a way of stimulating self-awareness and acknowledgement of their professional identity as journalists, aside from being men of letters. But they also sought to project this image to the world outside. In this way, it was possible to show society how journalism worked and to shatter the bohemian image of the profession that was propagated among much of contemporary society. This is the sense that can be attributed to the description of life in the newspaper offices that we can find in works by Mesonero Romanos onwards. Between the late nineteenth and early twentieth centuries, when the profession had become consolidated, speculations about the trade were materialized in different publications that endeavoured, in light of the experienced gained over an entire century, to show both young journalists and those unfamiliar with the profession the workings of an industry that was not always well understood. Outstanding examples of such publications were the satirical *Manual del perfecto periodista* (Manual for the Perfect Journalist) of 1891, by the brothers Carlos and Ángel Ossorio y Gallardo; *El libro del periodista* [*The Journalist's Book*] of 1912, by Basilio Álvarez; *Tratado de periodismo* [*Treatise on Journalism*] of 1901, by Augusto Jerez Perchet; *El periodismo* [*Journalism*] of 1906, by Modesto Sánchez Ortiz; and *El arte del periodista* [*The Art of the Journalist*] of 1906), by Rafael Mainar.[55] Also at the end of the nineteenth century, there seemed to be an emerging interest in the genealogy of the profession; in other words, to incorporate journalists into a tradition, to make them part of a collective to which figures of

54 'La vida de Madrid' (Life in Madrid), *El Observador*, 12 December 1834 (Mariano José Larra, *Obras completas. I. Artículos* (Madrid: Cátedra, 2009), 690).

55 A study of these publications can be found in Jorge Miguel Rodríguez, 'Rasgos de la figura del periodista en los primeros tratados de periodismo en España. Hacia una identidad profesional (1891–1912)', *Revista de comunicación* 15 (2016), 86–110.

unquestionable reputation had belonged. The clearest example of this is the renowned *Ensayo de un catálogo de periodistas españoles del siglo XIX* [*Essay on a Catalogue of Spanish Journalists of the Nineteenth Century*], by Manuel Ossorio y Bernard (1903–1904). In spite of the author's description of his work as no more than a 'simple listing of those who had devoted their efforts to the journalistic endeavour',[56] in fact it served as a mirror for novice journalists, while contributing to revive figures that were practically forgotten at the time the book was published. The same interest in delineating a 'canon of Spanish journalism' can be found in the proposal for the School of Journalism put forward by the Press Association of Madrid, one of whose chairs was to be named 'Famous Spanish Journalists' and consisted of a series of lectures entrusted to 'different speakers'.[57] These initiatives had been preceded long before by others, such as those by Manuel Eduardo de Gorostiza, with his *Galería en miniatura de los más célebres periodistas y articulistas de Madrid* [*Miniature Gallery of Madrid's Most Famous Journalists and Columnists*] of 1822, and Juan Pérez Calvo, with his *Galería de la Prensa. Colección de retratos políticos de los periodistas de España, hechos al daguerrotipo* [*Collection of Political Portraits of the Journalists of Spain, Made in Daguerreotype*] of 1846.

The creation of incorporated societies and associations was perhaps one of the most evident projects as it brought visibility to the collective in the professional world and balanced the individualism of certain journalists whose first point of reference as professionals was their newspaper office. This was in imitation of what had been done by other trades through the creation of entities that exceeded the limits of the actual company and defended journalists' work as a professional activity like any other in the modern productive society. These societies also became spaces for debate on the problems besetting the industry, and a shared space was carved out in which to defend common interests. Without entering into the connection between many journalists (in their facet of writers) with the Association of Writers and Artists that was founded in Madrid in 1872, the first of such

56 Manuel Ossorio Bernard, *Ensayo de un catálogo de periodistas españoles del siglo XIX* (Madrid: Imprenta y litografía J. Palacios, 1903), V.

57 *Revista Política y Parlamentaria* (30 December 1899).

groups emerged towards the end of the nineteenth century in the form of mutual societies. A first attempt was made between 1891 and 1892.[58] The Press Association of Madrid was founded in 1895 with backing from Alfredo Vicenti, the editor of *El Globo*, and its president was for many years Miguel Moya, the editor of *El Liberal*. Among others, press associations were founded in Málaga (1905), the Balearic Islands and Oviedo (1908), and Gijón (1910), and the Journalists' Association of Barcelona was founded in 1915.[59] Their creation was proof that journalism was being considered an autonomous activity of literary writing and an attempt by journalists to present themselves to society as an occupation that was clearly differentiated from other professional sectors. These were not trade union-style organizations created to defend the rights of journalists as workers. In fact, their members ranged from newswriters to the owners of the mastheads, which did not stop the interests of the different groups from clashing. The best-known conflict was the one that took place when, after the founding in 1919 of the Spanish Journalists' Union – a trade union associated with the General Union of Workers (UGT) – the first journalists' strike was called in Madrid to demand better pay and working conditions. The journalists asked the president of the Press Association of Madrid, Miguel Moya, for assistance. Moya faced a major conflict because, while his obligation as president was to defend his colleagues, he also had strong links to the owners of the newspapers and was also the chairman of the company Sociedad Editorial de España (known as 'El Trust'). Moya finally resigned from the leadership of the Press Association of Madrid.[60]

58 José Francos Rodríguez, *Cuando el rey era niño … De las memorias de un gacetillero (1890–1892)* (Madrid: Imprenta de J. Morales 1895), 89.

59 See García Galindo ('Las primeras sociedades españolas de periodistas: entre el socorro mutuo, los intereses profesionales y la libertad de expresión', in Santiago Castillo, ed., *Solidaridad desde abajo: trabajadores y socorros mutuos* (Madrid: UGT, 1994)), who located the creation of the ephemeral Press League in 1869. The Press Union of Málaga also existed in 1877. The formation of journalists' associations mainly took place in the twentieth century. See Luis Fernando Ramos Fernández, *La profesión periodística en España, regulación jurídica y consecuencias éticas* (Madrid: UCM, 1997), 131–266.

60 The situation in Spain was similar to that in other European countries, such as the United Kingdom, where the first professional association were incorporated. The

Apart from these matters, and despite their unstable position within the so-called middle-class professions, the possibilities journalists had to influence public opinion were always much greater than those of any other professional at the time. Mention was made of this previously when dealing with the appearance of the subject of journalistic ethics as a constant concern in certain professionals obsessed with reassertion of their reputation in society. Making the information they published credible also depended on the image they gave as professionals. This is the reason for resorting to the previously described strategies, such as the duelling, in order to support their assertions in the newspapers. Risking one's own life confirmed the veracity of the published information. Many journalists were involved in duels. This occasionally served to make a name for themselves by challenging important figures. In most other cases, it was to defend the honour of their work.[61] Some lost their life as a result, such as Augusto Suárez de Figueroa, who died in 1904 as the last of many duels he had fought throughout his career as a journalist. Where the duellists are concerned, it is difficult to discern whether they accepted the risk in order to defend the honour of the profession or their own reputation as men. Or even, although this is mere conjecture, whether they had come to so closely identify the profession with their personal identity as to understand any attack on the former as an insult to their standing as respectable gentlemen. The politician and journalist Nicolás María Rivero, editor of *La Discusión*, can be seen as a good example of this. Rivera fought a duel with General Caballero de Rodas as a result of criticism levelled against the officer by a member of his newspaper's editorial staff. Rodas had stated

---

National Association of Journalists was founded in 1884, changing its name to the Institute of Journalists in 1886. The National Union of Journalists, the trade union for journalists, was not founded until 1907 (Hampton, 1999). The Association syndicale professionnelle des journalistes républicains français was founded in France in 1887 (Delporte, *Les journalistes en France, 1880–1950*, 86).

61 See Juan Carlos Mateos Fernández, 'Cuestión de honor: Los periodistas se baten en duelo', *Historia y comunicación social* 3 (1998), 323–42 and Raquel Sánchez, 'Honor de periodistas: Libertad de prensa y reputación pública en la España liberal', in Raquel Sánchez and José Antonio Guillén Berrendero, eds, *La cultura de la espada: De honor, duelos y otros lances* (Madrid: Dykinson, 2019), 305–32.

that a printed correction would be enough for him to feel his reputation restored. However, the editor of *La Discusión* refused to rectify opinions that had already been published. Although he did not know which of his newswriters had caused the offence, Rivero did not hesitate to back him up by stating, as told by Martínez Olmedilla: 'There is never to be a correction in my newspaper. I answer, in whatever manner I please, for what is published in *La Discusión*.'[62]

The gradual specialization of the tasks within journalism also helped project a different image of the profession, which does not mean that all its facets were equally appreciated by the reading public. Descriptions of the world of newspapers show how the young *gacetillero* gathering information co-existed with the experienced journalist, a man of thought, who projected his knowledge of life into writing political analysis. Both – the dynamic youth and the level-headed older man – were two faces of an industry that was able in this way to unite its bohemian and adventurous facet with its pensive and intellectual side. The latter enjoyed greater prestige even within the actual newspaper industry given the connection between the traditional pensive and educating role that had been attributed to men of letters since the eighteenth century. By the end of the nineteenth century, the image of the pensive journalist, writer of editorials, fitted in well with that of the modern intellectual, the result of the nineteenth-century man of letters adapting to the times of the popular press. His analysis, which sometimes risked his freedom by defying the authorities, showed a strong determination to seek justice that would reinforce his credibility and, by extension, the reputation of the profession. At times, he would even influence the political situation of the nations, as occurred with the articles by Castelar published in *La Democracia* in the spring of 1865 and in the triggering by the press of the backlash by the intellectual classes against the Montjuïc Trial of 1896. Thus, intellectual bravery was added to the set of virtues that came to form the image of the profession of journalism and allowed the accusations of ideological perfidiousness so often levelled at the profession to be countered. What is more, intellectual bravery conformed perfectly

62 Martínez Olmedilla, *Periódicos de Madrid*, 137; also in Luis de Armiñán, *El duelo en mi tiempo* (Madrid: Editora Nacional, 1950), 50.

to the requirements of a new model of active and dynamic masculinity for which the journalist was a superb fit. Unlike the serious and respectable man inherent to professions such as medicine and law, the journalist was a physically or intellectually active man. However, a new figure would match this profile better than any other type of journalist: the *reportero* or reporter. This was a nimble and fast man on a quest for news, overcoming all sorts of obstacles to achieve his goal, which was to beat everybody else to a story or scoop. Based on this, Roch wrote an epic narrative on the theme of journalism in which the figure of the *reporter*, as the name was used in Spanish at the time, was embodied by Alfredo Escobar:

> Alfredo Escobar is simply a journalist, a great journalist in the modern sense, full of initiative, blessed with inventiveness, somewhat in the American style, able to do everything and to try anything in order to obtain a *reportage*. In order to find new and original information, he was the first Spanish journalist to ascend in a hot-air balloon and an aeroplane; he has entered into a cage with wild beasts, accompanied by their tamer, at the Parish Circus; he has gone on long journeys, and would be able to attempt and expedition to the moon, or to hell itself.[63]

Originating with the *gacetillero*, that is, the cub reporter or young journalist who went out in search of news, this modern style of reporting reached its peak in the initial decades of the twentieth century when the reporter became the new star of the newspaper business owing to the restlessness and adventure popularly associated with his work.[64] The journalist and writer Juan Más y Pi defined him in this way: '*Reporter*, that is to say, a man who lives his life to the full, who does not withdraw into himself, who does not dig his heels into the folds of his ego like a stylite, there at the top of his pillar. *Reporter*, that is to say, a man who lives ... '[65] The figure of the Spanish reporter was born out of the combination his precursor, the reviled *gacetillero*, and the war correspondent. With regard to the former, as previously explained, the intrusive nature of this journalist who pried

63 León Roch, *75 años de periodismo*, 195.

64 A study on the origin of the figure of the reporter in Ángeles Ezama, 'Primeros datos sobre la presencia del reportero en la prensa española', *Anales de literatura española* 26 (2014), 167–86.

65 Ezama, 'Primeros datos sobre la presencia del reportero en la prensa española', 178.

into the private affairs of individuals, had tainted the public image of the profession. By the time of the Bourbon Restoration, the *periodista de sucesos*, the journalist who reported on crimes and incidents, was the epitome of this negative image. This, however, was paradoxical considering that the crime story was the most popular genre consumed by the public. The war correspondent, on the other hand, offered a more appealing side of the profession because he combined the bravery of a soldier with the intellectual analysis and commitment with the truth of a man of letters. The figure of the war correspondent emerged in Spain during the Spanish-Moroccan War (1859–1860), through the coverage of events given by Pedro Antonio de Alarcón, Gaspar Núñez de Arce and the quintessential reporter for the Spanish press at the time, Francisco Peris Mencheta.[66]

Conclusion

The profession of journalism provides us with a very interesting vantage point from which to view the construction of the public sphere in Spain in the nineteenth century. First of all, there was a major change in the careers open to men of letters, who faced the challenges brought on by the economic transformation of the time more successfully than is usually admitted, allowing greater public exposure for their activity. Furthermore, it facilitates understanding into the dynamics of the conflict arising from the overlap between the rights of freedom of expression and press and the safeguarding of privacy and the reputation of individuals. In fact, drawing the line between freedom of expression and defamation was a difficult task for the jurists of the time. All of this revolved around the figure of the journalist, who, while not achieving the prestige or remuneration of other professionals, wielded great influence. In his hands was the ability to shape and guide public opinion and the possibility to make or destroy

66 Ángel Martínez Salazar, 'Pero no, la guerra no es bonita. Aproximación a la figura del corresponsal de guerra', *Sancho el Sabio. Revista de Cultura e Investigación Vasca* 7 (1997), 107.

reputations. The strength of journalism stems from this, but also its weakness. Throughout these pages, an endeavour has been made to deal with certain points that revolve around this dilemma, although much remains to be analysed. This subject is filled with challenges for the historian.[67]

67 This work forms part of the research project 'Culture of Honour, Politics and Public Sphere in Liberal Spain (1833–1890)' (PGC2018-093698-B-I00), financed by the Spanish Ministry of Science, Innovation and Universities/FEDER. No reference has been made here to the professionalization of women in the field of journalism owing to the special characteristics of the topic, which would require more detailed analysis.

PART V

Teaching Professionals

EDUARDO HIGUERAS CASTAÑEDA

Education in the Public Sphere

The Construction of the Reputation of Primary Teachers in Mid-Nineteenth-Century Spain

ABSTRACT

The process of professionalization of schoolteachers in Spain advanced in parallel with the building of the liberal state. The expansion of primary schools was one of the bases of the liberal national project. However, the liberal-moderate legislation, far from considering the teacher as a state official, attributed to him tasks typical of a priest, which pursued social control of the lower classes. Deficiencies in their formal education, dependence on the spoils system and poverty were the characteristics of this semi-profession throughout the entire nineteenth century. Even so, in the juncture of democratic opening of 1868–1873, teachers found the opportunity to vindicate themselves in the public sphere as 'workers of civilization' and representatives of the State. On this matter, the aim of this chapter consists in analysing the strategies they implemented to project a respectable image and demand their full professionalization.

Introduction

The Public Education Act of 1857 provided Spain with a lasting framework for the development of a national educational system. It was intended to produce 'citizens who will be more useful, the moralized and educated they are'.[1] The value of education as a condition of progress and cornerstone of citizenship was a commonplace in the different versions of liberal tradition. In this sense, the role of teachers was crucial: 'It is a prerequisite that a career in education should offer at every level such advantages of stability, decorum and remuneration that it may be embraced by competent men with their minds made up not to abandon it for others.'[2]

1 *Diario de Sesiones de las Cortes* [henceforth *DSC*] 11 (14 May 1857), appendix 1, 67.

2 *DSC* 11 (14 May 1857), appendix 1, 67.

However, teachers knew nothing of these advantages throughout the nineteenth century. On the contrary, this profession was characterized by serious training deficiencies, job insecurity and dependence upon the clergy and patronage networks.[3]

The Moyano Law, as it was known, underwent few significant changes during its life of over a hundred years. The first moderations were addressed after the 1868 Revolution, with the proclamation of freedom of education. These novelties were eliminated with the Bourbon Restoration in 1875 and, until the turn of the century, the situation of teachers remained almost unaltered, as did the stereotypical image generally attributed to them: that of the poor, hungry employee, despite the fact that they represented 'civilization' as opposed to ignorance. In this context, teachers strove to intervene in the public sphere in defence of the professional dignity of a collective mistreated by the State and united by an adverse situation.[4]

3 Ignacio Martín Jiménez, 'Ser maestro en la España del siglo XIX', *Historia Social* 33 (1999), 3–23.

4 The primary teacher has occupied a prominent position in the output of historians of communication in Spain. For example, the historiographical accounts by Aida Terrón, 'Estatuto socioeconómico y activismo sindical del profesorado', in Jean-Louis Guereña, Julio Ruiz Berrio and Alejandro Tiana Ferrer, eds, *Nuevas miradas historiográficas sobre la educación en la España de los siglos XIX y XX* (Madrid: IFIE, 2010), 185–208; and older, but still useful, by Narciso de Gabriel, 'La formación del magisterio', in Jean-Louis Guereña, Alejandro Tiana Ferrer and Julio Ruiz Berrio, eds, *Historia de la educación en la España contemporánea: diez años de investigación* (Madrid: CIDE, 1994), 215–66, focused above all on the training of primary school teachers. The professionalization of primary education, however, has attracted less attention. Significant in this respect, are the contributions by Narciso de Gabriel, 'Historia de la profesión docente en España', in A. Novoa and Julio Ruiz Berrio, eds, *A historia da Educação en Espanha e Portugal* (Lisboa: Sociedade Portuguesa da Ciencias da Educaço-Sociedad Española de Historia de la Educación, 1993), 137–56; Narciso de Gabriel, 'La profesionalización del magisterio en España (siglos XIX-XX): literatura, biografías, memorialística', *Historia y Memoria de la Educación* 1 (2015), 59–92; Cándido Ruiz Rodrigo, 'Referencias bibliográficas y documentales en torno a la problemática socio-profesional del magisterio', *Historia de la Educación* 16 (1997), 531–41; and Agustín Escolano, 'Memoria de la formación de maestros', *Aula* 8 (1996), 311–27.

During the first half of the nineteenth century, doctrinaire liberal legislation denied teachers the status of state representative. Quite to the contrary, they were considered to be exercising their function in representation of families. Given that primary schools were not regarded as the first step on the educational ladder, but as an institution intended to reproduce social hierarchies with teaching focused on traditional values, neither were teachers offered real advanced training. The title of primary teacher reflected a superficial ability and was only necessary to exercise in so-called 'complete' schools, which were not the most numerous in Spain.[5] Which is why this occupation could be regarded as a semi-profession. However, teachers, like members of other more affluent professional collectives, sought to assert the public dimension of their activity, as a fundamental collective for the progress of society, which could not dispense with their expert knowledge in the battle against ignorance.[6]

Education and clericalism during the reign of Isabel II

The concept of public school took shape in Spain in opposition to the schools run by the Church. In this sense, one can situate in the mid-eighteenth century an initial precedent for the professionalization of teachers as a guild.[7] A 1743 Royal Decree granted the *Hermandad de San Casiano* exclusive capacity to issue the title of teacher, a profession

5 'Liberal educational legislation in Spain differentiated, within public schools, between elementary and superior. The former could be, in turn, complete and incomplete. This differentiation was reflected in primary teachers' salaries and the level of training required of them. In practice, most Spanish primary schools were elementary and incomplete.'

6 Their strategies, in this respect, differed little from those deployed by doctors or engineers. See Darina Martykánová and Víctor Manel Núñez García, 'Ciencia, patria y honor: los médicos e ingenieros y la masculinidad romántica en España', *Studia histórica* 38 (2020), 45–75.

7 Julio Ruiz Berrio, 'La escuela pública', in Guereña, Ruiz Berrio and Tiana Ferrer, eds, *Historia de la Educación en la España Contemporánea*, 78–81.

equated in terms of privileges with 'those that exercise Liberal Arts in a literary degree'. From the perspective of enlightened reformism, teachers could make an effective contribution to 'the public cause', improving children's 'habits' by instilling 'in them the spirit of good citizens'. This legislation regulated access to the profession, which was linked to the definition of a pre-modern concept of citizenship. Logically, what prevailed were values of obedience to the king, 'to one's elders' and, of course, to the Catholic religion.[8]

However, beyond its guild origins, the starting point of the slow process of professionalization of Spanish public education coincided with the unfolding of the liberal state, during its critical phase at the end of the 1830s, when the definitive break with absolutism was confirmed in Spain. The law of 21 July 1838, Moderate[9] in inspiration, provided for the expansion of primary teaching upon the basis of a new school network organized by municipalities. The law differentiated between two types of public school: localities of fewer than a hundred inhabitants could have an 'incomplete' school, while the rest would have to fund 'complete' schools. The fundamental difference lay in the fact that, while the latter were to be run by a teacher with a professional qualification, this requirement did not apply to the former. In practice, most town councils found it impossible to finance a 'complete' school, which hampered the development of primary teaching.

The expansion of a public-school network constituted a fundamental tool in the affirmation of the liberal state as opposed to the Church. Thus, the teacher represented a crucial element of the process of national construction. Which suggests that schools and teachers were intended to become vectors of secularization, since private education was practically monopolized by religious orders. All of this involved regulation of access

8 This legislation, and others, is included in the *Real provisión de Su Magestad y señores del consejo en que se prescriben los requisitos que han de concurrir en las personas que se dediquen al magisterio de las primeras letras, y los que han de preceder para su examen, con lo demás que contiene* (Zaragoza: Imprenta del Rey nuestro Señor, 1771), 3.

9 The Moderate Party (Partido Moderado) upheld the ideas of Doctrinaire Liberalism in Spain.

to the public teaching system via specific professional training. Hence, the creation of teacher-training colleges, in which future public teachers were trained. 'Among the considerable number of obstacles hampering progress in primary education, one of the most significant is without a doubt the ignorance of teachers', declared the military governor of La Coruña at the inauguration of a teacher-training college in 1845. For this reason, this new institution was presented as 'a sign of civilization'.[10]

'Strengthening, moralising and instructing society' was the task of teachers, in the words of the director of the aforementioned school. Pupils of teacher-training colleges should, in this sense, contribute to teaching so that citizens were 'moral and virtuous as a matter of conviction and of habit' and thus avoid 'confusion, ruin and social dissolution'.[11] A task that, in practice, involved taking on a nationalizing endeavour that was not feasible with the teachers practising until then. Above all, because their lack of training undermined the prestige of the profession, 'the ridiculous image of the primary teacher has finally vanished from the face of the earth and it is publically and proudly stated that henceforth the teacher and not the cannon shall be the arbiter of the fate of the world'.[12] In 1841, Laureano Figuerola, when still a pupil at the Escuela Normal de Maestros [Central Teacher School], founded four years earlier, developed these arguments further:

> A central teacher training college ... will shortly produce a growing number of teachers in order to staff provincial teacher-training colleges, and, lending primary education a uniform and vigorous direction, to *nationalize*, one might say, that group of regions known as Spain, which instead of being a state, presents conflicting interests and even attitudes of hostility due to the spirit of provincialism that dominates those towns.[13]

10 *Discursos pronunciados en la apertura de la Escuela Normal de Instrucción Primaria de la Provincia de la Coruña celebrada el día 2 de julio de 1843* (La Coruña: Imprenta de D. Domingo Puga, 1845), 3.

11 *Discursos pronunciados en la apertura de la Escuela Normal*, 11.

12 *Discursos pronunciados en la apertura de la Escuela Normal*, 19.

13 Laureano Figuerola, *Manual completo de enseñanza simultánea, mutua y mixta* (Madrid: Imprenta de Yenes, 1841), VI–VII.

Figuerola's language was that of a progressive liberal. He was a staunch advocate of primary education as the engine of progress that facilitated advancement of the middle and working classes. Schooling was also one of the keys to the construction of a progressive vision of national sovereignty and the broadening of the sphere of citizenship, which had more to do with the idea of capacity than with that of wealth. However, the vision regarding education, its goals and, consequently, the function of teachers in the school system, differed in the various ramifications of liberal culture that, at that time, were already clearly delimited. To the left of progressive liberalism, a democratic culture was beginning to form that took shape in the republican movement. Primary education, in this case, appeared as a civil right. The State, therefore, had to guarantee universal, free, lay schooling, which involved the consideration of teachers as true civil servants with a secularizing mission.

It was not, however, the progressive liberal vision, or the republican option, that prevailed in the design of the educational system and the construction of the school network, but the criteria of doctrinaire liberalism. Indeed, it was the Moderates who shaped the Spanish liberal state from the second half of the 1840s onwards and occupied power, in almost uninterrupted fashion, until the Revolution of September 1868. With the signing of the 1851 Concordat, the State committed itself to sustaining the clergy budget. The Church, moreover, guaranteed itself not only the capacity to establish institutions of private education, but also supervision of 'the purity of the doctrine of faith … and of the religious education of the young … even in public schools'.[14] Teachers, therefore, appeared as the builders of a nation that, according to the Moderate project, was essentially Catholic.[15]

The revolution of 1854 and the opening of a Parliament in which the Catholic unity of Spain was debated did not alter this educational framework. In 1855, writer Juan Eugenio de Hartzenbusch, director of the Escuela Normal de Maestros, addressed his pupils at the opening ceremony of the new academic year:

14 Gregorio Alonso, *La nación en capilla. Ciudadanía católica y cuestión religiosa en España, 1793–1874* (Granada: Comares, 2014), 201.

15 Ángel Luis López Villaverde, *El poder de la Iglesia en la España contemporánea. La llave de las almas y de las aulas* (Madrid: La Catarata, 2013), 72.

> The post of primary school teacher is not only serious, it is almost sacred. In Spain, as in other countries, there are … many millions of individuals who, needing a religious and civil education, more or less complete, can receive only that provided by the teacher, the son of these colleges. The farm hand, the craftsman, the office clerk, all those parents with limited means, who employ their day, outside or inside the home, in a task that allows for no interruption if it is to be productive, have to place their children in the hands of primary school teachers, to be taught and educated; and the state … wants the teacher that substitutes the parent to do so in positive fashion. You are going to fulfil the role of parent, and of good parent; because the state, which cannot prevent in the natural parent the existence of defects or even vices, can and should demand that the educational parent possess only desirable garments; it has no choice but to accept the former; but the latter it trains, experiments with and chooses; and if her does not meet the necessary requirements, he is not included among the first … and the most useful propagators of the Enlightenment.[16]

The Enlightenment to which he referred implied an education that was, above all, religious: 'The first thing man should teach man is the history of mankind; and the primitive, the only true history of mankind, is the history of our faith.' For that reason, among 'the circumstances' that should 'grace the teacher', the main one was 'being an exemplary Christian'. If he fulfilled that condition, 'though his science were not great', he would be sufficiently 'useful to his country'. That was the education required by the working classes, upon whom the labour of teachers was focused. It was no longer a question of laying the foundations for the expansion of liberal citizenship via the spread of the Enlightenment, but of ensuring social order on the basis of Christian values. In order to achieve this objective, the State did not need a body of civil servants with specialized training, nor selection of those most capable of practising primary teaching. He did not even conceal from his pupils the fact that the only reward they should expect in their professional career was the satisfaction of making a sacrifice to a socially relevant end: 'he who dedicates himself to this profession, in fact demonstrates little ambition'.[17]

Thus, the image of the teacher was likened, firstly, to the figure of the parent, whom the former replaced by decision of the State so as to

16 Juan Eugenio de Hartzenbusch, *Discurso pronunciado en la escuela normal central de instrucción primaria* (Madrid: Imprenta Nacional, 1855).

17 Hartzenbusch, *Discurso pronunciado*.

complete a Catholic education: that which baptism entrusted, specifically, to parents and, in accordance with gender roles within the family, to mothers. School, therefore, was identified as an extension of the domestic environment, and the role of the teacher, indirectly, acquired female connotations. Secondly, the teacher was definitively presented as 'a secondary socializing agent',[18] given that he fulfilled functions formed within Catholic parameters, with the aim of reproducing social hierarchies, a task also undertaken by the clergy.

It was, indeed, growing social unrest that facilitated moderate liberalism's return to power in 1856. The Moderate shift narrowed the margins of political participation and accentuated concern over public order and social control. The function attributed to teachers, in this respect, did not vary in relation to the parameters indicated, but the religious component in teaching and clerical control of education was reinforced. That same year, in October, Eugenio de Hartzenbusch's replacement as director of the Escuela Normal de Maestros delivered a new speech to the future teachers on the occasion of the beginning of the academic year. The only difference vis-à-vis that of his predecessor was the emphasis on the school's evangelizing function:

> In the century of transition in which we live, a century in which anarchy reigns over ideas, in which anything goes … ; in which everything is questioned and everything is allowed, however absurd it be; in which authority is denied and everything is conceded to reason, in which beliefs waiver and faith is lost, the teacher has a great duty, which is to teach children the truths of the Gospel with more determination than ever, shape and strengthen their Catholic faith and teach them fear of God …, without which there is not nor can be true happiness or stable society, nor any man who fulfils his duties as is required by the law of God.[19]

18 Félix Ortega and Agustín Velasco, *La profesión de maestro: un estudio sociológico del magisterio en Castilla-La Mancha* (Madrid: CIDE, 1991), 19.

19 *Discurso pronunciado por Don Basilio Sebastián Castellanos, Director de la Escuela Normal Central de Instrucción Primaria en 26 de octubre de 1857, con motivo de la Inauguración del curso escolástico de 1857 a 1858* (Madrid: Imprenta Militar de don Pedro Montero, 1858), 15.

Only a month earlier, the new Public Education Act, the aforementioned Moyano Law, came into force, regulating every level of the educational system. It established the definitive basis for the shaping of public schools and education in Spain. Its first article established as the basis of children's education, teaching of 'the Christian doctrine and notions of sacred history'. Section III regulated 'professional teaching'. This included 'that of primary teachers', equated with 'that of veterinarian' or 'that of master builder'. On the one hand, it recognized primary teachers as professionals. However, this was a qualification that was held in lower social esteem than both university studies and even secondary education. In fact, the level required was clearly lower. Among the 'professionals' recognized by the Moyano Law, only primary school teachers were required to study the Catechism and the Bible. There was significantly more religious content in their training than pedagogical training.[20]

The situation of primary teaching, in the mid-nineteenth century, was deplorable. It clearly reflected the inability, disinterest even, on the part of the Moderate government regarding completion of the nationalization of the working classes via the expansion of public schooling, configured as a residual institution on the Spanish educational landscape. When the Moyano Law was passed, around 9,000 municipalities remained outside the school network. Over half of the schools that existed were incomplete. As a result, almost 47 per cent of primary teachers taught without a title or below their qualifications, if they had any.[21] Their salary, in these cases, was similar, or even lower than, that of a day labourer.[22] In other words, they lived on the breadline. It is logical, in these circumstances, that many primary teachers had to recur to a complementary source of income. As explained by Ignacio Martín, secondary school teacher, at the end of the century:

20 *Gaceta de Madrid* 1710 (10 September 1857).

21 Jean-Louis Guereña, 'La estadística escolar', in Guereña, Ruiz Berrio and Tiana Ferrer, eds, *Historia de la educación en la España contemporánea*, 73–4.

22 'Almost 60 per cent of teachers earn less than an Andalusian labourer', notes Martín Jiménez, 'Ser maestro en la España del siglo XIX', 9.

> The old primary teacher, miserably paid as such, was forced to seek extra work, lest he die of hunger; in other words, in the village he was sexton, bell-ringer, secretary and, possibly, bailiff, in short, he combined in one person all the menial jobs in the municipality. Could the primary teacher enjoy any prestige with such an outrageous combination of positions? The noble primary teacher, the mentor of childhood …, at the service of coarse locals and their servants![23]

It was not, ultimately, an attractive job for the middle classes or for the sectors of the working classes that sought to consolidate their social advancement. In fact, the vast majority of primary teachers (almost 75 per cent) came from rural areas and from relatively humble families.[24] They were, generally, the children of small landowners who could not aspire to improve the socio-economic situation of their parents or, quite simply, were unsuited to manual labour. 'The only people who aspired to be primary teachers were those incapable of following another career or working in art or industry, defectors from ecclesiastical studies, the disabled and the odd army discharge', claimed Serafín Casas.[25] This typology was customary, although the characterization may appear exaggerated. Primary education was a heterogeneous collective in which internal categories could also be identified. Among these, 'superior' primary teachers, with a year more of teacher-training than 'elementary' primary teachers, might be said to have been an elite that was particularly active in its defence of the profession.

Poor training had a direct effect upon the low prestige of primary teachers and became one of the fundamental obstacles to completion of the professionalization of this collective. Moreover, the new legislation maintained the division between complete or incomplete schools. All of them continued to be run by local councils, but the former were now obligatory in localities with a population of over 500. This meant leaving most schools staffed by unqualified primary teachers, appointed by town councils without more requirements than the possession of a 'certificate of aptitude

23 Martín Jiménez, 'Ser maestro en la España del siglo XIX', 9. Serafín Casas Abad, *El maestro de escuela de ayer y el profesor de instrucción primaria de hoy* (Huesca: Imprenta de Jacobo María Pérez, 1887), 12.

24 Martín Jiménez, 'Ser maestro en la España del siglo XIX', 9.

25 Casas Abad, *El maestro de escuela de ayer y el profesor de instrucción primaria de hoy*, 14.

and morality' issued by the local authorities. Only exceptionally did people embark upon the career via public examinations. Unqualified practice, therefore, became the norm. Hence, the position of primary teacher established itself as a semi-profession. Not only were they denied the status of state-paid employees, but the qualifications obtained in teacher-training colleges did not prevent other collectives from exercising as teachers. Finally, low salaries and the establishment of state and local controls over schools rendered primary teachers completely dependent upon patronage networks and ecclesiastical power, which generally went hand in hand.

This control over the practice of primary teaching was twofold. In the first place, the State exercised supervision by means of inspectors. However, in the daily life of primary teachers, the most significant role was played by provincial and, above all, local education boards, which had the capacity to initiate proceedings, suspend salaries or even expel teachers from schools if they identified inappropriate conduct.[26] These boards were formed, in accordance with the law, the local mayor, a member of the clergy, an alderman and 'three or more fathers'. With the exception of the clergyman, appointed by the diocese, the remaining board members were designated by the civil governor, who in turn was the key element in the liberal administration's centralized framework. Primary teachers, thus, were subordinated from a point of view of religious morality, the government's political orientation and approval by local patronage networks.

The memoirs written in the mid-1880s by primary teacher Valero Almudévar, posted to a village in the Pyrenees in 1864, are particularly illustrative in this respect: 'This corporation – he explained, in reference to the local boards – is generally responsible for suppressing the primary teacher's freedom, and causing him to lose his professional dignity, if the teacher is weak, or resort to loans in order to feed his poor family.'[27] Therefore, primary teachers had to follow the conduct guidelines established by the boards, which often took advantage of the slightest pretext to interfere in their professional work. In fact, their position rendered them especially

26 Martín Jiménez, 'Ser maestro en la España del siglo XIX', 12–4.

27 Valero Almudévar, *Páginas originales. Memorias de un maestro de escuela dedicadas al Excmo. Sr. D. Práxedes Mateo Sagasta* (Madrid: Est. Tip. De M. P. Montoya y compañía, 1886), 42–3.

qualified to intervene in electoral processes. If electoral legislation included them as voters 'through capacity', this was not a consequence of their meagre training, nor, logically, of their non-existent independence, but specifically due to their malleability. They were, inevitably, docile voters that, moreover, could be used to request their pupils' fathers' votes.[28]

This latter function, in truth, could prove difficult, because the figure of the primary teacher, in general, was not particularly respected in towns and villages, as Ortega y Velasco have argued.[29] This was confirmed, once again, by teacher Valero Almudévar's experience: 'People have a certain mistrust of primary teachers, based on ignorance and fanaticism, since they are regarded as leeches bleeding the municipal budget dry as employees paid directly from the municipal treasury.'[30] This was established an ultimate degree of scrutiny of the conduct of primary teachers, obliged to live apart from a community that, on the one hand, considered them a burden and, on the other, demanded exemplary behaviour from the point of view of family life and leisure activities. The primary teacher, furthermore, found himself in an intermediate position, condemned to isolation. Given his training, as modest as it was, he was in a superior position to the working classes. That did not mean, however, that his place was among local elites, from whom he was separated by poverty.

In this fashion, job insecurity, the presence of unqualified teachers, *caciquismo*, clericalism, 'ignorance' and 'fanaticism', constituted limitations upon the possibilities of professionalizing primary teachers. Which is why they sought to construct an image in opposition to these categories in order to defend their classification as civil servants and their alignment with middle-class professionals. In the mid-1860s, Spain was suffering a devastating economic crisis. In this context, the politicization of the working classes was driven by the republican and progressive opposition. The monarchy retreated to increasingly Moderate positions, with growing influence on the part of the neo-Catholic sector, which followed the antiliberal principles advocated by Pope Pious IX. It was logical for many

28 Martín Jiménez, 'Ser maestro en la España del siglo XIX', 15.

29 'El maestro está en la comunidad, pero no forma parte de ella', wrote Ortega and Velasco, *La profesión de maestro*, 21.

30 Almudévar, *Páginas originales*, 42.

primary teachers to sympathize with the revolutionary project, given that its secularizing proposals involved, in theory, a change in their status. After all, according to the democratic vision, the primary teacher was the cornerstone of national regeneration.[31]

One cannot, of course, generalize with regard to the revolutionary sympathies of a collective that, although it shared the same adverse conditions, was heterogeneous. Many primary teachers owed their position to clientelistic favours, and all had entered their schools with reports of exemplary religious conduct that, moreover, they were obliged to observe. In other words, primary teachers, more than via a system of public examination, had been selected because they conformed to the guidelines that distanced them from revolutionary terrain. But primary teachers with an elementary and, above all, a higher qualification, presented a particular profile. A possible interpretation is that the very configuration of the school in the doctrinaire state set them against the system since defence of the professionalization of primary education involved eliminating Church interference and replacing the residual function assigned them by Moderate legislation with genuine public employee status. In accordance with these coordinates, the demands voiced by primary teachers could be adapted to the project of nation envisaged by progressives and democrats.

It is not easy to identify primary teachers that were openly involved in the democratic protests of the 1860s. However, there is good reason to interpret that many of them were not alien to these demonstrations. Above all because the neo-Catholic media themselves began to brand schools as 'focal points of immorality' where teachers, who were known for their 'bad habits', taught 'bad books' to their pupils. In 1895, those kinds of accusations led Galician teacher Domingo Erosa to publish a novel in defence of the dignity of his profession from an openly liberal stance. With the eloquent title *El maestro de escuela o el civilizador del mundo* [*The Teacher or the Civilizer of the World*] the author contrasted the unqualified teacher, without training, vocation or awareness of his duties, with the qualified

31 'The primary school teacher was one of the key figures in the new society advocated by republicanism', writes Octavio Ruiz-Manjón, 'La cultura política del republicanismo español', in Guadalupe Gómez Ferrer, ed., *La época de la Restauración (1875–1902). Vol. II, Civilización y cultura* (Madrid: Espasa, 2002), 184.

teacher, 'a dignified, distinguished and esteemed figure', who one day would rise 'to the forefront of society in order to civilize the world, to enlighten the masses' continuing 'the sublime work that Jesus Christ himself began here on Earth'.[32]

Erosa planned to publish a second novel with an equally meaningful title: *El mártir de la civilización moderna* [*The Martyr of the Modern Civilization*]. Although it did not see the light of day, he did express his intention to portray the primary teacher as 'the main state functionary … the true civilizer of the world …, tireless worker in the divine task of our social regeneration', like a 'Jesus Christ preaching the truth', even if he did so in the desert: 'despite his lofty mission – continued the author – most of society, far from offering him the recognition he deserves, despises him … and denies him the social considerations to which he is rightly entitled'.[33] For that reason, Domingo Erosa claimed for primary teachers the same rights that were enjoyed by state functionaries, with the exception of those who lacked a qualification, and demanded the abolition of the local boards, instruments in the hands of *caciques* and the Church. In other words, he defended the dignity of the primary teacher and the complete professionalization of primary education. And he did so, moreover, while exhibiting his cultural training.

This novel is a good example of the type of strategy that those primary teachers most determined to defend their occupation could articulate so as to dignify their profession in an increasingly restricted public sphere. The final years of the Moderate regime were characterized, specifically, by the monarchy's authoritarian shift in response to the progressive-democratic revolutionary challenge. The institutional shut-down had a major impact upon qualified primary teachers. Isabel II's last government, neo-Catholic in its orientation, decided to close the teacher-training colleges, regarded as focal points of subversion. However, little is known of the political involvement of primary teachers in this context, the fact that the government

32 The work is analysed by Narciso de Gabriel, 'La profesionalización del magisterio en España (siglo XIX-XX): literatura, biografías, memorialística', *Historia y memoria de la educación* 1 (2015), 59–92. The quotations on pp. 62 and 66.

33 Gabriel, 'La profesionalización del magisterio en España', 68.

had them in its sights is a clear indication that their professional demands had merged with the revolutionary protest.

The verdict of the commission that drafted the new law on primary education,[34] which was to replace the Moyano Law, made this clear. The preparation of primary teachers in teacher-training colleges had instilled in them the illusory hope of equating themselves with secondary school and university teachers. That ambition, in turn, led to political positions that were incompatible with the goals of education, according to the conservative vision. There was condemnation of 'the academic tone' that the law of 1857 assigned to the training of primary teachers, as it led to confusion. Primary education, by nature, constituted a different sphere to that of secondary and university education. The former entered the terrain of benevolence, by virtue of a Christian ideal of charity towards poor families. Primary school was not the path towards 'scientific careers, neither were primary school teachers university professors'. Most certainly, they did not represent the State, but the family and the Church. Literally, it was explained that the people could live 'without wisdom', but not without a Christian education. Primary teachers, in short, needed less pedagogy and more conformity with their function as Catholic fathers in school:

> The inclusion of primary teachers, even in unreal fashion, in the public teaching faculty, inevitably had the painful consequence of the senseless determination to abandon that modest and peaceful environment that good sense assigns to primary education. Perhaps through unfamiliarity with the true nature of that education, through confusing it with other professions that, though analogous in terms of the objective, necessarily inhabit another social sphere, some primary teachers, already *seeking in political follies the achievement of malformed ambitions*, converting into reason and occasion for their own dissipation the notions of the science they received to educate and indoctrinate children, have provided with their conduct and their teaching grounds for bitter grievances … that will surely end and leave a more practical and popular organization, *even if it appears less academic*, of primary schools.[35]

The new law aimed to tackle the teaching problem by replacing primary teachers, in villages of fewer than 500 inhabitants, with priests. This

34 This can be consulted in *DSC* 65 (22 April 1868), appendix 1.

35 Included in the *DSC* 5 (2 January 1868), appendix, 2.

resolved the issue of unqualified maestros, but also the issue of those that had possessed the title but did not exercise in complete schools. In relation to other localities, the law sought to make a career in primary education available to any graduate in secondary education, with the requirement of a certificate in moral aptitude, while it reinforced clerical tutelage. It was clear that primary teachers coming out of teacher-training colleges had not conformed to the priestly stereotype, or resigned themselves to leading the ascetic life assigned them by the Moderate school. After the revolutionary break of 1868, which ended the reign of Isabel II, primary education found a framework of opportunities conducive to organizing itself as a professional movement in order to fulfil its demands.

The corporate mobilization of primary education in the Democratic Sexennium (1868–1874)

The Revolution of September 1868 constituted an unprecedented opening of the political framework in liberal Spain. As well as universal male suffrage, the revolutionary councils, first, and the provisional government, from October onwards, paved the way to the recognition of the individual rights enshrined in the Constitution of 1869. In turn, a secularizing process began that directly affected the educational system. The first decision taken by the new Minister for Internal Development, Ruiz Zorrilla, was the repeal of the 1868 Primary Education Law, the re-establishment of teacher-training colleges and the recognition of teaching freedom.[36] The democratic legislation, however, had contradictory effects for primary teachers. Above all, because what prevailed was a liberal-radical orientation that, while it freed schools of clerical supervision, promoted the creation of new private schools.[37]

36 Decree declaring free education and repealing the aforementioned decrees relating to public education, of 21 October 1868, *Gaceta de Madrid* 269 (22 October 1868).

37 Eduardo Higueras Castañeda, 'La materialización legislativa del liberalismo radical en el Sexenio Democrático: las reformas de Ruiz Zorrilla en el ministerio de

The Moyano Law of 1857 was provisionally reinstated, while the Constituent Assembly was entrusted with the adoption of a new Public Education Act.[38] In fact, that initiative did not come to fruition, so the Moderate educational model of primary education remained in force, although some aspects were adapted to the new democratic context: the clergy disappeared from the teaching boards and primary teachers were granted the right to choose textbooks. Local and provincial institutions were assigned new functions in educational matters. The most significant was the possibility of founding new schools, albeit public but privately financed. In practice, however, they took advantage of these powers to establish new secondary schools and universities, while they neglected primary schools. The delays in paying primary teachers, in many cases, grew longer, which forced the government to make repeated arrangements to protect teachers.[39]

The new political context created a new concept of nation based on the universalization of individual rights. The nationalizing role of primary school teachers, therefore, again took centre stage. The government, in the words of Minister Echegaray, was intent on improving 'the fortunes of such a wretched class, so worthy of consideration, on which depends the future and the freedom of our nation; for ignorant peoples will always be subject to the yoke of despotism'.[40] In this way, they were entrusted with the task of educating new citizens about democratic principles. Thus, they distributed among schools copies of *La Constitución española, puesta en diálogo, y con explicaciones convenientes para la inteligencia de los niños* [*The Spanish Constitution, in a Dialogue, and with Explanations Adapted to the Children's Understanding*] and of the *Cartilla de la Constitución democrática*

Fomento (1868–1869)', in Ana Eulalia Aparicio Guerrero and Raúl Navarro Olivas, eds, *Imágenes humanísticas para una sociedad educativa* (Cuenca: UCLM, 2018), 175–200.

38 Ruiz Zorrilla's draft Law on Education, which was neither debated nor adopted, can be consulted in the *DSC* 57 (23 April 1869), appendix 1, 57.

39 Mercedes Suárez Pazos, 'Las reformas educativas durante el Sexenio Revolucionario', in Rafael Serrano García, ed., *España, 1868–1874. Nuevos enfoques sobre el Sexenio Democrático* (Valladolid: Junta de Castilla y León, 2002), 139–57.

40 *DSC* 222 (19 February 1870), 5915.

Española [*The Primer of the Democratic Spanish Constitution*].[41] The recipients of these works were not only children, but adults attending night schools and, of course, the primary teachers themselves.

After the September Revolution, the salary situation of primary teachers had not improved. Although less dependent upon the clergy, they were now more tied to the town councils, which paid their salaries directly, bypassing the primary teaching boards. The patronage networks, although fragmented by the political change, remained in place. What was most important, however, was that the new democratic context opened up the possibility of defending their claims via the right to association, to freedom of speech and even universal suffrage. Despite the isolation in which most of them found themselves, primary teachers took advantage of the opening of the framework of opportunities to organize themselves.

During those years, different strategies were deployed to project a professional image in the public space. They assumed, in this sense, the discourse of progressives and democrats vis-à-vis primary education, which identified them as workers of civilization, enlighteners of the people in the face of despotism, as the bedrock, in short, of civil liberties. At the same time, however, they challenged those ideas with their shared experience of insecurity, sacrifice and submission to municipal powers, to demand, above all, their full transformation into functionaries. To this end, they should increase the prestige of a profession weighed down by unqualified practice and training deficiencies. Improving their professional competence was one of the objectives of primary education press, which witnessed an authentic boom during the Democratic Sexennium (1868–1874). Most of these journals, moreover, followed a liberal-democratic line.[42]

41 Gabriel Fernández, *La Constitución española, puesta en diálogo para la inteligencia de los niños y del pueblo* (1869); *Cartilla de la Constitución democrática española, promulgada el día 6 de junio de 1869, dispuesta en diálogo claro y sencillo por la redacción del periódico de Instrucción Primaria, El Magisterio Español, para la enseñanza en todas las escuelas de instrucción primaria y normales de la Nación* (Madrid: Imprenta de Manuel Tello, 1870).

42 See Antonio Checa Godoy, *Historia de la prensa pedagógica en España* (Sevilla: Universidad de Sevilla, 2002), 53–4.

The expansion of the professional press was a clear symptom of the development of a corporative awareness among primary teachers. Behind these kinds of publications, by and large, was the initiative of higher primary teachers and teacher-training college teachers. Many of the latter, however, took up their pens to present themselves as men of letters in cultural and even political periodicals. More than an extra source of income, they were seeking to equate their status to that of other professionals with a far more prestigious reputation, at that time, than that of primary teachers. Illustrative, in this sense, is the example of Melitón Escamilla, a higher primary teacher who over a period of years rose from a primary school in a Manchego village to the teacher-training college of the province of Cuenca.[43]

From 1869 onwards, he was a regular contributor to *El Eco de Cuenca*, the progressive party's local newspaper. He began by publishing some works of poetry. He soon started writing articles related to history and education. It was not long before he was defending openly political positions, in line with the newspaper for which he was writing.[44] Escamilla had secured his position via public examination, which afforded him more independence than most primary teachers. Some of the newspaper's editors occupied posts in both the capital's city council and the provincial government and, politically, it suited him to maintain a mutual understanding with these individuals. Above all, however, his collaborations enabled him to hobnob with secondary school professors and liberal professionals who wrote in this newspaper.

One of these collaborators was the director of the teacher-training college, Mariano Sánchez Almonacid, a veteran liberal who had good connections with important political leaders in the province, such as the former mayor of Madrid, Fermín Caballero. In mid-1871, Escamilla, almost certainly through Sánchez Almonacid, wrote to Caballero inviting him to write the dedication of the draft of a work on pedagogy. At the same time, he confessed: 'My current financial situation is, unfortunately, quite

43 His profesional career is covered in the *Gaceta de Instrucción Pública* 448 (23 March 1900).

44 See *El Eco de Cuenca* (13, 16 and 29 October 1869 and 11 December 1869).

pitiful.'[45] Of course, Caballero took care of the printing: 'It was not my intention, in dedicating this little work to Your Excellency, that he should sacrifice the 3,000 reals that might be the cost of a print run of 500 or 600 copies, which we would donate to the *Bibliotecas Populares*, which is the purpose of the project.'[46]

Caballero was the prototype of the liberal great man, rich and influential, keen to demonstrate his commitment to popular education and progress in his province. For that reason, in 1872, Escamilla, after publishing a new work entitled *La verdad de la Educación* [*The Truth of Education*],[47] wrote and requested that he employ 'his powerful and effective influence', and ask the members of three Provincial Boards of Primary Education not to eliminate from the budgets sent for approval by primary teachers the item designated for the acquisition of this work. Escamilla had spent his savings on the publication of this pamphlet. It was obvious that rural primary teachers could not afford to buy it, but they could acquire it via their school budgets: 'I am poor, very poor, Your Excellency; I have spent on the printing what I had in order to feed my children: If I now suffer, as I fear, this misfortune, I shall be completely lost.'[48]

Escamilla's intellectual output can be analysed on different levels. Apart from contributing to the professional advancement of his colleagues, it was a way of asserting his own intellectual preparation and his professional competence. Secondly, one should not overlook how he used the pitiful situation of primary teaching to highlight the disinterested sacrifice he had made in the name of a higher cause: popular education, the guarantee of civil liberties. A sacrifice that entitled him to recognition and favours on

45 Melitón Escamilla Campos to Fermín Caballero (Cuenca, 6 April 1871), Real Academia de la Historia [therefore: RAH], Archivo Fermín Caballero Morgáez, Correspondencia, 9/4709.

46 Melitón Escamilla to Fermín Caballero (Cuenca, 23 April 1871), RAH, Archivo Fermín Caballero Morgáez, Correspondencia, 9/4709.

47 Melitón Escamilla, *La verdad de la educación. Obrita de lectura para los niños que frecuentan las escuelas y dedica a los profesores de primera enseñanza de esta provincia* (Cuenca: Imprenta de F. Gómez, 1872). Copies of Escamilla's first work, entitled *La Educación*, have not been identified.

48 Melitón Escamilla to Fermín Caballero (Cuenca, 19 July 1872), RAH, Archivo Fermín Caballero Morgáez, Correspondencia, 9/4709.

the part of the progressive leaders with whom he associated, which could benefit his professional future. It was, in short, a strategy of personal advancement that, once again, shows how the professional progress of primary teachers largely depended on their capacity to project a respectable image in the public sphere.

In 1871, Escamilla promoted the creation of a professional journal, *El Magisterio Conquense* [*The Teaching of Cuenca*]. In the first extant issue of this publication, he introduced himself 'as a humble teacher [and] novice journalist, always interested in helping that benevolent, deserving and suffering class' to which he belonged. From this platform, he identified the primary teacher as 'the nation's first soldier … the state's first servant …, that gigantic figure of the century, amidst his poverty and the onerous martyrdom to which he is continually exposed'. He portrayed, ultimately, a stereotype born of the civic discourse on education. But most interesting was his recognition of the primary teacher as representative of the State, not of the municipality or of families, which was why he requested of the Minister for Internal Development that the payment of primary teachers cease to correspond to the town councils, and be transferred to either the State or the provincial councils:

> Either of them would enable this powerful, albeit humble, social entity, to acquire prestige and respectability among the people that need its help to know and determine their own interests, and also to determine their rights, set against the unavoidable duties that each and every right implies, both in the individual's awareness of his private acts, and in his relationship with society.[49]

The appearance of this newspaper was further evidence of the corporative awareness of primary teachers. It provided them with a means via which to circulate useful information and improve their training with articles on education, but also to share experiences, call attention to their situation and channel their grievances. That trend could be traced back to the initial moments prior to the opening of the 1869 Constituent Assembly. In January of that year, a meeting was held between 'primary school teachers of [the province of Cuenca] to attempt to designate the people that should

49 *El Magisterio Conquense* 3 (15 January 1871).

represent their interests in the ensuing Assembly'.[50] The notion of a primary school teacher as a candidate was a chimera: not even with the support of their colleagues could they meet the costs of an election campaign. But they could offer their votes and their ability to drum up votes in towns and villages for a liberal leader with sufficient prestige and commitment to the educational cause. They chose, of course, Fermín Caballero, who declined the invitation.

Despite the failure of the primary teachers' candidacy, it is worth noting that, for the first time, this collective was organizing itself in order take the initiative in the political field in autonomous fashion. The September Revolution had initiated an intense process of politicization to which primary teachers were not alien. The example of Pedro Benita, primary teacher in Villar de Cañas, a small village in the same province, is interesting. In December 1869, he published a statement in *El Eco de Cuenca* to assert his 'decency as a public man, as a primary school teacher' and his 'political dignity as citizen'. He had been accused of abandoning the school for three days to attend a republican demonstration. His writing shows how primary teachers found in political militancy a means of asserting themselves as active citizens, even in collectives opposed to the prevailing system, as was the case of the republicans following the adoption of the monarchic Constitution of 1869:

> Still young, and occupied until a few years ago with providing myself with a humble career with which and through honest work to satisfy my needs, the years have passed for me without knowing what politics is or even bothering to learn; and … with the advent of the era that initiated the September Revolution, … I attempted to study the leanings of all [the parties] and embraced with faith and decision the flag of the republic.[51]

Pedro Benita was the promoter and president of the local committee of the Federal Republican Party in this village. A year earlier, that political involvement would have been inconceivable for a primary teacher, above all

50 Ramón Escribano to Fermín Caballero (2 January 1869), RAH, Archivo Fermín Caballero, Correspondencia, 9/4706.

51 The article is dated 6 December 1869 and was published in the supplement of the *El Eco de Cuenca* (15 December 1869).

in the case of an option that ideologically was clearly secular in nature and directly opposed to the supervision of teaching by the Catholic Church. Even in the context of rural Spain in 1869, in spite of the proclamation of the freedom of teaching and of the provision of religious freedom in the Constitution, his stance could generate professional problems. His case, however, was not exceptional. In an analysis of the republican elites of the province of Jaen that developed their political activity between 1849 and 1923, Santiago Jaen identified primary teachers as the second largest professional group.[52]

Political rights, thus, enabled primary teachers to demand their recognition as professionals, but also as public men capable of defending themselves against clientelist pressures. Juan José Martínez Duque, primary teacher at the school in Canalejas, another small village in the province of Cuenca, addressed Ruiz Zorrilla in 1871. The Minister for Internal Development had designated a one-time provision to cover municipal debts with primary teachers. In this case, complaints about non-payment had borne fruit. However, many town councils, in opposition to primary teachers, attempted to prejudice them by paralysing the payment process. This is the situation that Duque was denouncing:

> Two weeks having passed since the publication of that humanitarian provision, with its contents having been ignored ... by many mayors who, far from contributing to the consolidation of the good, legal and fair, are ... parasitic plants in society ..., as an immediate consequence of their proven ignorance, despotic *caciquismo*, frenzied manners, bad faith and worse heart who, not satisfied with their work – some of them contributing to the annihilation of popular education by any means suggested by their villainous inclination – in denying primary teachers what is owed them, openly delay ... submitting to the financial authorities of the provincial capitals, the documents attesting to these debts.[53]

Martínez Duque presented himself as 'the last of the Nation's primary teachers'. Although he was in charge of 'a village public school', he

52 Santiago Jaén Milla, *Entre tierra y plomo. Historia del republicanismo Jiennense, 1849–1923* (Barcelona: Carena, 2014), 492–5.

53 Juan José Martínez Duque to Manuel Ruiz Zorrilla (Canalejas, 25 March 1871), Legado Rodolfo Llopis, Fundación Mediterráneo, file 42, nº 255.

represented 'the benevolent and neglected class of primary school teachers' as a whole. In other words, he defended the concept of primary teachers as functionaries and their professional dignity as specialists in teaching and representatives of the State. In turn, he demonstrated their capacity to defend themselves in the public arena in full awareness of their social function, their political rights and a cultural level that placed them above the ignorance of local authorities. He sought, ultimately, to show that primary teachers, 'victims of hunger and vulnerability, of insult and scorn', were capable of asserting their professional honour:

> To partly avoid the repetition of events that excessively demote and humiliate primary teachers before their peers, the next Constituent Assembly, evincing its highest standards and enlightenment and wisdom, should address with the necessary deliberation such an important issue for present and future generations, determining among other things *that H.M.'s government declare primary education to be free and obligatory, considering it a public service sustained by provincial funds; and declare as unfit for public office any person unable to read or write from the first of January, 1873.*[54]

Attainment of the status of functionary was the goal of primary school teachers, and the political context favoured their demands. In the democratic imaginary, they appeared as the architects of civic virtue. This rhetoric was not accompanied by immediate advantages, but it did help their grievances to be heard. On occasions, they met with success. Associationism was the next step towards institutionalizing a growing corporative awareness. Mention has already been made of how the primary teachers of Cuenca met early in 1869. Three years later, they assembled once again, to organize a primary teaching association. In April 1872, Melitón Escamilla again wrote to Fermín Caballero to inform him of the foundation of a 'professional society' called *La Auxiliadora* [*The Helper*] which he paced under the latter's protection:

> At the meeting on the 1st of this month attended by various primary teachers from this province in the capital, in order to set up a friendly society to attend to their most urgent needs in the event of illness or significant delay in payment of their salaries,

54 Juan José Martínez Duque to Manuel Ruiz Zorrilla (Canalejas, 25 March 1871), Legado Rodolfo Llopis, Fundación Mediterráneo, file 42, nº 255.

> they unanimously agreed … to appoint Your Excellency as Honorary President of said association.[55]

This was a fundamental step in the mobilization of primary teachers. In this sense, three significant circumstances should be underlined. Firstly, *La Auxiliadora* was the first mutual society to be founded in this province. Primary teachers were, therefore, the first collective to organize themselves professionally so as to defend their labour rights, which refutes the generalized idea that, throughout the nineteenth century, they barely mobilized themselves. In addition, this association constituted the platform that underpinned *El Magisterio Conquense*, which became one of the longest-lived journals in the province.[56] Thus, as well as providing mutual support when necessary, they had an instrument with which to channel their grievances and maintain the cohesion of the group with the exchange of information and the publication of communiqués by *La Auxiliadora*.

Finally, far from being an isolated initiative, this associative impulse can be perceived as a response to a mobilization on a national scale: '*El Magisterio Conquense* subscribes to the Junta Central Provisional de Maestros de Madrid [Provisional Central Board of Primary Teachers of Madrid], and hopes that this rapid movement towards professional association will be the lever that removes the obstacles currently facing the enlightenment and well-being of society.'[57] Galician primary teacher Roque Goy, at the same time, promoted similar associations in Lugo and La Coruña, as did Ildefonso Fernández in Toledo.[58] Even if little is known about the associationism of primary teachers in the nineteenth century, this evidence is sufficient to interpret that, in the context of freedoms during the

55 José Ruiz and Melitón Escamilla to Fermín Caballero (Cuenca, 2 April 1872), RAH, Archivo Fermín Caballero Morgáez, 9/4709.

56 After the founding of this association, the journal was subtitled the 'official organ of *La Auxiliadora*', *El Magisterio Conquense* (8 January 1873). With some interruptions, it was published until 1923. See Ángel Luis López Villaverde and Isidro Sánchez, *Historia y evolución de la prensa conquense, 1811–1939* (Cuenca: UCLM, 1998), 85.

57 *El Magisterio Conquense* (January 1873).

58 Gabriel, 'La profesionalización del magisterio en España (siglos XIX-XX)', 78.

Sexennium (1868–1874), the mobilization of primary education acquired a significant dimension.

The dialogue between the corporative demands of primary teachers and the reformist proposals of the progressive-radical government brought nearer the objective of converting primary teachers into public officials. In October 1872, Manuel Becerra presented in Parliament a draft law declaring primary education to be obligatory and mandating the State to pay 'two thirds of the fixed annual salary of all primary school teachers'.[59] The remainder would be the responsibility of provincial governments. This was the third time that the democratic leader had presented a project of this nature. For that reason, when in December of that year he was appointed minister in the government of Ruiz Zorrilla, the definitive adoption of the new law appeared likely.

The project, however, was not even debated. It was thwarted by Amadeus of Savoy's abdication in February 1873. The immediate proclamation of the Republic could have given primary teachers fresh hope, given that the republicans had been the staunchest advocates of obligatory, secular education provided by the State. The opening of the Constituent Assembly, however, delayed the question again, and it was definitively abandoned with the series of coups d'états that brought an end to the democratic experience. In 1875, following the Bourbons return to the throne, Manuel de Orovio, author of the 1868 neo-Catholic Education Law, became the new Minister for Internal Development in the first Restoration government. With his appointment, the Moderate framework of education was completely re-established.

59 This can be consulted in the DSC 37 (26 October 1872), appendix 12. This project, with few variations, had already been presented on two occasions, in 1870 and in 1871. See DSC 320 (19 December 1870), appendix 1 and 39 (19 May 1871), appendix 3.

Conclusions

At the beginning of the twentieth century, the watchword among primary teaching associations was that 'the emancipation of primary teachers will be the work of the primary teachers themselves'. In 1901, an important step was taken towards the goal of professionalization with the formation of the Asociación Nacional del Magisterio Primario [National Association of Primary Education] and the inclusion, for the first time, of their salaries in the General State Budget. From that point onwards, corporative associationism expanded upon the basis of friendly societies and, in many cases, was linked to working-class unionism.[60] On the road towards this new upsurge in the mobilezation of primary teachers, a fundamental element was the new openness of the political system resulting from the 1883 Press Law and the 1886 Law on Associations.

The Moderate watershed of 1875 delayed the goal of public employee status and consolidated the priestly stereotype of primary teachers, who, in line with the discourse of the new powers, continued to exercise a catechizing function. Their semi-professional status was accentuated during the final quarter of the nineteenth century. This was largely a consequence of the new powers granted to religious orders in order to found private schools, which in turn prompted a lay response from the democratic movement. The Institución Libre de Enseñanza [Free Educational Institute] and the lay schools promoted an image of primary teachers in keeping with the stereotype of the worker of civilization and denounced the precarious situation of primary teaching. Many teachers found in republicanism a militant channel via which to demand their professionalization.[61]

The republicans, indeed, repeatedly employed the image of the poverty of primary teachers in contrast with the opulence of the clergy. If the

60 Aida Terrón Bañuelos, 'Coordenadas del asociacionismo profesional de docentes. Estado de la cuestión en España', *Historia y Memoria de la Educación* 1 (2015), 93–130.

61 Sergio Sánchez Collantes, *El pueblo a escena. Republicanismos y tradición democrática en la Asturias del siglo XIX* (Oviedo: Real Instituto de Estudios Asturianos, 2019), 691–4.

former, hungry and emaciated, represented civilization and progress, priests symbolized reactionaryism, under a State that abandoned schools to protect the Church.[62] However, the resurgent pedagogical press established a clear fissure line between publications of a secular orientation and Catholic journals,[63] a division that was barely evident in primary education press during the Democratic Sexennium (1868–1874). The new professional associations left behind internal conflict within primary teaching to focus on the corporative defence of the acquisition of public employee status, an objective that was close in 1873 but was not attained until well into the twentieth century.[64]

62 Eloquent in this respect, are the caricatures published by *El Solfeo* (2 June 1875, 9 December 1875, 11 Decemer1875, 18 May 1876 or 26 April 1876).

63 Milagros Tapia Bon, 'La prensa profesional del magisterio en Cantabria (1896–1936)', *Cabás* 8 (2012), 45–62.

64 This work is part of the research project entitled 'Cultura del honor, política y esfera pública en la España Liberal (1833–1890)' (ref. number PGC2018-093698-B-I00) and financed by the Spanish Ministry of Science, Innovation and Universities.

CRISTINA DEL PRADO HIGUERA

Professionalization of Female Teachers in the Nineteenth Century

ABSTRACT
Throughout the nineteenth century, teaching became feminized and opening a workplace for women in a profession that, traditionally, had been defined as totally masculine. Teaching was the first professional field to which women had access. Some teachers who were educated above the average for their sex were the first to formulate demands and develop a feminist consciousness in education systems. In this chapter, we have raised some questions that help us understand the role played by teachers during the nineteenth and early twentieth centuries in the national education system of Spain. For this, we have analysed how education over the centuries has been an instrument of political power and social control based on political and partisan interests, hence the interest in relating the process of professionalization of the teaching work of women, with the political and legislative transformations in the Spanish educational system.

I have never again felt more intensely the worth of what I was doing. I said to myself, there can be no more beautiful vocation than this. This was the miracle of the profession I was beginning to experience and which kept me happy despite the snow and the gloomy kitchen, despite how little it apparently gave me and how much I had to give.[1]

Introduction

Studies in the historiography of education have focused on the figure of the male teacher but have rarely examined the history of female teachers. This distinction, being a male or female teacher, had very different

1 Josefina Aldecoa, *Historia de una Maestra* (Madrid: Santillana, 2011), 40.

connotations in the social, cultural, economic, political and religious spheres in the nineteenth and early twentieth centuries. It was during this period that a process of feminization of teaching took place, as women began to enter a profession that had traditionally been defined as exclusively male. Teaching was the first professional field to which women had access. Those female teachers who were better educated than the average for their sex were among the first to make demands and develop a feminist consciousness in education systems.[2]

Female teachers have played a decisive role in society over the centuries, despite the fact that their work has generally been undervalued or overlooked by social scientists and researchers. However, they did appear as protagonists in some of the novels of writers such as Benito Pérez Galdós, for example, in *La desheredada* [*The disinherited*], *El amigo Manso* [*The friend Manso*], *Doctor Centeno*, *La Primera República* [*The First Republic*], *Razón de la sinrazón* [*The reason of unreason*] and *El caballero encantado* [*The enchanted gentleman*], giving a voice to women such as Pascuala, Florina and Atenaida. Their stories shed light on what life was like for each of them, painting an accurate portrait of the professional profile of female teachers.[3] There is also the writer Josefina Aldecoa,[4] who narrates the experiences of Gabriela López Pardo in a very accurate and faithful account of the life of a female teacher at the beginning of the twentieth century. Her book is one of the best testimonies and novels about the life and work of a female teacher in rural schools in Spain.

Thus, it could be said that literature has provided some glimpses into the figure of the female teacher; nevertheless, several questions remain unanswered in the historiography of the nineteenth century. Some of the questions we need to ask ourselves in order to understand the role played by female teachers in the Spanish education system in the nineteenth century include, for example: what cultural and intellectual training did they receive? What was their social background? What differences were there

2 Pilar Ballarín, 'Maestras, innovación y cambios', *Arenal* 6/1 (1999), 81–110.

3 Fermín Ezpeleta, 'Sobre maestros y maestras en las novelas de Galdós'. *Actas del Congreso Internacional Galdosiano* (Las Palmas de Gran Canaria: Casa Museo Pérez Galdós, 2013), 246.

4 Aldecoa, *Historia de una Maestra*, 48.

between male and female teachers in the education system in the nineteenth century? What was their professional role throughout the nineteenth century? These questions lead to the basic issue concerning the education system, on which I shall focus: how did the education system change during the nineteenth century and what role did female teachers play in this change?

In order to answer the above questions, I have employed historiographic methods in this study in order to describe and analyse various events in the history of education, focusing on the figure of the female teacher in the nineteenth and early twentieth centuries. Besides the extensive literature on the subject, I have also analysed unpublished documents held in various archives.

The theoretical approach adopted in this study analyses education over the centuries as an instrument of political power and social control in the service of political and partisan interests, hence the interest in relating the process of professionalization of female teaching to political and legislative change in the Spanish education system.

The main European antecedents of our study period are located in the seventeenth and eighteenth centuries, which witnessed the creation of the first 'schoolmasters training colleges, and the religious orders became pioneers in these matters, particularly the Jesuits, Piarists and the congregation of St. John Baptist de la Salle, founded in Reims in 1684'.[5] France and Germany were the first countries where such state-wide teacher-training institutions were established.

In order to understand the education process throughout the nineteenth century, it is essential to go back to the eighteenth century and consider the legacy left by the Enlightenment. This was a period in which the education of women was reconsidered and became one of the most interesting points of debate among philosophers and thinkers of the time.

From the eighteenth century onwards, the state authorities encouraged and required schoolmasters to undergo professional training, creating specific institutions for this purpose. Condorcet's *Report on Public Education*

5 Isabel Gutiérrez, 'Contexto histórico en el que se produce la creación de las Escuelas Normales', *Revista Interuniversitaria de Formación del Profesorado* 5 (1989), 46.

stressed that the teaching profession formed character and required a special disposition,[6] noting that 'the function of teaching supposes the habit and the taste for a sedentary and well-regulated life; it requires a straight and gentle character, patience and zeal, kindness and a kind of dignity'.[7]

Institutions such as the Sociedades Económicas de Amigos del País [Economic Societies of Friends of the Country] also played an important role in the construction of the Enlightenment ideal of education, offering effective help to the monarchy in its endeavours to extend primary education to various parts of the kingdom. Although the Sociedad Económica Vascongada [Basque Economic Society] had existed since 1765, the first such society to obtain royal approval was the one in Madrid, in 1775. By 1808, ninety-five societies had been formed throughout the kingdom, and had to adapt themselves to the model dictated by the Crown. Besides their educational project, their other main activities targeted agriculture and industry with the aim of stimulating social change.[8] The Economic Societies focused primarily on a practical education, reflecting their Enlightenment ideals. Women were their principal target and indeed, pressure from women was decisive in the monarchy's acceptance of free education for women and girls.

On 12 January 1779, a Royal Decree declared that women were free to work in manufacturing, despite opposition from the guilds. The most important initiative in this respect was the foundation by some societies of the so-called Escuelas Patrióticas [Patriotic Schools], with a strongly economic and cultural nature.[9] The main purpose of these schools was to improve the economic status of disadvantaged families in order to prevent many women from resorting to begging or prostitution. Although it was a less widespread practice, some societies such as those in Seville and Aragon

6 Nicolas Condorcet, *Cinco Memorias sobre la Instrucción Pública y otros escritos* (Madrid: Morata, 2001).

7 Nicolas Condorcet, *Escritos Pedagógicos* (Madrid: Espasa Calpe, 1992), 128.

8 Raúl Mínguez, *Alumnas y maestras. La educación de las mujeres en España durante el proceso de formación de la feminidad liberal burguesa* (Master's Dissertation, Universidad de Valencia, 2009), 38.

9 María Consolación Calderón, ed., *Las Reales Sociedades Económicas de Amigos del País y el Espíritu Ilustrado* (Sevilla: Real Sociedad Económica Sevillana de Amigos del País, 2001).

also founded what were known as friendly or elementary schools, which adhered to the dictates of the Royal Decree of 11 May 1783. These established girls' schools in Spain and assumed the obligation to teach women to read and write, as stated in article 1. It is worth noting that when this law was enacted, female teachers were still practically illiterate, yet nonetheless were placed in charge of the girls' schools.

Meanwhile, the Real Sociedad Matritense [Royal Society of Madrid] was notable among such societies for the role women played in it. The question of whether to admit women as members had been raised at the very moment of its foundation in 1775, and the debate continued until 1786, with participants who included Jovellanos and the educationalist Josefa Amar y Borbón. This latter had managed to join the Real Sociedad Aragonesa [Royal Economic Society of Aragon] in 1782 and was the first woman to belong to this association. In 1787, she also became a member of the Junta de Damas de Honor y Mérito de la Sociedad Económica Matritense [Economic Society of Madrid's Board of Ladies of Honour and Merit], which consisted of fourteen women with Enlightenment ideals and in which, for the first time, women met for reasons other than prayer.[10] It is worth mentioning that it was a Royal Order issued by Carlos III and dated 27 August 1787 that granted the admission of female members of merit and honour to the regular and separate boards. Thus, in the eighteenth century, state policies contributed to the progress of education, with the aim of tackling economic decline and creating useful citizens. Jovellanos represented the culmination of this eighteenth-century trend and served as a bridge to the nineteenth century.[11] According to the sociologist Sonsoles San Román, 'the teaching profession was the only alternative to the priesthood, and was therefore defined in very similar terms'.[12]

It was in the nineteenth century that an education system began to take definitive shape, and it was established in 1834. Successive liberal governments enacted a series of laws, plans and regulations outlining education

10 Sonsoles San Román, *Las primeras maestras. Los orígenes del proceso de feminización docente en España* (Barcelona: Ariel, 1998), 62.

11 Estíbaliz Ruiz de Azúa, 'La enseñanza pública primaria a mediados del siglo XIX', in *Madrid en la sociedad del siglo XIX* (Madrid: Comunidad de Madrid, 1986), 416.

12 San Román, *Las primeras maestras*, 63.

levels, new teacher-training institutions and education administration in general.

Teacher-training institutions played a fundamental role in private education in nineteenth-century Spain, and were protected by the various moderate governments by the Concordat of 1851 and even by the Moyano Law of 1857. These governments allowed the Church to participate in public education without requiring teachers to hold a professional qualification, enabling these latter to open schools without a prior deposit, as stated in article 153 of the Law.[13]

Below, I shall conduct a detailed analysis, based on a historiographical review, of the advances and setbacks in education in the last half of the eighteenth century and throughout the nineteenth century. It should be noted that the ideology of the government in power determined the level of importance given to education in the affairs of the State and the interest or lack of it in promoting the professionalization of female teachers in Spain.

Advances and setbacks in the education system and public education in Spain in the eighteenth and nineteenth centuries

In order to analyse advances and setbacks in the education system, we must go back in history to the reign of Fernando VI (1746–1759), which marked the beginning of a period that witnessed various economic, political and education reforms. Basically, he expanded the network of schools in Madrid, considering education a matter of national interest that required the intervention of the public authorities and particularly of the State.[14] It should be remembered that for many years during the Ancien

13 Mª Carmen Simón Palmer, *La enseñanza privada seglar en Madrid. 1820–1868* (Madrid: Instituto de Estudios Madrileños, 1974).

14 Antonio Viñao Frago, 'Godoy y la educación en la España de su tiempo. El Instituto Pestalozziano', in Miguel Ángel Melón, Emilio La Parra and Fernando Tomás Pérez Gonzáñez, eds, *Manuel Godoy y su tiempo*, vol. 2 (Badajoz: Junta de Extremadura, 2003), 86.

Régime, no education policy existed on the part of the state authorities, the local institutions or of the Church.

Nonetheless, King Carlos III (1716–1788) 'showed great interest in the education of women. During the final years of his reign, female teaching in public schools began to take its first steps and the model emerged in Spain of the illiterate female teacher',[15] as I shall discuss later on. The king launched a series of initiatives, including the creation of the Colegio Académico del Noble Arte de Primeras Letras [Academic College of the Noble Art of First Letters] by Royal Provision of 22 December 1780, establishing that the people responsible for educating girls would be respectable midwives who had received sufficient instruction to teach.[16]

After the demise of the St Cassian Corporation, the king felt compelled to found a modern academic institution. Years later, in 1781, its statutes were approved,[17] obliging all teachers with a school in Madrid to join. Subsequently, the government regulated access to the teaching profession for both male and female teachers, and decreed that male teachers could only have boys in their classrooms while female teachers could only have girls.

By the end of the eighteenth century, new voices and works on education had emerged. One such was the French philosopher and mathematician Nicolas de Condorcet (1743–1794), whose Enlightenment ideas anticipated what would become a new concept of education. He viewed education as a driver for change and social reform, but above all as a means to develop what he called instruction in democracy. In his report to the Assembly, he advocated universal education in order to achieve true human

15 San Román, *Las primeras maestras*, 53.

16 The professions of midwife and teacher were practically the only ones that middle-class women could enter in the nineteenth century. From 1804 onwards, midwives had to sit examinations at the Royal Colleges of Surgery, and in 1861, hospitals in Madrid, Barcelona, Granada, Seville, Valencia and Valladolid were authorized to have a delivery room and give women the education necessary to obtain a teaching qualification. As we shall see below, midwives had to wait until the middle of the century to receive training in the teacher-training institutions known at the time as 'normal schools'.

17 Julio Ruiz Berrio, 'Maestros y escuelas de Madrid en el Antiguo Régimen', *Cuadernos de Historia Moderna* special issue 3 (2004), 113–35.

equality, proposing the right to an equal education for all members of the same nation: 'A curriculum based not only on reading, writing and arithmetic, but also on knowledge of one's own country, of moral ideas and of social legislation, will accomplish equality in education for all, even if only in private education.'[18] Importantly, Nicolas de Condorcet's thinking exerted a considerable influence on the Quintana Plan proposed to the Cortes of Cádiz and approved in 1821.

As the historian Raquel Sánchez has observed:

> The education of girls was a priority concern for women, who devoted themselves to the practice of charity as early as the eighteenth century. Aware that lower-class women could find themselves in a situation where they had to work (orphaned, a husband's illness, widowhood, lack of resources, etc.), they were very conscious of the importance of training girls in productive activities. Hence, the first female teachers were not educators in the modern sense, that is, transmitters of intellectual knowledge, but women who taught girls useful skills such as sewing, embroidery and, in general terms, work that could be done with the hands.[19]

Until the nineteenth century, education was virtually unregulated:

> The lower classes feel no need for their children to receive primary education, nor do the children require it. Furthermore, as children, they learn their parents' occupations, carrying out agricultural or livestock tasks in the rural world, and in the urban world working in family workshops and professions as apprentices. One must consider the negligible or null importance of education for society.[20]

With the accession of Carlos IV to the throne (1788–1808), the so-called Escuelas Reales [Royal Schools] were founded by Royal Decree on 25 December 1791, with the aim of revitalizing elementary education. These schools were free, funded by the Crown, and were attended by poor pupils sent by the Charity Board and the children of servants of the Royal

18 Isabel Gutiérrez Zuloaga, 'La creación de las Escuelas Normales en España', *Revista Interuniversitaria de Formación del Profesorado*, 5 (1989), 45.

19 Raquel Sánchez, *Señoras fuera de casa. Mujeres del siglo XIX: la conquista del espacio público* (Madrid: Catarata, 2019), 57.

20 Juan Antonio Lorenzo, 'Hacia la profesionalización y modernización del Magisterio (1898–1936)', *Revista Complutense de Educación* 6/2, 205.

Household. The intention was to provide the same teacher and method as the Court moved around the Royal Residences. However, some of the schools were in a deplorable state, as reflected in the complaint made by several headmasters: 'In view of the pitiful state in which they find themselves, eight headmasters of the free Royal Elementary Schools beg for some relief as regards their accrued salaries, having already exhausted all the resources they had, including the sale of their furniture.'[21] As for the title of Royal Schoolmaster, this was issued by the Council of Castile at the suggestion of the Brotherhood of St Cassian.[22] Title holders had two assistants, who later usually obtained the position of Royal Schoolmaster. By Royal Order of 9 July 1806, the Real Instituto Militar Pestalozziano [Royal Pestalozzian Military Academy] was created and Godoy, an advocate of the Pestalozzian method, appointed Francisco Woitel as head of the school, which subsequently closed in 1808.

With the accession of José I to the Spanish throne (1808–1813), his Francophile supporters in Spain hoped that liberalism would bring about a change in teacher-training. Title IX, articles 366 and 367 of the 1812 Constitution established the obligation to provide a free, universal education. The constitutionalists focused their endeavours on creating a national

21 Archivo Histórico Nacional, Consejos 49615, Exp.32, 10.2 (1812).

22 In the reign of Felipe IV (1621–1665), some schoolmasters founded the Congregation of St Cassian, selecting this Italian martyr as their patron saint with the aim of protecting themselves and acquiring the privilege of protecting other schoolmasters in the kingdom, and this became the first teachers' association. In the mid-eighteenth century, Schoolmasters' Brotherhoods emerged, which were governed by ordinances issued by the Council of Castile. These ordinances established the types of examination that could be taken, which depended on the place where these were held, and the subjects they would cover, which included reading, spelling, arithmetic and knowledge of Christian doctrine. In the reign of the Bourbons, schoolmasters benefited from the privileges enjoyed by the other liberal professions, enabling them to appoint inspectors known as visitors, to monitor the schools. In 1743, they were granted the prerogative of examining prospective schoolmasters and of appointing visitors to inspect schools. Thus, began a system of accreditation by teacher examiners chosen by the directors of the Brotherhood of Schoolmasters with the approval of the authorities, which remained in force until the beginning of the nineteenth century.

education system and promoting primary education, with the aim of ensuring that every village with up to 100 inhabitants would have a school.

When the liberals came to power under the mandate of Juan Moscoso de Altamira (1788–1854), first Count of Fontao and Minister of the Interior, the first national education system was inaugurated, incorporating female teachers in public schools for children. The liberal educationalist Pablo Montesino (1781–1849) exerted a decisive influence at the time, revolutionizing the education system by creating nursery schools and writing the *Manual para los maestros de Escuelas de Párvulos* [*Manual for nursery school teachers*],[23] in which he equated the schoolmistress's role to that of a mother and the maternal care of children in the public space.

Such was the confidence in public education as a means to modernize Spain that it was extended to all children through article 366 of the 1812 Constitution. Education was viewed as the driver of liberal transformation: 'The liberals saw education as one of the most important instruments of political change; hence the need to secularize the education system and place it under the control of the Spanish State.'[24] Accordingly, we can conclude that in 1812, it was considered of interest to foster a cultured, progressive nation; however, this goal gradually lost its primacy over the course of the century, and illiteracy remained widespread in Spanish society.

Despite the endeavours and advances of the liberals up until the beginning of the nineteenth century, when Fernando VII came to power (1814–1833), Spain witnessed a severe social backlash, especially in the field of education because it remained in the hands of the Church. Royal Decree of 18 July 1816 recommended that girls' schools be established in convents, endowing girls' education with a clearly and strictly religious nature.

Although this retrograde step in Spanish society and the education system remained evident for many years during the reign of Fernando VII, the situation was partially rectified with the Liberal Triennium. During this period, education once again acquired – albeit timidly – some prominence on the political agenda. In 1821, the *Reglamento General de la*

23 Pablo Montesino, *Manual para los maestros de Escuelas de Párvulos* (Madrid: Imprenta Nacional, 1840).

24 Ruiz de Azúa, 'La enseñanza pública primaria a mediados del siglo XIX', 414.

Instrucción Pública [*General Regulation of Public Education*] established equality of access to education for all citizens, and for the first time, it was stipulated that girls should be taught to count. From 1823 onwards, public schools offering primary education proliferated, most of which were run by Francophiles and liberals who had returned from exile. A year later, in 1824, the Calomarde Plan was enacted, implementing an education reform distinguishing between four types of school.

By the mid-nineteenth century, the education system had progressed in line with the new laws and regulations, but conditions for the teaching profession remained poor. For example, the salary was too low to support teachers, who were often obliged to combine this work with other jobs in order to survive, which had a very negative impact on their teaching performance. Schools also lacked sufficient technical resources to support learning.

In relation to the conditions of education in Spain, Miguel Artola has observed that precedence had been given to economic development over education,[25] and this had obstructed the goal of creating a country whose citizens had sufficient education to participate in its institutions. The liberals wished to prioritize education because according to their ideology, political achievements inevitably depended on public education and this should therefore be given greater importance in order to facilitate the establishment and consolidation of the middle classes.[26]

Subsequently, in the reign of Isabel II (1833–1868), her governments showed signs of progress and instability which were echoed in education. Secondary schools were established in 1847 and special schools in 1855. In addition, a series of regulations and laws were passed that affected the progress of the education system in Spain, including the Instruction for the Regime and Government of the Kingdom's Elementary Schools of 21 October 1834, which included the foundation of a teacher-training institution and re-established the Escuela de Enseñanza Mutua [School of Mutual Education]; the Royal Decree of 4 August 1836; the Law of 21

25 Miguel Artola, *La burguesía revolucionaria 1870–1874* (Madrid: Alianza, 1975).

26 Ruiz de Azúa, 'La enseñanza pública primaria a mediados del siglo XIX', 415.

July 1838 and the Regulations of 28 November 1838; and the first Law on Public Education, better known as the Moyano Law, in 1857.

Also, of interest, in 1836, the Jesuits were expelled and restrictive measures against religious orders were introduced. This curtailed the presence and role of the Jesuits in education and meant that most private schools were secularized during the reign of Isabel II.

The regent, María Cristina, had previously created a commission responsible for drawing up a general plan for primary education and establishing mutual education schools and above all, 'a Escuela Normal [Normal School] to instruct teachers from the provinces, who must then extend this beneficial method to their provinces'. From then on, Spain began to construct a national education system. On 4 August 1836, the Plan for Public Education was enacted, obliging town councils to open schools for children. On 21 July 1838, the Law on Primary Education was passed, giving legal substance to the 1821 Regulation[27] and influencing the Pidal Plan of 1845 and the Moyano Law of 1857. This was achieved thanks to the educational endeavours of Pablo Montesino and Gil de Zárate, the latter being highly cognizant of the precarious state of primary education in Spain. On 8 March 1839, the Schoolmaster's Training College–Central Seminary was inaugurated in Madrid at number 80, Calle Ancha de San Bernardo, occupying the confiscated former convent of the Franciscan nuns of Santa Clara.

Several years later, the Pidal Plan, passed on 17 September 1845, targeted secondary and university education, completing the various levels of education. Antonio Gil de Zárate (1844–1851) was a key figure in state administration and in education; his prime objective was to advance public education, which he believed had been treated 'with reluctance and meanness'.

However, despite the progress made by the mid-nineteenth century, in 1846 there were still more than 6,847 male teachers with qualifications and 5,937 without, while in the case of female teachers, 1,141 were qualified and 1,264 were not. By 1850, these figures had risen to 1,871 qualified and

27 San Román, *Las primeras maestras*, 65.

2,195 unqualified female teachers.[28] Accordingly, on 17 July 1857, Minister Claudio Moyano's Law on Public Education, better known as the Moyano Law, was passed. This laid the foundations for the Ministry of Development to exercise authority over all universities through a Higher Council of Public Education. In primary education, the teacher-training colleges were improved, and one was established in every university. The central institution was located in Madrid, and this was where the teaching staff of the other teacher-training colleges in Spain received their training. One of the most notable of the issues addressed was that of the prolonged interruptions in the payment of teachers' salaries, and a minimum salary of 1,100 *reales* was established, which could be paid in cash or in kind.[29]

Despite these reforms, illiteracy rates remained high in Spain: in 1860, 80 per cent of the population was illiterate, compared with a rate of 32 per cent in France at the same time. Half of school-age children were illiterate and 42 per cent of primary school teachers did not hold a specific qualification. In response to these illiteracy rates, the Law on Primary Education of 2 June 1868 represented a step forwards for the education of women, given that female education in the first half of the nineteenth century had been limited to primary education and the so-called 'accomplishments'.[30]

In light of the historiographical overview given here, it can be concluded that although these laws were decisive and important in shaping the education system in Spain, they did not fundamentally change the situation of education for women. The statistics for 1870 show that 81 per cent remained illiterate. The State neglected to prioritize educational progress, and it was left to private education to meet this need.

28 Vicente Palacio Atard, *La España del siglo XIX 1808–1898* (Madrid: Espasa Calpe,1988), 321.

29 San Román, *Las primeras maestras. Los orígenes del proceso de feminización docente en España*,123.

30 Enrique Guerrero, ed., *Historia de la educación en España. Del Despotismo Ilustrado a las Cortes de Cádiz* (Madrid: Ministerio de Educación y Ciencia, 1985).

The professionalization and working conditions of female teachers in the nineteenth century

The above brief historical overview of advances and setbacks in the Spanish education system from the eighteenth to the nineteenth century demonstrates the disparity that existed between different political and ideological stances regarding women's education. As noted earlier, this was the result of different conceptions of women, their social role and their contribution to the nation's progress.

Esther Cortada has rejected the idea of the feminization of teaching, arguing that women had long been involved in educational tasks, albeit not in public schools. In her view, 'the closest precedent of the schoolmistress should not be sought in the model of the mother responsible for the education of her sons and daughters, but in the figure of the seamstress',[31] contending that women's access to public teaching in the nineteenth century was a professional achievement rather than a concession.

Although I believe Cortada's perspective is correct, it remains the case that all the changes which occurred in the nineteenth century regarding the professionalization of female teachers were supported by legislative measures that accelerated or delayed women's participation in the education system. The political development of the system was no minor element in the professional achievement noted by Cortada. Examples of these legislative measures, which were decisive in the professionalization of female teachers, include the aforementioned Constitution of 1812 and what was known as the Quintana Report of 1813 which distinguished between the education of men, which should be public, and the education of women, which should be private, domestic and based solely on moral aspects.

31 Esther Cortada Andreu, 'De la calcetera a la maestra de escuela: expectativas y activismo profesional', *Arenal* 6/1 (1999), 31–53; Esther Cortada Andreu, 'El acceso de las maestras al magisterio público en el siglo XIX: ¿Concesión o logro profesional?', *Historia Social* 38 (2000), 35–55; and Esther Cortada Andreu, '*Hostilidad, negociación y conciencia profesional: el día a día de las maestras del siglo XIX*', *Ayer* 45 (2002), 223–50.

This relationship between education legislation and social change continued to develop, prompting radical changes such as that established in the Draft Decree for the General Organization of Public Education of 7 March 1814, which transformed all previous legislation by providing, in article 115, for the establishment of public schools in which girls would be taught to read and write and adults would be taught the work and skills proper to their sex. Meanwhile, article 116 stipulated that these schools would be run by the government and provincial councils, including the schools opened for girls. Arguing that the measure was dictated by a scarcity of financial resources, Royal Decree of 8 July 1816 encouraged convents elsewhere in Spain to establish girls' schools to teach 'the mysteries of the faith, the formation of customs and the rudiments of women's work, so necessary in society'.[32]

During the Liberal Triennium and before the death of Fernando VII, the most significant education initiative was Calomarde's Plan and Regulation for Primary Schools, approved by Royal Decree on 16 February 1825. The most important aspect of the Calomarde Plan was the distinction between four types of school, distinguished by different curricula and salaries. In girls' schools, the following were established as core subjects: Christian doctrine, reading and writing, while needlework varied according to the type of school. However, it does not seem to have mattered much to the legislators that some female teachers were illiterate, because article 199 stated that 'the very precise teaching of writing and counting shall be given either by the schoolmistress herself, or with the help of a schoolmaster or trainee who has reached the age of forty years old'.

However, Royal Decree of 4 August 1836, which included a General Plan for Public Education known as the Duke of Rivas Plan, represented a retrograde step as regards the access to free education advocated by early liberalism. Even at primary level, all families except the very poor were required to pay a contribution towards their children's education.[33] The

32 Consuelo Flecha García, *Las mujeres en la legislación educativa española. Enseñanza Primaria y Normal en los siglos XVIII y XIX* (Sevilla: GIHUS/KRONOS, 1997).

33 Isabel Gutiérrez Zuloaga, 'Contexto Histórico en el que se produce la creación de las Escuelas de España', *Revista Interuniversitaria de Formación del Profesorado* 5 (1989), 51.

Duke of Rivas Plan distinguished, for the first time, between complete and incomplete elementary schools and higher primary schools, a classification that would later be included in the Moyano Law. The only article that mentioned girls' schools was article 21, which simply provided for the establishment of such schools 'wherever resources permit, accommodating the teaching in these schools to the corresponding elementary and higher schools for boys, but with the modifications and in the manner corresponding to the sex'. With regard to teacher-training, the obligation was established for the first time to found men's teacher-training colleges in Madrid and the provinces, but nothing was said about similar colleges for women. The moderates, who continued in power, were obliged to make a pact with the progressives to enact a new education law. Reaching agreement on secondary and higher education proved difficult, as the progressives wanted secondary education to be free, whereas the moderates inclined towards an elitist model of secondary and higher education. The Marquis of Someruelos advocated the enactment of a Provisional Plan for Primary Education by means of a law passed on 21 July 1838.

Throughout the nineteenth century, Spain attempted to follow in the footsteps of other European countries as regards education. In 1837, the first nursery school was created; in 1876, the Escuela Modelo Jardines de Infancia [Froebel Kindergarten Model School] was founded; and years later, the decrees of 17 March and 13 August 1882 were approved. The former placed female teachers in charge of the public nursery schools and instituted a general board of directors for this education, while the latter reorganized the Escuela Nacional de Maestras [Schoolmistresses' Central Training College]. Both represented far-reaching reforms that laid the foundations for progress in the inclusion of female teachers in the education system.

In relation to the above, the sociologist Sonsoles San Román has defined the female teaching profession according to various prototypes. According to her classification, the first female teachers who emerged as such were the so-called illiterate teachers (1783–1838), who carried out their tasks in public schools and were practically unable to read or write; their primary function was to teach domestic skills to girls from the most disadvantaged classes who were denied any kind of instruction.[34] This model continued well into the nineteenth century in some villages.[35] The maternal female teacher (1838–1876) formed the second model, in which nursery schools played an important role in an attempt to tackle a problem for the working classes, who had nowhere to leave their children, while the third model was that of the rational-intuitive female teacher (1868–1882) associated with the thinking of three important eighteenth-century philosophers: Rousseau, Kant and Condorcet. The first female teacher model was characterized by teaching household management, needlework and the rudiments of the Catholic faith; the second by acting as a complement to male teachers in the classroom; and the third by being better trained because of having studied at a teacher-training college.[36]

Regarding the training of female teachers, this seems to have aroused little concern, and in many respects, they followed in the footsteps of male teachers. At first, it was considered sufficient for them to have a knowledge of Christian doctrine and to be examined by a bishop. They had to obtain a licence from the Examination Board after having proved their 'purity of blood', their good conduct and that of their husbands if they were married and that they had not engaged in 'vile or mechanical' trades. The rationale for such requirements was that the aim in girls' schools was to teach home economics and religion.[37]

In 1839, the first examination regulations were published for the qualification of schoolmistress, and by Royal Order of 1 January 1839, the examinations included subjects such as religion and morals, reading and writing, counting by whole numbers and domestic tasks, whereas male teachers were

34 San Román, *Las primeras maestras*, 58.

35 The newspaper *La Época* reported on the subject: 'The Civil Governor of the province of Valencia has suspended a schoolmistress from her post at the girls' school of Fuente Encarroz on the grounds that the said lady does not know how to read or write. If this is so, how did she obtain the qualification?' *La Época* (17 February 1883).

36 San Román, *Las primeras maestras*, 78.

37 Lorenzo, 'Hacia la profesionalización y modernización del Magisterio (1898–1936)', 215.

examined on a greater range of knowledge.[38] In addition, female teachers had to be at least 25 years old to be eligible for the post. The salary they earnt was approximately twenty *reales* a year. As stated in the Royal Decree of 23 September 1847, female teachers were paid one third less than the salary assigned to male teachers, for performing the same duties; they were also usually provided with room and board at the school.

In general, male teachers salaries were very low, but the situation was even worse for female teachers regardless of whether they worked in private or public schools. Elementary schoolmasters in Madrid earnt a salary of approximately six *reales* a day. However, with the Plan for Elementary Schools of 1825, their situation improved and they were paid around 8,000 *reales*. However, female teachers in the same post were paid around 3,000 *reales*. Salaries also differed according to location; the pay was higher in a major capital than in a minor city or a town with a population of more than a thousand inhabitants. In other words, the smaller the population, the lower the salary.[39]

Several years later, the 1857 law regulating education known as the Moyano Law, drafted at the instigation of Claudio Moyano, represented 'the most important advance, obliging the establishment of public elementary schools for girls in all towns with 500 residents. Also noteworthy was article 114, with its recommendation to establish teacher-training colleges for women to improve their training. The following year, the Escuela Normal Central de Maestras de Madrid [Schoolmistresses' Central Training College] was founded in Madrid, although three such teacher-training colleges already existed in the provinces prior to the Moyano Law.'[40] The different education received by boys and girls was echoed in the different training given to male and female teachers, as the subjects required to obtain the qualification were the same as those stipulated for girls in primary

38 Around the year 1370, following the Royal Decree of Enrique II, schoolmasters began to be obliged to pass various tests in order to be able to teach, which represented the first precedent of teacher evaluation. Teacher accreditation and guild organization was also strongly influenced by hierarchical evaluation systems.

39 Julio Ruiz Berrio, *Política escolar de España del siglo XIX (1808–1833)* (Madrid: CSIC, 1970), 150.

40 Mínguez Blasco, *Alumnas y maestras*, 57.

education, with the addition of the principles of education and teaching methods.[41]

In this respect, the Moyano Law was decisive for women's entry into the profession. As it was incompatible with holding other positions, men saw teaching as a temporary occupation, whereas for many years it was the only dignified profession open to women that enabled them to attain economic and personal emancipation. To obtain the qualification of elementary schoolmistress, it was more than sufficient to learn Christian doctrine and notions of sacred history, reading, writing, Spanish grammar and spelling, the principles of arithmetic and the tasks considered 'proper to their sex'.

> Despite these limitations, there is no doubt that the Moyano Law provided a major impetus to the creation of a professional body of secular female teachers, which was soon threatened, however, by the Law on Primary Education of 2 June 1868. The so-called Orovio Law, of clear neo-Catholic inspiration, endowed the ecclesiastical authorities with a major role in primary education, promoting the expansion of religious schools and suppressing teacher training colleges by entrusting teacher training for women to religious institutions. However, the law had a negligible impact as it was repealed following the Revolution of the same year.[42]

It should be noted that in the last sixty years of the nineteenth century, one of the main demands was wage equality, something that was not legally recognized in Spain until 1883.[43] On 5 October of that same year, the Minister of Development, Germán Gamazo, noted that public education had been very poorly funded and consequently increased the budgetary

41 This distinction between boys' and girls' education continued into the early twentieth century according to Josefina Aldecoa, who 'had observed in the previous schools – all mixed – that boys were livelier, quicker to understand, more interested in everything and unafraid of making mistakes. The girls were more attentive and more consistent; they worked patiently and finished their work carefully, but they were more passive. Trained from birth to be as submissive as possible, girls are too embarrassed to participate; they think they won't know or won't be able … that's why I preferred to have them together. It seemed to me that they were more motivated … together they developed better as people'. Aldecoa, *Historia de una Maestra*, 165.

42 Mínguez Blasco, *Alumnas y maestras*, 58.

43 Other Western countries achieved this in the early twentieth century.

allocation to 860,000 *pesetas*. Some 250,000 *pesetas* were assigned for the construction of schools, as stipulated by the Law on Public Education. This Royal Decree also increased the wages of male and female public-school teachers who earnt 250 *pesetas* or less.

In addition, it was stipulated that schools had to meet the following material conditions:

> The building must have an entrance hall, a school room or rooms, a playground, a garden, room for a public library and the necessary facilities for pupil hygiene. The schoolrooms shall not have a capacity for more than sixty pupils each; they shall have a surface area of 1.25 square metres per seat; the ceiling height shall be such as to give an area of five cubic metres per pupil. The size of the playground shall correspond to an area of five square metres per pupil; the schoolrooms shall be orientated in accordance with local climatic conditions. If the teachers' quarters are to be located in the same buildings as the schools, they shall be given separate entrances with no direct communication.[44]

Although legislative advances were important in the process of professionalization of the teaching profession and women's education, until the mid-nineteenth century state institutions evinced Spain's incapacity – primarily economic – to support projects such as the continuous and widespread training of female teachers. Hence, although the legal climate was favourable, the weakness of public institutions delayed the social changes called for by middle-class women in particular, who were demanding a better academic education. In this scenario, as we shall see in the following section, private initiative and civil society would play a key role in women's education.

44 Archivo de la Fundación Fernando de Castro – Asociación para la Enseñanza de la Mujer (hereafter: AFFC – AEM), leg. 4–7.

The role of Fernando de Castro in the professional and academic education of women in Spain

The analysis presented in this section is based on research conducted in the archives of the Fernando de Castro Foundation. In accordance with the historiographic method, information and data were obtained that enabled an analysis of the role played by Fernando de Castro (1814–1874) in the academic education of women in nineteenth-century Spain, which had not existed until then.

Fernando de Castro positioned himself as the harbinger of initiatives that sought to improve the education of middle-class women and achieve their social revitalization.[45] As part of his endeavours, on 1 December 1869 he inaugurated the School for Governesses,[46] and several years later, on 11 July 1871, he founded the Association for Women's Education with the aim of fostering primary and secondary education for women, as well as other studies such as commerce, the post office and telegraphy. The association brought together various schools for women and exerted a decisive influence on their progress and social advancement in Spain by improving their academic and occupational education.

In 1868, Krausist and Institutionist initiatives increased education opportunities for middle-class women. The Escuela de Institutrices [School for Governesses] was unquestionably the most brilliant and long-lasting practical implementation of Krausism in the field of women's education. Castro also created the school of Higher Primary Education, filling a gap in Spanish public education. The subjects taught included the physical and natural sciences, French language, arts and crafts, the principles of education, gymnastics, drawing and singing. These higher primary public

45 Ramón Chacón, *Don Fernando de Castro y el problema del catolicismo liberal en España* (Madrid: Fundación Fernando de Castro, 2006), 75.

46 On one of his trips to Germany and Switzerland, Fernando de Castro had the opportunity to attend an International Charity Conference and learn about the Froebel method, presented by Baroness Bertha von Marenholtz-Bulow, an experience that exerted a decisive influence on his subsequent projects for the instruction and education of women.

schools provided entry to professions such as teaching, commerce, medicine and many others, which would soon become accessible to women.[47]

In his various posts – for example, he was appointed rector of the Central University of Madrid on 4 October 1868 and the provisional government confirmed his appointment by a decree of 22 October 1868 –[48] Castro always promoted the education of women, considering them the heart of the family and the representative of the moral element.[49] However, the statistics for 1870 recorded that only 9 per cent of women could read and write, that is, 716,000 women out of a total population of 7,900,000 inhabitants.[50] Aware of this situation, he undertook to organized a series of Sunday lectures in the auditorium of the Central University from 21 February to 23 April 1867.[51] The subjects he proposed included the history of women's education, hygiene, legislation and the mother's influence on her children, while the lecturers included Castro himself, Francisco Pi y Margall, Labra, Canalejas and Echegaray.[52]

At the same time as these conferences were becoming established, other vigorous institutions also began to emerge, and on 1 December 1869 the School for Governesses was created. Although it had neither financial means nor official approval, it was attached to the Schoolmistresses' Training College and the first course was delivered in 1869. Fernando de Castro was still rector at the time, and he gave a speech to the new governesses in which he summed up the immeasurable importance of the work of female teachers:

47 AFFC – AEM, leg. 4–6.

48 Rafael Serrano García, *Fernando de Castro. Un obrero de la Humanidad* (León: Junta de Castilla y León, 2010), 320.

49 Fernando de Castro, *Compendio razonado de historia General*, vol. 3 (Madrid: Imprenta Fermín Martínez García,1872), 101.

50 Chacón, *Don Fernando de Castro*, 74.

51 In the same year, Faustina Sáez de Melgar directed the Ladies' Artistic and Literary Athenaeum and was also editor of the women's journal *La Violeta, Revista Hispanoamericana*, a publication that by Royal Order in 1864 was declared an official textbook in the teacher-training colleges for women and higher schools for girls.

52 Chacón, *Don Fernando de Castro*, 72.

> Those of you who aspire to the qualification of schoolmistress or governess, to the profession of teaching, emboldened to devote your lives to one of the noblest and most peaceful of occupations, which is to instil human culture in the world through education and instruction, far from causing tears to spill, you shall wipe them away, driving out the shadows of ignorance and opening the door to the senses and to reason through which knowledge of God, of the world and of the splendour of truth, beauty and virtue shall enter the soul.[53]

In June 1870, the first sixty female students were enrolled and examined at the Central University. Castro drew a clear distinction between the position of governess and that of schoolmistress. His idea was that the former required more training than the latter because governesses lived with their pupils and were therefore both teacher and companion: 'schoolmistresses and governesses, those who teach and those who both educate and teach that the work of human culture is not purely intellectual, but also moral, affective and religious'.[54] In 1870, Fernando de Castro became acting president of the Escuela de Institutrices.

Created within the framework of the Asociación para la Enseñanza de la Mujer [Association for Women's Education], the Escuela de Institutrices became a benchmark in women's education at the time. The first article of its regulations stated that its objective was 'to provide young women with the essential elements of intellectual, moral and social culture proper to women and to prepare those who are to devote themselves to teaching and education'.[55] To be admitted to the school, students had to pass examinations in expressive writing, correct normal writing and fundamentals of arithmetic. The qualification of governess was obtained after three years of study, and the subjects taught were advanced Spanish grammar, arithmetic, physics and chemistry, geography, geology and mineralogy, botany and zoology, hygiene and domestic health care, world history, Spanish history, theory of literature and the fine arts, history of Spanish literature, history

53 Fernando de Castro, 'Discurso pronunciado en la Escuela Normal de Maestras', *Boletín – Revista de la Universidad de Madrid* 2 (1870), 354–9.

54 Rosa María Capel, 'La educación de la mujer en el mudo contemporáneo', in *El trabajo y la educación de la mujer en España (1900–1930)* (Madrid: Ministerio de Cultura, Madrid, 1982), 330–1.

55 AFFC – AEM, leg. 5–6.

of the fine arts, anthropology or knowledge of human nature, principally of the faculties of the soul, and the moral duties of women in society and in the family (teaching, music, drawing and French). The subjects were taught in weekly lessons, except for drawing and French, which were delivered in alternating lessons, and music, which was taught every day.[56] Non-compulsory subjects were also studied in order to obtain the qualification, and these included English, German, Italian or French, painting and the art of reading. Students paid per enrolled subject. A one-year subject cost twenty-five *pesetas*, a single subject cost twelve *pesetas*, two subjects cost twenty *pesetas* and three subjects cost thirty *pesetas*. In a meeting held on 20 March 1880, the Sociedad Económica Matritense advised that justice should be done to this education institution, which was essential in Spain and raised the country's cultural level.[57]

Besides the Escuela de Institutrices, the Asociación para la Enseñanza de la Mujer also established the Escuela de Comercio para Señoras [Ladies' Commercial School] in 1878, the Post and Telegraph School in 1883 and the Elementary Primary School on 1 March 1884. Subsequently, a preparatory school for entry into the Escuela Normal Central de Maestras was also founded.[58] All of these institutions trained women for future new professions. A new Escuela de Profesores de Párvulos [Nursery School Teacher Training College] was inaugurated in December 1884 after having been abolished by Royal Decree of 4 July 1884, with the aim providing continuity as far as the meagre resources of a private foundation would allow.

Fernando de Castro contended that 'the education of infants is the exclusive competence of women, and of those who devote themselves to this occupation it requires particular intelligence, instruction, feelings and habits; these are universally recognized truths … it was the duty of the Association to exalt the principles scorned by the Royal Decree of 4 July 1884 and to organized the Escuela de Profesores de Párvulos College as

56 Asociación para la Enseñanza de la Mujer, *Bases de la misma y Reglamento de sus escuelas* (Madrid: Imprenta de U. Gómez, 1882).

57 AFFC – AEM, Reseña Histórica, leg. 83–4.

58 AFFC – AEM, Reseña histórica, leg. 94.

far as possible with the same teachers who had worked in the suppressed official one'.[59]

The origins of the Escuela Normal Central in Spain: A historical review from 1858 to 1900

The Escuela Normal de Maestras was created by Royal Order of Isabel II on 24 February 1858, and the first Escuela Normal Femenina [Schoolmistresses' Training College] was inaugurated in Madrid on 21 March 1858. Prior to this, such colleges had been established in Pamplona in 1847, in Badajoz and Logroño in 1851, in Navarre in 1856 and in Cuenca, Granada, Huesca, Salamanca and Seville in 1858. In the provinces, a basic elementary education qualified candidates for entry to the colleges, whereas in Madrid, admission required a higher elementary education. This influenced the training that such colleges delivered. Arising in response to the need created by discrimination in women's education, these colleges were established twenty years after similar institutions had been founded to train male teachers.[60] They emerged under the auspices of the Law on Public Education of 9 September 1857, article 114 of which states: 'The Government shall ensure that Escuelas Normales de Maestras are established to improve the education of girls.' They were created in almost all provinces and were run by the provincial councils.

These teacher-training colleges initially received no government funding and therefore struggled to survive throughout the nineteenth century and well into the twentieth century. After the 1880 Regulation, the eligible age for admission ranged from 15 to 30 years old. The first teacher-training college in Madrid was initially located in Calle Valverde, but was later moved to no. 4, Calle Arco de Santa María. Its first director was Ramona Aparicio Rodríguez, who had obtained her official teaching

59 AFFC – AEM, Curso 1886–1887, Prospecto, *El Liberal*.

60 The Schoolmasters' Teacher Training College was established on 8 March 1838 under the direction of Pablo Montesino.

qualification in 1837, and she remained in charge until her death in 1881. After 1869, she combined this position with the direction of the Escuela de Institutrices. On her death, she was succeeded by Carmen Rojo, who besides being a qualified teacher when she applied for the post, also held the qualification of governess, which more closely reflected the college curriculum and endowed her with a higher cultural and scientific level. Members of the appointments committee included the president of the Association for Women's Education, Manuel Ruiz de Quevedo.

These two institutions would have much in common over the years, as noted previously. Candidates for admission had to prove good moral and religious conduct, be in good physical condition and not suffer from any contagious diseases. In addition, they had to provide references from the parish priest and the civil authorities. The reason given for these requirements was that schoolmistresses played a social role as a model and example for their pupils.

In order to gain admission to the teacher-training college, candidates sat examinations to demonstrate the required level of knowledge, initially defined as having an education in elementary subjects for girls but after 1882, as having received a higher education. One striking test candidates had to pass was to make a man's shirt, sewn in the Spanish style.[61] Initially, the course lasted for two years, one for the elementary qualification and the other for the higher qualification. However, the course was extended after 1881 to two years for the elementary level and one more for the higher level.[62]

The main goal of the Escuela Normal de Maestras was to motivate female students in their education. It was not until 1870 that the study of the Spanish Constitution was included by decree. Also, by Royal Decree, of 24 August 1878, students began learning music with a professional teacher, and on 27 September 1879, the teaching of drawing was included. Scientific subjects such as the natural sciences, commerce and geometry were not included in the curriculum, although they were taught at the Escuela de

61 Antonia Fernández and Juana Anadón, 'La Escuela Normal de Maestras, Central del Reino, 1858–1900', in *Madrid en la Sociedad del siglo XIX* (Madrid: Comunidad de Madrid,1989), 397.

62 Fernández and Anadón, 'La Escuela Normal de Maestras', 398.

Institutrices, where students learnt subjects such as arithmetic, physics and chemistry, geography, geology and mineralogy, botany and zoology.[63]

The Escuela Normal de Maestras evidenced a curriculum that reflected social expectations and stereotypes of women at the time: female teachers were basically trained to educate girls to be good wives and mothers, rather than citizens capable of meeting new professional challenges. Furthermore, their training did not fulfil the purpose for which it was created – awakening students' motivation – because the college did not even have a library to enable students to consult books and support their reading. In addition, the subject given the greatest importance and taught in the best classroom was handicrafts, and the examination in this subject was one of the most dreaded.[64] This neglect of an academic education led to the emergence of other private institutions for women's education, as discussed earlier.

When the liberal party came to power in 1881, education once again acquired major importance, and training for female teachers was modernized. The Moyano Law was modified, endowing a larger allocation for education, 'although the teacher training qualification for women's education had been created in 1882. Three years later, in 1885, only one female teacher was teaching in the teacher training colleges, compared to 367 male teachers in the public sector and 71 in the private sector; figures that indicate that the social climate was not yet favourable to the incorporation of women at higher levels.'[65]

In 1882, an education conference was held which laid the foundations for reform of the teacher-training colleges, with the result that women were permitted to teach in nursery schools, thus opening up a new professional path for them.

From this moment on, a series of decrees were issued in an attempt to equalized the profession for men and women. The decree of 13 August 1882 brought the years of study for female teachers into line with those for male teachers, incorporated new subjects and above all, brought about a change in teaching methodology. The professionals involved in these

63 AFFC – AEM, leg. 49.

64 Fernández and Anadón, 'La Escuela Normal de Maestras', 399.

65 San Román, *Las primeras maestras*, 224.

changes included Rafael Torres Campos, Adela Riquelme, Concepción Saiz and Casilda Mexía, all of whom had been very closely associated with the Asociación para la Enseñanza de la Mujer and Fernando de Castro and were also staunch advocates of the new teaching methods.

In the late nineteenth century, the Budget Law of 28 June 1898 authorized the reorganization of the teacher-training colleges and shortly afterwards, a new curriculum was established.[66] This law took into account previous reforms, raising them to statutory level and providing resources for 'the continuance of the three established levels of teacher-training: elementary, higher and normal, although reducing the first one to two 5-month courses. In addition, the two Escuelas Normales Centrales in Madrid will continue: one for men and another for women in each university district, while all other provinces shall have at least one Escuela Normal Elemental [Elementary Teacher Training College].'[67]

> The curriculum in the elementary teacher training colleges included the following subjects: Christian doctrine and sacred history, Spanish language, geography, history, arithmetic, geometry, drawing, calligraphy, physics, chemistry, natural history, handicrafts, physiology, hygiene, gymnastics, education and teaching practice with notions of school legislation. The subjects for female teachers' elementary studies were the same as those for male teachers, with the addition of the usual domestic skills and sewing.[68]

Meanwhile, the two-year curriculum of the higher teacher-training colleges included 'religion and morals, general grammar, language and literature, geography, history, arithmetic, geometry, algebra, physics, chemistry, natural history, geology, biology, handicrafts, anthropology, psychology, complete theory of education, law and school legislation, physiology, hygiene, gymnastics, teaching theory and practice, artistic drawing, calligraphy, French, music and singing. The curriculum specified how subjects were to be delivered: some were taught cyclically, others in each year.'[69]

66 Royal Decree of 23 September 1898, reorganizing the teacher-training colleges, in *Colección Legislativa de Instrucción Pública* (1898), 152–91.

67 Lorenzo, 'Hacia la profesionalización y modernización del Magisterio', 110.

68 Lorenzo, 'Hacia la profesionalización y modernización del Magisterio', 112.

69 Lorenzo, 'Hacia la profesionalización y modernización del Magisterio', 114.

Candidates for admission had to fulfil a series of requirements, including being 16 years old, having a certificate of good conduct and having passed an entrance examination.

The institution was gradually endowed with new and improved facilities, such as a library, a laboratory, an office for the different subjects and a school museum, and it was moved to Calle de Barco, to gain more space. The programmes were expanded to include practical and highly didactic subjects taught by specialists in the field, such as arithmetic, French and the fine arts. The curriculum continued to change until the beginning of the twentieth century, but never reduced its disciplinary scope. Successive governments realized the role of education in shaping free citizens.[70]

It was not until the Plan of 6 July 1900 that male and female teachers' programmes and timetables were unified, establishing specializations in science or literature at the Normal level, which were also reflected in the public examinations for teachers. By the late nineteenth century, all governments had become aware of the need to educate women and above all, to train those who would later hold great responsibility in their hands.

Thus, throughout the nineteenth century, attempts were made to improve the professionalization of female teachers in Spain, where education was always viewed as a path towards modernizing the country and its democracy. The legislative and political development that has been reconstructed reflects this push for modernization through the creation of teacher-training colleges for men and women, not always in the hands of the State, but with the contribution of non-governmental organizations and leaders such as Fernando de Castro. Nonetheless, although the nineteenth century witnessed a period of revitalization in which important advances were made, social recognition of female teachers and the institutions involved in their training remained inadequate.

70 Fernández and Anadón, 'La Escuela Normal de Maestras', 400.

PART VI

Other Professionals

DAVID MARTÍNEZ-VILCHES

An Anti-liberal Profession in Modern Society

The Parish Priest (1833–1868)

ABSTRACT
After the fall of the Ancien Régime in Spain, parish clergy adapted to the post-revolutionary context during the reign of Isabel II (1833–1868). Their education and organization were normalized to place the priests at the service of the Church and the State, and the public image of these religious figures was redefined in tune with the new social values. Consequently, parish priests were no longer the last rung of a privileged estate, but a professional group which worked in favour of general welfare.

Introduction[1]

Parish priests were the part of the Catholic Church in greatest contact with Spanish society, given that they were entrusted with the task of tending to the spiritual needs of the faithful. They were the most direct intermediaries between the spiritual world and parishioners, and were the ones to administer the sacraments and perform the rituals that marked symbolic milestones of their lives on earth, such as baptism, marriage and funerals. Moreover, the parish was a social and anthropological reality in itself and served as a point of reference for local identity, often clearly expressed through dedication to a particular saint. Major changes took place in the nineteenth century that notably affected the Church, but parishes continued to be the unifying element of their respective communities, while the individual parishes played an important social role. Nevertheless, the

1 This chapter is part of the research project 'Cultura del honor, política y esfera pública en la España liberal (1833–1890)' funded by the Ministry of Science, Innovation and Universities (PGC2018-093698-B-I00) and the University Faculty Training programme (FPU 17/00545).

new reality meant a decisive change in the general perception held of the clergy, and parish priests in particular, in line with the new principles on which Spain's liberal society were organized.[2]

Firstly, the Church ceased to be one of the estates of the realm and became an institution. Although it had inherited many of its earlier privileges, it had to provide a useful service to the citizens of the country. Much of the clergy – the regular clergy and members of cathedral chapters – performed roles related to worship that did not meet the requirement of providing a public service. Parish priests, however, who were at the front line in providing the cure of souls, that is, pastoral care, were of particular importance to the liberal government that had come to power in Spain. After the revolutions that had taken place in the country in the early years of the century, it sought stability through a moderate doctrinal formula and no longer saw the Church as an enemy but an ally to ensure order in Spanish society, which professed itself constitutionally to be Catholic, Apostolic and Roman.[3] For this reason, both the liberals and the Church

2 As shown by different studies made in other countries, not only predominantly Catholic ones: *La parrocchia in Italia nell'età contemporanea* (Naples: Edizione Dehoniane, 1982); Gregory L. Freeze, *The Parish in Nineteenth-Century Russia. Crisis, Reform, Counter-Reform* (Princeton: Princeton University Press, 1983); Jacques Lafon, *Les prêtres, les fidèles et l'État: le ménage à trois du XIXe siècle* (Paris: Beauchesne, 1987); William David Bowman, *Priests and Parish in Vienna. 1780 to 1800* (Boston: Humanities Press, 1999); N. J. G. Pounds, *A History of the English Parish. The Culture of Religion from Augustine to Victoria* (Cambridge: Cambridge University Press, 2004); Samuel Gicquel, *Prêtres de Bretagne au XIXe siècle* (Rennes: Presses Universitaires de Rennes, 2008); Sérgio Ribeiro Pinto, *Servidores de Deus e funcionários de César. O clero paroquial da Monarquia à República (1882–1917)* (Maia: Cosmorama, 2017).

3 José María Portillo Valdés, 'De la Monarquía Católica a la Nación de los Católicos', in Xosé Ramón Barreiro Fernández, ed., *O liberalismo nos seus contextos: un estado da cuestión* (Santiago de Compostela: Universidade de Santiago de Compostela, 2008), 165–84; Gregorio Alonso, *La nación en capilla. Ciudadanía católica y cuestión religiosa en España (1793–1874)* (Granada: Comares, 2014); Jesús Millán and María Cruz Romeo, 'La nación católica en el liberalismo. Las perspectivas sobre la unidad religiosa en la España liberal, 1808–1868', *Historia y Política* 34 (2015), 183–209.

called for a suitable system for training clerics in seminaries, and a sustainable system of parishes that catered to all citizens.

Parish priests, through the professionalization of the priesthood and the public service they provided, took part in the construction of a liberal nation-state in Spain.[4] The nation-state of Spain, 'the State', was the new configuration of power that had been brought to the country by liberalism. It differed greatly from the absolute monarchy that preceded it, which had proven to be untenable during the reign of King Fernando VII. After the crisis of the Ancien Régime, the liberal revolution would bring about this new reality, whose existence is very often taken for granted, while its construction, carried out mainly by moderates, would last throughout the entire nineteenth century. This new figure in Spain's history came to take over – or at least that was the intention – some of the roles traditionally held by the Church. A good example of this was everything associated with control of the information about the population, a task for which parish clerics had centuries of experience given that the basic demographic indicators of births, marriages and deaths were noted in parish records. With the creation of the government statistics office in the nineteenth century, the State took over these tasks from the Church and conducted the first population censuses. However, the civil authorities required the services of parish priests for this purpose, as they knew that parish records were a reliable source with which to compare the new headcount and that priests could be enlisted as civil servants in order to carry out the census. Furthermore, another component of this participation of the secular clergy in the construction of the State was the organization of the corps of military chaplains entrusted with providing the cure of souls to the faithful who served in the armed forces.

Finally, the public image of the priest had to adapt to the new class society that had with liberalism. Freedom of the press had left the clergy in a position of weakness, given that the Church was the target of anti-clerical tirades, although parish priests did not come under as much attack as the

4 Together with other professions, such as engineers. See Darina Martykánová and Juan Pan-Montojo, 'Los constructores del Estado: los ingenieros españoles y el poder público en el contexto europeo (1840–1900)', *Historia y Política* 43 (2020), 57–86.

regular clergy. In any case, a large number of Catholic texts defended the work of priests as beneficial for society, not only in the religious but also the temporal domain, particularly with regard to tasks such as administration of the sacrament of confession and preaching of the Divine Word. In this sense, the priest appeared as the 'doctor of the soul', which can be likened somewhat to the physician or medical doctor, although he could also be seen as the latter's antithesis: while one embodied religion, the other represented reason. Furthermore, the texts addressed to parish priests stressed the important mission they were performing, and how they had to carry it out in the most virtuous manner possible, particularly with regard to their contact with women. What lay behind all these discourses was the design of a celibate and religious masculinity that the parish priest embodied, and its fit with the modern society.

Professionalization of the training for the priesthood

The priesthood underwent a phenomenon of professionalization during the nineteenth century, both in regard to the training of priests and their appointment to parishes in order to conduct pastoral duties. This process was largely guided by the liberal state, whose aim was to ensure the loyalty of parish priests owing to their influence over parishioners from the pulpit and confessional, and to turn the parish into an organization that catered to the spiritual needs of parishioners. It is quite obvious that this point was of concern to a State that had to guarantee the provision of 'spiritual pasture' to citizens who were constitutionally defined as Catholics. Moreover, this was a subject of the greatest interest to the liberal elites, who understood religion to be one of the sources of social order and political stability in the new post-revolutionary situation. In turn, the Church was very interested in the training of priests, not only to enable them to carry out their mission with greater effectiveness, but more particularly in order to prevent any deviation from orthodoxy at a time of ideological rearming against liberalism being undertaken by Pope Pius IX. Consequently, the professionalization of parish priests, as with so many other religious matters in liberal Spain, fell into the turbulent field of the relations between the Church and State.

The need to train priests arose from a religious reality that was gradually being resolved in Spain, with varying degrees of success, through the decrees of the Council of Trent requiring the building of seminaries in each diocese, the reason they are known as 'conciliar' (Tridentine) seminaries in Spain.[5] In addition to ensuring the providing the population with proper spiritual care, at stake was the prestige of the Catholic Church, which was competing with other creeds in a Europe that had become religiously fragmented in the wake of the Reformation. In the nineteenth century, the training of the secular clergy took on greater importance in the light of the transformations brought about by modernity and highlighted the role of the parish priest as a force against upheaval and at the service of social order, particularly after the revolutionary period of the first three decades and with the liberal system being put into place under moderate leadership. It is what a former student of the Seminary of San Sebastián in Málaga, Antonio R. de Vargas, called 'the sacred ministry of reconciliation' to which the clergy were called, precisely at a time when Spain 'was once again recovering its eminently Catholic character, after having experienced one of those terrible situations that upset the political, social and religious body'.[6] And this meant properly training future clerics in Tridentine seminaries that would have to be spiritual bastions against modernity and impiety. Therefore, Catholic apologetics conceived the role of the seminaries from a reactionary political and religious viewpoint, which was actually the transposition of the anti-liberal and anti-modern definition of the Church that took shape in the time of Pius IX.

This political reality behind the question of the seminaries is clearly brought to light in the *Apuntes* [*Notes*] written by Antonio María Claret [Saint Anthony Mary Claret] on the government of a diocese and which,

5 Francisco Martín Hernández, *Los seminarios españoles (1563–1700). Historia y pedagogía* (Salamanca: Sígueme, 1964); Francisco Martín Hernández, *Los seminarios españoles en la época de la Ilustración. Ensayo de una pedagogía eclesiástica en el siglo XVIII* (Madrid: CSIC, 1973).

6 Antonio R. de Vargas, *Instrucción sobre los seminarios eclesiásticos llamados conciliares* (Montevideo: Imp. de la Caridad, 1844), n.p. (in the draft text of 'Advertencia').

after being sent to the rest of the Spanish episcopate to know the opinion they merited, were ultimately published. Claret believed that was essential that there should be a seminary in each diocese that was a 'true nursery for good priests', who would make be the best assistants for the bishop as he carried out his pastoral labours, whereas 'bad clerics' would hinder his work.[7] 'Bad clerics', according to Claret, were the 'worst enemies of the Church'. This had been demonstrated during the French Revolution, when apostasy was concealed under the guise of the juring or constitutional clergy, who behaved like the 'whitewashed tombs' referenced by Christ in the Gospel.[8] This moral opposition between 'good' and 'bad' clerics summarized the Church's fears about heterodoxy and internal dissent in the words of one of the most outstanding and counter-revolutionary figures of the episcopate during the reign of Queen Isabel II.[9] The identification of error as sin, and the equal condemnation of both, called to mind the dangers that liberalism and rationalism posed to the faith and society. For this reason, by preserving the purity of the former, the seminaries also served to ensure the order in the latter. This perception was echoed by the rector of the seminary in Seville to his students in his speech to mark the beginning of the academic year in September 1863 in the mention of the 'religious and social importance' of the seminaries:

> It cannot be doubted, gentlemen; the science of the flesh must be fought by the science of the spirit; the doctrines of error by the doctrine of truth; and teaching,

7 Antonio María Claret, *Apuntes que para su uso personal y para el régimen de la diócesis escribía y tenía siempre a la vista el arzobispo de Santiago de Cuba, D. Antonio María Claret y Clará* (Madrid: Imp. de la Esperanza, 1857), 32.

8 Claret, *Apuntes para el régimen de la diócesis*, 18–21. The importance of the seminaries is again described in Antonio María Claret, *El colegial o seminarista teórica y prácticamente instruido*, 2 vols (Barcelona: Librería Religiosa, 1861), I, 7–16.

9 Described as 'Spartan conservatism' by Pedro Carlos González Cuevas, *Historia de las derechas españolas de la Ilustración a nuestros días* (Madrid: Biblioteca Nueva, 2000), 114. Other appraisals of Claret's ideology along very similar lines in David Martínez-Vilches, 'En la puerta de la voluntad regia: Antonio María Claret y el confesor real en el régimen liberal (1857–1868)', in Raquel Sánchez and David San Narciso, eds, *La cuestión de Palacio: Corte y cortesanos en la España contemporánea* (Granada: Comares, 2018), 146–50.

> which has risen from the bottom of the abyss by another teaching, which has descended from heaven. This sublime science, this purest of doctrines and this celestial teaching is communicated through Religion to the priesthood, for which the youth is fittingly prepared, in order to convey to the peoples through its means their inestimable benefits.[10]

It can be inferred from all of this that the training of future parish priests was affected by the doctrinal incompatibility between Catholicism and modernity asserted by the nineteenth-century Church, and it was made evident in the curriculum for seminaries approved on 28 September 1852. It had largely been produced by the nuncio Giovanni Brunelli after consultation with the episcopate, and its anti-regalism was continued in the Royal Decree of 21 May of the same year that abolished the faculties of theology in civilian universities.[11] The curriculum envisaged four stages of studies in grammar and humanities (four years), philosophy (three years), theology (seven years) and canon law (three years). The degree of *bachiller* [baccalaureate] was conferred after four years of theology studies, with the licentiate degree and doctorate conferred after six and seven years, respectively. Nonetheless, a shorter course was also created, theoretically for late vocations, but it was actually encouraged by bishops to enable vacancies in parishes to be filled. Moreover, the curriculum set out the duration of academic years and classes, enrolment fees, examinations and grades, and – a matter of the greatest importance – the text books with which the future priests would be trained. Analysis of this bibliography, which is essentially of foreign authorship, gives a clear indication of the concern for orthodoxy, which repressed the enlightened school of religious thought of the previous century. On the other hand, no reference was made to the teaching role

10 Manuel González y Sánchez, *Discurso sobre la importancia religiosa y social de los seminarios conciliares* (Seville: Librería Española y Extrangera de D. J. M. Geofrin, 1863), 25.

11 A well-known study on this particular point is that by Melquíades Andrés Martín, *La supresión de las facultades de Teología en las universidades españolas* (Burgos: Aldecoa, 1976). See also Beatriz Comella Gutiérrez, 'El devenir pedagógico de los seminarios conciliares españoles en la Edad Contemporánea', *Hispania Sacra* 64/Extra 1 (2014), 339–71.

because it was a duty perceived as a springboard to greater privileges – even to the Church hierarchy – and not a destination in itself.[12]

However, if the teaching role seemed vague, the sense of student efforts also did not go much further than that of the cure of souls, which meant that knowledge was reduced to an instrumental dimension and, moreover, aroused misgivings among a large number of Catholic authors. Claret wrote of the 'brotherhood' that should exist between science and virtue, spirit and letters, but warned seminarians that they were studying 'not to be seen as wise and erudite, not for mundane interests and purposes, but to know God better and to love him'; and that they should have 'the spirit of mortification that consists of reading and studying what is appropriate in the proper manner and at the proper time'.[13] Nonetheless, there were also those who demanded that clerics should have a degree of modern knowledge in order to manage with ease in the world in which they were meant to live, although they should on no account share the new ideologies of the age. Indeed, as can be seen in the *Novísimo manual de curas* [*Latest Manual for Priests*] by Antonio Covián, the nineteenth century was such an 'investigative century', that parish priests should not 'be indifferent to scientific advancements'. In Covián's opinion, the French clergy provided good examples of priests interested in 'legitimate advances'. Study and knowledge could prove highly useful to the priest 'because in all ages it was necessary to defend religion from the attacks of its enemies, and this need grows in times such as that in which we live'.[14] Or, in the words of the controversial prelate Pedro Cirilo Uriz of Pamplona: 'God free us from an ignorant

12 Decree of 28 September 1852, *Gaceta de Madrid* (30 September 1852). We refer to the study of this curriculum made by José Manuel Cuenca Toribio, 'Notas para el estudio de los seminarios españoles en el pontificado de Pío IX', *Saitabi: Revista de la Facultat de Geografia i Història* 23 (1973), 61–5. With regard to teaching in seminaries as part of the *cursus honorum* of the ecclesiastical hierarchy in the middle decades of the nineteenth century, by the same author: *Sociología de una élite de poder de España e Hispanoamérica contemporáneas: la Jerarquía eclesiástica (1789–1965)* (Córdoba: Escudero, 1976), 143–57.

13 Claret, *Apuntes para el régimen de la diócesis*, 102–3. See also Claret, *El colegial o seminarista*, I, 32–6.

14 Antonio Covián, *Novísimo manual de curas o breve compendio del ministerio parroquial* (Madrid: Imp. de Alhambra y comp., 1847), XXII–XXIII. Originally

priest!'[15] Still, those pleas were not materialized in the training of priests at that time. This would have to wait until the following pontificate when the Church doctrine offered an alternative to rationalism that was more in tune with the modern world.

In terms of the events that took place with regard to seminaries during the reign of Isabel II, the text of the Concordat of 1851 between Spain and the Vatican mandated that the government, with the prior agreement of the Holy See, was to establish general seminaries for ecclesiastical studies in dioceses where none existed, but leaving admission criteria for young men in the hands of the archbishop and bishops and that their administration should adhere to the decrees of the Council of Trent. As a result, with the creation of seminaries in Oviedo (1851), Santander (1852) and Minorca (1858), there were sixty-six Tridentine seminaries in fifty-nine dioceses by the end of Isabel II's reign.[16] It should be borne in mind that these were not only centres of religious education, but also institutions of an ambiguous nature that could be also be likened to secondary schools, as was finally acknowledged after different legislative vicissitudes in 1866. This came as no surprise given that most of the students attending seminaries were day students,[17] which reveals the influence of the Church over the middle classes, the competition these schools posed for government schools and the undermining of the education system at secondary level where the seminaries were independent of the education authorities.[18]

---

published in 1815, the quote is from the foreword by the author to the reprint issued in 1847.

15 Pedro Cirilo Uriz y Labayru, *Carta pastoral que el Ilmo. señor D. Pedro Cirilo Uriz y Labayru, obispo de Pamplona, dirige al clero de su diócesis* (Pamplona: Imp. de Francisco Erasun y Rada, 1862), quoted by José Manuel Cuenca Toribio, *Sociedad y clero en la España del siglo XIX* (Córdoba: Publicaciones del Monte de Piedad y Caja de Ahorros de Córdoba, 1980), 23.

16 *Anuario de la Instrucción pública para el año académico de 1867 a 1868* (Madrid: Imp. del Colegio de Sordo-Mudos y de Ciegos, 1868), 334–8. It contains a list by diocese, with their rectors and secretaries.

17 Instituto Nacional de Estadística, Fondo Documental, *Anuarios*, years 1858, 1859–1860 and 1866–1867, <http://www.ine.es/inebaseweb/libros.do?tntp=25687>, accessed 1 March 2021.

18 Cuenca Toribio, 'Notas para el estudio de los seminarios españoles', 55–8.

On the other hand, as a result of the concerns of the Church of the time, the bishops enacted rules and edicts to regulate every detail of daily life in the seminaries. Their provisions governed everything concerning the institution (rector, vice-rector, secretary and librarian), the teaching staff, students (admission criteria, enrolment fees, personal items to be brought to the seminary) and service staff (sacristans, servants, storekeeper, refectorian, infirmarian, doorman and cook). Those detailed documents also set out the type of food to be served, the clothing to be worn by students, the duration of the academic year, daily activities (also in summer), justified absences from seminaries, teaching methods, examinations and offences and punishments.[19] As explained by Professor José Manuel Cuenca Toribio: 'The ghetto complex suffered by the nineteenth-century Church aids understanding for anybody who might be tempted to see excessive authority as the best means of safeguarding seminarians from the errors of the century.'[20] In this sense, prelates made the utmost effort to ensure compliance with the rules and to make their seminaries places of retreat and good manners. One example of this obsession is evident in a report submitted by Gregorio María López, the Bishop of Palencia, to the nuncio Lorenzo Barilli. It tells of how, after taking possession of the bishopric, he had meticulously inspected the diocesan seminary, where he was made aware of 'many failings'. He corrected them by expelling certain students,

19 An example of this is *Constituciones del Seminario Conciliar de Sta. María de la Asunción en la Ciudad de Oviedo* (Oviedo: Imp. y Litografía de Martínez Hermanos, 1851).

20 Cuenca Toribio, 'Notas para el estudio de los seminarios españoles', 66. See also the monographs available on a number of similar seminaries during this period: Vicente Cárcel Ortí, *Segunda época del Seminario Conciliar de Valencia (1845–1896)* (Castellón de la Plana: Sociedad Castellanense de Cultura, 1969); Marie-Hélène Buisine-Soubeyroux, 'El seminario conciliar de Logroño en la segunda mitad del XIX', *Brocar: Cuadernos de Investigación Histórica* 21 (1997), 311–20; José Antonio Vázquez Vilanova, 'Los estudios en los seminarios españoles del siglo XIX. El ejemplo de la diócesis compostelana', *Hispania Sacra* 54/109 (2002), 227–42; Francisco González Lozano, *Historia pedagógica del Seminario Conciliar de San Atón, 1851–1962* (Badajoz: Fundación Caja Badajoz, 2015); Pedro Cabello Morales, *La Córdoba del seminario. El Seminario Conciliar de San Pelagio en la prensa local cordobesa, 1850–1939* (Córdoba: Almuzara, 2018).

imposing strict discipline and specifying spiritual exercises for the students. He then expressed his satisfaction with the results: 'I will say without fear of error that the present year rather resembles a convent than a seminary.'[21]

Aside from the seminaries, the other matter that had a bearing on the professionalization of the secular clergy in the new liberal context was the organization of everything associated with the parishes themselves. Matters related to the adaptation of the number of parishes to the populations of their corresponding parishioners and the provision of priests to head them were considered particularly urgent. This 'parish arrangement', together with the revision of diocesan boundaries stemmed from the regalist intention that the monarchy, by virtue of its patronage over the Church in its territories, should take the initiative of streamlining the ecclesiastic structure whose territorial implementation had inherited many features from the past that hindered the cure of souls. In the nineteenth century, with the implementation of the liberal system and the dismantling of the Ancien Régime, came the added necessity of adapting the drastic reduction in the rents that filled the coffers of the Church and its institutions caused by the abolition of tithes and the intermittent but intense process of expropriation of Church property. The parish arrangement must therefore be understood as a substantial part of the general arrangement of the clergy and in close association with the matter of providing an endowment to support public worship and the clergy that the liberals promised the Church, which placed the livelihood of the Church at the mercy of the State in economic terms.[22]

However, the break in relations between Spain and the Holy See and the economic hardship that initially beset the liberal state hindered

21 Gregorio María López to Lorenzo Barilli, Plasencia (22 October 1864), Archivio Apostolico Vaticano, Archivio della Nunziatura di Madrid (AAV, NM), vol. 454, sez. XLV, tit. 38, ff. 992–7.

22 Vicente Cárcel Ortí, *Política eclesial de los gobiernos liberales españoles (1830–1840)* (Pamplona: Universidad de Navarra, 1975); Alfredo Verdoy Herranz, 'El debate parlamentario sobre culto y clero. De las Constituyentes de 1837 a la firma del convenio con la Santa Sede', *Revista de Estudios Políticos* 93 (1996), 487–98; and Ricardo García, 'Desamortización y financiación del culto y el clero: la Constitución de 1837', *Revista Española de Derecho Canónico* 57/148 (2000), 71–127.

the effective implementations of the reforms regarding the cure of souls. Consequently, any projects created in this field were of a provisional nature until well into the reign of Isabel II. In this sense, the title of draft bill published in the then official state gazette *Gaceta de Madrid* in April 1838, *Proyecto de ley provisional de dotación del culto y el clero según su actual organización* [Draft Bill on the Endowment of Public Worship and the Clergy in Its Current Condition], is quite telling. Its preamble confirmed the intention of 'improving, as soon as it is feasible and the hardship suffered by the State allows it, the lot of the active parish clergy, until now poorly served and remunerated, but worthy of the particular preference of the Government and popular sympathy'. For this purpose, plans were made to divide parishes into four categories, which would be carried out by the diocesan boards with the agreement of the civil authorities: *de entrada* (entry level), *de primer ascenso* (first promotion), *de seguno ascenso* (second promotion) and *de término* (final level), with endowments adjusted upwards and able to be increased if permitted using leftover funds. This remuneration would be complemented by the use of rectories and their vegetable gardens and orchards, in the same conditions that had existed until then, and surplice and altarage fees.[23]

In any case, the implementation of any deep-seated reform within the Spanish Church would require the agreement of the Holy See; otherwise, any government action could be interpreted as an invasion of the exclusive competence of the religious authorities. This actually occurred in the wake of the revolution of 1840, when the new division of parishes in Madrid that was ordered by decree on 14 November was received with protests by the interim nuncio and auditor judge of the ecclesiastical court attached to the nunciature in Madrid, José Ramírez de Arellano, who pointed out the meddling by the civil authorities, which was particularly serious given the fact that the post of archbishop of Toledo, under whose jurisdiction Madrid lay, was vacant. This was not the first or last protest by Ramírez de Arellano against the religious policy of the liberal government, which came to a head with the banishment of this particular cleric and confiscation of

23 Draft bill, *Gaceta de Madrid* (17 April 1838). This bill was enacted in the law of 21 July 1838, *Gaceta de Madrid* (2 August 1838).

his income, and the closure of the nunciature and its ecclesiastical court in December 1840.[24] The following year, the Minister of Grace and Justice, José Alonso, pursued the issuance of a royal decree to suppress and merge parishes in localities where there were more than one. Alonso reasoned that the excessive number of parishes had made their endowment difficult, explaining that the confiscation measures and abolition of tithes and first fruits, meant that the parish clergy had to be maintained with the contributions made by parishioners, which would be very unequal if the parishes were not made more homogeneous. Therefore, exercising the rights of the monarchs of Spain's universal patronage of the Church, the minister ordered the bishops to propose to the government the mergers and suppressions of parishes they saw fit, based on information gathered by municipal and provincial councils and parish priests.[25]

This form of cooperation between the government and the dioceses continued throughout Isabel's effective reign, now under a moderate government, while a rapprochement was being reached between Spain and Rome. On 26 February 1844, the minister Luis Mayans sent a notice to the prelates obligating them to compile reports on the suppression, merger or erection of parishes and the appointment of chaplains or assistants known as 'coadjutors'.[26] The demarcation of parishes was one of the matters dealt with in the Concordat of 1851, continuing on with the conciliatory tone that left the initiative in the hands of the bishops, but which ultimately required the agreement of the government. The Concordat also created the framework for setting out the definitive parish arrangement. Firstly, a priest would be provided for vacant parishes by means of an open competitive selection process, and the government would appoint the priest from a *terna* or shortlist formed by ordinaries. As a consequence, the privilege of birthright, which had benefited clerics who had been baptized within a particular parish (known as *curas pilongos*, 'priests by the font'), would cease and the *terna* system was extended to all parishes under ecclesiastical

24 'Copia del expediente relativo al estrañamiento de estos reinos de D. José Ramírez de Arellano, Vice-gerente de la Nunciatura apostólica', published in the *Gaceta de Madrid* (1 January 1841).

25 Royal Decree of 11 December 1841, *Gaceta de Madrid* (13 December 1841).

26 Notice of 26 February 1844, *Gaceta de Madrid* (27 February 1844).

or lay patronage. In regard to the endowment of priests, the stipend was set at between 3,000 and 10,000 reales for urban parishes and a minimum of 2,200 reales for rural parishes, in addition to use of houses intended for their abode, lands that had not yet been sold and surplice and altarage fees. In turn, coadjutors who were appointed by prelates after the corresponding synodal selection process were allocated a salary of between 2,000 and 4,000 reales, plus their rightful share of parochial fees.

The scope of the text of the Concordat was subsequently set by Spanish law. On 21 November 1851, a royal decree considered vicariates, holdings, missions and parishes with their own priest in localities with fewer than fifty inhabitants as rural curacies, which could be first class (more than thirty-five inhabitants) or second class (all others). Moreover, it differentiated between *vicarios perpetuos* [perpetual vicars], priests who administered their vicariates or missions independently, who were also given the title of *párroco* [parish priest] or *cura propio* [own priest], and chaplains and rectors of missions dependent on the parish priest, who were classified as coadjutors. Another royal decree of the same date mandated that bishops were to appoint an archpriest or dean for each judicial district, known as a deanery, in order to act as vicar forane or rural vicar and assist in the tasks involved in implementing the new parish demarcation.[27]

Finally, on 3 January 1854, the long-awaited parish arrangement was approved, with José de Castro y Orozco as the Minister of Grace and Justice. The dioceses would maintain this division into deaneries, with mother parishes (divided into urban and rural) and other missions and sanctuaries, and each locality would have a number of parishes in accordance with its number of inhabitants. Clustered settlements with fewer than 4,000 inhabitants would have a single parish, above which the number of parishes would increase according to the number of residents. Conversely, in places with dispersed settlements, districts would be formed with a sufficient population in order to establish a parish, with the parish church situated in the most central location possible so that the residents living furthest away would not have more than an hour to walk there. However, in those districts whose parish churches were not accessible to part of the

27 Royal Decrees of 21 November 1851, *Gaceta de Madrid* (17 December 1851).

parishioners, missions would be established, and also wherever necessary in clustered settlements. But on no account were missions to exceed a third of the number of coadjutors of the mother parish (there would be one coadjutor for 800 individuals, upwards of which the number would rise proportionately).

According to the terms of the Concordat and the preceding legislative measures, parishes were divided into classes: rural parishes were classified as first and second class; urban parishes as *de entrada* [entry level], *de ascenso* [promotion] – three promotion-level parishes for each final level parish in each diocese – and *de término* [final level] – in the seat of the diocese, provincial capital or judicial district. Missions would have coadjutors dependent on the parish priest of the mother parishes, whose responsibilities would be set by their respective ordinaries. Curacies came with perpetual and conferred residential benefice, and therefore its holders could not lose them unless under the provisions of canon law. The responsibilities of coadjutors were set by bishops and were typically to tend to the sick and to administer the sacraments, except those of baptism and marriage. Moreover, the rules for setting the endowment of parish priests and coadjutors were laid down, which included taking into account the circumstances of the place and population. This meant that the maximum set out in the Concordat for final level parishes did not necessarily apply. Furthermore, the setting of endowments would not take into account the proceeds of surplice and altarage fees, emoluments, alms, rectories (*mansos* and *iglesarios*) and the pious works charged to the parish, and the value that curacies, tithes, first fruits and rent would have had in other times, except for certain exceptions.[28]

This parish arrangement served to organize and maintain the clergy entrusted with the cure of souls, who by the end of the reign of Isabel II numbered close to 37,000 individuals, of which fewer than half were parish priests.[29] This also had a decisive influence on their professionalization,

28 Royal Order of 3 January 1854, *Colección legislativa de España*, vol. 61 (Madrid: Imp. Nacional, 1854), 9–21. See also José Sánchez Rubio, *Arreglo parroquial testual y esplicado* (Madrid: Imp. de D. Manuel Martínez Maestre, 1854).

29 Instituto Nacional de Estadística, Fondo Documental, *Anuarios*, years 1858, 1859–1860 and 1866–1867, <http://www.ine.es/inebaseweb/libros.do?tntp=25687>, accessed 1 March 2021.

establishing the way to access curacies by means of a competitive selection process that candidates had to pass if they wanted to form part of the *ternas* that the prelates sent to the government so that appointments could be made. It also meant the end of the previous privileges, such as that of birthright, and the *terna* system was expanded to curacies under both ecclesiastical and lay patronage. And, no less important, a grading system was established for parishes with greater remuneration for the higher levels, which marked out the ecclesiastical career for priests and offered a horizon of expectations for their career development.

Between God and Caesar: Parish priests at the service of the State

From its inception, the liberal state – understood as the contemporary configuration of power that was separated from the monarchy in the modern age – found it needed support from the structures of the Church in order to deal with the situation of decomposition experienced by the Ancien Régime in Spain during the early decades of the nineteenth century. In fact, support from this parallel institution of power with a well-organized hierarchy that extended throughout the land had actually been sought by the monarchy in order to mobilize the population against the armies of the French Republic during the War of the Pyrenees (1793–1795). At that time, the Church had become the propaganda machine for the monarchy in order to stir up support for the war and spread the notion among the faithful of a 'monarchic patriotism' that identified subjects with their king by cloaking the counter-revolutionary cause in religiosity. As a consequence, the two governing institutions of the Ancien Régime in terms of temporal and spiritual power, the throne and the altar, were merged in order to give meaning to a diffuse and reactionary identity of 'motherland', which was threatened by the evils of the French Revolution. And in 1808, with the change in dynasty and outbreak of the Peninsular War, the counter-revolutionary message and its recourse to the triad of *Dios, Patria y Rey* [the Spanish equivalent of 'God, king and country'] would be preached from the pulpits in order to build up resistance against the French, but also to condemn liberal political ideals as an alternative to absolute monarchy.[30]

Therefore, it came as no surprise that the new liberal state that had been given shape by the Constitution of 1812 should attempt to make use of the services of the Church, particularly the parish priests, to assist it to take its first steps. A good example of this was the system designed for the 1810 general election to the *Cortes*, the newly formed parliamentary institution. It made use of the parishes in order to organize the exercise of the right of indirect universal male suffrage, which would be executed once the corresponding mass was concluded and after a 'vigorous appeal to the people' by the parish priest, who would also sign the voting record together with the mayor and the members of the municipal council.[31] The electoral system established in the Constitution of 1812 would also set out the same duties for the parish priest, who together with the parish councils would guarantee the 'greatest solemnity for the action'.[32] The parish church was thus converted into a space of political participation for the locality, at least symbolically, despite voting taking place at a different location, while assigning the parish priest with the task of providing civic education for his parishioners. Moreover, the religious liturgy surrounding the voting became a 'transfer of sacredness' from religion to politics that pursued the conversion of subjects into citizens while incorporating the new liberal state

30 Pedro Rújula, 'El nacimiento de un patriotismo monárquico', in Encarnación García Monerris, Ivana Frasquet and Carmen García Monerris, eds, *Cuando todo era posible. Liberalismo y antiliberalismo en España e Hispanoamérica (1780–1842)* (Madrid: Sílex, 2016), 73–94; Pedro Rújula, 'Realismo y contrarrevolución en la Guerra de la Independencia', *Ayer* 86 (2012), 45–66.

31 *Instrucción que deberá observarse para la elección de diputados a Cortes*, (Seville: Imp. Real, 1810), 5–8.

32 The quote is taken from Art. 46 of the Constitution of 1812. The subsequent article sets out that before the council meeting, a votive mass of the Holy Spirit was to be said in which the parish priest was to offer a 'speech corresponding to the circumstances'.

into the same bonds of loyalty that parishioners shared with the Church.[33] During the Trienio Liberal, the period of liberal government in Spain between 1820 and 1823, the clergy was again entrusted by the State with this non-spiritual task of educating parishioners in politics by explaining the constitution to them. But at that time, it became obvious that the greater part of the Church preferred to use the pulpit, not to extol the benefits of the liberal system, but to denounce it.[34]

The Liberal Revolution that took place in the 1830s took a very different course to those taken in 1812, and the uneasy relations between the Church and the State led to the parish being relieved of its role in elections, replaced by the judicial district. The removal of universal male suffrage and the drastic reduction in the number of voters made this new arrangement possible. Furthermore, the support for the Carlist cause shown by much of the clergy made it advisable to closely monitor what was said by priests. In this respect, a royal order was sent to prelates on 27 January 1834 'so that neither in the pulpit nor in the confessional is the opinion of the faithful to be lost, nor the sacred precept of obedience and cordial submission to the Her Majesty's legitimate Government to be weakened'.[35] There was no longer any attempt, as during the previous liberal experiences, to make clerics preach in favour of the new order, but they were not permitted to preach against it. Therefore, this was not a very revolutionary measure, but one that the actual text states was inspired by a previous royal order from 1801 to prevent excesses in the performance of the sacred ministry. During the Carlist Wars, these types of precautions by the government were stepped up given the actions taken by the clergy, who were aware of the animosity of the civil authorities. According to Father Claret, they would

33 Alonso, *La nación en capilla*, 43. Regarding the concept of the 'transfer of sacredness', see Mona Ozouf, *La fête révolutionnaire (1789–1799)* (París: Gallimard, 1976), 317–40.

34 Manuel Revuelta González, *Política religiosa de los liberales en el siglo XIX. Trienio Constitucional* (Madrid: CSIC, 1973), 124–26.

35 Royal Order of 27 January 1834, *Decretos de la Reina Nuestra Señora Isabel II*, vol. XIX (Madrid: Imp. Real, 1835), 35–6.

have to take the 'greatest care to not to say a political word in favour or against either of the two parties'.[36]

Nonetheless, not only did the new State undergoing construction watch the Church very closely, it also took on tasks it had previously performed – in an assisting role as an extension to the monarchy – and abandoned owing to its loss of political, social and economic power. The State was largely built on confrontation with the Church, but it also needed the latter's structures. While the Church had a hierarchically structured mechanism of operation throughout the country, the State was still in its infancy. As a result, the religious policy of the liberal government focused on making these structures more dependent on the liberal state than they were on Rome by reforming the Church and making it more 'national'. This created a very thorny situation, as the State continued with the regalist tradition of the Catholic Monarchy and required approval from the Holy See, which at the time was taking an increasingly anti-liberal stance. Despite this, the political exclusivism of the moderates in power brought about reconciliation between temporal and spiritual power, as sanctioned by the Concordat of 1851. The interest of the liberal authorities in the parish arrangement – as previously seen – is a good reflection of how the parishes were to be an instrument for use by the State to bring its authority to the people, turning the parish priests into its servants.

Another essential aspect that illustrates the way in which the State needed parish priests in order to make this possible is that of the obtaining of statistical information on the population. The political will of nineteenth-century governments to know whom they governed was not random. This knowledge was actually vital in such essential fields as taxation and political representation. Statistics were not meant to satisfy curiosity, but to be an instrument for the action of the government of the State as it took on greater roles and expanded its power over the country.[37] Nonetheless, the creation of a statistical system in Spain was a long process, which did not

36 Antonio María Claret, *Autobiografía y escritos complementarios*, ed. by José María Viñas and Jesús Bermejo (Buenos Aires: Claretiana, 2008), 265.

37 Michel Armatte, 'El papel de la estadística en la construcción del Estado nación', in Marc Barbut and José María Arribas Macho, eds, *Estadística y Sociedad* (Madrid: UNED, 2002), 17–43; Libby Schweber, *Disciplining Statistics. Demography and Vital Statistics in France and England, 1830–1885* (Duham-London: Duke

come to fruition until well into the reign of Isabel II.[38] The first attempts at creating a civil registry during Espartero's regency were very precarious, as shown by the fact that the Ministry of Government sent a royal circular order in May 1845 to political leaders determining that parish priests and other priests responsible for parishes could baptize newborn babies and bury the dead without previously obtaining a certificate from the head of the civil registry.[39] This was clearly proof that the public administration was not yet able to perform certain duties that had for centuries been under the control of parish priests.

Momentum in the field of statistics gathering was finally gaining pace under the moderates and took shape during the middle decades of the reign of Isabel II with the founding of the General Statistics Commission of the Kingdom in 1856, which would be entrusted with conducting Spain's first modern census in the following year. For this purpose, as a 'preparatory means', the diocesan authorities and the Tribunal of Military Orders were ordered to send the information available on the population of their respective districts, owing to the fact that ecclesiastical administration was established throughout the country and had had centuries of experience in these type of tasks.[40] Moreover, the regulation that implemented the method for conducting the census again made use of parish priests and parishes for the purpose of gathering information. Not only were parish priests present on the census boards at municipal and judicial district level – there were two members of the cathedral chapter present on provincial boards – but their parishes would also serve as circumscriptions

University Press, 2006); Alain Desrosières, *La politique des grands nombres. Histoire de la raison statistique* (París: La Découverte, 2010), 180–217.

38 Isabel Sánchez Casado, *La estadística del Estado en los períodos constitucionales* (Madrid: Movinter, 1983); José Ignacio Muro, Francesc Nadal and Luis Urteaga, *Geografía, estadística y catastro en España, 1856–1870* (Barcelona: Ediciones del Serbal, 1996); and, in particular, Juan Pro, *La construcción del Estado en España. Una historia del siglo XIX* (Madrid: Alianza, 2019), 405–63.

39 Royal Order of 24 May 1845, *Gaceta de Madrid* (01 June 1845). Nonetheless, the parish priests were obligated to send a note to the municipal authorities every month indicating the births, deaths and marriages in their parishes.

40 Letter of 5 February 1857, *Colección legislativa de Estadística* (Madrid: Imp. Nacional, 1862), 11.

for smaller sections of more populated municipalities, given that the names of all their inhabitants had to be recorded on the same day throughout the country. Furthermore, the law granted them the status of public employees while performing the duties of conducting the census.[41] This was why, in October 1858, when the vice-president of the statistics commission, Alejandro Oliván, requested the provincial governors provide information on the people who had shown the most outstanding participation in those tasks, mention was clearly made of the clergy, who 'generally played a praiseworthy part in the operations'.[42]

A new census would be conducted in 1860 to correct certain inaccuracies detected in the previous headcount, include other variables and adjust the census year to the European context.[43] As in 1857, the commission acknowledged that 'their work could never have been considered satisfactory had there been no assistance from the information contained in parish records, the only source of authenticity on the subject'. This was because it became evident that certain localities had concealed their real number of inhabitants during the previous headcount out of fear of the tax burden. The public administration, despite the enthusiasm with which it carried out its inquiries, 'was not certain in many instances to achieve the exactitude of the records where the Church with her holy devotion notes the entry and departure of individuals as they transit through this earthly world'. For this reason, Oliván requested that prelates should have the parish priests show the parish records to the statistics inspectors and commissioners.[44] Likewise, clerics would again be present on the municipal and judicial district boards.[45] In short, parish priests ultimately performed

41 Regulation of 14 March 1857, *Colección legislativa de Estadística*, 15–28.

42 Circular of 2 October 1858, *Colección legislativa de Estadística*, 164.

43 Thought was at first given to extend the census to Spain's overseas provinces, where parish priests would be of great importance as they, together with the native *gobernadorcillos* [governors and municipal judges] would direct the headcount for each locality and translate the documents and registers of inhabitants from the indigenous languages into Spanish. Royal Order of 27 November 1859, *Colección legislativa de Estadística*, 250–4.

44 Circular of 19 September 1860, *Colección legislativa de Estadística*, 301–2.

45 Regulation of 10 November 1860, *Colección legislativa de Estadística*, 312–23.

the tasks of civil servants, a circumstance that was in no way out of keeping with the laws of the time. In this respect, mention should be made of the chapter regarding falsification of public documents in the Penal Code of 1848 (which was applied to the members of the census boards), which created a distinction between clerics and civil servants, on the one hand, and other individuals, on the other, together with different penalties.[46]

Another of the aspects that demonstrated the participation of the secular clergy in the construction of the State was the figure of the military chaplain, entrusted with providing the cure of souls to those individuals who, while serving in Spain's armed forces, had no permanent residence. In 1762, the military vicariate was assigned by Pope Clement XIII to the patriarch of the West Indies, a title already held by the assistant chief chaplain of the Royal Chapel [the title of chief chaplain of the Royal Chapel, now honorary, was held by the archbishop of Santiago de Compostela], who held ecclesiastical jurisdiction over the royal palace. As a result, Spain's military vicariate was merged with the Patriarchate of the West Indies – an honorary ecclesiastical title created by the papacy – and the Royal Chaplaincy – typically held by an employee of the court appointed by the king – in the same person. As vicar general of the Spanish armed forces, the patriarch of the West Indies was given the same authority as that wielded by bishops in their respective dioceses, and he was assisted in this task by an auditor general, who was also the judge of the royal chapel, and subdelegate chaplains, church dignitaries responsible for negotiations regarding jurisdiction in each diocese. In turn, the cure of souls was performed directly by parish priests or military chaplains, who had the same obligations and rights as those of ordinary parish priests, to whom they had to accredit their ministry in order to say mass and administer the sacraments to their parishioners.[47]

As was to be expected, the military vicariate was a question of great importance for the liberals, who wanted to reform the Church, and especially for the progressives, who were wary of the Church. This came as

46 Arts. 226 and 227 of the Penal Code of 1848.

47 Joaquín Aguirre, *Curso de disciplina eclesiástica general y particular de España*, 2 edn (Madrid: Librería de Sánchez, 1857–1858), II, 381–4. See Félix Ruiz García, 'Patriarcado de Indias y Vicariato General Castrense', *Revista Española de Derecho Canónico* 23/65 (1967), 449–71.

no surprise seeing that this jurisdiction was delegated by Rome, a foreign power that was hostile to Spain during the early years of Isabel II's reign. This is why, after the progressives came to power in 1836 and furthered the liberal revolution, there was an attempt at an ambitious organization of the clergy that involved major changes to the military vicariate. The government's opinion on the reform and organization of the clergy, presented to the parliament on 21 May 1837, was to suppress the military vicariate and transfer the Patriarchate 'of Spain' – not of the West Indies – to the future archbishop of Madrid, as primate of Spain and 'head chaplain of the national armies', who would propose the nomination of chaplains after a competitive selection process.[48] The archbishop of Seville, Francisco Javier Cienfuegos, reacted to the project by sending a text to the parliament defining the military vicariate 'as a bishopric extended throughout the kingdom but without a fixed territory, created through papal bulls', with the reminder that because of those bulls, only the pope could authorize the exercise of that jurisdiction.[49] The reason for this was that new figure of head chaplain of the national armed forces did not involve any jurisdiction delegated by Rome, and this was because, as noted by the parliamentarian and canon Antonio Martínez de Velasco during parliamentary debate, 'it is an abuse that has placed the Church of Spain under the dominion of a foreign court'.[50]

In actual fact, that project dating from 1837 never came to fruition because in order for its provisions to take effect, the consent of the Holy See – the 'foreign court' referred to by Martínez de Velasco – was required, and Spain's relations with Rome would not be restored until years later. By that time, the Concordat of 1851 included the military vicariate of Spain among the exempted jurisdictions. The special regulation

48 *Diario de Sesiones de las Cortes Constituyentes* 208 (21 May 1837), appendix, 3551–2.

49 Francisco Javier Cienfuegos, 'Observaciones dirigidas al Soberano Congreso Nacional', *La Voz de la Religión* 2 (1838), 64–5.

50 *Diario de Sesiones de las Cortes Constituyentes* 291 (25 August 1837), 5584. For a comparison with the case of Portugal, which shares a number of similarities, see David Martínez-Vilches, 'Monstruosos patriarcados. Los patriarcados de Lisboa e Indias frente a la Revolución liberal en Portugal y España', *Hispania Sacra* 72/146 (2020), 515–23.

governing military chaplains was passed two years later, with Tomás Iglesias y Barcones as patriarch of the West Indies and vicar general of the Spanish armed forces, and similar special regulations were passed in 1867 governing subdelegate chaplains and chaplains of military parishes. These were divided into three classes: *de entrada* [entry level], who served in the infantry and reserve; *de ascenso* [promotion], in the cavalry corps and the General Veterans' Barracks; and *de término* [final level], in the artillery and engineers' corps, Queen's Guard and military colleges. In turn, the chaplaincies of the Supreme Court of War and the Navy, military hospitals, military outposts, castles, factories and armouries were considered fixed military parishes. Entry-level chaplains were recruited by a competitive selection process, meaning that clerics who wished to apply had to present a request to the patriarch, with the permission of his prelate and documents that accredited his services and merits. The selection process was held before the patriarch or auditor general, who designated judges. The judges submitted the *censuras* – qualifications obtained by the candidates in the armed forces – to the patriarch, who was responsible for creating the *terna* for each of the vacancies and submitting it to the Ministry of War. The chaplains of the fixed military parishes, however, were nominated directly by the patriarch.[51]

In short, the parish clergy played a remarkable role in the construction of the liberal state, once it had adopted a moderate stance and gained the conformity of the Church. The Spanish State developed by exerting control over areas of social reality that had previously been in the hands of clerics, such as population records, although, paradoxically, their agreement was needed in order for this expansion of roles to become a reality. Moreover, the State attempted to nationalize the areas of religion that directly affected it, such as the ecclesiastical jurisdiction applied to military chaplains, and although the exemption of that jurisdiction was ultimately upheld, the

51 *Reglamento del clero castrense. Aprobado por S. M. el 12 de octubre de 1853* (Manila: Imp. del Colegio de Santo Tomás, 1854); *Reglamento especial de los capellanes párrocos del ejército, hospitales, castillos y demás institutos militares de la Península y Ultramar, aprobado por S. M.* (Madrid: Imp. del Memorial de Infantería, 1867). See also Mateo Martínez, 'D. Tomás Iglesias y Barcones, un patriarca de Indias (1851–1874)', *Hispania Sacra* 25/49 (1972), 110–13.

military clerics became the object of specific regulation by the State that largely took over the organization of the parish arrangement. Therefore, the role of parish priests and their military counterparts was halfway between that of the sacred ministry and that of the public ministry, serving God, but also the new Caesar that was born out of the liberal revolution: the State.

'Doctors of the soul': Parish priests and modern society

Since the eighteenth century, the countries of Europe – Spain among them – had been undergoing a process of secularization that influenced individual consciousness and the institutions in which social life was played out. This process placed the Church in a position of weakness against a new hostile reality and made clerics the target of the criticism from the more liberal sectors. This invective was not levelled at Catholicism as a religious belief, but against the Church as an anachronistic structure of power owing to its privileges and counter-revolutionary stance, and its preferred target was the regular clergy, whose cultural functions were removed from the principle of providing a public service that was to rule in the new class society. However, parish priests were viewed more leniently because their work of providing pastoral care placed them in an important position in the community, particularly after the revolutions of the early part of the nineteenth century and the stabilization of the liberal system under the moderates. Regardless of this, for much of the clergy, including parish priests, the problem of where they fit in the modern society was not only political, but mainly cultural. Their existence would therefore have to be justified and the importance of the tasks they performed highlighted.

This intention was not only a reaction to the sense of a single entity that united the clergy among themselves; it was mainly a response to the accusations to which they had felt subjected, every time that the freedom of the press – which would encounter changing circumstances during the reign of Isabel II – left them exposed to public opinion. The appearance of the parish priest in the Spanish literature of the nineteenth century is a good gauge of this exposure to anti-clerical criticism. It came as no surprise to find a complaint by one priest to the nuncio Brunelli explaining that in certain localities, immoral dramas ridiculing the pope and ministers of religion were staged that the local authorities were no longer able to prohibit. And he added, bitterly: 'Several years ago there were restrictions that in my humble opinion should be re-established.'[52] Such attacks were not limited to the regular clergy, but were also levelled at parish clergy. In fact, one of the targets of anti-clericalism was one of the sacraments that was most associated with their pastoral work: the hearing of confession. According to the famous minor work by Jules Michelet that had soon begun to circulate among Spanish anti-clerical circles, confessors were accused of manipulating penitents in order 'to sever this woman from her family, to weaken her kindred ties, and, particularly, to undermine the rival authority – I mean, the husband's'.[53] And it was not only the educated upper classes who espoused this type of precaution, but it was also common among working classes to hear a husband say to his wife: 'I don't want a priest ruling over my home.'[54]

Therefore, the new class society that had introduced liberalism, which was as profane as it was deeply religious, demanded an adjustment to the figure of the parish priest that could be accommodated to its prevailing social principles and expectations. It was not a question of dogma, but one of reconfiguring the social position of priests, who without abandoning

52 Ignacio Carbó to Brunelli (n.d.), AAV, NM, vol. 364, f. 821. On the figure of the priest in the literature of the time, see Guadalupe Arbona and Paloma Fanconi, eds, *La figura del sacerdote en la literatura contemporánea: vasijas de barro* (Madrid: Encuentro, 2014).

53 Jules Michelet, *El sacerdote, la mujer y la familia*, trad. de A. Abella (Barcelona: Jané Hermanos, [1845]), 189 [English version quoted in the translation: *Priests, Women and Families* (London: The Protestant Evangelical Mission, 1874)]. For an analysis of this work, Paul Pelckmans, '"Le Prêtre, la Femme et la Famille": notes sur l'anticléricalisme de Michelet', *Romantisme* 23 (1979), 17–30; and on its circuclation in Spain, Enrique A. Sanabria, *Republicanism and Anticlerical Nationalism in Spain* (New York: Palgrave Macmillan, 2009), 128–9.

54 Claret, *Autobiografía*, 482. Regarding arguments against confession, see Diana Peschier, *Nineteenth-Century Anti-Catholic Discourses: The Case of Charlotte Brontë* (London: Palgrave Macmillan, 2005), 25–42.

fundamentalist religious and political assumptions could incorporate a certain dose of modernity to ensure the relevance of their work.[55] This was strongly expressed by Covián in his manual: 'We have blind faith in the future, and prominently featured in that future are the ministers of the Catholic Church.' This was because the 'religious question' was a 'social question, the most social, eminently social'.[56] After the impact of the revolution and after 'so much veneration of the principle of free examination', only religion, faithfully handed down by the parish priests, could rebuild a society broken down by individualism and angst:

> Well, at the front of this society, beside these men and amidst the perplexing noise of a superficial world that is shaken by convulsions, lives the parish priest, the true man of the people; the man who, without seeming grand, is just that; without airs, he holds the office of a true magistrate; without the trappings of authority, he pronounces laws in the towns and villages; although not a father, he has a large family; although not a physician, he is told of every ailment; although not a judge, he puts an end to all discord; without seeming wise, his counsel is requested; such a man who, when he is not speaking with God to save men, instructs and guides men to love God.[57]

Added to this positive contribution to shared life that Covián defended was the excellence inherent to the parochial task within the Church, which appeared time and time again in writings and sermons. Claret reminded parish priests that God had granted them a treble power that made them greater than the angels in heaven: 'the ministry of sacrifice, the ministry of reconciliation of sinners with God and the ministry of the Divine Word'. For this very reason, performing such a lofty role required 'excellent sanctity' through imitation of the figure of Christ.[58] This is one of the aspects most stressed by clerics, because the cure of souls required individuals who

55 Regarding the complex relationship between the Church and modernity, see Daniele Menozzi, 'Iglesia, modernidad y modernización en el siglo XIX', in Pedro Rújula and Francisco Javier Ramón Solans, eds, *El desafío de la revolución: reaccionarios, antiliberales y contrarrevolucionarios (siglos XVIII y XIX)* (Granada: Comares, 2017), 301–18.

56 Covián, *Novísimo manual de curas*, XIV.

57 Covián, *Novísimo manual de curas*, XVI.

58 Antonio María Claret, *Avisos a un sacerdote que acaba de hacer los ejercicios de san Ignacio* (Barcelona: Imp. de los Herederos de la V. Pla, 1847), 4.

were irreproachable. Ambition, excessive dealings with women, ignorance and avarice were flaws that, besides disgracing those who fell into such ways, tarnished the name of the Church and were used by detractors to attack it. Claret warned that 'even the bad ones want us to be good', while Iglesias y Barcones, the patriarch of the West Indies, recommended that military chaplains should combine 'preaching with the word and preaching with deeds', because it was outrageous 'to expect that others learn, and love, and observe the law, when they are seeing it battered and trampled, violated and debased by the one who pronounces it'.[59]

What is more, another of the components that gave shape to this new image of the parish priest was the likening, simultaneously with competition, to a profession that perfectly embodied the idea of progress: the physician. Priests were identified to a certain degree with doctors, although they were opposites in other cases. In Viladrau, Father Claret worked as a doctor, and he explained that as so many ill people came to him, he decided to spurn 'physical remedies' and only bless them and commend them to God. Even so, the patients were 'cured by faith and the trust with which they came'.[60] The case where the competition between priest and physician could be seen, which personified religion and science, respectively, was the different form of assistance provided in childbirth. Here, whereas physicians, when they were to be found, were there to facilitate labour and guarantee the life of the woman and her child, parish priests had to provide the spiritual assistance necessary in case something went wrong. Moreover, texts on holy embryology encouraged priests to refute doctors during difficult deliveries and pressure them to perform a caesarean so that the foetus could be baptized in case the woman died. And if the physician refused to do it, and there was no midwife, the priest had to pluck up his courage and perform the intervention himself, guaranteeing the baby's spiritual welfare, and perhaps even earthly salvation.[61] From the Catholic standpoint, the

59 The quotes are from Claret, *Autobiografía*, 198, and Tomás Iglesias y Barcones, *Exhortación pastoral que el Patriarca de las Indias dirige a todo el clero castrense del Ejército y Armada con motivo de la Santa Cuaresma* (Madrid: Aguado, 1867), 10, 12.

60 Claret, *Autobiografía*, 219.

61 Inocencio María Riesco Le Grand, *Tratado de embriología sagrada* (Madrid: Tip. Greco-latina, 1848), 243–50. The reference text continued to be that by Francesco

knowledge of the priest exceeded that of doctors, as could be read in an article sent from the village of Larín, in the province of A Coruña, to the newspaper *El Católico* in 1843:

> A married and pregnant woman has just died in this parish; she was close to giving birth in her normal term, but for three days was beset by strong and intense pains before succumbing to their violence. Two hours before her death, the creature was alive, as could be seen by the evident signs of its movement. In such a situation, the caesarean should have been done by opening the mother after she breathed her last in order to remove the foetus and perform the baptism if it were practicable. This is what the parish priest requested, and he went to great pains to achieve this, but in vain, because here and in other parts of the kingdom there is much neglect, much ignorance and concern from people about this point, with which certain physicians cooperate, although not all, owing to their apathy and lack of resolution, and even more to their ignorance and lack of knowledge.[62]

At other times, the parish priest was likened to a doctor, a 'doctor of the soul'. This simile had actually been in existence for a long time, but in the nineteenth century it was a recurring rhetorical device used to defend the moralizing work of the parish priest, in particular the administration of penance. The bishop of Pamplona Uriz y Labayru urged his clerics to be 'doctors of souls in their most secret illnesses' because this was what 'the sublime and celestial institution of the sacrament of confession' comprised.[63] A year after the bishop had pronounced these words to his diocesan clergy, the Franciscan missionary Pedro Gual published a strong defence of this sacrament, as expressed by its title: *La moralizadora y salvadora del mundo es la confesión sacramental* [*The Moralizer and Saviour of the World is Sacramental Confession*]. In his work, Gual divided the advantages of confession into three types. First were the individual advantages: humans had had a tendency to commit evil since the time of their forefathers, which meant that all individuals would ultimately fall into sin, but that it was possible to regain the state of grace and virtue through penance. The second

---

Emanuello Cangiamila, *Embriologia sacra, ovvero dell' uffizio de' sacerdoti, medici, e superiori, circa l'eterna salute de' bambini racchiusi nell' utero* (Milan: Giuseppe Cairoli, 1751), which was disseminated in Spain during the reign of King Charles III.

62 *El Católico* (27 January 1843), 210–11.

63 Quoted by Cuenca Toribio, *Sociedad y clero*, 25.

set of benefits provided by the sacrament was for the family because the confessor could and should act as a barrage against adultery and to ensure that the members of the family were on good terms with one another. Finally, confession benefited society as a whole, safeguarding the union of the family as its foundation and censuring habits that were harmful to the public interest. The parish priest, therefore, was not an annoying busybody for the penitent, but 'a compassionate *doctor* who inspired all the trust of a good friend'.[64] And to facilitate this task, there were a growing number of books that assisted clerics with confession, both in translation, such as the *Manual for Confessors* by Jean-Joseph Gaume (1844), which was reissued a number of times, or the very famous book by Claret, *Llave de oro* [*The Golden Key*] of 1857.[65]

Together with the ministry of penance was the ministry of the Word. While the former took place in a private setting, the confessional, the latter was performed publicly from the pulpit. For this reason, preaching had a counter-revolutionary connotation of opposition to the ideologies of the Enlightenment in the context of the free competition of discourses and ideas that liberalism had brought to Spain. However, for the most intransigent clerics, such as Father Claret, freedom of the press signified an attack on the Church by ending its ideological monopoly, and in so doing undermined the very pillars of society, which had 'withdrawn from the Church's Word, which is the Word of life and the Word of God', and had replaced it 'by a mob of obscure journalists and utterly ignorant charlatans'. Nonetheless, if the Church was to assert the Divine Word against other

64 Pedro Gual, *La moralizadora y salvadora del mundo es la confesión sacramental* (Barcelona: Librería Religiosa, 1863), 282 ff.; the final quote is taken from p. 286. See also *La confesión: o sea, amena controversia entre un abogado y un militar, sobre la institución divina del sacramento de la penitencia, su práctica y necesidad, sus ventajas y beneficios, tanto para la sociedad como para el individuo* (Madrid: Biblioteca Católica-Popular, 1845).

65 Jean-Joseph Gaume, *Manual de confesores*, 2 vols (Madrid: J. F. Palacios, 1844); Antonio María Claret, *Llave de oro o serie de reflexiones para abrir el corazón cerrado de los pobres pecadores* (Barcelona: Librería Religiosa, 1857). Or, in the case of children, Andrés Martínez de Novoa, *Ejercicios piadosos para disponer a los niños a los santos sacramentos de la penitencia i comunión, con instrucciones, oraciones, cánticos* (Madrid: Imp. de Eusebio Aguado, 1841).

opinions, parish priests had to improve their oratory skills, which often left much to be desired. Claret himself complained about 'those preachers who care more about adorning their speech than reforming habits, preaching things that are futile, airy, without substance, word games and bombastic clauses, and select and unintelligible terms'.[66] An anonymous letter sent to the nuncio Brunelli criticized a priest at Seville's Oratory of San Felipe Neri who aspired to become a bishop, but who 'has never been understood with regards to any subject in discourse in the cathedral of the Santo Spiritu [*sic*] and all believe he is incapable of this, and that he has neither the education or science necessary'.[67] A large number of collections of sacred oratory were subsequently published to make up for these failings and to allow priests to compose their own sermons, which was evidence that the training in this field given to future parish priests in seminaries was insufficient.[68]

Together with administration of the sacraments, one of the recurring topics in Catholic texts targeting parish priests was the conduct to be observed with parishioners. Clerics were not unaware of the fact that one of the most serious accusations that were levelled against them referred to the access they had to women and their consciences through their pastoral work, a situation that could give rise to misunderstandings and serve as a pretext for anybody who doubted the morality of the clergy. What lay behind these types of attacks was not only a hackneyed anti-clerical cliché, but also mistrust by liberal sectors of the counter-revolutionary alliance between the clergy and Catholic women, whose new model of femininity was removed from the previous misogynistic discourse and would come to

66 For the first quote, Claret, *Autobiografía*, 326, and Claret, *Avisos a un sacerdote*, 18–19 for the second.

67 Anonymous letter to Brunelli, Seville (15 November 1851), AAV, NM, vol. 346, ff. 764–5.

68 Juan Troncoso, *Biblioteca completa de oratoria sagrada, o colección selecta de discursos dogmáticos, panejíricos y morales para todas las festividades del año*, 12 vols (Madrid: Librería López, 1844–1848); Un Rector de Seminario, *Tesoro de la elocuencia sagrada o método práctico que enseña el medio fácil de componer y predicar discursos, conferencias y sermones de todos géneros* (Madrid: Librería de D. Leocadio López, 1853); José María Rodríguez, ed., *Tesoro de oratoria sagrada: o sea, repertorio universal de materias predicables*, 12 vols (Barcelona: Pons y Cia, 1858–1860).

play an important role in the spiritual reconquest of society.[69] In any case, the mistrust of clerics who had female company in their dwellings was generalized. These suspicions also fell upon the hierarchy: in 1857, the maid in the service of Francisco Landeira Sevilla, the bishop of Teruel, had stones thrown at her with cries of *obispa* [bishop's wife] as she rode in the prelate's carriage.[70] And while even bishops and their maids were not immune to such rumours, parish priests and their maids awakened all sorts of gossip, as reflected by José María Tenorio in his portrait of the priest's housekeeper:

> Taking into account the fact that the priest's housekeeper tends to be young and pretty as a rule, or at least plump and not unattractive; because these blessed gentlemen with very few exceptions have always insisted on taking on housekeepers approaching their twentieth and never past their thirtieth year, lacking what is prescribed in repeated ecclesiastical canons, a *fomes pecati* [*sic*] is discovered that has ever been the source of scandal for the masses, I say masses so that you will not imagine that I am speaking of what is known as the common people, because they look at things only by their appearances, nor should you think that those who meet to kill time in the café or tavern have thought exclusively of that housekeeper with pettiness or malice. Popes and councils, kings and lawmakers, writers of religious moral, and likewise many poets, all, all have endeavoured to censure this custom, giving rise to a mighty argument by these authorities in unison:
>
> That the priest should have
> A lively girl as his housekeeper,
> When it is better to have an old woman
> Tend to his home
> What is inferred?[71]

69 Raúl Mínguez Blasco, *Evas, Marías y Magdalenas: género y modernidad católica en la España liberal (1833–1875)* (Madrid: Centro de Estudios Políticos y Constitucionales, 2016), 61–130; David Martínez-Vilches, 'Sine labe concepta. La proyección de un modelo de feminidad católica a través de la Inmaculada Concepción en la España del siglo XIX', *Arenal: Revista de Historia de las Mujeres* 27/2 (2020), 495–518.

70 Giovanni Simeoni (business administrator at the nunciature in Madrid) to Domingo Canubio y Alberto (bishop of Segorbe) (15 January 1857), AAV, NM, vol. 349, ff. 44–5.

71 José María Tenorio, 'El ama del cura', in *Los españoles pintados por sí mismos* (Madrid: Gaspar y Roig, 1851), 22.

For this reason, every author advised parish priests to be scrupulous and disciplined when dealing with the opposite sex, particularly in the confessional. Father Claret, who said that he never looked women in the face when he had to speak to them because of his 'natural blushing', advised his readers to avoid conversations with them and, where they were obligated 'out of courtesy and tact', they should be 'brief and to the point, with eyes downcast. Do not trust your virtue and wisdom, because women cause virtuous Davids and wise Solomons to fall.'[72] One of the occasions on which both the decorum of the parish priest and the modesty of the female sex were fraught with danger was in the case of 'false devotees', women who claimed to have experienced visions, revelations or demonic possessions. In the book *Tesoro del sacerdote* [*The Priest's Treasure*] by the Jesuit José Mach, one could read that women 'naturally have a very vivid imagination, which leads them to learn fanciful things as if they were real and existing'. This inclination, added to 'the nerves that make them extremely susceptible', could create strange phenomena in them even for physicians, and that these could be mistaken for miracles. The priest was to behave prudently and not appear gullible, as he ran the risk of becoming involved in a scandal 'often with dishonour for religion and vilification by the public'.[73]

These precautions that were endlessly repeated in books written for the secular clergy were based on clerical celibacy, a topic that would begin to be analysed by literature in the light of the emotional needs extolled by bourgeois culture, but also by medical discourse, which found the absence of sexual relations to be the origin of many perversions.[74] For this very reason, clerics needed to extol celibacy, no longer just as a virtuous state,

72 Claret, *Avisos a un sacerdote*, 8. About his 'natural blushing', Claret, *Autobiografía*, 308–9.

73 José Mach, *Tesoro del sacerdote o repertorio de las principales cosas que ha de saber y practicar el sacerdote para santificarse a sí mismo, y santificar a los demás* (Barcelona: Imp. del Heredero de José Gorgas, 1861), 661–2.

74 Solange Hibbs-Lissorgues, 'El celibato en la literatura religiosa del siglo XIX', in Roberto Fernández and Jacques Soubeyroux, eds, *Historia social y literatura. Familia y clero en España (siglo XVIII y XIX)* (Lleida/Saint-Étienne: Milenio/Université Jean Monnet, 2004), 219–32; Francisco Vázquez García, 'La patologización del celibato en la medicina española (1820–1920)', *Asclepio* 70/2 (2018).

but also as a way of life that allowed priests to better serve their parishioners. In other words, these debates served to publicize the legitimacy of the priestly model of masculinity in modern society.[75] From the religious standpoint, abstinence did not imply a lack of affection, but the projection of the affections held by the father of a family to the rest of society in order to benefit religion and the common good. As a result, in the speech he gave upon being conferred with his doctorate at the Universidad Central, the priest Leonardo Fernández Villelga concluded, after an extremely positive deliberation on celibacy and refuting arguments against it, that 'celibate Catholic priests, regardless of what Protestants and their rationalite [*sic*] adepts may think, have always been and will be revered and lauded by all peoples with the honourable judgements of fathers of the poor, fathers of the motherland and masters of the true civilization'.[76]

In short, efforts were made by the clergy to highlight the importance of both the priest's religious and social role, protect the respectability of his public image and defend the model of celibate masculinity that it represented. In this way, the Church offered a modern figure of the parish priest, although his fit with modern times was not on liberal or rational terms, but based on the moral and religious principles of Catholicism that had taken a cautious approach in the face of the errors of the century.

75 See Angela Berlis, 'Celibate or Married Priests? Polemical Gender Discourse in Nineteenth-Century Catholicism', in Patrick Pasture and Jan Art, eds, *Gender and Christianity in Modern Europe. Beyond the Feminization Thesis* (Leuven: Leuven University Press, 2012), 57–71.

76 Leonardo Fernández Villelga, *El celibato eclesiástico, fundado en una antiquísima tradición, es muy conveniente a los sagrados ministros y muy útil a la sociedad* (Madrid: Establecimiento Tipográfico a cargo de D. Florencio Gamayo, 1863), 18. See also Antonio López-Quiroga, *Discurso canónico-legal sobre el celibato eclesiástico* (Madrid: Saavedra y Compañía, 1849); and Miguel Sanz Lafuente, *Memoria leída en la Real Academia de Ciencias Morales y Políticas sobre el celibato eclesiástico* (Madrid: Imp. Nacional, 1864).

Conclusion

After the fall of the Ancien Régime, the priesthood was defined by its social role in terms of the three elements analysed: the professionalization of parish priests, their participation in the construction of the State and the adaptation of their public image to modern times. As a result, parish priests were no longer the lowest rank of a privileged estate, but a profession that developed its religious vocation for the common good. As with so many other matters affecting liberal Spain, that involving the parish clergy had to be dealt with between the Church and the State, reconciling the interests of both institutions. The liberal state largely granted them the status of civil servants, which was combined with the anti-liberal religious orthodoxy that was defended by the Church with its encyclicals *Quanta cura* and *Syllabus errorum*. Given that the liberal system in Spain followed the path marked out by the moderates, both facets interrelated better than could be expected. While liberal politicians, after the highs and lows of the revolution, offered the Church a legislative framework that ensured its position of hegemony, the Church contributed to the social order by performing a labour of moderation whose main instruments were parish priests. At the same time, clerics were concerned about the public image of priests and erected a model of respectable priest that was appropriate to the moral principles of the class society. All these phenomena permitted not only the continuation of their parochial ministry, but also their social influence, at a time when the first voices were being raised from public platforms, newspapers and novels to attack the power of the Church.

DAVID SAN NARCISO

Merchants to Businessmen

The Professionalization of Entrepreneurs in Nineteenth-Century Spain

ABSTRACT
Businessmen acquired an enormous entity within the social imaginary of the nineteenth century. They emerged as the epitome of a world under construction in which money became a vehicle for social promotion and legitimization in the liberal public sphere. This chapter shows how merchants became real entrepreneurs in nineteenth-century Spain by professionalizing their occupations. To analyse this process, I first consider the group strategies they undertook: the construction of a professional discourse, its institutionalization in associations and the design of a specific training program in business schools. I then study the professional self-representation practices of these men. Thus, their professional workplace (the office), the way they dress or their places of sociability became symbolic markers of their public legitimacy as professionals. I always try to compare business with other disciplines – such as agriculture or industry – that underwent a similar professionalization process in structure and time.

Introduction[1]

In 1889, Emile Zola was preparing another instalment of his series on the Rougon-Macquart family. On this occasion, the book was about Aristide Rougon. Born into a merchant family in 1815, he became the epitome of those men who became rich in the 1850s and 1860s with the real estate and financial speculations during the Second French Empire. Undue enrichment was followed by ruin, which forced him to auction off his art collection, sell his palace and mortgage his social respectability. However,

1 This work is supported by the Ministry of Science, Innovation, and University of Spain (MICUE) under Grant PGC2018–093698–B–I00.

corruption and fraud enabled Aristide to regain his position of social pre-eminence. He thus exemplifies one of those lives that, with sudden rises and falls, lived the 'money rushes' in a world under construction in its political, economic and social facets. In his preliminary notes to the book, Zola expressed his opinion regarding these modern upstarts. Beyond the moral criticism of these behaviours, the book 'should not oppose our century of money to those formerly called centuries of honour'.[2] For him, the reason was evident: both concepts had merged in the nineteenth century to form one. Hence, 'money has become for many people the dignity of life: it makes us free, it is hygiene, property, health, almost even intelligence'.

Zola's words were, of course, not exceptional. They were part of the discourses made in the nineteenth century about figures who were equally admired and criticized: businessmen. The trope would be very recurrent among writers. Benito Pérez Galdós was perhaps one of those who used it most. In his series on the Torquemada family, he tells how a small neighbourhood loan shark became a modern and elitist financier.[3] However, his opinion changed drastically. If he saw them at the beginning of the century as respectable, hard-working and honest people, they degenerated gradually as conformist and corrupt men. At the same time, Narcís Oller published *La Febre d'Or* [*Gold Fever*] in very similar terms. In this case, he told the story of Gil Foix, a humble carpenter who, thanks to stock market investments, managed to get rich quickly and rise to the wealthiest classes of Barcelona. Although with a critical sense, through hyperboles, Oller highlighted the markers of social distinction that the emerging Catalan industrial and financial bourgeoisie tried to forge. In other words, those symbolic patterns that legitimized their social position and recognized them as social elites.[4]

2 Quote from the original manuscript in Éléonore Reverzy, *La chair de l'idée: poétique de l'allégorie dans les Rougon-Macquart* (Genève: Droz, 2007), 160.

3 Francisco Villacorta, 'Visión galdosiana de la sociedad de la Restauración: las novelas del ciclo de Torquemada', *Revista de Literatura* 81 (1979), 68–115.

4 Laureano Bonet, *Literatura, regionalismo y lucha de clases* (Barcelona: Universidad de Barcelona, 1983).

What these men of letters condensed in their writings was, thus, the feeling of a time. They portrayed figures with such entity that they were tangible, recognizable in the space and the organization of post-revolutionary society. During the nineteenth century, money was one of the main mechanisms and motors of social progress. On this pro-sociological basis, Liberalism understood that modern society has to be founded on the development of capabilities. In other words, they conceptualized society as a conglomerate of capable citizens characterized, beyond professional distinctions, by intellectual capital oriented towards the general interest.[5] Trade and the business world thereby become part of that sphere which enable men to participate legitimately in society.

However, from a sociological perspective, these businessmen have traditionally been perceived outside the domain of the professions, if not opposed to them.[6] While recognizing the challenges in identifying the individual or collective interest that moved them, Talcott Parsons himself contrasted both categories to define them. Therefore, he classified the professions by their rationality, functional specificity – based on technical competence – and universalism. On the contrary, he classified the business world by the quest for personal profit, particularism and functional specificity. In his opinion, their 'essential goals' were 'substantially the same, achievement of objectives and recognition'.[7] The difference thus lies in the paths to achieve it, 'which in turn are determined by the differences in the respective occupational situations'. In that way, their respective institutional patterns and social functions were decisive. As opposed to occupations, professions were defined by their close relationship with knowledge, their social function and their institutionalization. In the same sense, Harold L. Wilensky diagnosed a progressive professionalization of the occupations. Namely, an endeavour to acquire professional authority and status.[8] He

5 Pierre Rosanvallon, *Le moment Guizot* (Paris: Gallimard, 1985).

6 Lucila Finkel, *La sociología de las profesiones: legados y perspectivas* (PhD dissertation, Universidad Complutense de Madrid, 2015).

7 Talcott Parsons, 'The Professions and the Social Structure', *Social Forces* 17/4 (1939), 464.

8 Harold L. Wilensky, 'The Professionalization of Everyone?', *American Journal of Sociology* 70/2 (1964), 137–58.

identified five phases of this development. First, these men had to engage full-time in their occupation. This was followed by the establishment of training and recruitment and the creation of professional associations. Furthermore, they had to be politically mobilized to ensure them legal protection, public recognition and control on the professional practice. Finally, they provided themselves with a specific deontological code, behavioural patterns and distinctive professional ethics.

These functionalist theories were sternly criticized by symbolic interactionism. The advocates of this sociological perspective condemned this vision of professions as compact entities, enclosed in rigid theoretical schemes. In their opinion, the process should be the opposite: professions had to be deduced from social interactions and defined on the basis of social groups. In this way, they gave less importance to official structuring and pre-established classifications to emphasize the relationship between professional segments and society. Professions are thus social constructions based on certain shared beliefs about the meaning of the professional activity.[9] In short, they are social processes embedded in given contexts and, therefore, in continuous re-elaboration by the subjects and social groups. For example, Eliot Friedson showed how professions derive from particular positions of economic and political power. Far from being predetermined, they are in a continuous dialogue with the labour market.[10] For his part, Everett Hughes understood professions within a biographical process that challenged personal identities.[11] By focusing on this social dimension, professions acquire a noticeable historical, relational and diversified nature. In this way, as in the case of journalism,[12] some occupations can be studied within the logic of professionalization insofar as they historically formed a professional group.[13] Firstly, because they demand the exercise of a specific

9 Anselm Strauss and Rue Bucher, 'Professions in Process', *American Journal of Sociology* 66/4 (1961), 325–34.

10 Eliot Friedson, *Professionalism: The Third Logic* (Chicago: The University of Chicago Press, 2001).

11 Everett Hughes, *Men and Their Work* (Illinois: Free Press, 1958).

12 Meryl Aldridge and Julia Evetts, 'Rethinking the Concept of Professionalism: The Case of Journalism', *The British Journal of Sociology* 54/4 (2003), 547–64.

13 Paloma Fernández-Pérez, ed., *La profesionalización de las empresas familiares* (Madrid: LID, 2013).

activity, competence or authority. But these professionals also share a social world, a system of beliefs and a negotiated order with spaces for informal relations and operating rules.

This work avoids rigid theoretical notions of professions to understand them in their plastic and contextual sense as defined by Pierre Bourdieu.[14] That is, discussing the professions not as a subject matter in itself but as a methodological tool that allows 'taking seriously the work of aggregation and symbolic impositions that was necessary to produce it'.[15] Thus, I understand the profession as 'a structured space of social forces and struggles', as 'the social product of a historical work of construction of a group and a representation of groups'.[16] Based on its most social sense, I attempt to analyse businessmen as a privileged group concerning their social position and economic and cultural capital. To this end, I will first study the development of a specific discourse that would legitimize their public participation in defining their own scientific-technical space. This discursive level was developed alongside an important professional institutionalization through associations and regulated education. Furthermore, professional self-representation practices were implemented, giving them the legitimacy to participate in the country's capable elites. To portray themselves as respectable men, these entrepreneurs developed a range of symbolic legitimization strategies that essentially showed them as professionals at the nation's service.

14 For a work from this perspective see Maria Malatesta, *Professional Men, Professional Women. The European Professions from the 19th Century until Today* (London: SAGE, 2010).

15 Pierre Bourdieu, 'A Radical Doubt', in Loïc Wacquant and Pierre Bourdieu, eds, *An Invitation to Reflexive Sociology* (Chicago: The University of Chicago Press, 1992), 243.

16 Bourdieu, 'A Radical Doubt', 242–3.

Professional discourse and public legitimization

The business world encompassed a broad and diverse conglomerate of activities that based their legitimacy on work and money. Of course, this label included traditional businesses such as textiles or tobacco. Nevertheless, the development of technology and communications that the Industrial Revolution entailed created new challenges. Thus, there were improvements in both freight and passenger transport companies, particularly with the progress of the railway. And some new companies had to cover the latest needs, for example, those related to urban services such as gas or electricity. For all of them, the State's connection through the granting of monopolies was fundamental to guarantee their stability and business future. However, in the nineteenth century, this business category also included those engaged in financial investment and credit societies. In a world under construction, entrepreneurs were thus characterized by diversity and fluctuation from one business to another. Therefore, it was usual to see the same man investing in the stock market, managing a state monopoly and running a private company from another field at the same time. However, the diversity was not only in the typology of the companies, but also in their social position. The business world included everyone from small local merchants to high-level businessmen born, mostly, from these same socio-professional strata. Nonetheless, these internal differences were also present in other professions without their professional category being questioned.

Beyond this diversity, it is worth noting a uniform public discourse that sought to legitimize their social and professional position, transcending any political, geographical, or social differences. It was present, for example, in the institutionalized spaces they created as a professional group. In 1865, the programmatic manifesto of the Círculo de la Unión Mercantil [Circle of the Mercantile Union] of Madrid clearly stated their main discursive axes. Firstly, their firm universalism. Their orientation towards the collective made them appear as defenders of the national interest over any particular benefit. Thus, their profession was founded above all on their desire 'to develop themselves strong and powerful to give importance to the country and wealth to the State'.[17] Ultimately, commerce was 'the driving force of the classes' that 'provided the common good'. As José Luis Albareda, Minister of Public Works, said in 1882, 'studying people's trade, trying to moralize it, to defend its ideas and interests, is to work for the flag of general civilization'.[18] But above all it entailed 'the wealth, exaltation, and progress of the nation'.

Precisely for those reasons, businessmen persistently tried to emphasize their political independence. In the end, they will say 'trade and industry do not need the government to take them by the hand'.[19] Consequently, they defended that 'the welfare and future of the great social institutions should never be postponed by the party interest'. It could not be possible to sacrifice 'the great to the small, the sublime to the petty, the social and permanent to the momentary and mutable'. To political independence, they added their particular professional discourse based on scientific knowledge. They criticized 'the reigning confusion in all spheres of public administration' and 'the financial system' because it was not 'founded on the prescriptions of economic science'. They demanded professional control of the exercise of commerce, backed by the legitimacy of science and the knowledge of technical competence. Therefore, governments had 'to limit themselves to requesting the regulatory authority of collective forces'.

Finally, they vindicated commerce as a respectable profession. The opening speeches of the First Spanish Commercial Conference (1881) were particularly emphatic in this regard. Ramón Sainz, secretary of the conference, explained that 'the businessman is no longer the former merchant who had a lower social position despite his exploits and financial worth'.[20] Foremost, commerce was 'a distinctive nineteenth century idea' insofar as it was 'a thought of reform and progress, a source of prosperity for public wealth and social welfare'. Thus, entrepreneurs were legitimated to participate in the country's elites by their rise to the scientific status and their quest of the nation's general interest. Joaquín María Sanromá, president

17 *La Iberia* (23 December 1865).

18 S. A., *Actas del Congreso Nacional Mercantil* (Madrid: El porvenir literario, 1882), 41.

19 This quote and the subsequent ones are taken from *La Iberia* (23 December 1865).

20 S. A., Actas del Congreso Nacional Mercantil, 25 and 27.

of the conference, delved into these ideas. As early as 1865, he said that 'we are far from those times when the exercise of commerce, if it did not bring a blot, was at least unfavourable and the worst considered'.[21] In 1881, by contrast, the nation was no longer magnified 'by the brilliance of the sword and the magic of the conquests'. In modern society, he stated that 'national greatness lies in morality, credit, ships, desks, warehouses, and railways'. Thus, modern civilization was based on 'respect, consideration, and a kind of idolatry towards those men who wear with honour, profit, and pride the noblest title of sons of labour'.

These groups had a marked free trade and progressive tendency, bringing together an extremely broad and diverse merchant conglomeration of all classes. For this reason, they were swiftly questioned by protectionist institutions, such as Fomento de la Producción Nacional [Promotion of Domestic Production] or Fomento de la Producción Española [Promotion of Spanish Production].[22] In fact, Juan Güell – president of the *Junta de Fábricas de Cataluña* [Board of Manufacturers of Catalonia] and founder of the Instituto Industrial de Cataluña [Catalan Industrial Institute] – wrote an irate reply objecting to the premise of the Círculo de la Unión Mercantil [Circle of the Mercantile Union].[23] However, over and above these ideological differences, a growing consensus space emerged that converged with many of their opinions. Thus, two main issues structured their public discourse: commercial professionalization and the dignification of entrepreneurs.

This confluence was particularly apparent in the businessmen's involvement in politics. Indeed, many politicians were linked to the business world in one way or another. Politicians and businessmen had very close relationships, often being part of the same family and patronage networks.[24]

21 S. A., Actas del Congreso Nacional Mercantil, 27–8.

22 For this ideological and economic discussion see José María Serrano, 'Librecambio y protección en la España liberal', *Historia Contemporánea* 43 (2011), 623–52.

23 Juan Güell, *Causas económico-administrativas de los males actuales de España distintas de las que expone el Círculo de la Unión Mercantil* (Barcelona: Narciso Ramírez y Compañía, 1866).

24 Juan Pro, 'Poder político y poder económico en el Madrid de los moderados (1844–1854)', *Ayer* 66 (2007), 27–55; Mercedes Cabrera and Fernando del Rey, *El poder*

Likewise, the presence of business family names was common in Congress and particularly in the Senate. However, most of the time, their direct involvement was circumscribed to specific matters related to their technical and professional competence. Most of them were not the greatest and most illustrious parliamentary speakers. Their activities were often hidden in the final committees related to trade, taxes, or economics. Their interventions mainly referred to these same subjects. Nonetheless, their public discourse expressed the same ideas as those developed by these broad and diverse institutions. In this way, tropes and arguments were reproduced by businessmen regardless of their ideology and social status.

Firstly, the aversion they show for intervening in politics is remarkable. José María Ybarra even wrote in his will to his heirs that 'if one day you are offered a public position, excuse yourself as much as you can'.[25] Facing the professional concept of politics, they were called upon to participate by putting their knowledge at the nation's service. For example, in his first speech in the Senate, Manuel Girona already stated that he spoke 'as a practical businessman'.[26] He clarified that he did not 'understand political matters' and that he was not 'a politician'; he just was 'a man who knows a little about numbers by moving them around'. From this competent position, protected by economic science, he intervened in politics 'to propose remedies; the question is whether they are acceptable to the government'. These businessmen sought to appear publicly as independent figures, placed beyond the political struggle and pursuing the general interest. As Juan Manuel de Urquijo wrote in the 1880s, 'we do not make politics'.[27] Like many other business families, they always remained 'on the government's side in all matters of order and good government'. However, in economic

de los empresarios: política e intereses económicos en la España contemporánea, 1875–2000 (Madrid: Taurus, 2002).

25 Quote in Pablo Díaz-Morlán, *Los Ybarra: una dinastía de empresarios, 1801–2001* (Madrid: Marcial Pons, 2002), 133.

26 Diario de Sesiones del Senado, Legislature 1877, n. 50, 3 July 1877. Quote in 732, 736 and 737.

27 Quote in Onésimo Díaz-Hernández, *Los marqueses de Urquijo. El apogeo de una saga poderosa y los inicios del Banco Urquijo, 1870–1931* (Pamplona: EUNSA, 1998), 109.

ones, they felt empowered to intervene independently based on their scientific competence. And always, at least rhetorically, in search of the nation's wealth. For example, when Juan Güell died, the newspapers stressed that his parliamentary engagement was 'not to interfere in party matters ..., nor to support or overthrow any government, but only to defend the national industry'.[28] Antonio López's political attitude was also lauded in the same sense. Despite being a senator due to his noble status, he abstained from participating in political matters except on one occasion: 'to vote against the commercial treaty with France, which he considered to be a tragedy for the national industry'.[29]

These businessmen were also involved in local politics. The dynamics they followed were similar to their participation in parliament. In the first place, they often were mayors of their cities. With a certain imposture, José María Ybarra wrote in 1876 to his children that 'the only thing anyone can get from the City Council are disappointments'.[30] Nevertheless, this was the third time he had accepted the position. Along with those annoyances, the mayoral service also had political and no least economic influence. For example, José Campo governed Valencia between 1843 and 1847; but he had to resign after being caught up in a corruption scandal. In 1846, he founded the Sociedad Valenciana de Fomento [Valencian Promotion Society], a mixed public and private enterprise of which he was the main stockholder. This company bought some land that he, as mayor, reclassified for the construction of the city's enlargement.[31] However, he enriched himself with businesses related to the city, such as gas supplies or tax collection. His national and local political supports were essential to achieve this.

In any case, these men distinguished themselves by promoting improvements in the urban development and modernization from the city councils. Thus, they were remembered and praised for undertaking projects for urban improvement, water purification, lighting installation, transport

28 *La Ilustración Española y Americana* (5 January 1877).

29 *La Época* (18 January 1883).

30 Quote in María Sierra, 'La Casa Ybarra: Política de honor y política de interés', *Historia Social* 36 (2000), 18.

31 Telésforo Hernández, 'José Campo Pérez (1814–1889)', in Javier Vidal, ed., *Cien empresarios valencianos* (Madrid: LID, 2005), 53–64.

services, etc. Likewise, they privately play a prominent role in local patronage. As happened, for example, with Antonio López, the investments in his birth and residence localities were constant and abundant.[32] They focused mainly on education, charity and local development. In the end, this link with progress and modernity would be fundamental in their social legitimization but also in their professional one, showing them as some notables pursuing the general interest.

Professional organization and training

The professional public discourse was a determining aspect in the development of a collective awareness among businessmen of their social role and their duty towards the general interest. Meanwhile, there was also a range of measures to implement institutions of self-regulatory, unifying and training control. The first effort of unity was, perhaps, the one made towards professional institutionalization. From the eighteenth century onwards, there were already spaces for the coordination of professional activity. The *Juntas de Comercio* [Trade Boards] were created as a reflection mirror of the Sociedades Económicas de Amigos del País [Economic Societies of Friends of the Country], but focused on commerce. Their purposes were to protect the commercial activity, settle merchants' quarrels and promote trade studies. Until the Código de Comercio [Commercial Code] of 1829, they maintained administrative, training and judicial functions. Since the 1830s, liberalism has sought to delimit these competencies and integrate them into modern legislation.

However, the primary efforts to establish a professional organizational structure came in the 1850s, within the first cycle of modern associationism that Spain experienced.[33] The creation of the Círculo de la Unión Mercantil

32 Martín Rodrigo, *Los marqueses de Comillas, 1817–1925. Antonio y Claudio López* (Madrid: LID, 2000), 63–70.

33 Ramón Arnabat, *Asociaos y seréis fuertes. Sociabilidades, modernizaciones y ciudadanías en España, 1860–1930* (Zaragoza: Prensas de la Universidad de Zaragoza, 2019).

[Circle of the Mercantile Union] of Madrid was perhaps the first landmark in a long process that culminated at the end of the century. On 20 June 1858, a few merchants from Madrid met 'to establish a meeting point where they could centralize their forces and make the individuals of this great family known to each other'.[34] The meeting was a success. Besides appointing a commission to formalize the association, they succeeded in drafting an exposition for Junta de Comercio [Trade Board] of Madrid complaining about the poor railway service and the tariff disorder. Although longer than expected, the process had already begun. The commission initially worked to find a place to meet. The club's inauguration took place on 14 November 1858, with the attendance of roughly fifty founding members. As some newspapers pointed out then, 'the great merchant family had finally been brought together; an idea that had been tried so many times but had not been fulfilled until today'.[35] The drafting of statutes and the formation of working commissions completed the establishment of the business association. From then on, its growth was exponential. The membership rose to almost 300 and even forced them to search for a new headquarters and to increase the activation and maintenance fees.[36]

In 1865, the institutionalization process was so advanced that they decided to make their postulates and intentions explicit. In a meeting of nearly 400 businessmen, they approved the theoretical bases that were to guide the institution. But they also outlined a range of programmatic agreements to be implemented. Among them, there highlighted the communication with other business groups and the promotion of new ones where they did not yet exist. The ultimate objective was clear: to organize themselves professionally on a national level. The association called on 'all other sister corporations' to collectively encourage 'the regeneration of Spanish trade and industry, the reform of the country's economic administration, and the study of all the matters and questions that disturb our interests'.[37] To achieve this, they urged them to promote specific publications and to coordinate petitions to the Parliament. Furthermore, they

34 *La Corona* (24 June 1858).
35 *La Época* (15 November 1858).
36 *La España* (23 January1864).
37 *La Época* (8 December 1865).

added concrete actions to promote the defence of commercial interests. These included, for example, the announcement of 'prizes for authors of economic and administrative reform projects'; or the establishing of specific classes in their associations 'on all subjects related to the commercial institution'. Nevertheless, among the measures, the attempt to convene a national trade conference was noteworthy.

A few days after the meeting, the executive committee published a programmatic manifesto echoing the same ideas and measures. But above all, the union was essential to convene an annual trade conference, 'firstly in the capital and then in the provinces in decreasing order of trade importance'.[38] The goal was to present a united front to the country to directly influence 'public opinion, the queen of today and lady of the world'. This was the only way of guaranteeing that their claims would 'not get lost in the coffered ceilings of ministries and head offices' nor be buried 'in the desk of some section chief or business officer'. There were plenty of examples of these specific events at the international level. That was the case of 'France, Switzerland, Germany, England, and Belgium, the nations closest to the banner of civilization'. But their argument focused primarily on two professional meetings celebrated in Spain: 'that of our class of jurist [1863] and medical doctors [1864]'. If these two cases had held their meetings following the example of foreigners, businessmen could not be less 'because their profession is cosmopolitan and universal par excellence'. They demanded the same treatment as them based on how decisive these conferences had been in their professional development. After all, 'they form an epoch in the life of nations and the history of professions because they brought a real revolution in them'.

This revolution had to temper its aims and rhythms. The national institutional structure was created in 1881, in a very different economic and political context. Firstly, at the beginning of the year, the Asociación de Profesores Mercantiles [Association of Mercantile Professors] was founded in Madrid. Apparently, its initial objective was not national. Its first president, Enrique Lucini, wrote to a distrustful Antonio Torrent, head of the Academia Científico Mercantil de Barcelona [Scientific and Mercantile

38 This quote and the subsequent ones are taken from *La Iberia* (23 December 1865).

Academy of Barcelona], that he did not want 'to have any superiority over those established in the provinces'.[39] However, 'the fact of being installed closer to the highest powers of the nation' made the association 'the perfect intermediary for managing matters and complaints in those powers'. Its national orientation was definitively expressed in the 1890s. At that time, it changed its name to the Asociación Nacional de Profesores y Peritos Mercantiles [National Association of Professors and Mercantile Experts] 'to better show the new and varied aims of the institution'.[40] The process culminated in 1898 when the association was declared an official professional corporation 'due to its service to the general interests'.[41] This condition also obliged it 'to be at the disposal of the public administration to give its opinion on its particular matters'.

This association, with the support of the Círculo de la Unión Mercantil [Circle of the Mercantile Union], managed to complete the 1865 project and convened the first trade conference in 1881. The president of the meeting, Joaquín María Sanromá, pointed out the different reception that the proposal received in those specific contexts. If in 1865 'the idea, lacking strength and resources, passed like a shadow and fell into oblivion', in 1881 'the flame caught fire with astonishing speed'. In his opinion, this change was the result of two great achievements.[42] Firstly, 'a great conquest in the public opinion'. By 1881 not only were 'there hundreds of newspapers devoted exclusively to so-called material interests', but it had also been possible 'for even the major political newspapers' to have 'a special section reserved for economic, rental, and commercial matters'. This conquest was followed by that of 'a free, serious, and vigorous organization'. Sanromá argued that 'centralization and doctrinaire liberalism' turned the Juntas de Comercio [Trade Boards] into 'mere State wheels, … without their own purposes or

39 Quote in Javier Fernández-Aguado, *Historia de la Escuela de Comercio de Madrid y su influencia en la formación gerencial española, 1850–1970* (PhD dissertation, Universidad Complutense de Madrid, 1996), 320.

40 Enrique Lucini, *La Carrera Mercantil* (Madrid: Establecimiento Tipográfico de Ricardo Álvarez, 1894), 13.

41 *Gaceta de Madrid* (1 April 1898).

42 This quote and the subsequent ones are taken from S. A., *Actas del Congreso Nacional Mercantil*, 27–33.

ideals'. However, 'the organization of trade as a business has been succeeded by its organization as an idea'. The conference was therefore the culmination 'of this moral and scientific organization of trade'.

Between 11 and 19 December, prominent entrepreneurs, small merchants, specialist teachers and politicians met in Madrid. The meeting discussed trade priorities – mainly trade law and education – and proposed a range of reforms. The event was also supported by the Ministry of Public Works and other significant institutions, such as the Bank of Spain and the Madrid City Council. But above all, the conference elevated business and commerce to a professional status. As Sanromá concluded, 'in this century of discussion, struggle, and assemblies, every respectable class must begin by having two essential conditions: science and the word'. A hundred years earlier, 'if any tradesmen association had tried to discuss on the grounds of a university', they would have been expelled and told to 'go back to your occupations and leave the majesty of the chairs to us'. However, gathered in 1881 in the assembly hall of the Central University, they succeeded in showing 'that trade and science [...] are twin brothers who, concerned for the nation's welfare, wield their weapons to fight together'. Commerce had finally achieved the voice and the scientific legitimacy that qualified it as a respectable profession. This conference was also the first of a long series of meetings which, although not annual, would take place regularly from then on, as happened in 1886 and 1891. But it would also be the beginning of Spanish participation in the wave of international meetings held in the second half of the nineteenth century. Thus, Spain was part of the Comité Permanente de los Congresos de Enseñanza Técnica y Comercial [Standing Committee of the Congresses of Technical and Commercial Education] from the first one, held in Bordeaux in 1886.[43]

Professional institutionalization was early combined with a manifest interest in structuring formal training. The process was very similar to that experienced by other disciplines, such as agriculture or industry.[44] Trade

43 Société Philomathique de Bordeaux, *Congrès international ayant pour objet l'enseignement technique commercial et industriel* (Paris: Guillaumin et Cie, 1887), 5.

44 Juan Pan-Montojo, 'De la agronomía a la ingeniería agronómica: la reforma de la agricultura y la sociedad rural españolas, 1855–1931', *AREAS* 26 (2007), 75–93; José Manuel Cano, *Enseñanza e industrialización en España (1844–1868): medios humanos y materiales* (PhD dissertation, Universidad Nacional de Educación a

schools were born in the eighteenth century. Their germ was in the chairs of commerce created within the Juntas de Comercio [Trade Boards] that the Bourbon reforms established in certain cities.[45] Their aim was twofold: to increase the crown's power and to encourage trade improvements to recover the former economic vigour.[46] The Peninsular War broke, in part, the dynamic followed by some trade schools, such as those of Cádiz or Bilbao. But the philosophy of the Enlightenment remained within liberalism in the importance that political economy had since its origins.[47] For this reason,

---

Distancia, 2002); Darina Martykánová, 'Shaping a New Man: The Schools for the State Engineers in Nineteenth Century Spain (1830s–1900)', *Engineering Studies* 7 (2014), 87–107.

45 No global analysis is available. It is possible to see studies on the functioning of the schools of Barcelona in Jordi Mones, 'Enseñanza técnica y profesional y desarrollo socio-económico. El caso de la Junta de Comercio de Barcelona (1769–1851)', *Historia de la Educación* 4 (1985), 241–71; of Málaga in Manuel Morales, 'La Escuela de Comercio de Málaga (1887–1909). Proyección e inserción social', in Jean-René Aymes and Jean-Luis Guereña, eds, *L'Université en Espagne et en Amérique Latine du Moyen Âge à nos Jours* (Tours: Presses Universitaires François-Rabelais, 1991), 305–16; of Zaragoza in Jorge Infante, *La Escuela de Comercio de Zaragoza. Orígenes y desarrollo histórico* (PhD dissertation, Universidad de Zaragoza, 1991); of Madrid in Fernández-Aguado, *Historia de la Escuela de Comercio de Madrid*; of Valencia in María Carmen Cuéllar and Juan Ramón Rodríguez, *Los estudios mercantiles y la Escuela de Comercio de Valencia 1787–1975* (Valencia: Prensas de la Universidad de Valencia, 2000); of Cádiz in Fernando Guilloto, *La carrera de comercio en Cádiz. Del arte de la Contabilidad a las Ciencias Empresariales* (Cádiz: Publicaciones de la Universidad de Cádiz, 1994); and of Canarias in Julio Javier Menús, *Los estudios oficiales de Comercio y Empresariales en Canarias durante el siglo XX* (PhD dissertation, Universidad de Las Palmas de Gran Canaria, 2011).

46 Lucini, *La Carrera Mercantil*, 1–17; Agustín García, *La enseñanza mercantil en España y en el extranjero* (Cádiz: Cabello y Lozón, 1898), 69–72; Rafael Heredia, 'La enseñanza mercantil en los pueblos latinos', *Unión Ibero-Americana* 22/2 (1908), 16–24.

47 José Enrique Covarrubias, 'La ciencia del gobierno, la economía política y la utilidad en el ideario de Campomanes y Jovellanos', in Maria Pilar Martínez and Leonor Ludlow, eds, *Historia del pensamiento económico: del mercantilismo al liberalismo* (México: Universidad Nacional Autónoma de México, 2007), 27–46; Jesús Astigarraga and Juan Zabalza, "Economía Política' y 'Comercio' en los diccionarios y la literatura enciclopédica española del siglo XVIII', *Bulletin hispanique* 111/2 (2009), 387–427; Pablo Cervera, 'Disipando sombras, aportando

commercial training was always present in the training programs conceived by the liberals. The Reglamento General de la Instrucción Pública [General Regulation on Public Education] of 1821 already included the business schools among the studies 'required for certain professions in civilian life', along with medicine and veterinary science.[48] The definitive imposition of liberalism in the 1830s reincorporated these schools into the third cycle of the training scheme. Thus, the Plan General de Instrucción Pública [General Plan of Public Instruction] of 1836 integrated business schools into the so-called special schools, such as the Schools of Roads and Canals, Mining and Agriculture.[49]

The final step in the establishment of structured academic studies came in the 1850s. In 1847, the schools became part of the Dirección General de Instrucción Pública [Public Education Office] and started to be defrayed by the national budget.[50] In 1850, the commercial training program was definitively established. The government's aim was manifest: to give the schools 'the unity they lacked and to subordinate them to a single idea'.[51] This centralization meant above all uniformity of the training program 'to enlighten those who are engaged in the profession' or 'can be of great help to companies and enterprises'. Thus, it was divided into six subjects in three domains: the technical – mathematics and monetary systems, double-entry accounting system and commercial law; the theoretical – political economics, industrial and commercial geography; and the linguistic – English and French. In addition, they became part of the secondary schools.

However, the main endeavour for the creation of the training plan came in 1857 with Claudio Moyano as Minister of Public Works. The spirit of the century, with the increase in communications, showed how important trade was to the countries' development and progress. 'Already our grandfathers – the government said – considered commerce as a

---

luces. Economía española del siglo XVIII revisitada', *Cuadernos Dieciochistas* 20 (2019), 97–158.

48 S. A., *Reglamento General de Instrucción Pública* (Granada: Imprenta Nacional, 1821), 10.

49 *Gaceta de Madrid* (9 August 1836).

50 *Gaceta de Madrid* (10 October 1847).

51 *Gaceta de Madrid* (11 September 1850).

profession. Science later came to prescribe rules, to order its complicated operations.'[52] Previous laws had established 'a uniform and general plan' for commercial schools. However, they needed an update to the new scientific knowledge. To this end, the government added new subjects such as general commerce history, universal metrology, or applied commercial calculus. But the new law sought, first and foremost, to ensure 'the same rights as those of other similar careers'. The government thus established an organic plan for the business schools, which was complemented by specific regulations. Therefore, they structured the pedagogical process in two phases: an elementary one of three years – conducted in schools all over the country – and a higher stage of one more year, centralized in Madrid. The Ley de Instrucción Pública [Public Instruction Act] of the same year ratified this whole organizational and training program.[53] With this, Spain entered the process of formalizing commercial education that had started in Europe with the École de Commerce et d'Industrie [School of Commerce and Industry] of Paris (1820) and the Institut Supérieur [Higher Institute] of Antwerp (1852).[54]

The Public Instruction Act 1857 remained intact for thirty years, with its achievements and shortcomings. The development of the Second Industrial Revolution and, particularly, the crisis of 1873 and 1882 highlighted the modern challenges faced by the economy. Among others, these included the concentration of increasingly globalized enterprises and the need for a more specialized technology sector. In this context, the Spanish government resolved to reengage in commercial training. Its intention was 'to found it on a scientific basis as much as possible'.[55] In its view, the middle class had looked with disdain on the mercantile career, turning instead to the former so-called liberal professions. The government therefor sought 'to encourage a commercial spirit with higher elevation, dignity, and moral character'. After all, he said, 'the knowledge of the laws that regulate the

52 *Gaceta de Madrid* (23 March 1857).

53 *Gaceta de Madrid* (10 September 1857).

54 Adrien Jean–Guy Passant, 'Issues in European Business Education in the Mid-Nineteenth Century: A Comparative Perspective', *Business History* 58/7 (2016), 1118–45.

55 *Gaceta de Madrid* (17 August 1887).

exchange of property and the world's wealth is a function as higher as science or art'. To this end, the government offered 'a new rigorous, thoughtful preparation' based on a range of economic, statistical, geographical and linguistic knowledge. The law was inspired 'by the current noticeable movement in professional training towards the study of the principles and rules that govern them'. The case of England, 'where mercantile traditions were perpetuated within the family', was paradigmatic of the importance that training had acquired in economic development. Competition from other countries, 'where commercial training was more developed', had filled 'the city of London with foreigners because they were better qualified than the British'. England had therefore 'understood that practice was not enough' and founded 'business schools in every major city'.

Accordingly, the educational reform of 1887 was an essential element in the definitive professionalization of commerce. It granted independence to the business schools, but also modernized the training program – adding, for example, German – and promoted its higher education, raising the status of the Barcelona School. But, above all, the law sought to sanction the study of commerce as moral and to vindicate the professional status of an undervalued technical domain. As a result, their scientific and technical training was assimilated on equal terms with other liberal occupations professionalized in the nineteenth century. The official curricular organization and the structure of the training schools were followed by the foundation of private institutions. Among them was the Centro de Instrucción Comercial [Centre for Commercial Instruction].[56] Created in 1882 by the Círculo de la Unión Mercantil [Circle of the Mercantile Union] of Madrid, its target was the formation of commercial training of the lower classes. In this sense, it was a significant associative space for the commercial professionalization, particularly through its public conferences.

Likewise, commercial training also played a decisive role in women's education and professional development. In 1878, just seven years after the foundation of the Governess School, the Asociación para la Enseñanza de la Mujer [Association for the Education of Women] opened a business

56 Eugenio Sainz, *Monografía del Centro de Instrucción Comercial de Madrid* (Madrid: Establecimiento Tipográfico de Rodríguez Ojeda, 1908).

school. Its three-year training program copied the male curriculum. It was established based on practical skills – arithmetic, modern accounting techniques and statistics; theoretical ones – commercial law, political economy and commercial geography; and language ones – Spanish, English and French.[57] As Professor Rafael Torres Campos said, the incorporation of women into 'careers, professions, and jobs hitherto monopolized by one sex always demonstrated their aptitudes and conditions'.[58] Thus, women were to become involved in commerce after their positive results in the medical and educational fields. There were many reasons for this. In the first place, 'there were few professions like commerce in which household heads are so much in need of help'. In reality, he said 'wives and daughters' were already in the trade 'but they were engaged in the simplest tasks'. Hence, there was one very straightforward thing to do: 'to change their position through proper training' and allow them to share 'the business management with the household head'.

Besides this logistical support, women's commercial training was essential because of their role when they were widowed. When their husbands died, they handled the business management to ensure the survival of the family and to maintain the enterprises for their descendants.[59] The progressive José Luis Albareda alluded directly to these functions in his inaugural lecture at the first mercantile congress (1881). Their trade link, the then Minister of Public Works said, was critical 'in the mission that women had with the nation's political development'.[60] In the end, 'half of social life belongs to the fair sex'. That is why Spain had to assimilate itself to other countries and encourage women's participation 'in all enterprises, in all jobs, in all the aims of national commercial and industrial life'. For both men and women, education was fundamental to shape a profession

57 Asociación para la Enseñanza de la Mujer, *Bases-reglamento de la Escuela de Comercio para Señoras* (Madrid: M. Tello, 1878).

58 This quote and the subsequent ones are taken from *La Ilustración Española y Americana* (30 September 1878).

59 Raquel Sánchez, *Señoras fuera de casa. Mujeres del siglo XIX: la conquista del espacio público* (Madrid: Catarata, 2019), 76–91.

60 This quote and the subsequent ones are taken from S. A., *Actas del Congreso Nacional Mercantil*, 43–4.

based on knowledge and science. The goal was always to guarantee their specific economic independence, but also the general progress of the country.

Professional self-representation and performance

Such public discourse and organizational practices were complemented by a self-representation that gave them legitimacy and showed them as respectable men. For this purpose, they had to appear as real gentlemen, performing in the public space as a distinctive professional class. In this respect, the investment they made in symbolic capital was decisive. As Pierre Bourdieu stated, these economically powerful factions of the bourgeoisie confused the accumulation of equity with symbolic capital. Thus, they acquired 'a reputation for competence and an image of respectability and honourability that are easily converted into notable political positions'.[61]

The first and most visible of these investments were in housing conditions and material culture. These businessmen began to buy the palaces of the aristocrats in the power centres of the cities. However, far from being satisfied with just their acquisition, they dressed their antique golden halls with a modern and respectable taste. After buying his palace from the Count of Santa Coloma, in 1852 Ignacio Girona said to his son Manuel: 'We have to build a house like a banker because it is necessary to display opulence, especially for foreigners.'[62] Along with these acquisitions, they also promoted the new elites' symbolic spaces by investing in the urban enlargement that structured modern cities.[63] Here they also displayed the opulence that Ignacio Girona spoke of, giving it a modern character. Wealth

61 Pierre Bourdieu, *La distinction. Critique sociale du jugement* (Paris: Les Éditions de Minuit, 1979), 331.

62 Lluïsa Pla, *Los Girona. La gran burguesía catalana del siglo XIX* (Lleida: Milenio, 2017), 251.

63 Clementina Díez, *Arquitectura y clases sociales en el Madrid del siglo XIX* (Madrid: Siglo XXI, 1986).

manifested itself in many ways. Art was undoubtedly one of them. The investment they made in paintings, sculptures, books and antiques was truly impressive. Nevertheless, their collecting practice went beyond that traditional customs of the nobles, in which collections sought to show their legitimacy by anchoring them in history. These businessmen followed the rules of modern collecting in which, as Óscar Vázquez said, 'a collection's value – in the widest sense of the worth, significance, importance, use, and facility of exchange – was now measured partly by the collector's identity, rather than solely by that of the objects contained within'.[64] Moreover, images and writings favoured the dissemination of collections and made them more accessible to the public. Thus, collecting helped them to forge a specific identity with regard to the aristocracy and the public opinion, founding their particular museums. Alongside art, opulence was expressed in objects closely linked to the emerging concepts of modernity and comfort, almost always imported from France or England. Hence, houses were filled with iron and glass structures, and new spaces were created, such as billiards or gymnasiums. They also added all the modern commodities and technological innovations.

These material investments acquire greater importance due to the entity that the concept of the house had at that time. Its essence transcended its materiality as it referred, first of all, to the family's network of influence. Certainly, the new liberal society was built on nodes in which family connections and political and economic loyalties were invariably mixed. For example, the Ybarra's palace in Seville was known as 'the Big House', and its entity went beyond the ownership of the head of household to become a structuring place for the clan.[65] The concept had yet a particularly relevant sense for these businessmen in which family and business merged. It was frequent for them to settle the headquarters and even the offices of their enterprises in their homes. Thus, these material investments became symbolic, conferring legitimacy to their family and their profession. In that sense, one space stood out above other housing structures: the office.

64 Oscar Vázquez, *Inventing the Art Collection. Patrons, Markets, and the State in Nineteenth Century Spain* (Pennsylvania: Penn State University Press, 2010), 14.

65 Sierra, 'La Casa Ybarra', 10.

Jesús Cruz has shown how offices were conceived in bourgeois houses – or adapted in aristocratic ones – as a public or semi-public space.[66] There men worked, read, delivered correspondence and kept their money there. But they were also homosocial spaces of sociability where they met to talk or close business deals. Moreover, as the manliest place of the house, the office brough together all the material culture that expressed their role as heads of household, businessmen and respectable notables.

Besides this consolidation of professional space and self-representation within the houses, they developed specific symbolic practices. Some signs served as external markers of belonging to this socio-professional collective. The portraits they commissioned can provide us a guide to know them. Indeed, their varied propagandistic purposes speak eloquently about how crucial they were in their legitimization. From the imposing paintings to the small *carte de visite* [visiting cart], the portraits of businessmen acquired distinctive iconographic patterns. In all of them, the props surrounding them stood out above all else. These professional spaces are repeatedly reproduced, where the desk occupies a prominent place. The men appeared there with their bureaux covered with ledgers or treatises of political economics. But they were also surrounded by the material culture that showed their economic and social position. Sometimes they were absorbed in their work. At other times, they were portrayed with a thoughtful gaze. In any case, they always had a formal and reserved appearance and were dressed in black suits. It was precisely this garment that gave them an aura of respectability. Firmly associated with these middle classes, the black suit thus became the epitome of the modern, respectable man.[67] Therefore, as social psychologist John C. Flügel said, gentlemen had resigned to wear 'brighter, gayer, more elaborate and more varied forms of ornamentation' to assumed plain, black suit as distinctive markers.[68] In his view, two trends explained this drastic change. Firstly, 'the doctrine of brotherhood' defended by

66 Jesús Cruz, *The Rise of Middle-Class Culture in Nineteenth Century Spain* (Baton Rouge: Louisiana State University Press, 2011), 83–5 and 89.

67 Collin McKinney, 'Men in Black: Fashioning Masculinity in Nineteenth Century Spain', *Letras Hispanas* 8/2 (2012), 78–93.

68 This quote and the subsequent ones are taken from John C. Flügel, *The Psychology of Clothes* (London: Hogarth Press, 1930), 110–13.

the revolutions was finally and inevitably imposed. Likewise, 'the ideal of work had now become respectable'. Thus, suits ended up symbolizing the middle-class 'devotion to the principles of duty, renunciation, and self-control'. In the nineteenth century, the black suit would eventually take hold at the same time that liberals assumed power and legitimized their occupations. That is to say, as they gave professional status to business and became respectable men.

The suit was undoubtedly a clear distinctive, public sign of these businessmen. But it was complemented by many others, notably the fashionable vehicles, first on horseback and then by car. Referring to one of the popular figures (*costumbrista*, referring to 'custom') present in Madrid in the 1840s, the stockbroker Ramón de Castañeira remarked that the first thing they did to show their power was 'to buy a fashionable cabriolet'.[69] In his opinion, 'the coach is one of the means that men used to distinguish themselves from the crowd'. Therefore, they did not only use it for rides. The carriages were also useful as an exterior symbolic marker when they attended a business or a party. For example, José Safont was known 'for promoting himself in the business world' by appearing 'in his magnificent coach'.[70] This businessman and financier, 'someone who yesterday was just a furrier', publicly performed the role of a respectable man. In the end, all these men tended towards pomp and ostentation in their appearance and manners. Therefore, they were 'more lavish than elegant', being 'a mixture between aristocrats and commoners' that made them 'the embodiment of the present time'.[71]

Finally, besides the investments of symbolic capital and the assumption of certain markers, these men founded distinguished spaces of sociability related to their professional category. The most prominent businessmen shared equally the manly spaces that modulated the new elites, particularly the Casino.[72] However, they also created their ones. There, along

69 Ramón de Castañeira, 'El agente de bolsa', in *Los españoles pintados por sí mismos* (Madrid: I. Boix editor, 1844, vol. 2), 362.

70 *El Zurriago* (15 June 1841).

71 Castañeira, 'El agente de bolsa', 366.

72 María Zozaya, *Identidades en juego. Formas de representación social del poder de la élite en un espacio de sociabilidad masculino, 1836–1936* (Madrid: Siglo XXI, 2016).

with conferences on their profession, they had specialized libraries and distinguished spaces for collective entertainment and discussion. Due to their importance and impact, the commercial *ateneos* and casinos stood out, many of which coupled as complementary formative spaces to the professional associations. A police record from 1865 describes Madrid's one, with its interior, its activities and its varied social profile. The club was then in Mayor Street; located near the public square where the well-known Noche de San Daniel riots took place. Some men had to stay there after the disturbances that ended with fourteen students dead. Its halls were decorated with wooden furniture, paintings, carpets and fireplaces. The police search caught many of them 'with the games or hobbies of the place', such as reading or playing the pool.[73] The Catalan deputy José Brunet – who was involved in the railway development – and the Valencian senator Juan Bautista Romero – whose fortune was due to the silk business – took shelter there. Along with them, men of lesser political relevance took refuge. For example, this was the case of the brothers Cristóbal and Feliciano Domingo – printing prosecutor and trade employee, respectively; the historian and businessman Miguel Ruiz de Villanueva – concessionaire of one saltworks monopoly; and the shopkeeper Manuel Orozco and the corporate lawyer Pedro Pi. Thus, this space of sociability was defined by the fact that it brough together a varied social and geographical profile of men around one thing: their profession. In this sense, it was an essential element in shaping a sense of collective belonging based on professional identity.

Conclusion

During the nineteenth century, businessmen filled up novels, pamphlets and newspapers until they formed a recognizable type in the social imaginary. A large and diverse conglomerate of enterprises came together under this label. Some of them were traditional. Others were born with industrial development. But all were modified by the progressive

73 *La Discusión* (20 April 1865).

expansion of communications and technology. The social, geographical and economic profile of these men was equally varied. The business world included the small local merchant and the great capitalist, those who managed a state monopoly and chartered their ships to import or export products. Perhaps their only unifying link was that they all based their legitimacy on labour and money. As one newspaper said in 1883, the challenge was to reconcile 'two antagonistic elements: matter and spirit'.[74] Thus, it was necessary to differentiate 'intelligent, enlightened, and rolling money' from 'the selfish, brutal, and stationary one'.

However, despite this vast diversity, these men managed to overcome their differences and unite to legitimize their role in the contemporary world. First, they established a public discourse based on two principles: the technical expertise of economic science and the quest for the general nation's interest over any particular benefit. Based on the professionalization of their occupations, this discourse was shared by everyone, whether they were supporters of free trade or protectionism, large businessmen or local merchants. To this end, they did not hesitate to intervene actively in local and national politics. Its public interventions always emphasized their independence, scientific competence and determination to serve the national wealth. However, beyond the rhetoric, they made significant efforts at institutionalization. From the 1850s onwards, they founded their particular associations throughout the country until they became an official professional corporation. Besides, they made enormous attempts to conquer public opinion, holding regular meetings since 1881. They also joined forces to formalize a formal, independently controlled and scientific education.

In all these activities, there were constant allusions to other European countries and references to other professions such as medicine, law and engineering. Nevertheless, the aim was not only to equip them professionally but also to legitimize their social position. To show themselves as respectable men, they developed a range of symbolic strategies that led them to exhibit themselves essentially as professionals at the nation's service. For this purpose, they did not hesitate to invest large sums of money in palaces, art collections, or charity. Thus, economic capital became a lucrative

74 *El Liberal* (22 January 1883).

symbolic capital that gave them significant benefits by legitimizing them in the post-revolutionary society. Alongside this process, businessmen created a self-representation as a socio-professional group, with distinctive visual and performative features. Furthermore, they also configured specific professional spaces that varied from the home office to the business casinos and *ateneos*. All these things helped to portray a particular social type in the social imaginary. But they also prompted these businessmen to formulate a sense of collective identity based on their professional status.

Notes on Contributors

JOAQUÍN ÁLVAREZ BARRIENTOS holds a PhD in Hispanic Philology and is a tenured researcher at the Centro Superior de Investigaciones Científicas in Madrid. He has focused on the cultural history of modernity, particularly on the men of letters and the republic of letters, the cultural institutions, the popular literature and the theatre. His latest works are *El crimen de la escritura. Una historia de las falsificaciones literarias españolas* (2014), *Cultura y ciudad. Madrid, del incendio a la maqueta (1701–1833)* (2017), *Marcelino Menéndez Pelayo, Literatura y nación. Preliminares de historia literaria* (2019), *El actor borbónico (1700–1831)* (2019) and *El astrólogo y su gabinete. Autoría, ciencia y representación en los almanaques del siglo XVIII* (2020). He chairs the Spanish Society of Eighteenth-Century Studies and has been awarded the Prize Leandro Fernández Moratín by the Association of Stage Directors of Spain and the Prize of Research by the Royal Society Menéndez Pelayo.

DIEGO CAMENO MAYO is a PhD candidate in Late Modern History at the Universidad Complutense de Madrid. His doctoral dissertation deals with the process of formation and behaviour codes of the Spanish army during the reign of Isabel II. He has published 'El bicentenario del general Prim y la polémica sobre su asesinato en los medios de comunicación españoles' (*Revista Internacional de Historia de la Comunicación*, 2019), and several other works are in press.

AINHOA GILARRANZ-IBÁÑEZ is a postdoctoral researcher and lecturer at the Université Sorbonne Nouvelle-Paris 3. She focuses on the institutionalization of art in the context of nineteenth-century state building. Her publications include '¿Qué hace la nación por las artes?: problemáticas patrimoniales y modelos museísticos en las colecciones del Prado y la Trinidad' (*Hispania*, 2019), 'La arteria cultural del cuerpo estatal: el campo de las Bellas Artes en la construcción del Estado liberal español (1833–1874)' (*Revista de Historiografía*, 2019), 'Los nexos del arte: explorar las redes del pintor de Corte durante el reinado de Isabel II' (in R. Sánchez, ed., *Un rey para la nación. Monarquía y nacionalización en el siglo XIX*, 2019) and *El Estado y el arte: historia de una relación simbiótica durante la España liberal (1833–1875)* (2021).

CARMEN GONZÁLEZ CANALEJO is retired Senior Lecturer at the Universidad de Almería. She is an expert in female healthcare professions. Her publications include 'Análisis histórico de la situación de las enfermeras y matronas en España: Una perspectiva global' (*Raudem: Revista de estudios de las mujeres*, 2013), 'Cuidados y bienestar: el trabajo sanitario femenino en respuesta a la "cuestión social" (1857–1936)' (*Dynamis*, 2007) and 'Los procesos de profesionalización de la enfermería española desde el punto de vista de género', (in *Medicina y poder político: XVI Congreso de la Sociedad Española de Historia de la Medicina*, 2014).

MANUEL AMADOR GONZÁLEZ FUERTES is a secondary school teacher and researcher associated with the Universidad Complutense de Madrid. He is an expert in legal and judicial institutions of the eighteenth and nineteenth centuries. He has published the following works: *La organización institucional de la Cámara de Castilla en la época borbónica* (2003); 'La reestructuración de la administración judicial local en la Corona de Castilla (1700–1749)' (in A. Dubet and J. J. Ruiz Ibáñez, eds, *Las monarquías española y francesa (siglos XVI–XVIII): ¿dos modelos políticos?*, 2010); 'El control de la magistratura a través de los informes anuales remitidos a la Cámara de Castilla (siglos XVII–XVIII). Análisis de una fuente inédita' (*Memoria y Civilización*, 2019, with Fernando Negredo del Cerro) and '¿El hábito hace al monje? Institucionalización de la carrera judicial en España a finales del Antiguo Régimen' (*Studia Historica. Historia Moderna*, 2017).

EDUARDO HIGUERAS CASTAÑEDA is Lecturer at the Universidad Nacional de Educación a Distancia. He received his PhD in History from the Universidad de Castilla-La Mancha with an Extraordinary Doctoral Award (2016). His main lines of research focus on the origins of democratic mobilization and republican political culture in liberal Spain, mostly from a biographical perspective. Among his works, the book *Con los Borbones, jamás. Biografía de Manuel Ruiz Zorrilla, 1833–1895* (2016) can be highlighted. His other publications include 'Militares republicanos en la Restauración: de la rebelión al exilio (1883–1891)' (*Trocadero*, 2013), 'Prensa y partido en el republicanismo progresista: *El Porvenir* (1882–1885)' (*Historia Contemporánea*, 2015) and 'Radicales contra carlistas: la lucha por el espacio público en Cuenca durante el Sexenio Democrático (1868–1874)' (*Historia Constitucional*, 2019).

DAVID MARTÍNEZ-VILCHES is a PhD candidate in Late Modern History and researcher-in-training at the Universidad Complutense de Madrid. He has focused on religious history and currently works on his doctoral dissertation about the religious entourage of the Spanish court during the reign of Isabel II. Some of his recent publications include 'The Pious Crown. The Monarchy's Religious Devotions during the Reign of Isabel II' (in D. San Narciso, M. Barral and C. Armenteros, eds, *Monarchy and Liberalism in Spain. The Building of the Nation-State, 1780–1931*, 2021), 'Sine labe concepta. La proyección de un modelo de feminidad católica a través de la Inmaculada Concepción' (*Arenal. Revista de Historia de las* mujeres, 2020), 'Monstruosos patriarcados. Los Patriarcados de Lisboa e Indias frente a la revolución liberal en Portugal y España' (*Hispania* Sacra, 2020) and 'Vivir los días usados. Eduardo Zamacois en el exilio (1939–1971)' (*Ayer*, 2020).

DARINA MARTYKÁNOVÁ is Lecturer in Modern History at the Universidad Autónoma de Madrid. She is an expert in the history of technical professions and also studies masculinities and the discourse of progress. Her publications include *Reconstructing Ottoman Engineers. Archaeology of a Profession (1789–1914)* (2010), special issue 'Los ingenieros y el poder en la España contemporánea' (*Historia y Política*, 2020), 'Remover los obstáculos. Los ingenieros de caminos españoles y sus visiones del Estado durante la segunda mitad del siglo XIX' (*Historia y Política*, 2016) and 'Shaping a New Man: The Schools for the State Engineers in Nineteenth-Century Spain (1830s–1900)' (*Engineering Studies*, 2014). She chairs the jury of the 2021 Turriano Prize granted by the International Committee for the History of Technology to the best monographs in the history of technology written by early-career scholars.

RUBÉN MIRÓN-GONZÁLEZ holds a PhD in Human and Social Sciences from the Universidad de Almería, with Extraordinary Doctorate Award. He is Lecturer in History of Nursing at the Universidad de Alcalá de Henares. His publications include 'La enfermería profesional en España: orígen, avance y represión (S. XIX–XX)' (2013); 'Depuración franquista del personal sanitario de la Beneficencia Provincial de Almería' (*Híades*, 2015), *Asistencia y condiciones sociosanitarias de los exiliados españoles en el sur de Francia, 1936–1945* (2019); 'De ciencia de la enfermedad a ciencias de la salud: una aproximación histórica del abordaje multidisciplinar (S.XIX–XX)' (2020) and 'La enfermería en el exilio republicano español de 1939 a Francia: una aproximación para su estudio' (*Dynamis*, 2020).

VÍCTOR M. NÚÑEZ-GARCÍA is Lecturer in History of Medicine and Scientific Documentation at the Universidad de Sevilla. He has worked on the configuration of the liberal political system in Spain, and recently has focused on the transformations of medical professions and the image of physicians in nineteenth-century Spain. His publications include *Huelva en las Cortes: élites y poder político durante la Década Moderada (1843–1854)* (2007); 'Médicos en la Corte española del siglo XIX. Influencias, sociabilidad y práctica profesional' (*Asclepio: Revista de historia de la medicina y de la ciencia,* 2019, with M.ª L. Calero-Delgado and E. Bernal-Borrego); 'Ciencia, patria y honor: los médicos e ingenieros y la masculinidad romántica en España (1820–1860)' (*Studia Historica. Historia Contemporánea*, 2020, with Darina Martykánová); 'Los hospitales docentes en la España contemporánea: El caso de los hospitales clínicos universitarios' (*Dynamis*, 2021) and the special issue 'Ciencia, amor y sacrificio frente al fraude: el honor y las profesiones médicas en la Europa del siglo XIX' (*Dynamis*, 2021, with Darina Martykánová).

PABLO ORTEGA-DEL-CERRO holds a PhD in History from the Universidad de Murcia and is currently Juan de la Cierva postdoctoral researcher at the Centro Superior de Investigaciones Científicas. He has specialized in the Spanish navy and naval officers in the eighteenth and nineteenth centuries. His publications include *El devenir de la élite naval: experiencias de los oficiales de la Armada en tiempos de cambio, inicios del XVIII–finales del XIX* (2018), 'Redes de relación e integración social de los oficiales de la Armada en Ferrol, 1740–1870' (*Cuadernos de estudios gallegos*, 2019) and 'Los beneficios del mar: negocios e inversiones económicas de la oficialidad naval en el siglo XVIII' (*Estudis: Revista de historia moderna*, 2019).

JUAN PAN-MONTOJO is Full Professor of Modern History at the Universidad Autónoma de Madrid. His research interests include the history of economic policies, state institutions, networks and social and economic interest groups and the history of engineering. He is author of several monographs, articles and edited volumes, including *Apostolado, profesión y tecnología: una historia de los ingenieros agrónomos en España* (2005); 'De la agronomía a la ingeniería agronómica: la reforma de la agricultura y la sociedad rural españolas, 1855–1931' (*Áreas: Revista internacional de ciencias sociales*, 2007); 'Poderes privados y recursos públicos. Redes sociales, grupos de interés y políticas económicas, 1844–1975' (*Ayer*, 2007) and 'Ciudadanos y contribuyentes' (in Manuel Pérez Ledesma, ed., *De súbditos a ciudadanos: una historia de la ciudadanía de España*, 2007).

CRISTINA DEL PRADO HIGUERA is Lecturer in Late Modern History and Vice-Chancellor of University Extension at the Universidad Rey Juan Carlos. She has specialized in the study of upper classes and the history of women. Among her publications figure: *El Todo Madrid. La Corte, la Nobleza y sus espacios de sociabilidad en el siglo XIX* (2012); 'Fernando de Castro y la defensa por los derechos de la mujer en el siglo XIX' (in J. L. Rodríguez Jiménez and C. del Prado, eds, *Reflexiones sobre los Derechos Humanos*, 2017) and 'El mundo social de la monarquía isabelina: espacios de sociabilidad y espejo de la nación en las élites españolas' (in R. Sánchez, ed., *Un rey para la nación: monarquía y nacionalización en el siglo XIX*, 2019).

DAVID SAN NARCISO completed his PhD in Late Modern History at the Universidad Complutense de Madrid in 2020. He works on nineteenth-century Spanish history and specializes in the cultural perspectives of the monarchy, the informal power networks of elites and the construction of masculinity. He has published several articles in peer-reviewed journals such as *Ayer*, *Historia y Política*, *Nationalities Papers* and the *European Review of History*. He is the editor of *La cuestión de Palacio. Corte y cortesanos en la España contemporánea* (2018) and *Monarchy and Liberalism in Spain. The Building of the Nation-State, 1780–1931* (2021).

RAQUEL SÁNCHEZ is Professor of Modern History in the Faculty of Geography and History at the Universidad Complutense de Madrid. She has specialized in the cultural and political history of nineteenth-century Spain. She is the researcher-in-charge of the research project which supports this book. Her publications include *Mediación y transferencias culturales: Eugenio de Ochoa y las letras europeas* (2017), *El autor en España, 1900–1936* (2008), *Alcalá Galiano y el liberalismo español* (2005), 'How to Be a Man of Letters' (in G. Lawless and A. Ginger, eds, *Spain in the Nineteenth Century. New Essays on Experiences of Culture and Society*, 2018), 'Les collections de littérature espagnole et leurs lecteurs dans l'Europe du XIXème siècle. Transferts culturels et identité nationale' (in L. Braida and B. Ouvry-Vial, eds, *Lire en Europe. Textes, formes, lectures*, 2020), '*Revista Enciclopédica de la Civilización Europea*: un proyecto de mediación cultural en el exilio (1843)' (*Bulletin Hispanique*, 2017) and 'Hartzenbusch en el laberinto: carrera literaria y redes profesionales del escritor isabelino' (*Studi Ispanici*, 2018).

JAIME TRIBALDOS MILLA is a PhD candidate in Late Modern History and researcher-in-training at the Universidad Complutense de Madrid. Previously, he worked as a research assistant at the Institute of Language, Literature and Anthropology of the Consejo Superior de Investigaciones Científicas. His doctoral dissertation is a biographical reconstruction of Lt. Gen. and statesman Fernando Fernández de Córdova (1809–1883). He has published *La política exterior española del Gobierno largo de O'Donnell y del Sexenio Democrático: una perspectiva comparada* (2018), and several other works are in press.

Index

Hispanic Studies: Culture and Ideas

Edited by
Claudio Canaparo

This series aims to publish studies in the arts, humanities and social sciences, the main focus of which is the Hispanic World. The series invites proposals with interdisciplinary approaches to Hispanic culture in fields such as the history of concepts and ideas, the sociology of culture, the evolution of visual arts, the critique of literature, and the uses of historiography. It is not confined to a particular historical period.

Monographs as well as collected papers are welcome in English or Spanish.

Those interested in contributing to the series are invited to write with either the synopsis of a subject already in typescript or with a detailed project outline to either Professor Claudio Canaparo, Department of Iberian and Latin American Studies, School of Arts, Birkbeck College, 43 Gordon Square, London WC1H 0PD, UK, c.canaparo@sllc.bbk.ac.uk, or Peter Lang Ltd, oxford@peterlang.com.

Vol. 1 Antonio Sánchez
Postmodern Spain. A Cultural Analysis of 1980s–1990s Spanish Culture. 220 pages. 2007.
ISBN 978-3-03910-914-2

Vol. 2 Geneviève Fabry y Claudio Canaparo (eds)
El enigma de lo real. Las fronteras del realismo en la narrativa del siglo XX. 275 pages. 2007.
ISBN 978-3-03910-893-0

Vol. 3 William Rowlandson
Reading Lezama's *Paradiso*. 290 pages. 2007.
ISBN 978-3-03910-751-3

Vol. 4 Fernanda Peñaloza, Jason Wilson and Claudio Canaparo (eds)
Patagonia. Myths and Realities. 277 pages. 2010.
ISBN 978-3-03910-917-3

Vol. 5 Xon de Ros
Primitivismo y Modernismo. El legado de María Blanchard.
238 pages. 2007.
ISBN 978-3-03910-937-1

Vol. 6 Sergio Plata
Visions of Applied Mathematics. Strategy and Knowledge.
284 pages. 2007.
ISBN 978-3-03910-923-4

Vol. 7 Annick Louis
Borges ante el fascismo. 374 pages. 2007.
ISBN 978-3-03911-005-6

Vol. 8 Helen Oakley
From Revolution to Migration. A Study of Contemporary Cuban and Cuban-American Crime Fiction. 200 pages. 2012.
ISBN 978-3-03911-021-6

Vol. 9 Thea Pitman
Mexican Travel Writing. 209 pages. 2008.
ISBN 978-3-03911-020-9

Vol. 10 Francisco J. Borge
A New World for a New Nation. The Promotion of America in Early Modern England. 240 pages. 2007.
ISBN 978-3-03911-070-4

Vol. 11 Helena Buffery, Stuart Davis and Kirsty Hooper (eds)
Reading Iberia. Theory/History/Identity. 229 pages. 2007.
ISBN 978-3-03911-109-1

Vol. 12 Matías Bruera
Mapping the Tasteland. Explorations in Food and Wine in Argentinean and European Culture. 240 pages. 2014.
ISBN 978-3-03911-345-3

Vol. 13 Angela Romero-Astvaldsson
La obra narrativa de David Viñas. La nueva inflexión de *Prontuario* y *Claudia Conversa*. 300 pages. 2007.
ISBN 978-3-03911-100-8

Vol. 14 Aaron Kahn
The Ambivalence of Imperial Discourse. Cervantes's *La Numancia* within the 'Lost Generation' of Spanish Drama (1570–90).
243 pages. 2008.
ISBN 978-3-03911-098-8

Vol. 15 Turid Hagene
Negotiating Love in Post-Revolutionary Nicaragua. The role of love in the reproduction of gender asymmetry. 341 pages. 2008.
ISBN 978-3-03911-011-7

Vol. 16 Yolanda Rodríguez Pérez
The Dutch Revolt through Spanish Eyes. Self and Other in historical and literary texts of Golden Age Spain (c. 1548–1673). 346 pages. 2008.
ISBN 978-3-03911-136-7

Vol. 17 Stanley Black (ed.)
Juan Goytisolo. Territories of Life and Writing. 202 pages. 2007.
ISBN 978-3-03911-324-8

Vol. 18 María T. Sánchez
The Problems of Literary Translation. A Study of the Theory and Practice of Translation from English into Spanish. 269 pages. 2009.
ISBN 978-3-03911-326-2

Vol. 19 Aino Linda Rinhaug
Fernando Pessoa. A Ludicrous Self. *Forthcoming*.
ISBN 978-3-03911-909-7

Vol. 20 Ana Cruz García
Re(de-)generando identidades. Locura, feminidad y liberalización en Elena Garro, Susana Pagano, Ana Castillo y María Amparo Escandón.
259 pages. 2009.
ISBN 978-3-03911-524-2

Vol. 21 Idoya Puig (ed.)
Tradition and Modernity. Cervantes's Presence in Spanish Contemporary Literature. 221 pages. 2009.
ISBN 978-3-03911-526-6

Vol. 22 Charlotte Lange
Modos de parodia. Guillermo Cabrera Infante, Reinaldo Arenas, Jorge Ibargüengoitia y José Agustín. 252 pages. 2008.
ISBN 978-3-03911-554-9

Vol. 23 Claudio Canaparo
Geo-epistemology. Latin America and the Location of Knowledge. 284 pages. 2009.
ISBN 978-3-03911-573-0

Vol. 24 Jesús López-Peláez Casellas
"Honourable Murderers". El concepto del honor en *Othello* de Shakespeare y en los "dramas de honor" de Calderón. 321 pages. 2009.
ISBN 978-3-03911-825-0

Vol. 25 Marian Womack and Jennifer Wood (eds)
Beyond the Back Room. New Perspectives on Carmen Martín Gaite. 336 pages. 2011.
ISBN 978-3-03911-827-4

Vol. 26 Manuela Palacios and Laura Lojo (eds)
Writing Bonds. Irish and Galician Contemporary Women Poets. 232 pages. 2009.
ISBN 978-3-03911-834-2

Vol. 27 Myriam Osorio
Agencia femenina, agencia narrativa. Una lectura feminista de la obra en prosa de Albalucía Ángel. 180 pages. 2010.
ISBN 978-3-03911-893-3

Vol. 28 *Forthcoming*

Vol. 29 Soledad Pérez-Abadín Barro
Cortázar y Che Guevara. Lectura de *Reunión*. 182 pages. 2010.
ISBN 978-3-03911-919-6

Vol. 30 Gonzalo Pasamar
Apologia and Criticism. Historians and the History of Spain, 1500–2000. 301 pages. 2010.
ISBN 978-3-03911-920-2

Vol. 31 Victoria Carpenter (ed.)
(Re)Collecting the Past. History and Collective Memory in Latin American Narrative. 315 pages. 2010.
ISBN 978-3-03911-928-8

Vol. 32 Geneviève Fabry, Ilse Logie y Pablo Decock (eds.)
Los imaginarios apocalípticos en la literatura hispanoamericana contemporánea. 472 pages. 2010.
ISBN 978-3-03911-937-0

Vol. 33 Julian Vigo
Performative Bodies, Hybrid Tongues. Race, Gender, Sex and Modernity in Latin America and the Maghreb. 391 pages. 2010.
ISBN 978-3-03911-951-6

Vol. 34 Heike Pintor Pirzkall
La cooperación alemana al desarrollo. Factores condicionantes de su transformación en la década de los noventa y su impacto en América Latina. 374 pages. 2010.
ISBN 978-3-0343-0107-7

Vol. 35 Arturo Casas and Ben Bollig (eds)
Resistance and Emancipation. Cultural and Poetic Practices. 419 pages. 2011.
ISBN 978-3-0343-0160-2

Vol. 36 Pablo Decock
Las figuras paradójicas de César Aira. Un estudio semiótico y axiológico de la estereotipia y la autofiguración. 344 pages. 2014.
ISBN 978-3-0343-0169-5

Vol. 37 Guillermo Olivera
Laboratorios de la mediatización. La experimentación con materiales mediáticos, la teoría y la crítica cultural argentina, 1965–1978.
364 pages. 2011.
ISBN 978-3-0343-0201-2

Vol. 38 Guy Baron
Gender in Cuban Cinema. From the Modern to the Postmodern.
334 pages. 2011.
ISBN 978-3-0343-0229-6

Vol. 39 Claudio Canaparo
El imaginario Patagonia. Ensayo acerca de la evolución conceptual del espacio. 576 pages. 2011.
ISBN 978-3-0343-0287-6

Vol. 40 Inmaculada Murcia Serrano
Agua y destino. Introducción a la estética de Ramón Gaya.
220 pages. 2011.
ISBN 978-3-0343-0251-7

Vol. 41 Bill Richardson
Borges and Space. 266 pages. 2012.
ISBN 978-3-0343-0246-3

Vol. 42 *Forthcoming*

Vol. 43 Ann Frost
The Galician Works of Ramón del Valle-Inclán. Patterns of Repetition and Continuity. 241 pages. 2010.
ISBN 978-3-0343-0242-5

Vol. 44 Milagros López-Peláez Casellas
What About the Girls? Estrategias narrativas de resistencia en la primera literatura chicana. 265 pages. 2012.
ISBN 978-3-0343-0264-7

Vol. 45 Bill Richardson and Lorraine Kelly (eds)
Power, Place and Representation. Contested Sites of Dependence and Independence in Latin America. 268 pages. 2012.
ISBN 978-3-0343-0710-9

Vol. 46 Patricia D'Allemand
José María Samper. Nación y cultura en el siglo XIX colombiano. 177 pages. 2012.
ISBN 978-3-0343-0288-3

Vol. 47 *Forthcoming*

Vol. 48 Emilio Rosales
Baroja. La novela como laberinto. 163 pages. 2012.
ISBN 978-3-0343-0774-1

Vol. 49 Kristine Vanden Berghe
Las novelas de la rebelión zapatista. 171 pages. 2012.
ISBN 978-3-0343-0779-6

Vol. 50 William Rowlandson
Borges, Swedenborg and Mysticism. 267 pages. 2013.
ISBN 978-3-0343-0811-3

Vol. 51 Elena Rodríguez-Guridi
Exégesis del "error". Una reinterpretación de la praxis de escritura en *Libro de la vida*, *Novelas ejemplares* y *Desengaños amorosos.* 175 pages. 2013.
ISBN 978-3-0343-0817-5

Vol. 52 Eva Bru-Domínguez
Beyond Containment. Corporeality in Mercè Rodoreda's Literature. 235 pages. 2013
ISBN 978-3-0343-0888-5

Vol. 53 Gabriele Andreozzi (ed.)
Desaparición. Argentina's Human Rights Trials. 355 pages. 2014.
ISBN 978-3-0343-0857-1

Vol. 54 Mel Boland
Displacement in Isabel Allende's Fiction, 1982–2000.
212 pages. 2013.
ISBN 978-3-0343-0932-5

Vol. 55 Eduardo Tasis Moratinos
El exilio en la poesía de Tomás Segovia y Angelina Muñiz Huberman.
234 pages. 2014.
ISBN 978-3-0343-0941-7

Vol. 56 Santiago Pérez Isasi and Ângela Fernandes (eds)
Looking at Iberia. A Comparative European Perspective.
317 pages. 2013.
ISBN 978-3-0343-0934-9

Vol. 57 Daniel de Zubía Fernández
Señas del esplendor ausente. Itinerarios familiares en *Señas de identidad* y en *O Esplendor de Portugal*
373 pages. 2014.
ISBN 978-3-0343-0963-9

Vol. 58 Helena Usandizaga (ed.)
Palimpsestos de la antigua palabra. Inventario de mitos prehispánicos en la literatura latinoamericana
383 pages. 2013.
ISBN 978-3-0343-0967-7

Vol. 59 Raquel Sánchez and David Martínez-Vilches (eds)
Respectable Professionals: The Origins of the Liberal Professions in Nineteenth-Century Spain
422 pages. 2022.
ISBN 978-1-80079-450-4

Vol. 60 Guillermo Laín Corona
Proyecciones de Gabriel Miró en la narrativa del 27.
250 pages. 2013.
ISBN 978-3-0343-0952-3

Vol. 61 Javier Ordiz (ed.)
Estrategias y figuraciones de lo insólito en la narrativa mexicana (siglos XIX–XXI)
237 pages. 2014.
ISBN 978-3-0343-1729-0

Vol. 62 Anna Vives
Identidad en tiempos de vanguardia: narcisismo, genio y violencia en la obra de Salvador Dalí y Federico García Lorca.
323 pages. 2015.
ISBN 978-3-0343-1792-4

Vol. 63 C.A. Longhurst
Modernismo, noventayochismo y novela: España y Europa. Ensayo de literatura comparada.
262 pages. 2014.
ISBN 978-3-0343-1810-5

Vol. 64 *Forthcoming*

Vol. 65 Ángela Gracia Menéndez
Gaspar de Jovellanos: crítico, reformador y humanista ilustrado.
202 pages. 2015.
ISBN 978-3-0343-1849-5

Vol. 66 Michael W. Stannard
Galdós and Medicine.
240 pages. 2015.
ISBN 978-3-0343-1825-9

Vol. 67 Helena Usandizaga y Beatriz Ferrús (eds.)
Fragmentos de un nuevo pasado: inventario de mitos prehispánicos en la literatura latinoamericana actual.
467 pages. 2015.
ISBN 978-3-0343-1852-5

Vol. 68 Guillermo Laín Corona y Mazal Oaknín (eds.)
Literatura política y política literaria en España. Del Desastre del 98 a Felipe VI.
293 pages. 2015.
ISBN 978-3-0343-1889-1

Vol. 69 Claudio Canaparo
El mundo Ingaramo
176 pages. 2015.
ISBN 978-3-0343-1910-2

Vol. 70 Ana Bravo-Moreno
Desigualdades, diferencias y experiencias de (no) pertenencia en educación: perspectivas transdisciplinares en contextos de diversidad
246 pages. 2015.
ISBN 978-3-0343-1850-1

Vol. 71 Alvaro Quiroga-Cifuentes
The Colombian Political Novel 1951–1987: A Critical Contribution
263 pages. 2015.
ISBN 978-3-0343-1978-2

Vol. 72 Xavier Pla, Maximiliano Fuentes and Francesc Montero (eds)
A Civil War of Words: The Cultural Impact of the Great War in Catalonia, Spain, Europe and a Glance at Latin America
449 pages. 2016.
ISBN 978-3-0343-1950-8

Vol. 73 Pilar Molina Taracena
La poética de la poesía de la Guerra Civil española: diversidad en la unidad
248 pages. 2016.
ISBN 978-3-0343-1933-1

Vol. 74 Santiago Pérez Isasi, Raquel Baltazar, Isabel Araújo Branco, Rita Bueno Maia, Ana Bela Morais, Sara Rodrigues de Sousa (eds)
Los límites del Hispanismo: nuevos métodos, nuevas fronteras, nuevos géneros
236 pages. 2016.
ISBN 978-3-0343-2267-6

Vol. 75 Rogelio Guedea (ed.)
Países en tránsito: estudios de literatura comparada
158 pages. 2016.
ISBN 978-3-0343-1979-9

Vol. 76 Shlomy Mualem
Mazes and Amazements: Borges and Western Philosophy
282 pages. 2017.
ISBN 978-1-78707-197-1

Vol. 77 Anne-Marie Storrs
Loving's the Strange Thing: Jungian Individuation in the Fairy Tales of Carmen Martín Gaite
260 pages. 2018.
ISBN 978-1-78707-844-4

Vol. 78 Rogelio Guedea (ed.)
Margen al centro: Nuevas vertientes de la poesía ibero/americana contemporánea. 164 pages. 2018.
ISBN 978-1-78707-766-9

Vol. 79 Isaac Benabu
Textos «ilegibles»: Reflexiones sobre la representación de la comedia áurea. 172 pages. 2018.
ISBN 978-1-78874-167-5

Vol. 80 Ana Duffy
Of Silenced and Unheard Voices from the South: Argentinean Subalternity According to Luisa Valenzuela
208 pages. 2020.
ISBN 978-1-78997-252-8

Vol. 81 Dimitrina J. Semova, Eva Aladro Vico, Roxana Popelka, Sosa Sánchez (coord.)
Entender el Artivismo
324 pages. 2019.
ISBN 978-1-78874-434-8

Vol. 82 Claudia del Río
Ikebana política: notas, poemas y ejercicios (2005–2015)
194 pages. 2019.
ISBN 978-1-78997-232-0

Vol. 83 David Torollo
Mishle he-ʻarav: La tradición sapiencial hebrea en la Península Ibérica y Provenza, s. XII y XIII
632 pages. 2021.
ISBN 978-1-78997-920-6

Vol. 84 Carlos Uxó
El género policial en Cuba: Novela policial revolucionaria, neopolicial y teleseries
262 pages. 2021.
ISBN 978-1-78997-387-7

Vol. 85 Claudio Canaparo
La cuestión periférica: Heidegger, Derrida, Europa
630 pages. 2021.
ISBN 978-1-78997-988-6

www.ingramcontent.com/pod-product-compliance
Ingram Content Group UK Ltd.
Pitfield, Milton Keynes, MK11 3LW, UK
UKHW021853100926
8556IPUK00020B/1204

9 781800 794504